CONTENTS

PREFACE

Perhaps no phase of Franklin D. Roosevelt's career
is more controversial than his involvement in the events leading
to Pearl Harbor. James MacGregor Burns, for example, has
reported that in 1941 Roosevelt "once again was failing to supply the crucial factor of his own leadership in the equation of
public opinion." On the other side, in contrast to this picture of a
man moving only timidly to meet the forces charging toward him,
historians of the Charles A. Beard inclination believe that
Roosevelt so conducted foreign affairs "as to maneuver a foreign
country into firing the shot that brought on war." Much more
recently Noam Chomsky has written that "Japan's appeal to national interest, which was not totally without merit, becomes
merely ludicrous when translated into a justification for American
conquests in Asia."

A large number of well-researched books have been written
about certain aspects of the events leading to Pearl Harbor. Basil
Rauch has described FDR's foreign policy from Munich to the
American entry into the war. Herbert Feis has described the
diplomatic road to Pearl Harbor. Robert J. C. Butow has described the coming of the war from the Japanese side. Roberta
Wohlstetter has described the warnings of an attack and the
decisions made, and not made. David Kahn has written of how
the Japanese code was broken.

The story of Franklin Roosevelt and the coming of Pearl Harbor,
however, remained untold. Did he do as much as he could have
done? More? Less? Did he provoke a war because he could not
prepare for one? Was he interested primarily in extending his

personal power? Was he engaged in a rescue mission for Winston Churchill? Or, to the contrary, had Churchill tricked him into acts that ultimately led to war?

These are the questions for which I have sought answers. And because Franklin Roosevelt was the leader of a democracy, my search took me into the area of politics. This was not the partisan politics of favor seeking. It was, instead, the politics of the isolationists, the men of industry, the labor leaders, the military men: the American people. Without them Franklin Roosevelt could do nothing. With them he could do all that had to be done if he chose.

The story of Franklin Roosevelt and the coming of Pearl Harbor is the story of any President in time of crisis. It tells something of the powers that are available to a President and something of those that are not. In that story also is something of the standards by which to judge other Presidents and by which to judge the American people.

LEONARD BAKER

Roosevelt and Pearl Harbor

JANUARY: ". . . *the sacred fire of liberty*"

THE DAY began as this same day had begun twice before, with a prayer. "With Thy favor," beseeched the pastor, "to behold and bless Thy servant Franklin, the President of the United States, and all others in authority; and so replenish them with the grace of Thy Holy Spirit that they may always incline to Thy will and walk in Thy way."

This day was the third inauguration of Franklin Delano Roosevelt as President of the United States. Twice before he had raised his right hand and placed his left upon a family Bible and sworn to preserve and protect the Constitution. When he had done so in 1933 and in 1937, the act had been enveloped in an aura of hope. He had said to the American people on those two occasions that their problems were of their own making, and so could be their solutions. "The only thing we have to fear," he had said, "is fear itself." And then he had led the nation in the struggle against that fear. If the struggle had not been completely successful—and no struggle is as successful as that—Americans at least raised their heads again with pride.

Such hope did not exist this time, this third inauguration day. For the problems the Americans faced in the 1940s were not the problems they had faced in the 1930s. These new problems were not of their own making. The enemy no longer was within. It was without. "People sensed," Franklin Roosevelt himself later commented about this day, "that something was wrong with the world."

Across the seas from the United States the apostles of violence had gained control in Germany, Italy, and Japan. These men of

1

violence exuded confidence. A few days before Roosevelt was sworn in as President of the United States for the third time, Adolf Hitler had proclaimed, "The year 1941 will bring consummation of the greatest victory in our history." And with that threat from Germany was also a similar threat from Japan on the other side of the world. The day of Roosevelt's third inaugural, Japan's foreign minister Yosuke Matsuoka told his nation's parliament that the combine of Germany, Italy, and Japan ultimately would triumph. "Establishment of a new world order," he said, "the goal of the powerful triple pact, if only given time, will surely be accomplished. There is no room for doubt that it will be crowned with brilliant success."

One could trace the path of violence across the map: Czechoslovakia, Poland, France, Holland, then probably England; Manchuria, China, and soon most likely Southeast Asia.

And when this was done: the United States.

Adolf Hitler, the German leader, knew his real enemy was the United States. France was defeated. England lacked the manpower to assault continental Europe. Russia, not yet in the war, had manpower and a land mass but lacked the industrial base required to be an effective participant in a modern war. Only the United States had the manpower, the industrial strength combined with the land mass, to pose a threat to the mad dreams of the former wall painter turned despoiler of the world. The more perceptive observers in Europe understood this. In October, 1940, Herbert L. Matthews had reported in *The New York Times* from Rome that "the Axis is out to defeat President Roosevelt, not as a measure of interference in the internal policies of the United States but because of the President's foreign policy and because of everything which he stands for in the eyes of the Italians and Germans." And William L. Shirer in his chronicle *The Rise and Fall of the Third Reich* reports that the Nazi dictator fully understood, as his various private utterances made clear, that "the United States, as long as it was led by President Roosevelt, stood in the way of Hitler's grandiose plans for world conquest and the dividing up of the planet among the Tripartite powers."

Franklin Roosevelt recognized that danger to America from across the seas. But there were many, among the four hundred thousand persons attending his inaugural and among the millions of other Americans, who did not recognize that danger. They were found among the military, business, and labor leaders of the nation as well as among the average citizens who followed rather than led. Some were prisoners of their past, others of their greed, and some of their prejudices; many were prisoners of their fears. Whatever their motivation, they were against Franklin Roosevelt and the policy he planned to pursue through 1941.

And it was because of them that Franklin Roosevelt faced his greatest challenge. This man who had turned himself from a physical cripple to a political master, who had led a paralyzed nation from the path of despair to the road of decency, this man now must call the American nation to arms. He must plead and command, persuade and politick. This challenge was not only for Roosevelt, it also was for the office he held. Just how big was the Presidency? How powerful? At times of highly visible threats —such as the splitting of the nation eighty years before or the economic catastrophe eight years earlier—the Presidency had been big enough. The dangers then were so real, so personal, so easily felt by most citizens that there was no objection to the President doing what needed to be done—but always with the proviso that, if he did too much, the voters would countermand him at the polls. But could the Presidency be big and powerful enough when the dangers were not conceded to be so real, so personal, so easily felt?

On this day, January 20, 1941, the answers to the questions about the ability of Franklin Roosevelt and the powers of the Presidency were not clear.

But if the problems were different, many of the faces at this scene were familiar. There was Harold L. Ickes, still Secretary of the Interior after eight turbulent, effective, and honest years. There was Frances Perkins—"Ma" Perkins, the President called her—continuing as Secretary of Labor after eight years in which the labor unions had made the greatest legislative gains in their history, and continuing to wear her drab, dark dresses and three-cornered felt hats. Henry Morgenthau still headed the Treasury Department in his humorless and efficient fashion. He remained an aide and confidant to his old friend and neighbor, Franklin Roosevelt, but more and more he was turning his interest and his energies to meet the Nazi threat.

Cordell Hull, although in his seventies, was entering his ninth year as Secretary of State. He then still hoped that the nations of the world would act as one decent, honorable man would expect another decent, honorable man to act. But he was growing increasingly aware that his hopes would not be realized.

And there were other old friends, assistants, Cabinet members, newsmen whose experience with FDR went back to his years as governor of New York State. Some even could recall knowing FDR in the years before that, during the First World War when he was Assistant Secretary of the Navy and then in 1920 when he was the Democratic Party's unsuccessful vice presidential candidate.

There were faces, however, that had belonged at this scene, when it had been played in the 1930s, that no longer belonged. John Nance Garner—"Cactus Jack"—had been Franklin Roosevelt's vice president for eight years. Accepting this representative of the Bourbon South had been the price Franklin Roosevelt had had to pay back in 1932 if he wanted the nomination. But Jack Garner had not moved in the direction that Franklin Roosevelt had moved, and so this inaugural was his last official act. His place would be taken by Henry A. Wallace, a liberal who had been Secretary of Agriculture. But neither his liberalism nor his farm policies had gained Wallace the second spot on the Democratic ticket. He was a midwesterner, from Iowa. The isolationist sentiment there was strong, and Wallace was needed on the ticket to help carry that part of the nation. That, perhaps, was the first sign of the change. Before FDR had needed a running mate whose presence on the ticket would appease the conservative South. Now he needed a running mate who would appease the isolationist Midwest. Franklin Roosevelt was aware that his political problems no longer stemmed from wtithin the nation but from without.

There were other changes also. Once Joseph P. Kennedy, the Wall Street wheeler-dealer, would have been present at any Roosevelt affair as important as an inaugural. But no longer. Kennedy had been wise where many of his business contemporaries had not been, and had understood that FDR's economic revolution—termed the New Deal—was sound and healthy for America, sounder and healthier, at least, than other kinds of revolutions. FDR had appreciated Kennedy's support and had given him important appointments in his administration. Finally, in 1938, Roosevelt had named Joe Kennedy to be the American ambassador to the Court of St. James's in London. Because of the supposed antipathy between the British and the Irish, appointing an Irish Catholic to the post was considered a daring deed by

FDR, but the President carried it off with no sign of fear. He sent Kennedy to London with only this caution: "When you feel that British accent creeping up on you and your trousers riding up to the knee, take the first steamer home for a couple of weeks holiday." But Joe Kennedy had concluded that England could not stand before Germany, a conclusion that FDR did not share. By this third inaugural the once close relationship had been severed.

Instead of Kennedy on the inaugural platform this day there would be William S. Knudsen. A year earlier the presence of the head of the General Motors Corporation at a Franklin Roosevelt inaugural would not have been believed. Bill Knudsen and his company represented the "economic royalists" that the New Deal was against. This was the royalism of great concentrations of economic power, the fight against labor unions, at times a public-be-damned attitude. And the New Deal represented much that Bill Knudsen was against. Some years later he wrote of the New Deal: "When troublesome times came, politics took a sudden interest in what to do to live without working, and a brand new set of teachings came into the life of America. Doles, boondoggling, and government spending were tried. Although these failed utterly, they left a thought in the minds of men that there might be something to them. The family of breadwinners got constantly smaller because the youngsters had been told that manual labor was a detriment to the educational potential ability in this new and better world."

Knudsen had come to the United States as a twenty-year-old immigrant, worked hard, and become president of General Motors. Now in his sixties, a huge man more than six feet tall, Knudsen hated the Nazis who were occupying his native Denmark even more than he hated the New Deal. FDR wanted him in Washington because he stood high with the business community. If America were to meet the challenge from abroad, it must have the cooperation of that community. The leaders of that business community might not speak with FDR and other New Dealers, but they would talk to Bill Knudsen.

So Bill Knudsen sat on the inaugural stand this day, next to the Cabinet members. He and Franklin Roosevelt never would settle old arguments, but they would work together on new problems. That was a requirement for running the nation; running it well, that is: jettisoning old comrades and developing new ones. Many described it as ruthless.

There were other new faces. The Secretary of the Navy was

Frank Knox. Knox also was a Republican, not only by conviction, like Knudsen, but also by practice. He had been on the 1936 ticket that ran against FDR. But he also dramatized a significant point about professional politicians, the good ones that is. Sometimes they did not care about politics. Back in 1937, before there was any apparent possibility of being offered a Cabinet post, Frank Knox had written to FDR that "I should like to . . . assure you of my unequivocal support in any further measures you may find it necessary to take to maintain American self-respect and respect for America abroad in a world that has apparently gone drunk and mad."

Another Republican present on the platform was Henry L. Stimson, the new Secretary of War. Like Cordell Hull, Stimson was in his seventies. He was tall and thin, ramrod straight. A lawyer, he was by career a Republican administrator; but he had not hesitated to join the Democratic administration and to offer his talents and his immense prestige as a Republican to Roosevelt's efforts to call the nation to arms.

Franklin Roosevelt's New Deal administration in the 1930s had been considered a partisan administration; FDR was a Democrat, his men were Democrats, and their enemies were the Republicans. But FDR's partisanship was exaggerated. Roosevelt had an allegiance to the social welfare ends he was seeking. He supported liberals, such as George Norris, who agreed with his objectives even if they were not Democrats. He opposed Democrats who were against those objectives. His allegiance to the Democratic Party was minimal, seeing it only as an organizational tool for the gaining of his objectives.

When, as the New Deal came to a close and FDR realized he needed a war Cabinet for the 1940s, he determined that he must have an administration that would be avowedly bipartisan. This was a political decision. If Congress fought him on rearming, prominent Republicans in his Cabinet would be an invaluable aid. The Congressional Republicans would have a difficult time criticizing their own party leaders.

Roosevelt had first offered Knox the Navy Secretary post in the fall of 1939. Knox was interested: "The temptation to undertake the task you suggested was almost irresistible," he told FDR. But Knox had reservations. He did, he explained, have a responsibility to the Republican Party. "The only things that give me pause are the absence at the moment on the part of the public of any deep sense of crisis which would justify completely forgetting and obliterating party lines, and the fact that the addition of only one Republican to the Cabinet would not make it, in the public view, a coalition cabinet into which a member of the opposition could go without encountering overwhelming criticism which would be destructive of any reputation one may have built through a whole lifetime of pretty consistent party loyalty."

Roosevelt answered that the public did not (this was December, 1939) have "any deep sense of world crisis . . . and, therefore, I must also admit that your coming into the Cabinet might be construed as a political move rather than as a patriotic move." FDR said that naming two Republicans, as Knox wished, "might be misunderstood in both parties!" FDR said he would postpone making any Republican appointments for that particular time. But, he added, "if there should develop a real crisis such as you suggest . . . It would be necessary to put aside in large part strictly old fashioned party government, and the people would understand such a situation." When and if that happened, FDR said, he would renew his invitation to Knox.

In the spring of 1940, FDR believed the nation had a sufficient "crisis" mentality to accept Republicans in the administration. Knox would come in as Secretary of the Navy. But a new leader was also needed for the War Department. Felix Frankfurter, then an associate justice of the Supreme Court and an FDR adviser of many years, suggested Henry Stimson. Stimson was a Republican, had served in every Republican administration since that of William Howard Taft; he had been Secretary of State in the Herbert Hoover administration preceding FDR's entry into the White House. Frankfurter had known him for years, had worked for him, and worshiped him.

In May, Frankfurter arranged to bring Stimson and FDR together at a White House luncheon. A few weeks later Frankfurter suggested Stimson as Secretary of War and Robert P. Patterson, a federal judge and a Republican, as Stimson's assistant. "Stimson," Frankfurter insisted to FDR, "has been for so long associated in the public mind as a supporter of your foreign policy and he has been so completely out of sorts with his own party that no one would deem it a manifestation of the 'coalition' idea." Frankfurter, who knew FDR very well, was telling the President what the President undoubtedly wanted to hear. If the President chose Stimson, Frankfurter was suggesting, he would not be criticized for playing politics.

Once the Republicans had joined FDR's team, he considered

them full members, embracing them with respect and friendship. If they chose, they could become part of the intimate social life in the White House, including the poker games that gave FDR his best opportunities for relaxation. "We have two recruits who played with us Thursday night," Roosevelt told Harold Ickes a few days before the inaugural, "and we drank your health. Knudsen is good at the ancient game but Knox is worse than you are!"

There was another change this January day in 1941, in addition to the presence of former foes at Roosevelt's side. This change was noticeable perhaps only when one stared intently at the face of Franklin Roosevelt. He already had held the office of the President for eight years, as long as any man. Now, ten days before his fifty-ninth birthday, he would accept its burdens for another four years. From a distance he seemed much the same. Tall and handsome, his shoulders the massive size that comes to cripples who use crutches instead of legs, the smile ever confident; he looked much as he did eight years earlier when he first rallied the nation. But as one came closer to FDR, one noticed the hair was thinner and grayer, the lines in his face deeper. Those who knew him realized that the illnesses, the colds, and the bouts with flu that plagued him now seemed more serious, took longer to leave him, and, when they were gone, left him weaker.

FDR had begun his inauguration day with a special service at St. John's Church, the small stucco church across Lafayette Square from the White House where he had begun his first and second inaugurals also. The spectators there easily could see a difference. Franklin Roosevelt was helped with the arm of his son James. In Washington this was a familiar sight: the father and son, a handsome pair. But this morning the father was helped by a Marine captain. James Roosevelt was in the uniform of his country. And this was a change and a challenge and a dread. Across the nation, in the coming months, fathers and mothers would have to face the prospect of their sons donning the uniform of their country and, if necessary, fighting for their country. For many, fighting would mean dying.

There was another change this morning at that church service, one perhaps that Roosevelt alone could appreciate. The President described himself as a Christian and a Democrat, meaning that he believed he had an obligation to his fellow men and the political process was his means of fulfilling that obligation. Much in his background—the baronial family estate, the parents who taught responsibility, his wife Eleanor, the times in which he lived, his own innate sense of decency—had formed his concept of a religious person. But one of the strongest influences in that development had been Endicott Peabody.

Endicott Peabody had founded a boy's preparatory school called Groton and had dedicated it to teaching young men to be constructive, responsible, and decent. Franklin Roosevelt had been one of those young men, and he never forgot what he had been taught and he never forgot the man who had taught him. When Franklin and Eleanor Roosevelt were married in 1905, Endicott Peabody performed the ceremony. And when Franklin Roosevelt was inaugurated President in 1933 and in 1937, it was Endicott Peabody who began those days for his former pupil by mounting the pulpit at St. John's to ask the Lord's blessing on the nation and the man who would lead it.

But Endicott Peabody now was eighty-four years of age, retired in Tucson, Arizona. He could no longer be with his young pupil. "Eleanor and I," Franklin Roosevelt wrote to his former teacher, "deeply missed you and Mrs. Peabody." He began that letter to "Mr. Peabody." Franklin Roosevelt had reached the highest position available to an American, the White House, but he never overcame his awe and respect for his old mentor. It always was "Mr. Peabody."

But more than this man's presence was missing. The values he had imparted to his young charges—being constructive and valuable, being decent—seemed so lacking this day in the world facing the United States, a world that had fallen from the brink of sanity into the pit of madness. It had become, it seemed, a world in which destruction and death reigned supreme. It was a world in which decency had been the first casualty.

The service this morning was conducted by the Reverend Frank R. Wilson, rector of St. James's Episcopal Church at Hyde Park, New York, the Roosevelt family church. FDR was a senior warden there, following a tradition that saw the landed gentry in America being the stalwart citizens of their community. It was Reverend Wilson who had called on the Almighty to watch and bless Franklin Roosevelt.

As part of the service, the Twentieth Psalm was read responsively. In this Psalm it is said that "Some trust in chariots, and some in horses: but we will remember the name of the Lord our God. They are brought down and fallen: but we are risen, and stand upright." It was a valid prayer this day that those who trust in chariots and horses, in the gods of war, would fall before those who trusted in the God of love. It was a prayer, of course, that had been offered many times before and which would be offered many times again. But its repetition did not in any way demean its urgency.

After the service at St. John's there was the bustle of moving the inaugural processional to the Capitol where the ceremony would take place. The presidential car left at 11:40 A.M.

"Samuel, how are you?" shouted FDR as Sam Rayburn entered the car.

And then to Alben W. Barkley, the President said, good-naturedly: "Alben, can you get in there?"

They were massive men with big, muscular, chunky bodies. But they were massive men in other ways also. Sam Rayburn's family had been poor dirt farmers in Texas. Now he was the Speaker of the House of Representatives. For a House member there is no greater honor. Alben Barkley had come from the hills of Kentucky. A loyal Democrat, he was "regular as a metronome." The reward for his service had been his election by the Democrats in the Senate to be their leader. And Roosevelt, born to wealth and prestige, had come from Groton and Harvard, Columbia and Wall Street. Together these three men had bested the money-changers, the industrialists; they had awakened the sleeping, helped the poor, defended the farmer, and strengthened the working man. Catholic and Protestant, Jew and Negro, city dweller and small-town resident; all had benefited from the Washington battles these three had fought and won. They had used their physical strength. They had cashed in on the favors owed them. They had used all their tricks, relied on their cunning ways. And now they must do so again, with an even greater energy. For however great the battles they had fought in the past, even greater ones loomed before them.

The wind came from the north, sharp and cold, as the procession moved toward the home of the Congress. Still, the sky was clear. And the sun was warm. It was a sharp contrast to the 1933 inaugural when a damp and gray chill had hung over the proceedings, and it was in even sharper contrast to the 1937 swearing-in when snow had enveloped the participants.

Once on the inaugural platform, John Nance Garner swore

in his successor, Henry Wallace. When that was done, Roosevelt turned and embraced "Cactus Jack." Their relationship had turned from friendship to opposition, but now all that was done. There had been many times when the two men had been together, and as John Nance Garner finished his last official act as a member of government after four decades of service, FDR wanted him to know he was appreciated and that he was leaving in good grace. The seventy-two-year-old Garner seemed to understand what Roosevelt was trying to say by that embrace. Friends saw him struggling against the tears welling up in his eyes.

Then it was Roosevelt's moment to take the oath of the President of the United States for the third time. Chief Justice of the United States Charles Evans Hughes stepped forward. It was eleven minutes after twelve.

Franklin Roosevelt placed his hand on the Bible that had been brought into the Roosevelt family in the 1600s. When FDR had first come to Washington as President-elect in 1933, he had carried that Bible with him.

His hand reached out to touch the opened page. His fingers rested on these words: "Though I speak with the tongues of men, and of angels, and have not charity, I am become as sounding brass, or a tinkling cymbal . . . and though I have all faith, so that I could remove mountains, and have not charity, I am nothing. . . ."

He raised his right hand and solemnly intoned the words that formally made him President of the United States for the third time, the first man ever to be sworn into that office for three terms. "I do solemnly swear," he said, "that I will faithfully execute the office of President of the United States and will, to the best of my ability, preserve, protect and defend the Constitution of the United States."

Then it was time for his inaugural speech. People look to a President's inaugural speech for the setting of the tone of the coming four years. Franklin Roosevelt did not disappoint them. In his first inaugural he had made clear that he expected the American people to rally behind him in the fight against the economic depression engulfing the nation. This led to the great mass of legislation designed to make right the economic system. In his second inaugural in 1937, he made clear that he expected all branches of the government to adhere to the people's mandate. This led to his bruising fight with the Supreme

Court in 1937. He appeared to lose that fight; the Congress refused to increase the size of the Court's membership so FDR could "pack" it with liberals friendly to his legislative program. But it was a fight which he actually won as the Court adopted a more liberal position. The Court defeated its enemy by joining him.

And so this speech in 1941 would set the tone for the coming four years. In his earlier inaugural addresses FDR had barely noticed anything outside of the continental borders of the United States. In the first there had been a fleeting reference to world trade and the declaration of the good neighbor policy toward Latin America. The 1937 speech made no reference to foreign affairs. It had been concerned only with the dangers within.

The speech Franklin Roosevelt was about to read was concerned, in contrast, only with the danger from without. He began slowly. "On each national day of inauguration since 1789," he said, "the people have renewed their sense of dedication to the United States." He continued that a time now had come for Americans to recall what was their place in history "and to rediscover what we are and what we may be." If Americans do not, he said, "we risk the real peril of isolation and inaction." The word "isolation" was not in his text; he said it inadvertently. But thinking of those Americans who would ignore the dangers of a hostile world, FDR thought the addition improved the speech.

He then spoke of the democratic spirit. It "is no mere recent phase in human history," he said. "It is human history. . . . In the Americas its impact has been irresistible. America has been the New World in all tongues, to all peoples, not because this continent was a new-found land, but because all those who came here believed they could create upon this continent a new life—a life that should be new in freedom. . . ."

To describe this spirit he found words in the first inaugural address of George Washington, "the sacred fire of liberty." And then Franklin Roosevelt told his countrymen, "If we lose that sacred fire—if we let it be smothered with doubt and fear—then we shall reject the destiny which Washington strove so valiantly and so triumphantly to establish. The preservation of the spirit and faith of the Nation does, and will, furnish the highest justification for every sacrifice that we may make in the cause of national defense."

And he concluded by saying that "In the face of great perils never before encountered, our strong purpose is to protect and to perpetuate the integrity of democracy.

"For this we muster the spirit of America, and the faith of America.

"We do not retreat. We are not content to stand still. As Americans, we go forward, in the service of our country, by the will of God."

The speech was completed in only sixteen minutes. It was one of the shortest inaugural addresses on record. Some understood the speech as the call it was meant to be, while others did not. Harold Ickes, for example, considered the address "admirably suited to the times," while a new Republican senator from Ohio, Harold H. Burton, thought the speech "an appeal for a living and progressive America, which if not applied to a military solution too radically, is good." But, of course, a call to arms always implies that the arms may have to be used.

When the actual inaugural ceremony was completed, the festival of the presidential inauguration turned to the anticipated hoopla. Since Thomas Jefferson was inaugurated in 1801 as the nation's third president, the states traditionally had sent a little bit of color and razzle-dazzle to be part of the inaugural parade from the Capitol, along Pennsylvania Avenue to the White House. In recent years these state contributions had been drum and bugle corps, high school bands, fraternal groups, floats. Almost without exception, the parades had been fun.

Not this time. There were no drum and bugle corps and no high school bands, no festive floats adorned with pretty girls, and no middle-aged men wearing the funny hats of their fraternal orders. Instead, there were riflemen of the United States Army, wearing drab khaki and marching with bayonets fixed, their eyes staring intently before them beneath steel helmets. And there was the rumbling of tanks, big military trucks, the heavy guns. Then, overhead, the blue sky suddenly darkened. Almost three hundred military aircraft crowded the sky, aiming at the White House from every direction. Their silver, red-tipped bodies came over the rooftops of the quiet city toward the parade stand where Franklin Roosevelt reviewed America's military might, their droning controlled, powerful and angry. This was America's air might, more airplanes than most Americans ever had seen at one time. The Navy sent eighty fighter and scout airplanes from the aircraft carrier *Wasp*, stationed at Norfolk, Virginia. The Army was represented by six pursuit and bombardment groups. There were eighteen Flying Fortresses, the big, lumbering bombers that were indicative of the belief that the next war would not be defensive. Flying Fortresses carried bombs to the enemy.

The parade was businesslike, totally without pomp. It was the American military showing itself to its commander-in-chief, the President. From the reviewing stand in front of the White House, he smiled and waved. But some thought he seemed more serious this time than he had been on the two previous occasions of his inauguration as President—more thoughtful, more concerned.

One soldier's wife, present at the parade, recalled that "Above the rumble of these mechanized forces could be heard the wild cheers of the immense crowds." And Mrs. George C. Marshall thought that "Possibly in the thunder of those forces the huge throng could hear the not-so-distant battle that would shape the destiny of America and of the entire world." It was this battle that Franklin Roosevelt heard.

The battle that Franklin Roosevelt heard was not heard by many members of America's military forces.

Harvey H. Bundy, a civilian aide to Stimson, said of the military bureaucracy he and Stimson had found in the War Department: "Of course the general staff had to be completely revamped. General George C. Marshall [Army chief of staff] had to improve the general staff and throw out a lot of people who were not adequate for the operation of the war. Often they were colonels who had come up through camp life in peacetime and lost their self-starters."

The established members of the military feared making decisions. If their choices were wrong, they believed their mistakes would become stamped forever on their records. Better to do nothing than make a mistake and lose the opportunity to rise slowly but inexorably through the military caste system until reaching the inevitable successful retirement.

Decisions had to be made; new techniques of warfare had to be explored; new weapons developed. Henry Stimson and George Marshall ultimately realized these decisions must be made by civilians. The military had neither the courage nor the background to make them. This was particularly true with the development of new weapons, which became almost entirely the province of a civilian committee. Harvey Bundy later recalled:

The problem was in alerting the whole army to the importance of scientific development of all kinds, including such things as the amphibious boat. And later on, of course, well I can't tell you how many scientific developments there were; proximity fuses, radar. All of those things were civilian developments. If there was any value in our work at the War Department in that field, it was because [Secretary Stimson] was absolutely determined . . . and then the Secretary would hit the army over the head, and the process of pushing, pushing, pushing for the acceptance of new inventions and the development of new inventions.

The army, with its peacetime tempo, just thought new inventions took years and years and "we've got to get on with this war." As a matter of fact the new inventions, particularly in the radar field, were moving along so fast that they could be used in this war, and were. Why, if they hadn't had the proximity fuse, I don't know what would have happened to England with the V-1, because those were being knocked down by proximity fuses.

It was not only the "tempo" of military life that dissuaded the military men from advocating new weapons; they were caught up in the romance of a distant past. They anticipated fighting the next war as they had fought the previous war, or even the one before that. One lesson that should have been learned from the First World War, for example, was that horse cavalry was a fighting technique of the past. It had been outmatched by the airplane and by mechanized cavalry—the armored car, the truck, and most especially the tank. But the horse soldier simply could not accept this.

"Piffle to the contrary notwithstanding," said a cavalry major named George S. Patton in 1929, "cavalry will bear its part in the next war as it has done in all that have preceded it . . . the future is big with glorious opportunities for cavalry." And he ended that 1929 speech by invoking memories of the American Civil War: "As J. E. B. Stuart used to sing, 'If you want to have a good time, jine the cavalry.' "

On the eve of the Second World War the cavalry soldiers still remained devoted to the past. "The advent of machines, be they guns, tanks, armored cars, or airplanes," said an Army major general named Guy V. Henry, "have in no way diminished the value of cavalry; but have, on the contrary, rendered cavalry—which fully cooperates with and exploits them—more powerful than ever in its history."

When war did come in 1939 and the mechanized divisions of

Nazi Germany swept across Europe, there should have been no question left about the ineffectiveness of horse cavalry. But there were such questions. When FDR's third term began, the European war was seventeen months old and continental Europe had fallen before Hitler's soldiers. However, in January, 1941, George Patton still was marshaling his arguments in support of the horse cavalry. He said then:

Let us assume that a charge must traverse a distance of five hundred yards to reach the enemy. Records of most colleges show that a trained runner with spikes and running clothes takes fifty seconds to cover a quarter of a mile. It is then more than generous to assume that an infantry soldier in battle kit will take at least 150 seconds to negotiate five hundred yards. A cavalry horse charges at least twenty miles an hour, so will cover five hundred yards in fifty-one seconds, or at least three times as fast. Let us assume further that the front silhouette of a mounted man is twice as large as that of a dismounted man. Against an equal intensity of fire, then, the chances of a cavalryman and his horse being hit is only two thirds as great as that of an infantryman.

That argument could have been appropriate in the American Civil War. It was dangerously inappropriate eighty years later. A horse could not charge a machine gun or a tank. It could traverse an open field quickly but not a gutted ash heap of a city pocked with land mines.

In 1941 an Englishman, Harold Nicolson, made a comment about his own nation's military which is appropriate to the American military at the same time. "I have no doubt that we shall win in the end," said Nicolson. "But we shall have to learn the new technique, the secret of mobile warfare." The secret was mechanization, and this the cavalryman resisted. The excitement of the charging horses, the whir of a saber through the air, the gloss of the riding boot—all this was too romantic to surrender. The American military would learn. George Patton himself would become the great exponent and the brilliant user of the tank. But the lesson would not be accepted easily. The lesson was, of course, more than mechanization. It was, rather, that there is nothing romantic about modern warfare.

The battle that Franklin Roosevelt heard was not heard by many leaders of America's industrial machine.

As FDR recited the presidential oath for a third time, the War

Department was preparing a memorandum for Robert Patterson to give to the President. This memorandum demonstrated the critical impact on the rearmament effort of those industrial leaders not hearing the rumble of war across the seas. "On January 10th," it read, ". . . the United States Army had only sixty-three heavy bombers, thirty-three medium bombers and 193 pursuit planes fit for combat against a modern air force. None of these had armor or leakproof tanks. . . . The shortage in combat planes is critical, in view of the acute emergency facing this country. Continuance of the present situation is fraught with the gravest danger. Not only is the weakness extreme in the event of war, but the training of our pilots in modern tactical types is being seriously hampered."

There were many reasons why American industry was reluctant to cooperate with Roosevelt, and he could understand some of them. One member of an industry would not be happy about giving up his share of the civilian market to produce military goods, leaving the way open for his competitors to gobble up all his customers. Another very practical problem, pointed out by FDR himself, was typified by the rubber industry. The government's objective was to have the tire companies lay in a year's supply of rubber. "Well, naturally," conceded the President, "the tire companies were not going out into the market to store another six months' or a year's supply at the present prices because they are away up high. I would do the same thing if I were making tires myself."

There were other reasons. Some American industrial leaders simply could not get over their distrust and fear of FDR. That American business was doing better as 1941 began, after eight years of the New Deal, than it had ever before done was irrelevant to these men who could not or would not overcome their prejudices. Others were isolationists and objected to the United States taking any action that might appear warlike, such as arming for defense.

Most important, however, in this opposition was the fear of losing dollars in profits. The success of the business comeback was earning industry the kind of profits that it had been without for some years. The year 1941, for example, was the best year the automobile industry had had since 1929. What was wrong with Roosevelt, the businessmen wanted to know, that he expects us to divert our resources, our factories, our energies, our skilled labor from these profitable peacetime pursuits to wartime production? Why, everyone knows, they argued, that the war will not last long. England cannot hold out more than a few weeks; then we can deal with Hitler. "It was," commented Robert Patterson, "the old question of business as usual."

A study for the Army Air Force reported of this period that "Concerns engaged in production for the civilian competitive market were indisposed to take defense work if by so doing they would lose any of their civilian customers. They even urged the procurement officers to give the defense work to competitors." All blame did not lie with the producers. The study also asserted that the American public, for the first time in a decade with money to spend beyond what was necessary for the minimum necessities of life, wanted some luxuries. The study asserted that the public "in general, seemed to believe that the country would prepare for war and conduct all its regular peacetime pursuits at the same time." It could not be done, of course. The economy would not support both guns and butter.

Even the smaller industries were reluctant to become involved in defense work. The War Department did make efforts to enlist many of the smaller businessmen. Exhibits were staged around the nation with displays of items that could be easily produced by a small company. But the response was poor. "What do we know about making bombs?" said the small manufacturers, according to Robert Patterson, who was concerned primarily with production.

And when a small businessman finally was persuaded to join the war effort, he often found himself in trouble with a large contractor. The War Department, trying to speed up production, recommended to large contractors that they subcontract out as much work as possible. The Army Air Force study explained what happened. "Prime contractors," it said, "were able to find good reasons for not letting out a larger proportion of the work and to put various obstacles in the way. They could not find suitable subcontractors. If firms were suggested to them, they did not trust the management, or did not believe the men could work to close enough tolerances, or could not arrange terms. If persuaded to license other firms, they often delayed sending the proper drawings and production models."

One army man, involved in production, summed it up this

way: "Well, these subcontractors have gotten a lot of runaround from these prime contractors, and we're breaking it up here as fast as we can."

Large companies balked at farming out work for a variety of reasons. They did not wish to divulge patents or techniques of operation. They did not wish to build up competitors. They did not wish to surrender what seemed to be potential profits. Also, they figured they could make more money if they resisted the push. They told Robert Patterson that the talk about subcontracting was only "flag waving." If he really were serious about subcontracting, they said, then he should increase delivery schedules so that subcontracting would become a necessity and, also, he should pay bonuses for accelerated production. Patterson, besieged on all sides by pressures for the defense dollar, refused.

The battle that Franklin Roosevelt heard was not heard by many of America's labor leaders.

When the New Deal had begun in 1933, the American working man was at the bottom of the economic pyramid, subject to the whim and caprice of an employer who was often arrogant and callous. The working man had little defense against this kind of attitude. The lone working man had no power. One of the great contributions of the New Deal was the extension of legal authority to the labor unions. By joining together in a labor organization, the working men developed a power equal to that of business and could bargain with business. Roosevelt had insisted on the unions receiving this cloak of legality. Protected by this cloak, working men had the means to obtain whatever they sought.

As the rearmament effort began, labor had two goals. They were enunciated in the administration by Sidney Hillman, the labor union representative in the defense production effort. Hillman wanted to be certain that the gains achieved by labor during the New Deal were not lost, and he hoped to guide defense expansion so that it would employ many of the millions still without work. The businessmen guiding the defense expansion had different ideas. Some simply opposed labor unions, as did many of the companies to which defense contracts would be offered. Others genuinely were concerned about using national defense as a club for enforcing labor laws.

For labor leaders the issues involved were more than an extra few cents an hour for their union members, more than a reduction in the work week. The union had enabled the working man to achieve a dignity and a sense of security that he had never before had. These achievements, common in later years, were too newly tasted at the beginning of the 1940s to be surrendered easily. John L. Lewis, head of the United Mine Workers union, realized as soon as the defense effort began that pressures would be on to reduce labor's gains. His face and character had been scarred by too many experiences watching dead coal miners being carried out of unsafe mines to permit that to happen.

He discussed the matter with Hillman. The specific point was a 1937 ruling by the government that the various labor laws did not authorize withholding of federal contracts from a company that failed to grant labor its rights. To secure its rights, the union must work through the National Labor Relations Board and the courts. This was a lengthy process and the war could be over before it was finished. Lewis argued that if the government could be persuaded to withhold contracts from companies not in compliance with federal labor laws, that would be an immediate punishment. Industry would be hit where it hurts—in its profits.

Hillman assured Lewis that a policy was being worked out, but offered few details. Hillman realized the result would not be near what Lewis wanted. This Hillman-Lewis discussion had been in the summer of 1940, shortly after Hillman joined the defense effort. A few weeks later, on Labor Day, the policy was announced. It promised that a consideration in the choice of new plant sites would be the availability of the labor supply. The policy also promised that "all work carried on as part of the defense program should comply with federal statutory provisions affecting labor wherever such provisions are applicable." No one was quite certain what the promise meant. It turned out not to mean much.

In the fall of 1940 several companies seeking defense contracts had been having troubles with labor unions. Many of them were found by the National Labor Relations Board, an agency of the federal government, to be in violation of the federal labor laws. The Ford Motor Company particularly had been cited several times. Theoretically, at least, such NLRB pronouncements could bar the company from receiving a federal contract. Not so, said Attorney General Robert H. Jackson. He ruled that such decisions by the NLRB would not prohibit a government agency from awarding a contract to the company.

The businessmen and Republicans running the defense effort found the concern of labor unions to be a bother. "I regret to say," said Robert Patterson to a member of the Roosevelt administration in November, 1940, "that I am unable to inform you as to the total number of contracts placed with companies held to be in violation of the National Labor Relations Act by the Labor Board. It would be a long and difficult job to assemble this information, since it would require a search of the files of the Labor Board and a comparison of them with all the contracts made by the War Department."

But if labor could not hold its gains by federal enforcement, and if court challenges were lengthy, there was one other weapon available to the labor union members: the strike.

The battle that Franklin Roosevelt heard was not heard by many members of the general public.

This public indifference toward rearming was well described in one government study: "It was difficult to arouse any considerable public interest in planning for a hypothetical future war; yet without such interest the appropriations and staff necessary for a thorough planning job were not forthcoming. On the other hand—especially in the early and mid-1930s—it was virtually impossible to conduct any public discussion of even minimum plans for military preparedness without generating accusations of 'militarism,' 'warmongering,' and the like. A significant section of the general public was suspicious of 'war' plans, a 'War' Department, and other instrumentalities with similar nomenclature which failed to distinguish between aggressive intention and defensive preparation."

This public hostility was reflected in Congress many times. Once, when George Marshall was appearing before a House committee, he was criticized for not having requested money for an army housing survey. Why had he not done so? Marshall, permitting his temper to show, snapped: "I would say very much for the same reason that we did not come to your committee with formal recommendations for adequate ammunition. I wanted to have about $150 million worth of ammunition appropriated for in the spring of 1939 . . . but I did not present the request to this committee. I also wanted about $300 million for ordnance at that particular time: $110 million, including about $37 million for ammunition, was provided." The committee took the scolding for its parsimony in silence.

Another time a member of Congress asked Marshall if the army was not seeking more than it needed. The time was immediately after the fall of France in the summer of 1940, and the chief of staff was astonished that anyone could doubt or question the growing danger. "My relief of mind would be tremendous," he replied, "if we just had too much of something besides patriotism and spirit."

Some years later Marshall recalled that period in a discussion with his biographer, Forrest C. Pogue. "People have forgotten today," Marshall said in 1957, "what a difficult time we had raising an army, how bitter was the opposition in raising it, how strong was the influence of the Middle West. . . . We had to move cautiously. If I had ignored public opinion, if I had ignored the reaction of Congress, we would literally have gotten nowhere."

Although the Congress was Democratically controlled, it was not overly responsive to Franklin Roosevelt. The day FDR was inaugurated for a third term, he was both feared and disliked by Congressional Democrats. Many suspected he was pushing the United States toward war because he wished to be a war president. Others resented his having violated the tradition that said a president does not seek a third term. His political power had been weakened in the eyes of Congressional Democrats because of his unsuccessful attempt in 1938 to purge those party members who had opposed him.

And the Republicans, still, were largely isolationists. This was so even though the party's 1940 presidential candidate and its 1941 titular leader, Wendell L. Willkie, was openly supporting FDR's foreign policy, and in some instances was even more forthright than was the President. In addition to this isolationist sentiment, the Republicans in Congress saw in FDR all the evil of the past eight years personified. It was he who had effectively struck at the *laissez-faire* economics they worshiped. It was he who had assisted the Negroes, the Jews, members of all minorities to climb up the American success ladder. It was he who had persuaded the United States to accept the premise that wealth must be better distributed. It was he who had accomplished a revolution. That he had done so within the traditional American framework did not make him any more attractive to his enemies, who hated his accomplishments rather than his techniques.

Those troubles on Capitol Hill were dangerous to the defense effort because of the desperate need to do so much so fast. Comparing the 1941 situation with the situation in 1917, when the

United States entered the First World War, demonstrated how serious the situation was. In 1917, at least five powerful nations—Britain, France, Italy, Russia, and Japan—were fighting Germany and keeping her penned behind battle lines in Europe. In 1941 only one of those nations was fighting Germany—England. The others either were fighting on Germany's side or giving Germany considerable support.

Also in 1917 those five nations fighting Germany had effective control over both the Atlantic and the Pacific oceans. In 1941 the British navy patrolled the Atlantic Ocean alone, and the heavy odds it was against prevented it from doing an effective job.

In 1917, as in 1941, the United States military had no heavy weapons—the field guns, the tanks, and the airplanes with which modern warfare is fought. But the United States in 1917 was able to purchase almost all it needed of such weapons from France and England. In 1941 those two nations had no such weapons for sale. The United States could produce them, of course, but two years are required to develop a war industry.

Finally, in 1917, American troops could be sent to Europe with less than adequate training. Because warfare then was trench warfare, American soldiers could be placed in the trenches next to experienced French and English troops and pick up some practical knowhow before actually entering combat. But the war in 1941, as it was developing, was not stabilized and did not permit such on-the-job training.

This situation was pointed up by George Marshall when he said, "Democratic governments devote their resources primarily to improving the standard of living of their people. Therefore, when attacked by nations which have concentrated on preparations for a war of conquest, the initial successes inevitably will go to the aggressors. This was the case with the democracies of western Europe and later on was found true in the case of the United States." When Robert Patterson pointed out that "free men will fight better than slaves," he did not mean that free men would fight better without proper training and modern equipment.

And the final group that did not hear the battle that Franklin Roosevelt heard was the natural climax of the mixture of a general public reluctant to rearm, the businessman's desire to retain profits, and the labor union leader's hope to retain his gains—the isolationist movement.

Perhaps because he had grown up in the East, which had a

European orientation, and perhaps because of his early education in Europe and travels there, Roosevelt never believed the
United States could sever itself from Europe. When the First
World War broke out in Europe, for example, Henry Ford announced he would devote a million dollars to oppose American
rearmament. FDR scoffed at such an approach. "Most of these
worthies," he said to his wife Eleanor, "are like Henry Ford, who
until he saw a chance for publicity free of charge, thought a submarine was something to eat."

"The isolation of the United States is at an end," Woodrow
Wilson had said in 1918, "not because we chose to go into the
politics of the world, but because by the sheer genius of this people and the growth of our power we have become a determining
factor in the history of mankind, and after you have become a
determining factor you cannot remain isolated, whether you want
to or not."

FDR agreed. In 1935 he told Colonel E. M. House, Wilson's
old associate, that the trouble with isolationists is they believe that
the United States "can and should withdraw wholly within
ourselves and cut off all but the most perfunctory relationships
with other nations. They imagine that if the civilization of Europe
is about to destroy itself through internal strife, it might just as
well go ahead and do it and that the United States can stand
idly by."

There were several reasons for that belief by the isolationists.
Americans were not then a mobile society. Once a family settled,
particularly in the Midwest and the far West, it rarely moved. It
had no relationship with Europe, except for bad memories, perhaps, and saw no reason to develop any new relationship. Also
there was much disillusionment with the concept of intervention.
The United States had entered the First World War to "make
the world safe for democracy," according to the slogan at the
time, and also to end war. "The war to end wars" did not turn
out, it appeared, to be quite so decisive, and democracy did not
appear to be any safer after the war than it had been before.

Led by Senators Gerald P. Nye, Republican of North Dakota,
and Burton K. Wheeler, Democrat of Montana, a group of politicians seized on this feeling of disillusionment and exploited it.
In the mid-1930s, Senator Nye led a Congressional investigation of
profiteering during the First World War. He produced a sordid
story of munition makers profiting from the war. The Nye com-

mittee also claimed that the United States had been led into the First World War by Wall Street bankers. Germany had not really started the war, the committee charged. France and England, it said, had been the actual villains.

Professor Wayne S. Cole of Indiana University, who made a thorough study of Senator Nye and his impact and involvement in foreign relations, reports: "At the same time Nye and his committee stressed the business 'villain' in their analyses of foreign affairs, a second villain gradually began to loom larger in their finding and thinking: government, and particularly the executive branch of the government. Its role in promoting international friction and war was increasingly emphasized by Nye from 1934 onward."

Despite its historical inaccuracies, the Nye committee produced a favorable response among the American people. They did not want another war, and the findings of the Nye committee told them that they should not become involved in another conflict.

Then there were those who believed that all of the talk about war was just that—talk—and nothing more. It was only a plot to increase FDR's power, to make him a dictator. Had not the Nye committee stressed the "villain" role of the Presidency? Or the talk of war was only a plot to increase profits, to strengthen labor unions—almost anything except a legitimate concern.

In an effort to counter the isolationist movement, a group of prominent American citizens in 1940 organized the Committee to Defend America by Aiding the Allies. The logical choice for a chairman was William Allen White, the newspaper editor from Emporia, Kansas. He could touch all points. White was a Republican, which of the two major political parties then had the greater number of isolationists. He was from the Midwest, which was then the center of isolationism. He was a political progressive. Since before the Bull Moose campaign of 1912, he had had been identified with the causes that, twenty years later, people wished they had supported. He also was a good friend of Roosevelt's as well as being a man with close contacts in the New York publishing and business worlds.

The White group had one high point. This came in the summer of 1940 when the appointments of Stimson and Knox to the Cabinet were made. The announcement came as the Republicans were gathering for their 1940 presidential convention. The Republicans immediately saw the appointments as a political trick by the President. The party's national chairman, John Hamilton, shouted both Knox and Stimson out of the Republican Party. When a few Democrats in the Senate made sounds about joining Republican senators in voting against confirming the appointments, FDR knew he had a fight on his hands.

He called in White, who agreed to help. The President, said White, "sent me to Senator Jimmy Byrnes, who gave me the doubtful committee members. That night we had telegrams going into their states asking for help." By the next morning, Sunday, the influential people across the country who had heard from White began responding. There were telegrams, calls, and visits to the committee members. Knox and Stimson were confirmed.

"I feel," said White a few days after the vote, "like Father Coughlin or Frankenstein, and I am duly and properly scared, humble, and a bit ashamed that one man should have such power!"

By the end of 1940 his committee had more than seven hundred local chapters. It had collected approximately a quarter of a million dollars. The group provided speakers, information for mailings, and lobbied in Congress. Its basic purpose, at least at the beginning, was to assure military assistance to those nations fighting Germany. But there was a dispute within its membership whether the committee should go beyond that. In December, 1940, White had made public comments suggesting that the committee opposed entry of the United States into the war. Some committee members believed the opposite. Others agreed that the United States should not enter the war but did not believe it was a wise tactical choice to proclaim such a belief. The result of the dispute was that White resigned as active chairman of the group, pleading ill health, and became the committee's "honorary chairman." Without White as its leader, the committee did not regain the momentum it once had. None of the other officers enjoyed the popular esteem that White had amassed over almost forty years as a leader of progressive causes.

The real significance of the White committee perhaps may not be found in its own accomplishments but in the accomplishments of the group set up to counter it. This was the America First Committee.

At the time that William Allen White's committee to aid the allies was developing in 1940, a young law student at Yale

University was also becoming increasingly concerned about the international situation, but from a different point of view. This student was Robert Douglas Stuart, Jr., of Chicago. As an undergraduate at Yale he had studied international relations. After graduating in 1937 and before entering law school, he had traveled through Europe. Back at Yale, in law school, he continued his interest in foreign affairs. His concern was that the United States might be pulled into the wars of Europe, where Stuart did not believe America belonged.

Stuart was not just any boy from around the corner. He was the son of the first vice president of the Quaker Oats Company, and could bring to his cause some wealth, a good education, charm and intelligence, and—perhaps most important—a wide acquaintance with the wealthy men of business.

His movement started as a small discussion group at Yale. Some of his fellow law students participated, as well as a couple of professors from the school. At the end of the 1939–40 school year, Stuart and his friends sent out a mimeographed letter to various colleges asking for volunteers to spend part of the summer months working in opposition to American intervention in the war. The students, as indicated by a petition they circulated then, believed the United States should stay out of the European war, "even if Great Britain is on the verge of defeat." The group consented to America aiding Britain but only, it stressed, on a "cash-and-carry" basis.

At the same time that Stuart and his college friends were interested in the noninterventionist cause, a businessman in Chicago named Robert E. Wood also was talking with some of his friends about what should be done to promote the same cause. It was natural that the two forces—the young college students and the mature businessman—should come together. As Wood explained it some years later, "A young idealistic college student by the name of Bobby Stuart, son of my next-door neighbor, formed this chapter at Yale, and they came to me, and I helped them some financially." Wood served as chairman of the group during its lifetime. "They couldn't get any man of substance to head the movement, because it wasn't too popular with the so-called best people. I finally said, 'I'll take the acting chairmanship.' Well, they never did find anybody who'd bear the brickbats."

At the time Wood was chairman of the board of the Sears,

Roebuck Company. Then in his early sixties, he was a brilliant choice to head the Committee. Wood brought to the America First Committee a perspective that can come only to a man with sixty years of successful living behind him, a reputation for probity in the United States, and wealthy friends who were willing to ante up money so the Committee could get started.

At a time when many businessmen considered any reform in the American economic system to be a socialist tide that must be halted, Wood willingly acknowledged that such reforms must come. He supported Roosevelt in the 1932 election, when a number of businessmen did. Robert Wood also, however, supported FDR in the 1936 election when many of FDR's former business supporters deserted him.

But Wood did not believe the United States should become involved in the European conflict. There are two possible explanations for his belief. Both or one may be correct. And they may not only apply to him but to many other noninterventionists also. The first was suggested by Henry Wallace, then Secretary of Agriculture, to FDR in 1939. Wallace said:

> [Wood's attitude] is a common one in certain parts of the Middle West. He thinks, first, that Hitler has economic justice on his side; second, he is a strong believer in the barter of American farm products for German manufactured goods; third, he thinks the farmer is in an impossible situation as long as the Central European market for farm products is cut off. Previous to 1933, Germany took about 1,800,000 bales of cotton from us each year, and about 150,000,000 pounds of lard. During 1938 she imported less than one-quarter million bales of our cotton and less than one million pounds of our lard. During January and February of this year her rate of import has been lower than in 1938, amounting to about one-fifth of her pre-1933 quantity in the case of cotton and less than one percent in the case of lard. World events and our foreign policy have combined—the trade agreements to the contrary notwithstanding—to make it necessary for us to make internal adjustments in agriculture which are almost impossible.

Certainly if the United States had been friendlier to Germany in the 1930s, the farmer in the Midwest, who was the best customer then for General Wood's mail order house, would have been in a better financial condition.

The other explanation for Wood's isolationism comes from Wood himself. Shortly after the European war broke out in September, 1939, Wood returned from Alaska to find what he considered a disturbing situation in the United States. According to the news reports he read, many officials in Washington believed American entry into the war to be inevitable. Robert Wood sat down and wrote a letter to his friend, the President.

It seems to me that the issue is plain. We went into the war twenty-two years ago to save democracy. We know how it was saved and how a peace was made which really created Hitler and Hitlerism. Today, we are called on to aid in a war to smash Hitler, and if we do aid, just as certainly shall we see another peace made which will in turn create another Hitler. All nations, including our own, are staggering under a load of debts piled up as a result of past wars. Another long war would complete the ruin of all. The only possible way of preserving our own institutions is to stay out of the conflict at any cost, to stand firmly on this continent, with the strongest defense possible, both military and naval. If the British Empire should go down in the conflict, Canada would probably annex herself to us. On the other hand, if we go into the war, we may find that we have lost our present and future liberties and have a complete upset in our social system. We shall lose all the social gains that have been made over the last six years, we shall see the money put into the health, recreation and upbuilding of our people dissipated in paying for a war to preserve the British and French empires.

Roosevelt answered that Wood should discount newspaper speculation. Officials in Washington in the fall of 1939 did not believe the United States must enter the European war, said FDR. He added, "So, my dear friend, stop being disturbed and get both of your feet back on the ground."

Wood never would be calmed, however. Later he bluntly told FDR, "I have been afraid that your policy would involve us in the European war. You know I am no pacifist and I am perfectly willing to serve and fight for my country, but I believe its involvement in the war abroad would be disastrous to us and not in our interest." Wood concluded, "If we do not become involved in the war, I shall be the first to say that I was wrong." He never made such a concession.

At the beginning, the America First Committee concentrated on national advertising campaigns. After the 1940 election, however, the Committee encouraged the formation of local chapters as the William Allen White committee had done. Ultimately there were four to five hundred local chapters with a total membership claimed to be between eight hundred thousand and one million persons. After the initial financial start with the help of General Wood, the Committee became self-supporting through donations by members.

The local chapter in New York City, for example, recruited 5,636 members in its first twenty-three weeks and collected $8,407.95. While some of the contributions to America First were in the thousands of dollars, there was no single individual or group bankrolling the committee after its start. It drew its financial support from all areas of the United States and from all economic levels. That, of course, is why it was such a threat to FDR's foreign policy.

Despite the youthful enthusiasm of Stuart and the respectable conservatism of Wood, America First and the entire isolationist movement lacked a galvanizing force. This was illustrated four days after FDR's third inaugural by an ex-Congressman named John J. O'Connor. A conservative, O'Connor had the distinction of being the only successful object of FDR's 1938 attempt to purge disloyal Democrats from Congress. From that point on, O'Connor could not support FDR's policies.

"We have no Borah," said O'Connor to a friend on January 24, "and I have no faith in the vacillating Wheeler being able to do the job. I keep thinking of Senator [Hiram] Johnson (Republican) of California, but perhaps he is too old. Willkie has a great opportunity, which he twice muffed. First in the campaign and then since. I cannot follow Joe Kennedy's inconsistency. If Roosevelt cannot win the so-called leaders over completely to his side by calling them to the White House and smiling at them, he at least does a ninety percent job on them, so that they meet themselves coming back because of the fear of offending the throne."

What the isolationist movement lacked was a dynamic, and even romantic, personality to capture the American imagination. It needed someone to evoke moral fervor and lead a crusade. It needed someone whose presence would attract the crowds and whose words then would convince them. The movement would find that personality in 1941. At almost the same moment John O'Connor was expressing his lament, Charles A. Lindbergh, Jr., was appearing before a House committee.

"I believe," he said to the committee, "the fault of the war is about evenly divided in Europe, and the causes of it." He said he preferred to see neither side win. This man whose exploits as an aviator had made him a romantic hero to America and who drew no moral distinction between the aggression of Germany and the defense of England ultimately would become the galvanizing force the isolationist movement lacked.

These then were the ones who did not hear the rumble of battle as Franklin Roosevelt heard it—those military men who saw the future as if it were the past, those business leaders who would not concede that success also demands sacrifice, the labor leaders with victory too recently gained to be lost, and those members of the general public who listened to the music of peace as if there were no other sound. "Frankly and definitely," Franklin Roosevelt told them all in January, 1941, "there is danger ahead—danger against which we must prepare. . . . We well know that we cannot escape danger, or the fear of it, by crawling into bed and pulling the covers over our heads." If they heard his words, they ignored his meaning.

Looking back at the year 1941, General George Marshall later described Roosevelt's call to arms in this manner: "It involved, in effect, a great experiment in democracy, a test of the ability of a government such as ours to prepare itself in time of peace against the ruthless and arbitrary action of other governments whose leaders take such measures as they see fit, and strike when and where they will with sudden and terrific violence."

As Franklin Roosevelt's third inauguration day ended, no man could speak with assurance of how that test would be resolved.

FEBRUARY: "... the United States fleet in Hawaiian waters can be destroyed"

ON FEBRUARY 19, 1941, General George Marshall, the Army chief of staff, told a meeting of twenty-nine of his top military advisers that "Out in Hawaii the Fleet is anchored but they have to be prepared against any surprise attack." But he added to them, "I don't say any probable attack but they have to be prepared against a surprise attack from a trick ship or torpedo planes."

The threat of war between Japan and the United States had existed since the early 1920s. It had been then that the United States adopted a policy of keeping its fleet in the Pacific to block Japan's imperialist trends. The American fleet, with its headquarters at the Pearl Harbor base in the Hawaiian Islands served to protect the Pacific territories and the West Coast of the United States as the British fleet in the Atlantic protected the Atlantic territories and the East Coast of the United States. Admiral Harold R. Stark, chief of naval operations, told the commander of the Pacific fleet, "You are there because of the deterrent effect which it is thought your presence may have on the Japs going into the East Indies."

But, of course, a deterrent also can be a target, if an aggressor is bold enough, and also, perhaps, foolish enough. The danger of a Japanese attack on the American fleet always existed. The United States realized it was taking a risk.

That Japan and the United States might fight each other had an extra tragic touch beyond the tragedy of war itself. The United States, along with Great Britain, had been Japan's godparents. Until the middle of the 1800s, Japan had been a nation locked away from the world. The United States and Britain introduced Japan to the world and the world to Japan. But Japan learned its lessons well, much too well. It leaped quickly from the feudal world of the sword to the modern world of the machine gun. In less than a hundred years it made a jump that other nations had accomplished only over centuries. The result was, as Samuel Eliot Morison has described it, Japan's "inability to make a competent synthesis between power and responsibility."

During the 1930s Japan moved into Manchuria and China. It harassed Americans in Asia. It threatened all of Southeast Asia. The rationale was that land was needed for population expansion and that natural resources were required. But the reason went much deeper than any apparent needs. Japan had quickly acquired the technology of the warship and the airplane. Its ethic, however, was of the samurai's sword. What one wanted, this ethic said, one took. The trappings of a modern civilization were the means by which Japan could achieve a barbarian dream.

The only power capable of stopping Japan from achieving this dream was the United States. No other nation in Asia had sufficient power. What happened in the 1920s and 1930s was a tortured chain of circumstances and mistakes. The Japanese exclusion act of 1924, by which the United States blocked the immigration of Japanese people into the United States, was a nasty slap in the face to a proud people. Then the first belligerent moves by the Japanese were not met forcefully by the United States, nor were later moves. Franklin Roosevelt understood that to block Japan's aggressive journey meant courting war with Japan. The United States was not prepared in the 1930s to fight such a war, either militarily or emotionally. FDR's cousin, Theodore Roosevelt, had advised America to carry a big stick. But carrying such a stick means being willing, at some time, to use it. One cannot use a big stick made of paper.

Not being stopped herself and seeing Germany seeming to do so well in Europe, the path for Japan appeared clear. On September 27, 1940, she signed a treaty of alliance with Germany and Italy. This Tripartite Pact brought together the three major world nations that believed in militarism as a policy. The three would conquer the world and then divide it among themselves. This greed and the willingness to use guns to satisfy their hunger were the common denominators that brought together Germany, Italy, and Japan. The great opponent of all three was the

United States. By the way the Tripartite Pact was written, it guaranteed that if one of the three nations went to war against the United States, the other two would join the conflict.

Franklin Roosevelt recognized the threat of war in the Pacific against the United States by Japan. A few days before his third inaugural, he called in Secretary of State Cordell Hull, Secretary of War Henry Stimson, Navy Secretary Frank Knox, and the top uniformed men. What concerned him, FDR told them, was the possibility of Germany and Japan simultaneously making war against the United States. The chances of such a sudden attack, FDR estimated, were one in five.

He cautioned the military men against expecting to have a considerable period of time in which to arm against such a double enemy. "We must be ready," George Marshall reported FDR as saying, "to act with what we had available."

That the United States would someday have to act seemed inevitable early in 1941. The American ambassador to Japan, Joseph C. Grew, wrote FDR that "it seems to me to be increasingly clear that we are bound to have a showdown someday, and the principal question at issue is whether it is to our advantage to have that showdown sooner or to have it later."

The implication of that remark was that perhaps the United States should not wait until it was attacked at a time to the enemy's advantage; perhaps it would be wise for the United States to choose the time of warfare—to initiate or provoke a "preventive" war.

Grew's letter had been written in terms of strategy and not of morality. FDR answered him in the same terms. For the United States to make war against Japan, FDR explained, would have a negative impact on the worldwide struggle against the Axis powers of Germany and Italy as well as Japan.

"I believe," FDR wrote, "that the fundamental proposition is that we must recognize that the hostilities in Europe, in Africa, and in Asia are all parts of a single world conflict. We must, consequently, recognize that our interests are menaced both in Europe and in the Far East. . . ."

Grew had raised the question of whether the United States was not afraid to take on Japan because a war in the Pacific would hamper Britain's effort against Germany. That supposition was correct. That was one of the reasons deterring the United States from being more aggressive toward Japan. Wrote Roosevelt to Grew:

It seems to me that we must consider whether, if Japan should gain possession of the region of the Netherlands East Indies and the Malay Peninsula, the chances of England's winning in her struggle with Germany would not be decreased thereby.

The British Isles, the British in those Isles, have been able to exist and to defend themselves not only because they have prepared strong local defenses but also because as the heart and nerve center of the British Empire they have been able to draw upon vast resources for their sustenance and to bring into operation against their enemies economic, military and naval pressures on a worldwide scale. . . . Our strategy of giving them assistance toward ensuring our own security must envisage both sending of supplies to England and helping to prevent a closing of channels of communication to and from various parts of the world, so that other important sources of supply will not be denied to the British and be added to the assets of the other side.

Grew, like many other people, was not certain that was a proper policy. "It may become open to question," he recorded in his diary, "whether we can afford to await a British victory and whether we should allow Japan to dig in throughout areas where she now visualizes far-flung control. That question, I think, will depend upon the tempo of the Japanese advance." Then he added, "In the meantime let us keep our powder dry."

In early 1941, the tempo of the Japanese advance through Asia quickened. From many sources, both among members of the diplomatic corps in Japan and from the few friendly Japanese officials Grew cultivated, the American ambassador heard reports of growing hostility toward the United States and of plans to move into Southeast Asia.

Shigenori Togo, one of the more prominent members of the Japanese government in 1941 and considered by some to be one of its more moderate members, later tried to justify the acts committed by his country. The blame, he said, lay with the United States. "The Russo-Japanese war (in the early 1900s)," he later wrote, "marked a turning point in Japanese-American relations, an epoch from which the policy of the United States developed in the direction of restraint of Japan's expansion on the continent."

That statement can be a justification only if one can accept that Japan had the right to gain territory, to expand on the Asian continent, by military means. Should the United States have stood by without trying to impose restraints on Japan while Japan attacked Manchuria and China and threatened Southeast

Asia and the Pacific islands? Japan still was the samurai in a world trying to find something better than the warrior.

If Japan attacked the United States, the American naval base at Pearl Harbor would be a primary target.

The base is located on the southern or lee side of Oahu, one of the eight principal islands of what in 1941 was the Territory of Hawaii. Its position was considered strategic: 2,000 miles from San Francisco, 4,767 miles from Manila in the Philippines, and 3,430 miles from Tokyo. Officially the base was the headquarters of the Fourteenth Naval District. This included, in addition to the Hawaiian Islands, a number of other Pacific posts—Midway, Wake, Johnson, Palmyra, and the Canton islands. These other posts, however, were considered minor and were designed primarily to serve or protect Pearl Harbor.

Pearl Harbor itself was a natural harbor. The only entrance was from the south by way of a channel which had been blasted through the coral reef barricade. The entrance began at Keahi and Holokahiki points, was 375 yards wide, 3,500 yards long, and forty-five feet deep at its shallowest point. This entrance was guarded by two protective devices; one to the seaward side consisted of a combined antitorpedo net and antiboat boom, and a second on the inner side with an antitorpedo net but without the antiboat boom.

This base was the natural object of any Japanese attack because, for Japan to move aggressively in the Pacific, the American fleet must be destroyed. A European war would be a land war with great armies moving across that continent. A Pacific war must be a sea war. Ships must travel great distances to deliver an invading army, to bring airplanes within range of targets, to support land operations. The Pacific Ocean was a highway and the American fleet controlled that highway.

There was one man in Japan very much aware of the danger posed to his country's ambitions by the American fleet. His name was Isoroku Yamamoto and he had grown up on the bleak island of Nagaoka in northern Japan at the time Franklin Roosevelt was growing up at Hyde Park and in 1941 was commander-in-chief of the Japanese navy. In the early 1940s Yamamoto was pictured in the United States as having grown up hearing terrible stories about the "barbarians who come in their black ships, break down the doors of Japan, threaten the Son of Heaven, trample upon ancient customs, demand indemnities." These "barbarians" were Americans. At the age of seventeen, according to this version of Yamamoto's life, this young man joined the Japanese navy determined to "return Commodore Perry's visit."

A quarter of a century later a new version of Yamamoto's life appeared. Relying primarily on friends and defenders of Yamamoto, this account pictured Yamamoto as the son of a retiring schoolmaster and as a friend of the few Americans he knew in his youth. The picture of Yamamoto passionately hating the "barbarians" from America is "far from the truth," so this account goes.

In whichever account lies the real truth, to the people of Japan in the early 1940s the truth was that Yamamoto was a fierce militarist who sought to extend his nation's power by armed force. In a Japanese account of his life written in 1943, for example, he was pictured as always eager to fight and, if necessary, die for his country. When Yamamoto had been a student, one of his teachers asked him about his future plans. Yamamoto replied that he would like to do such a thing as would surprise the world. Once in the navy he told a friend of his that he had cremated one half of himself at the time of the Russo-Japanese war and that he was waiting for an opportunity to sacrifice the other half for the cause of his country. To his fellow naval officers Yamamoto was known as one who always kept everything in order in the drawers of his desk because, as Yamamoto explained, anyone whose things were in disorder could not be said to be prepared for battle.

Yamamoto also definitely was not a fool. To a friend of his he wrote on January 24, 1941:

Should hostilities break out between Japan and the United States it is not enough that we take Guam and the Philippines or even Hawaii and San Francisco. We would have to march into Washington and sign the treaty in the White House. I wonder if our politicians who speak so lightly of a Japanese-American war have confidence as to the outcome and are prepared to make the necessary sacrifices.

The statement was not a boast. Rather it was a hard assessment of the military situation facing Japan; too hard, actually. Later even Yamamoto himself would disagree with it. At the end of 1941 the Japanese government would broadcast a slightly altered version of that statement, to make it appear that Yamamoto was boasting. "I am looking forward," this government version said, "to dictating peace to the United States in the White House at Washington." Although the statement was inaccurate, Yamamoto never made any effort to correct it. After his death, his eulogist wrote that Yamamoto "said that Japan should not aim only at Guam, the Philippines, Hawaii, or San Francisco, but at the surrender of the enemy at Washington." Yamamoto may not have intended to boast, but the people of Japan wanted to believe that he did.

A war between the United States and Japan, Yamamoto understood, could not be won, as he said, unless "the United States fleet in Hawaiian waters can be destroyed." The point made by Yamamoto involved too daring a concept for most of his colleagues in the navy. Because of his position, however, a feasibility study was ordered.

"My Peruvian colleague," Ambassador Joseph Grew wired Secretary of State Hull late in January, "told a member of my staff that he had heard from many sources, including a Japanese source, that the Japanese military forces planned, in the event of trouble with the United States, to attempt a surprise mass attack on Pearl Harbor using all of their military facilities. He added that although the project seemed fantastic, the fact that he had heard it from many sources prompted him to pass on the information."

The possibility of a Japanese attack on the American fleet seemed preposterous to the United States Navy. The report would have been dismissed without any attention except that Ambassador Grew and the State Department seemed so concerned. So the Navy investigated and, a few days after Grew's telegram had been received, sent the following assurances to the commander-in-chief of the Pacific fleet:

> The Division of Naval Intelligence places no credence in these rumors. Furthermore, based on known data regarding the present disposition and employment of Japanese naval and army forces, no move against Pearl Harbor appears imminent or planned in the foreseeable future.

In addition to the confidence the American Navy had in itself, another reason why it discounted the possibility of an attack on Pearl Harbor was the shallowness of the water there. An attack on the American fleet while at anchor must be by air, using either dive bombers or planes launching torpedoes. The torpedo planes were the best method of attack against big ships, and no torpedoes known to the American Navy could be launched from the air in the shallow Pearl Harbor waters.

Also there was a feeling within the Navy that it would be foolhardy for an enemy to attack a fleet in a harbor such as Pearl Harbor. No reason existed for such complacency.

In 1937 the American fleet was moving through the Pacific engaging in war exercises. The fleet had split up into two sections, the Blue and the Black. The Blue fleet was at Pearl Harbor. The Black fleet was moving toward them from the north; Admiral Ernest J. King was in charge of this attacking force.

"By golly," a Navy contemporary of Admiral King's has said of King's 1937 maneuver, "he took his carriers north of Oahu, launched his airplanes in bad weather, and swooped through the favoring storm clouds, and appeared over the fleet, to the startled consternation of everyone concerned."

The American Navy should have paid attention to the lesson learned from that mock attack on Pearl Harbor back in 1937. But the military was not learning very well then—even when it had a second chance. This second chance was the British attack November 11, 1940, against the Italian fleet based at Taranto. Taranto is a magnificent natural harbor in the heel of Italy. Well defended, it was considered as impregnable as Pearl Harbor. Using aircraft from the carrier *Illustrious,* the British swooped in with both dive bombers and torpedo-carrying airplanes. The attack disabled half the Italian fleet and shifted the naval power in the Mediterranean Sea to the British.

There were lessons to be learned, if the pupil was alert.

Actually whatever concern existed in American military offices about the fleet at Pearl Harbor being a subject for attack as well as a deterrent was more in Army circles than in Navy. In an early morning meeting on June 17, 1940, in George Marshall's office, Marshall "thinking out loud," as he said, had asked, "Should not Hawaii have some big bombers?" He pointed out that "It is possible that opponents in the Pacific would be four-fifths of the way to Hawaii before we knew that they had moved. Would five or ten Flying Fortresses at Hawaii alter this picture?"

The answer offered by another general at the meeting was: no, the presence of a few more bombers would not make much difference. "We are weak in pursuit," the explanation continued, "and any small force would be destroyed." The answer continued that if the United States could get reserves of ammunition and bombs to Hawaii, the big planes, if needed, could be there in three days after an emergency arose. Marshall commented that three days might be fatal. Another general suggested that an attack might come with less than twenty-four hours warning.

No one suggested the possibility then of an attack without any warning.

Several months later, in October, Henry Stimson, the Secretary of War, had spoken to FDR about defenses at Hawaii and Pearl Harbor. "I told him," said Secretary Stimson of that session with the President, "that our real need was more anti-aircraft guns and troops and more heavy bombers; that the defense of the group of the Hawaiian Islands depended on command of the air from Oahu."

By the time Roosevelt was inaugurated in January, 1941, the Navy was beginning to realize its fleet might be in some danger at Pearl Harbor. "If war eventuates with Japan," Navy Secretary Frank Knox said to Stimson, "it is believed easily possible that hostilities would be initiated by a surprise attack upon the Fleet or the Naval Base at Pearl Harbor."

This, continued Knox, had prompted a new study of the fleet's security at the base. In the order of possibility, Knox said, the dangers were of an air bomber attack, an air torpedo plane attack, sabotage, submarine attack, mining of the harbor, and bombardment by gun fire. Said Knox, "Defense against all but the first two of these dangers [the air bomber and air torpedo plane] appears to have been provided for satisfactorily."

Still what concern existed about Pearl Harbor was within the Army. The new Army commander there was Major General Walter C. Short. Marshall told him that "My impression of the Hawaiian problem has been that if no serious harm is done us during the first six hours of known hostilities, thereafter the existing defenses would discourage an enemy against the hazard of an attack."

Despite that warning to Short, Marshall did not believe a surprise attack against Pearl Harbor a basis for serious concern. "I do not feel that it is a possibility or even a probability," he said. Marshall's difficulty then was that he looked at Pearl Harbor as the traditional army man would, in terms of land to attack, hold, and occupy. He did not appreciate that sufficient damage to the United States could be done simply by the first of those three—the attack. He made this clear in a conversation with Secretary of War Stimson. Stimson was explaining the President's view that the fleet should be kept at Pearl Harbor. The chief of staff disagreed. Marshall said that American heavy bombers and new pursuit airplanes, when combined with the land force at Pearl Harbor, would be too much for the Japanese to consider attacking. An invasion attempt, he argued, would be defeated. He did not understand then that the problem was the existence of the fleet rather than who held the land.

Against this background of growing hostility between Japan and the United States, a six-foot, two hundred pound Japanese navy admiral presented himself in Washington early in February, 1941. His name was Kichisaburo Nomura and he was the new ambassador from his country to the United States. Japan's foreign minister, Matsuoka, had cabled confidential instructions for the new ambassador. The United States had broken the Japanese code and learned, even before Nomura did, that the United States could avoid war by recognizing Japanese authority in the western Pacific. It meant giving Japanese military aggression carte blanche.

"These instructions," said an amazed FDR to a State Department official, "seem to me to be the product of a mind which is disturbed and unable to think quietly or logically."

On February 12, Nomura presented his credentials to Secretary of State Cordell Hull. The meeting was marked by a coolness that barely met the demands of protocol. The two men made what Hull described as "somewhat brief" preliminary remarks, then Hull offered to arrange a session with the President. "He then handed me his credentials," Hull wrote, "and the conversation ended. There was no effort by either of us to enter into any discussion of anything."

A question has always hung over the position of Nomura: What was the purpose of his coming to the United States?

One State Department official who spent much of 1941 dealing with Nomura later remarked that "Admiral Nomura was one of the finest men that I've known, a man of high character, absolutely patriotic." The official added, "He was inexperienced in the field of diplomacy because he was not a diplomat." Among the Japanese, Nomura had a reputation of being pro-American, or at least one not anxious for war with the United States. He also had known Roosevelt for years. It was easy from this background to conclude, as many at the time did, that Japan was genuinely interested in a rapprochement with the United States. History offers a more realistic assessment: Nomura was the dupe of militarists in the government who sent him to the United States to mislead the American government into believing Japan genuinely was interested in peace.

Nomura and FDR had first met when Nomura was stationed in Washington during the First World War. It was natural that Nomura, a navy man, would meet Roosevelt, then Assistant Secretary of the Navy. After the war, with Nomura back in Japan, they corresponded occasionally. Most of this correspondence was letters of congratulations to FDR from Nomura on occasions of Roosevelt being elected to office. FDR usually wrote polite and friendly answers. When Nomura was about to formally present his credentials at the White House, FDR said of him, Nomura "is an old friend of mine."

The two men met February 14, with FDR greeting Nomura in what Hull, who was present, called a "marked spirit of cordiality and personal friendliness." Roosevelt recalled his association with Nomura years earlier, and then said he proposed to call Nomura by his title of Admiral rather than Ambassador. FDR then said, as Hull recorded it, that "they were friends and they could at all times talk candidly as friends about the relations and related affairs of the two countries."

The President then reviewed some of the difficulties between the nations and pointed out that the American people were concerned about the course Japan was taking. Twice the President spoke of the Tripartite Pact, which Americans were interpreting as Japan's surrender to Germany on the question of whether to make war. Roosevelt then suggested that Nomura meet on occasion with Hull to discuss problems in the Pacific.

"The President," Hull wrote, "finally said it would not do this country any good nor Japan any good, but both of them harm, to get into a war. The Ambassador gave his prompt assent to this."

Nomura spoke in a friendly fashion to FDR, giving the appearance of earnestness and of a sincere desire to preserve peace between the two nations. He was critical of the military group in his nation as representing the chief obstacle to the continuing peaceful relations between the two nations. As he spoke, the feasibility study of Admiral Yamamoto's proposal for an attack against Pearl Harbor was beginning.

FDR had made such an effort with Nomura because he was anxious to keep Japan at bay. His crucial problem then, as he saw it, was not fighting Japan but assisting England. Since the War of 1812 between the United States and England and the proclamation of the Monroe Doctrine a few years later, when the United States asserted its authority over the western hemisphere, England and the United States had had a satisfactory *modus vivendi*. With the possible single serious exception of the Civil War, when England was sympathetic to the Confederacy, England generally stayed out of the affairs of the American hemisphere. More important, her fleet controlled the Atlantic, shielding the United States from the wars of Europe. Some thought of the Atlantic as an impassable barrier. It was nothing of the kind. It was a sea route, a water highway, as passable as any other highway. The only reason it had been a barrier through the years was that the British fleet patrolled it. American isolationism had been possible not because the ocean was a fortress wall but because of British guns. If those guns were lost to Germany, there would be no protection.

That was the reason behind America's effort to assist England. It was not an effort which, in February, 1941, appeared destined for success. Joe Kennedy, who had been in England as the American ambassador, did not believe England could survive the Nazi attacks. He said Great Britain was finished, and for that reason was removed as ambassador. However, no one could say his thesis was overly pessimistic. England's prospects were bleak. Germany had conquered continental Europe with a minimum of difficulty. The jump across the English Channel did not seem too far. Germany continued to be well-armed and devoted to war as a means of achieving policy. England was a badly-battered defender of freedom.

Probably because of his distaste for fascism, certainly because of his concern for a United States facing Germany without England as a buffer between them, FDR would not abandon his effort to save England. This effort was managed on the American side by Roosevelt himself and on the English side by Winston Churchill. Rarely in the world's history had there been such a remarkable combination, so personal, so vital, and so significant.

The two men originally had met during the First World War, although Churchill did not recall the meeting in later years. Like FDR, an advocate of military preparedness, Churchill had urged the development of a strong air force in the years before the First World War. During the early years of the war he was First Lord of the Admiralty. Later he was minister of munitions and made visits to the United States in hopes of securing military assistance. It was on such a trip the Assistant Secretary of the American Navy first met him.

"Just back from lunch with Winston Churchill," Franklin Roosevelt wrote Eleanor in the summer of 1917. "He saw the President yesterday and apparently had a pretty satisfactory talk."

Churchill was in his forties during the First World War. He was a squarely built man with red hair who had never outgrown his early reputation as a dashing soldier, traveler, writer, and entertaining lecturer. His romantic life must have intrigued the young Roosevelt with his staid Wall Street law office background. Roosevelt obviously was impressed by Churchill. For example, after a meeting with Wilson, FDR wrote Eleanor, "The more I think over the talk with the President, the more I am encouraged to think that he has begun to catch on, but then it will take lots more of the Churchill type of attack."

In the years following the First World War, Roosevelt and Churchill did not meet again. But FDR did not forget the Englishman. After the Second World War began, Churchill was brought into the Neville Chamberlain cabinet as First Lord of the Admiralty. That was the position he had first held in World War I.

A few days after joining the cabinet, Churchill received the following letter:

My Dear Churchill:
It is because you and I occupied similar positions in the World War that I want you to know how glad I am that you are back again in the Admiralty. Your problems are, I realize, complicated by new factors but the essential is not very different. What I want you and the Prime Minister to know is that I shall at all times welcome it if you will keep me in touch personally with anything you want me to know about. You can always send sealed letters through your pouch or my pouch.
I am glad you did the Marlboro volumes before this thing started—and I much enjoyed reading them.

That letter from Franklin Roosevelt is typical of his correspondence. A courteous congratulations, a statement of encouragement, the expression of interest and the request to be kept informed, and then finally the personal note about Churchill's writing; all reflected a gracious man.

Churchill quickly responded with his thanks, signing his letter "Naval Person." And so began a remarkable correspondence. The letters over the next five years would total in the hundreds. They would be warm personal notes, or lengthy explanations of policy; some were frantic pleas for assistance or curt comments against a projected plan or person. These letters between "FDR," as the President signed his letters, and "Naval Person" (later "Former Naval Person") forged a liaison between two men and two nations. It was a liaison based on mutual trust and confidence, and a shared belief in the evils of Nazism and the virtues of democracy. To Churchill, Franklin Roosevelt was a great man, a warm friend, and the foremost champion of democracy in the fight the world then faced against fascism.

In May, 1940, Neville Chamberlain resigned as Prime Minister of England and Churchill became that nation's new Prime Minister, heading a coalition cabinet. Roosevelt considered Winston Churchill the best man England had. He undoubtedly was.

Winston Churchill, by the time he became Prime Minister, was acknowledged to be the world's finest orator. In a world that included orators of the quality of Franklin Roosevelt and Adolf Hitler, that was high praise for Winston Churchill. For a time his oratory was England's only weapon. He promised any invader that the English people would fight him on the beaches, in the streets, in the homes—"We shall never surrender." And he told his countrymen, "Let us therefore brace ourselves to our duties, and so bear ourselves that, if the British Empire and its Commonwealth last for a thousand years, men will say, 'This was their finest hour.' "

When Britain was without military arms, when its air force was exhausted, when its incoming supplies were ravaged by German U-boats, the vision of the English citizen fighting off all attackers in defense of his home, as conjured up by a pugnacious bulldog of a man who had become the British prime minister, was sufficient to frighten off Adolf Hitler.

Winston Churchill knew he needed more than oratory. He needed American assistance. When the battle of France was drawing to a close in May, 1940, he telegraphed FDR that an invasion of Britain was expected shortly. Churchill promised that the British people would give a good account of themselves. "But if American assistance is to play any part," he cautioned, "it must be available soon."

And then two days later he was even more blunt. He pointed out in a message to the President that he could not bind future British governments. If American aid was not forthcoming, Churchill said, it was entirely possible that some future prime minister might bargain away the British fleet to the Germans in hope of peace. Unspoken was the significance of the threat, without the British fleet as a guard, the Atlantic Ocean would be open to a Nazi army moving toward the United States. "Excuse me, Mr. President," Churchill concluded, "putting this nightmare bluntly."

Churchill had only pointed out a reality of the situation, and it was a mark of the maturity of the two men, the sender and the receiver, that they could be so honest with each other.

As he entered his third term as President, Roosevelt was more and more haunted by the vision of England holding out valiantly against Germany, suffering the loss of its youth, its riches, and its energies. On the eve of his inaugural, Roosevelt was host at the White House to Wendell Willkie, the man he had defeated in the election almost three months earlier. Willkie was about to leave on a fact-finding trip to England for FDR. The two men chatted for a few minutes and then FDR asked Willkie to deliver a note to Churchill. Grabbing a piece of his personal stationery and a pen, FDR scrawled out a short note.

A few weeks earlier England had suffered the worst fire bombing of the entire war. Bombs dropped by German airplanes had started 1,500 fires in London. Because of the German air attacks, more than a million Englishmen were on duty as air raid wardens, auxiliary fire fighters, medical assistants, and in other special jobs. The number of civilians wounded by German bombs was approaching forty thousand and the civilian death toll had climbed over twenty-five thousand. England's army was in a state of collapse. The country's back was against the wall as Franklin Roosevelt began his note to Winston Churchill.

"Wendell Willkie will give you this," wrote the President. "He is truly helping to keep politics out over here." The President began a new paragraph: "I think," he wrote, "this verse applies to your people as it does to us." Then he scrawled these five lines:

> Sail on, O Ship of State!
> Sail on, O Union, strong and great!
> Humanity with all its fears,
> With all the hopes of future years,
> Is hanging breathless on thy fate!

Both Roosevelt and Churchill had a similar quality. Each could arouse a man to do more than that man thought possible for him to do. Churchill could call on his people to make one more sacrifice, to take one additional risk, to stand even more solidly in defense of their nation—and they did. Roosevelt, on the eve of his third inaugural, called on Winston Churchill never to waver, never to forget the great stakes for which he was playing. And Churchill never forgot. "These splendid lines . . ." Churchill said of that letter "were an inspiration."

Roosevelt wished a closer relationship with Churchill than letters could bring. FDR and Churchill then could not meet, neither man could leave his country for any length of time. FDR did what for him was the next best thing. He sent the man closest to him to England. He was Harry L. Hopkins. The relationship between these two men was unique. Perhaps no President and an assistant were quite as close as were FDR and Hopkins. Jean Monnet, a Frenchman who knew both FDR and Hopkins well in this period, later said of Hopkins' relationship with FDR, "There was a kind of osmosis between him and Roosevelt. The President was the man of synthesis—of the big view. Hopkins was the organizer. He became the informal chief of staff, 'the president in charge of action,' you might say."

Not everyone had quite so positive a view of the Hopkins-FDR relationship. Harold Ickes, perhaps twinged by jealousy, made clear that he did not like Hopkins and did not like the influence that Ickes believed Hopkins had with the President.

Wendell Willkie once asked FDR why he kept Hopkins on his staff. "You surely must realize," Willkie said to the President of Hopkins, "that people distrust him and they resent his influence."

Roosevelt answered, as Willkie recalled it, this way: "Someday you may well be sitting here where I am now as President of the United States. And when you are, you'll be looking at that door over there and knowing that practically everybody who walks through it wants something out of you. You'll learn what a lonely job this is, and you'll discover the need for somebody like Harry Hopkins who asks for nothing except to serve you."

By the 1940s Harry Hopkins was in his fifties. He had devoted most of his life to social welfare causes. When FDR had first been elected governor of New York, he picked Hopkins to administer the Temporary Relief Administration. In two years Hopkins spent $140 million. When FDR became president, he asked Hopkins to do the same job nationally. Hopkins accepted and from 1933 until 1938 he spent $8.5 billion. Then he became ill and resigned, but in 1940 he moved into the White House to work directly for the President.

"The only way he is working," said FDR of his assistant, "is that I have got him over in the White House and I put him to bed every night at a reasonable hour and I see that he gets proper food and he is coming along strong. Doctor Roosevelt! There is nothing like it!"

Hopkins' strength in government was his presidential support, so he did not hesitate to be sarcastic with others. During a Cabinet meeting, when one Cabinet member permitted his interest to noticeably stray, Hopkins passed him a note. "Now listen carefully," it read, "because the class is in session. *Act* & *Look* interested."

In appearance Hopkins was a scrawny man who always seemed as if he believed he should be doing something else, something of greater importance than being with whoever was talking to him. "He gives off a suggestion," commented *Fortune* magazine, "of quick cigarets, thinning hair, brief sarcasm, fraying suits of clothes and wholly understandable preoccupation."

Hopkins often was underrated. A friend once described him as a "hick." He added, "Harry will always be a hick. He still gets a small-towner's thrill out of going to a New York nightclub and spotting famous people." *Time* magazine reported that comment and then added, "Yet Harry Hopkins is certainly as sophisticated a hick as ever came down the road; the hayseed on him has charmed more notables than an ascot tie ever would have."

It was this "hick" who was going to the land of the ascot tie at Franklin Roosevelt's direction.

Steve Early, the White House press secretary, was the first to inform Hopkins. "You're elected to go to England," he told him.

Hopkins had been at work in the White House room he used as both a bedroom and an office when Early's telephone call had come. After hanging up the telephone, he walked over to the presidential office in the west wing of the White House. "Did you say that, Boss?" he asked.

The President acknowledged that he had decided to send Hopkins to London.

"Well," said Hopkins, "I'm going." He continued, "I'm going right away. I'm not going to hang around here. I know what you'll want me to do, go over to the State Department for instructions and get the view of a lot of people. I won't learn anything that way; all I need is a long talk with you."

The President accepted Hopkins' terms. They had a long talk over the weekend, and Hopkins left for London by clipper.

"I am sending over to London Harry Hopkins for two or three weeks so that he can talk to Churchill like an Iowa farmer," explained Roosevelt.

When the President was pressed by newsmen as to whether Hopkins would have "any mission to perform," he answered, "No, you can't get anything exciting. He's just going over to say 'How do you do' to a lot of my friends."

But it was exciting. Hopkins was going to London as the President's eyes and ears. Much of the President's attitude toward England—could it stand before Hitler? should it be helped? was Churchill leading it properly?—would be determined by the reports filed by Hopkins. No one knew this better, perhaps, than Felix Frankfurter. He understood Roosevelt and Hopkins and the relationship between them; he also understood the significance of the Hopkins trip. And Felix Frankfurter was not one to deny himself the opportunity of acting.

He stopped by to see his friend, the Right Honorable Richard G. Casey, Australian minister in the United States. Justice Frankfurter explained to his friend that Prime Minister Churchill should understand several things about Hopkins. First, Frankfurter said, Hopkins is passionately antitotalitarian; he would be sympathetic to the British situation. But, Frankfurter stressed this second point, Hopkins reveres Franklin Roosevelt, reacts negatively to anyone who does not hold the President in high regard, and also suspects that the Prime Minister is such a person. Frankfurter then suggested that the surest way of making the Hopkins trip a success from the British viewpoint was to make certain that Winston Churchill expressed his great admiration for FDR in an early meeting with Hopkins.

Lord Casey immediately telegraphed a summary of the Frankfurter conversation to a friend in London. "I saw the Prime Minister last night," the friend telegraphed back, "and conveyed your point. He is most grateful and will certainly act on it."

The meeting between Hopkins and Churchill was a resounding success. Each man heard what he wanted to hear. Churchill impressed Hopkins with his high regard for President Roosevelt. Hopkins impressed Churchill with his statement that "The President is determined that we shall win the war together. Make no mistake about it."

Hopkins spent several weeks with the Prime Minister. He was shown everything about England's war effort that he wanted to see. All his questions were answered. He spoke with most of the Englishmen prominent in the war effort. Again he was assisted. Harold Laski, the teacher and British socialist and good friend of both Frankfurter and Roosevelt, led Hopkins down the right paths.

"This is an apology for speaking with all this frankness," Laski told Hopkins, "but I am assuming that I may say to you precisely what I should have said in similar circumstances if I were talking at the White House or discussing it all with F.F."

And then in a memorandum Laski suggested persons for Hopkins to see. Of one man: "His specialty is bombers. He is completely up-to-date. He knows the Ministry up to the last moment. A little slow, nevertheless complete integrity." Of the Labour Party leaders: "If you see Attlee with the others, it is imperative to make him talk and not to let any of the others take away the conversation." Of a union official: "By emphasizing to him the importance of great measures, you could swing an influence into the conduct of the Government of quite vital importance." And of Churchill: "What matters is the adequacy of the team and not the place in the hierarchy that the accident of years has produced. Some clearly secondrate men are in the Government, some equally clearly firstrate men are left outside."

Roosevelt was quite pleased with the way the Hopkins–Churchill relationship developed. At a Cabinet meeting Roosevelt, never a humble man, praised himself for his choice of the Iowan as his personal emissary to Churchill. Harold Ickes was skeptical. "I suspect," he thought, "that if, as his personal representative, the President should send to London a man with the bubonic plague, Churchill would, nevertheless, see a good deal of him." And Ickes probably was correct.

Hopkins left England confident the British, although facing difficult times, ultimately would survive. "The people here," he reported to Roosevelt, "are amazing, from Churchill down."

Although FDR in 1940 had thought in terms of materiel assistance to England, he also realized that the United States had to take certain precautions in the event it was involved in war. This realization had long been apparent to the American military men. The result was the "ABC-1" conferences in early 1941; they ran through February and ended in March. The very fact they existed was a danger. "War might have exploded at once," wrote Robert Patterson, "had rumors of ABC-1 gained circulation, and the United States was far from ready."

The conferences were a series of secret strategy sessions held in Washington between American and British military leaders. Congress, if it had learned of the sessions, might have interpreted them as steps toward war and would have, in fear, balked at any rearmament action. The Axis powers also might have interpreted the sessions in the same manner and seized upon the conferences as a pretext to launch a war against the United States. The distinction between precautions in the event war came and steps toward war was a subtle one that easily could have been ignored in the emotions of the time.

The most pressing question, in the event war came, was the disposition of the American fleet. Its primary purpose had been to stand between Japan and the Pacific islands as well as the American west coast. If war broke out, could the United States continue to depend upon the British fleet guarding the Atlantic? Admiral Harold Stark, chief of naval operations, had first suggested that a meeting between American and British military leaders would be advisable to find answers to such questions. General Marshall agreed the idea was sound.

On December 2, 1940, a colonel on the War Department's general staff wrote a memorandum stating that the British would send to Washington a group of military officers for discussions. "In order to insure secrecy," wrote the colonel, "these officers will be sent as additions to the British Purchasing Commission."

There were six British military men. They wore civilian clothes and were attached, as far as the public knew, to the commission charged with obtaining war supplies in the United States. Their first session with their American counterparts was on January 29, nine days after Franklin Roosevelt had been sworn in as president for the third time.

Sumner Welles, Under Secretary of State, had been expected to welcome the British delegation formally at that session, but he was not present. At no time did a Cabinet member attend any of the ABC sessions. None could be accused of being aware of it. Admiral Stark and General Marshall did attend the opening session, but only long enough to make welcoming speeches. In his talk, Marshall warned that public knowledge of the meetings would have disastrous results in Congress.

After Admiral Stark and General Marshall left, the delegations got down to business. Both the Americans and the British made clear they were there only to discuss; neither side could commit its leaders or its nation. There were fourteen meetings, the last one on March 27. The English in these sessions, naturally, were interested in involving the United States as far as possible in the war. The Americans, just as naturally, were very cautious about sounding as if they were interested in doing more than a neutral nation should be doing.

The British wanted the United States to assume the responsibility of defending Singapore, a British outpost in the Pacific. In case war broke out with the Japanese, the British could not themselves hold Singapore because they were concentrating their main strength in Europe. The Pacific post, they maintained, was not only important strategically but also had great significance as a British possession. If it fell, who would retain faith in the ability of England to stand before the Axis?

The Americans would not go along with this, however. They believed it beyond their assignment to make such a decision. Also they did not believe Singapore to be of sufficient military importance to warrant taking ships and men from other Pacific bases which might be more important.

From the conference did emerge agreement in substantial areas. The United States would sell much of its developing aircraft production to the British. A primary purpose of the Allies would be to protect Great Britain against invasion. The Americans and the British would join together in additional attempts to persuade the Japanese to avoid war. But the most important result to emerge from the ABC conferences was the Anglo-American agreement that should the United States and England find themselves at war with Germany and Japan, the major effort would be made against Germany. The President and the military agreed that of the two great enemies the United States faced, Germany and Japan, Germany was the more serious threat. She was the one that must be blocked at all costs. Of those two warring nations, Germany had the manpower, the industrial resources, the conquered land masses, and the absolute lack of moral scruples that made her overshadow Japan as a danger to England and the United States.

This "Germany first" strategy was important to the British; Hitler was at England's doorstep. But it also was in keeping with American thinking. The strategy was not imposed upon the United States; it was welcomed by the United States.

As early as April, 1939, in some exploratory studies by the Joint Planning Committee in Washington, it was decided that if war came, "There can be no doubt that the vital interests of the United States would require offensive measures in the Atlantic against Germany and Italy to preserve the vital security of the Caribbean and the Panama Canal. If this is done it will be necessary to assume a defensive attitude in the eastern Pacific."

George Marshall quickly came to that approach. In June, 1940, he asked a meeting of his staff: "Are we not forced into a question of reframing our naval policy, that is into purely defensive action in the Pacific with a main effort on the Atlantic side?"

Three months later, in September, Japan signed the Tripartite Pact with Germany and Italy. Sitting up in his bed one morning, discussing Japan's joining the Axis, Roosevelt continued to insist that Hitlerism was the great enemy of Western civilization. He wondered if the Pact were not merely a diversion to turn the United States away from Europe. If it were, he insisted, it would not work. The United States would hold the Atlantic line as well as the Pacific line. But, he explained, the Pacific action would be a delaying one while the Atlantic action would be an aggressive one. The policy would be "Germany first."

The fear was that if Germany won, it would close off a major source of America's trade as well as open Latin America to German exploitation and military conquest. Japan represented a threat in the Pacific, but not that much of a physical threat to the western hemisphere.

In November, 1940, Admiral Stark presented a paper that became known as "Plan Dog," after the crucial point in Paragraph

D. "Shall we direct our efforts toward an eventual strong offensive in the Atlantic as an ally of the British, and a defensive in the
Pacific?" he asked, pointing out that "Any strength that we might
send to the Far East would, by just so much, reduce the force of our
blows against Germany and Italy."

That memorandum by Stark also raised another issue, one that
many in Washington preferred to ignore. If the United States
wanted to see Germany defeated, it must consider entering the
war itself. "Purely naval assistance," he wrote, "would not, in
my opinion, assure final victory for Great Britain. Victory would
probably depend upon her ability ultimately to make a land offensive against the Axis powers. For making a successful land
offensive, British manpower is insufficient. I believe that the
United States, in addition to sending naval assistance, would also
need to send large air and land forces to Europe or Africa, or
both, and to participate strongly in this land offensive."

This memorandum would be the sword hanging over all their
heads as the American planners worked in 1941. As sympathetic
as Roosevelt would be to the British cause, and as much as he
would have the United States contribute to that cause, he and his
military men knew the essential step that the United States
must take was to join with England in fighting Germany. England simply could not do it herself. But that step Roosevelt
could not and would not take.

There was no dispute with this Germany-first strategy.
Marshall agreed with Stark. The formal American military position in December, 1940, was that although "our interests in the
Far East are very important, it would, however, be incorrect to
consider that they are as important to us as is the integrity of the
western hemisphere, or as important as preventing the defeat of
the British commonwealth."

Roosevelt accepted this, willingly. At a White House meeting
January 16, four days before his third inaugural, FDR told his
military leaders that if war came, the United States would take
the defensive in the Pacific and the offensive in the Atlantic.

The Germany-first policy would dominate American thinking
through 1945. It was not a policy imposed upon an innocent
United States by a deceitful England. The Germany-first concept
always had been the policy of the American military and of the
President.

The ABC meetings produced a report. It summed up the conclusions reached in the meetings and, stamped "SECRET," it was

sent around to the top government officials for approval. There were only one hundred twenty-five copies of the report, each one numbered for security. Admiral Stark and General Marshall gave their approval to the report. The President never did, in writing, but there was no doubt he agreed with the conclusions. Roosevelt's keen political eye did manage to catch a potentially embarrassing line. The report he received said the purpose of the meetings had been to determine the best means of defeating Germany and the other Axis powers "should the United States desire to resort to war." When the report left his desk, the line read "should the United States be compelled to resort to war." He did not desire war and he did not wish an historian to later find any document suggesting that he or the United States did desire war.

The United States made no commitments to the British at the ABC meetings that it had not already made to itself. Nor was the United States led into any traps. Instead, the United States and England emerged with a better understanding of what could be expected of the other—if war came.

Robert Patterson, who had been so concerned at the possible explosion if the public had learned of the ABC meetings, later reported that "The secret was kept, however. The plan gave us some basis for evolving our war plants and time to decide which things came first."

In that month of February as he wrestled with the problem of a sly and ever more dangerous Japan and with the question of assisting England, FDR had another issue thrown at him. On the surface it involved the question of should the United States help feed the starving areas of Europe conquered by Germany. Beneath the surface was the question of the future of the French fleet.

In 1940, when France had fallen to Germany, Churchill begged the French to allow their fleet to sail to British ports so that the French ships could be used on the side of the Allies. To block this, Hitler promised the fallen French leaders that the fleet could be inactivated and that he would not use it in Germany's cause. This was still the situation in 1941. But the collaborationist Vichy government showed inclinations of wanting to turn the fleet over to Hitler. That would have given Hitler a tremendous military advantage, and a chief concern of the British and the Americans was to block that from happening.

"The one supreme purpose of the Laval-Darlan group," said

Secretary Hull of the Vichy government, "seemed to be to whip-saw French sentiment around by utilizing the food relief question in a most dastardly way so that this group might get the upper hand at Vichy, and with the support of changed French sentiment turn the Navy over to Hitler." He made that comment in February to Lord Halifax, the British ambassador to the United States. It was Britain that was blocking the food shipments from the United States to Europe.

Almost as soon as the Germans had pushed the British off the European continent at Dunkirk in 1940, stories began circulating in the United States that the Nazis were treating the occupied nations with decency and that there would be no obstacles placed in the way of American efforts to feed the hungry Europeans. Some of the stories were "plants" by German agents or German sympathizers. Others sincerely believed they had seen examples of the Germans' decency and were happy to advocate that the United States assist beleaguered peoples. Feeding the hungry, they pointed out, was, after all, an American tradition.

From his tower suite at the Waldorf-Astoria in New York, Herbert Hoover, Franklin Roosevelt's old enemy, was leading the campaign to supply food for Europe. Hoover had been President when the 1929 Depression struck. With his high, stiff shirt collar and small-knotted tie, with his neatly parted hair and his paunch pushing out at his vest, Hoover seemed the prototype of the small-town lawyer or banker who was the hero to the American people in the 1920s. An engineer and a humanitarian, as well as a self-made millionaire, Hoover lacked the ability to govern in time of crisis. Unwilling to act decisively when the Depression struck, during the next three years he presided over the disintegration of the American economy and much of the fabric of its social and moral life as well. In the election of November, 1932, the American voters repudiated Hoover and chose Franklin Roosevelt to replace him in the White House. Hoover did not take his loss with grace, nor did he ever reconcile himself to it. His anger and resentment was directed at FDR. On occasions Hoover had hopes of regaining his party's banner and defeating FDR at the polls. But in 1936 William Allen White rallied the Midwesterners behind Governor Alf M. Landon of Kansas and pushed him into the nominee's position. In 1937 Hoover had hoped he could use FDR's attack on the Supreme Court—"court packing" Hoover named it—as an issue with which to regain leadership of the Republicans; but in this he failed. In 1940 the Republicans turned to Wendell Willkie, a vigorous personality who probably did as well against FDR as any Republican could have done. As 1941 began, Hoover was in his mid-sixties; the prospects of his ever having another chance as a presidential candidate were remote. Still, he could try to embarrass the man in the White House and also perhaps hurt him politically.

Feeding the Europeans in the conquered lands was a "natural" issue for Hoover. His original fame had come during the First World War when he had served with great distinction as chairman of the American Relief Committee in London, as chairman of the Commission for Relief in Belgium, and finally as United States Food Administrator. He won such deserved glory saving war-ravaged Europeans from starvation that he was prominently considered as a presidential candidate in 1920 by both the Democrats and the Republicans; his Republican inclinations were then unknown. The issue in 1941 then would not be a manufactured one for Herbert Hoover. It would be a natural result of his desire to see the hungry fed, mixed with his dislike of England, his isolationism, and his hatred of FDR.

Hoover's campaign for the United States to feed the conquered Europeans disturbed FDR. Roosevelt believed that Hoover was becoming altogether too successful in drumming up public support for his cause. At one point, Roosevelt talked to a friend of his who was an officer in the J. P. Morgan banking company. Could the friend do anything to keep Hoover quiet? The friend said he would try, but he was not successful.

Hoover claimed any food sent to the European nations could be restricted to those who needed it, that the Germans could be blocked from stealing the food. But few in the Roosevelt administration believed that. They argued that food to Europe would be food to Germany. There also was another point. The British were blockading continental Europe. If American ships tried to run that blockade to deliver food, the British would stop them. That would present a delicate situation, one that the United States preferred to avoid.

England made clear its belief that it should not be asked to permit the sending of food to German-occupied Europe. An official British government statement said that "His Majesty's Government" had given "most sympathetic attention" to Herbert Hoover's proposals, "all the more so because His Majesty's Government have had in mind the noble services rendered by Mr. Hoover to the people of Belgium and other countries during and after the last war." But England had concluded, the statement said, that "any such scheme [to feed Europe] must be of material assistance to Germany's war effort and would thereby postpone the day of liberation of these peoples from German subjugation. They are therefore not able to give permission for the passage of food through the blockade."

Realizing that its refusal could be used as a propaganda weapon against it, particularly in the United States where it needed support, England closed its formal statement in this way:

Great Britain is risking starvation and undergoing every conceivable hardship in the fight for freedom not only for herself but for all freedom-loving peoples. We cannot in these circumstances endanger our existence and imperil our cause by weakening our blockade. The British people who are in the firing line have through their representatives in Parliament expressed their determination not to give assistance to Germany such as would result from the adoption of Mr. Hoover's proposal. We trust that all those who share our love for freedom and hope for our victory will sympathize with and support our attitude.

The polite tone of the English statement belied the anger the British people felt at that situation. They saw no suggestion made that Germany, which was occupying the European nations, stop withdrawing food supplies from the occupied countries. They saw no suggestion made that Germany stop the ravishment of these lands. They saw no suggestion made that Germany stop the forced recruitment of labor, including agricultural workers, from the occupied lands. All such suggestions would have done more, in the British view, to relieve hunger in occupied Europe than any American shipments. And the British saw no suggestion made that the Germans make any efforts in return for receiving such food from the United States. All that the British saw was the implication that they were responsible for the starvation in Europe. The people of England, who were selling off their empire to pay for the cost of the war, who were watching their cities being destroyed by German bombs, who understood that once again a generation of their young men would be lost on the fields of Europe, could not accept responsibility for food conditions in Europe.

A few days before FDR's third inaugural, the French ambassador to the United States, Gaston Henry-Haye, paid a formal call on Secretary of State Cordell Hull. He spoke "very earnestly and strongly about the urgency" of obtaining food for France, both occupied and unoccupied.

Hull began his answer with a courteous and diplomatic response. The United States, he said, retains to the fullest extent its ancient friendship for France and her people and is watching every opportunity to assist France. It must be made clear, however, continued the Secretary, that the United States deeply believes that the success of Great Britain against Germany was crucial to the future welfare of both France and the United States. Then, as he warmed to his subject, Hull became less diplomatic. He told the French ambassador that he was greatly surprised to find some friends of America "continuously" urging Great Britain to lift the blockade. "At the same time," continued the Secretary, "there has not been heard one whisper by these food relief leaders about facing Germany and reminding her that she has robbed the people of their foodstuffs and caused them to go out into the world seeking to replace that which has been stolen from them." He continued at the same level for a few moments. Hull obviously had been irritated by the constant references by persons such as Hoover and in the pleadings of Ambassador Henry-Haye that the United States and Great Britain were at fault, while such references ignored German responsibility.

"The Ambassador did not attempt to dispute what I said," Hull recorded later, "but nodded his head as though he did not feel justified in taking issue with it."

Herbert Hoover continued to press the issue. Late in January he met with Lord Halifax, the British ambassador to the United States. Hoover told the ambassador that a food crisis would erupt in Belgium by the middle of February. Unless the British government lifted its blockade of the European continent so that the Belgians could be fed with American food, Hoover threatened to launch a "paralyzing" movement against the British in the United States. Halifax replied that Great Britain had decided weeks earlier not to lift the blockade and that there was nothing further to discuss.

But Halifax was worried. How capable, he asked Secretary of State Hull, was Hoover of carrying out his threat? Hull assured the British ambassador that there was no cause for concern. If Hoover made any such effort, the response would be that Germany should be approached first about its plans to feed the peoples it had conquered. When satisfactory answers were supplied, Hull continued, "it would then be time to turn to Great Britain and take up the blockade question with her." Lord Halifax agreed on the wisdom of that approach.

Food for Europe was obviously a major domestic political issue in the United States. Evidence mounted that the Germans also understood the political value of the issue. The American ambassador in Vichy France was an old FDR friend, a retired navy admiral named William D. Leahy. The day after FDR's third inaugural, Leahy met in France with a representative of the Red Cross. Their subject was food. The Red Cross representative stated bluntly, Leahy reported, that "The Germans have now in France vast quantities of food in storage, particularly wheat; that the Germans in France are well fed. That the Germans may permit food conditions in the cities to become desperate and then make political capital by feeding the population from their stored reserves."

In February Leahy met with Admiral Jean Darlan, a prominent official in the Vichy government. As Leahy reported to FDR, the conversation made clear that the food issue could develop into a major propaganda instrument of the Axis. "He is very much concerned," said Leahy of Darlan, "about recent British naval action in stopping ships carrying food to parts of the French empire in which, according to him, it could not possibly be of use to Germany, and he stated categorically that if this British action continues it will be necessary for him to announce publicly that the starvation of the French people is due to the action of the Churchill government. He also said that it may be necessary for him to convoy ships carrying food and to sink any British ships that attempt to interfere."

FDR was using the issue militarily. If the United States did not supply the food, pressure would increase on Germany. Either it must supply the food itself or it must cope with the discontent of a hungry people. This could shorten the war. There were two other factors bolstering FDR's position. The first was that Germany had invaded these lands and had assumed the responsibility for them. Most of the hunger experienced in France and Belgium and the other conquered nations was caused either by Germany stealing food from them and transferring it to its own people or by the ravaging of the land by German invaders. The second mitigating factor was the belief—and the evidence supporting this belief would mount substantially during 1941—that any food sent to the occupied nations would be diverted to Germany.

Still, to head off the developing political issue, FDR did authorize the shipment of two boatloads of wheat to unoccupied France. The British agreed to this; their blockade would not stop the ships. Later, FDR permitted the sending of food for infants.

Hull explained to Halifax that the small shipments of food were being allowed to blunt the Vichy attempts to build up support in France for the turning over of the French fleet to Germany. Halifax understood the situation and did not object. But he suggested that Hull try to coax as much as possible from the French in exchange for its food shipments. Hull should tell the French that it might be a profitable idea to respond in kind to the British lifting the blockade for the two wheat ships. For example, Halifax suggested, the French could join in a plan for "rigid supervision" to prevent Germans from infiltrating into French Africa, and the French could move their naval vessels away from continental Europe, where they were an easy prey for Germany, toward French North Africa.

As a device for preventing the Germans from getting hold of the French fleet, the American policy succeeded. The American food trickling into France was sufficient to blunt the Darlan efforts. He never could build up sufficient animosity toward England among the French to justify the turning over of the fleet to Germany. In 1942, when Hitler broke all promises to France and seized the unoccupied territory, German forces moved on the French port of Toulon to take possession of the fleet. French sailors scuttled their ships rather than see them used by the Germans.

As would often happen during the Second World War, Germany worked against its own best interests. Its demands for cooperation from Vichy France and the willingness of the leaders of that government to collaborate with Germany became apparent to the American people. The political issue in the United States involving food for France, instead of feeding France, became one of *not* feeding France.

"The efforts of Admiral Darlan and others of the government," FDR wrote to William Leahy, "to increase collaboration with Germany has definitely compromised our program of assistance to France. The two flour shipments which go forward this week represent a certain contribution, but this cannot be continued unless we receive positive evidence not only from the Marshal but from his Government that our efforts to aid are creating a positive resistance to German demands for further collaboration in support of their military aims."

FDR's personal inclinations were to help feed the Europeans. But he could not do so unless he could produce some gains to show the British. Also, he needed such gains for America's own position; he needed reasonable assurance that such food would not build up the United States' potential enemy, Germany. "I feel," he told Leahy, "as if every time we get some real collaboration for the good of the French, especially for the children, started, Darlan and some others say or do some stupid or not wholly above-board thing which results in complete stoppage of all we would like to do."

Leahy, who had been sympathetic at first to the cause of feeding France, gradually became disillusioned with the Vichy government and its prospects of ever being anything more than an adjunct of the Third Reich. He ultimately would advise FDR to continue distribution of baby food. "In regard to all other shipments to continental France," he quickly added, "it is my opinion that the present collaborationist attitude of Vichy fully justifies and points to the military advantage of clamping down tight on the blockade." He recommended "clamping down" even if it involved "engaging escorting French naval vessels."

Eventually there would be no question that any food sent to Europe by the United States, except baby food, would be stolen by the Germans. William Leahy, at one point, slipped across the French border into Spain. At Barcelona he met FDR's aide, Myron C. Taylor. The shipment of baby food should be continued, Leahy reported to Taylor. It was helpful to morale and created a friendliness for the United States. It did reach its destination. Germany, however, takes all the other food "she dares." Leahy was certain, Taylor reported, that "If America sent food, generally Germany would take equivalent."

There was even some question of whether food for infants would reach its destination. Harold Denny reported in *The New York Times* that ". . . a shipment of canned milk arrived [in Greece] as the gift of Premier Mussolini of Italy for poor children of Athens and Piraeus. It was immediately confiscated by the Germans."

Food to Europe then would be food to Germany, the enemy. And food, like everything else, was a weapon of war. It could be as serious a weapon and as deadly a weapon as a rifle bullet. This was the second major issue behind the food for Europe campaign.

Germany used food as it used all of its assets. Its soldiers, its striking force, were allowed the best diets. The workers who built the weapons for that striking force were permitted second-level diets. When it had begun planning for war in the mid-1930s, Germany had understood the military value of food as well as it understood the value of an air force and of the tank. It tried to increase food production so that it could be self-sufficient when war came and Germany also tried to educate its people to the new diets a war might make necessary.

But Germany's plans for food, like its plans for other items of military value, counted on a quick victory. More intensive farming methods may have resulted in higher grain and potato production, but they also depleted the soil. As the war progressed, other difficulties in the production of food showed. Shortages of farm labor developed as more young men were needed for the army. The farmers ran out of fertilizers. Trains to haul the grain and the other farm goods no longer were available.

According to information available to the United States government early in 1941, Germany had enough bread grains to last until sometime in 1942. Potatoes were in ample supply, but there would be distribution problems. Germany, the United States knew, had come into a windfall supply of meat as a result of a slaughter of animals in the Netherlands and in Denmark. But by the winter of 1941, according to American estimates, the German meat supply would begin to dwindle. Either meat rations would have to be reduced among the population generally, or the rations going to manual workers would have to be reduced.

Also, the United States expected that Germany would be facing a shortage in fats, vitamins, and minerals. Germany would be unable to continue its prevailing level of food rations in a protracted war. The foodstuffs it was taking from the occupied nations—and that action was causing the food shortages in those countries—was to build up its own military position. The food supplies of conquered Europe were being used as an integral part of the total German war effort. This analysis of the food situation meant that the longer the war, the less chance of Germany fighting effectively. And so for FDR it all came back to assisting England. The longer she could keep Germany involved in hostilities, the greater would be the opportunity for Germany's defeat. Time was against the Axis powers.

MARCH: *"Suppose my neighbor's home catches fire . . ."*

THE MORNING of Sunday, March 9, Winston Churchill awoke at his country estate Chequers to find his secretary waiting with a message. Harry Hopkins had called from Washington during the night while the Prime Minister was sleeping. Churchill heard Hopkins' message and then quickly sent him a reply.

"Thank God for your news," said the Churchill answer to Hopkins. "The strain is serious."

The news telephoned across the Atlantic by Hopkins was that the Senate had approved the lend-lease program. Churchill was to later describe this program as the most unsordid act in all of human history.

When William Leahy heard the news in Vichy France, he thought, "This definitely puts the United States in a position from which it must, for its own security, take any action that is necessary to insure the success of Great Britain in the present war."

Both estimates were correct.

The lend-lease program committed the United States to becoming the arsenal of democracy. The United States would manufacture the weapons of war while the English would fight the Germans with those weapons.

The British need for American assistance had been apparent as soon as the war had begun in 1939. "There is no question that the war is going to be conducted with eyes constantly on the United States," Joe Kennedy had reported to the President from the American embassy in London when the war was only one week old. "Unless the war comes to a standstill and it is a stalemate between the Germans and the French on the Maginot and Siegfried lines, the English are going to think of every way of maintaining favorable public opinion in the United States, figuring that sooner or later they can obtain real help from America."

During the First World War, when they were fighting together, England and the United States had cooperated on military matters. This concept of cooperation had faded after that war. In 1938, however, the two nations agreed to offer each other's fleet assistance in case both nations were involved in a war with Japan. The agreement, although a loose one, did reestablish the concept of military cooperation between the two nations.

In November, 1939, as a second step in reviving the concept of military cooperation, FDR had persuaded Congress to amend the neutrality laws so that England and France could buy weapons of war on a "cash and carry" basis. Not only had FDR approved of the sales then but he had also established a policy of making a large part of America's military production available for sale in England.

By the time of the battle of Dunkirk in 1940, when Britain rescued its army from the European continent, the concept of cooperation between England and the United States had not yet evolved enough in detail to have much meaning. George Marshall has best summed up the situation the British and the Americans were then in. "Immediately after Dunkirk in 1940," he said, "the British Isles were in effect defenseless so far as organized and equipped ground forces were concerned. Practically all their field army equipment had been lost and an immediate invasion was threatened. . . . For the United States the military issue immediately at stake was the security of the British fleet to dominate the Atlantic."

Churchill appealed to the United States for assistance. He had the manpower, the British soldiers rescued at Dunkirk, but he needed weapons for them.

The United States, in the summer of 1940, was desperately short of weapons itself. It did have, lying about from the First World War, 500,000 Enfield rifles plus some other equipment. This equipment was not modern, but would be needed if the United States suddenly were at war. Could this be given to England? Members of the American general staff argued that providing England with any equipment would be only wasting it. England, they believed, could not last against Germany. That was the expert advice given to Roosevelt.

But FDR was skeptical of it. Knowing something of the sea and something of naval requirements, FDR realized that an invasion of England would require a much greater quantity of small sea craft than Germany had available or had the prospect of acquiring quickly. Also FDR was willing to give more weight to an unmeasurable quality called national spirit than were his military chieftains. He had seen that spirit organize behind him to fight the Depression eight years earlier. He believed he was seeing it mass behind Churchill to fight Germany.

So he rejected the professional military opinion that England would not survive.

A 1926 law, which appeared to allow the United States to sell surplus military equipment for cash, was found. With misgivings, George Marshall declared the rifles and the other equipment surplus. Roosevelt was delighted. He told Henry Morgenthau to give the shipment of the "surplus" goods priority. "Give it an extra push every morning and every night," he directed, "until it is on board ship!"

"It was," said Churchill of the Roosevelt action, "a supreme act of faith and leadership for the United States to deprive themselves of this very considerable mass of arms for the sake of a country which many deemed already beaten."

After the rifles, the immediate need of England was for destroyers. Churchill asked for the ships in May, 1940. Roosevelt responded that the sale of destroyers required Congressional authorization which, for political reasons, would not be forthcoming. Churchill kept pressing for the ships. After the fall of France, he said, the Germans had the entire French coastline to use as launching sites for submarines, as well as Norway. At the same time German air attacks against British shipping had been serious. In the last ten days of July four British destroyers were sunk and seven were damaged.

"Mr. President," said Winston Churchill, "with great respect I must tell you that in the long history of the world this is a thing to do *now*."

Franklin Roosevelt resolved to act, but he could not act illegally. Ben Cohen, one of his close aides from the New Deal days and still a government official, told FDR that the destroy-

ers could be released to the British "if their release for such purpose would, as at least some naval authorities believe, strengthen
rather than weaken the defense position of the United States."

FDR told Frank Knox that giving the ships, or "releasing"
them in Ben Cohen's phrase, would not stand up legally. "Also,"
he said, "I fear Congress is in no mood at the present time to
allow any form of sale." A little later perhaps, FDR suggested
to Navy Secretary Knox, Congress might be persuaded to allow
the sale of the ships to Canada. This would release Canadian
ships to assist England.

But England could not wait. Three weeks after Cohen's memorandum to the President, Churchill informed a sympathetic
Henry Morgenthau that "The need of American destroyers is
more urgent than ever in view of the losses and the need of
coping with the invasion threat. . . . There is nothing that America
can do at this moment that would be of greater help than to send
fifty destroyers, except sending one hundred."

A solution was quick to come. A group of the nation's most
prestigious lawyers sent a letter to the editor of *The New York
Times* in which they claimed that the President had the legal
authority to sell over-age destroyers that were then not in use.
The letter was developed by Ben Cohen and Dean Acheson.
Acheson represented the epitome of the "Washington lawyer."
He moved with ease from private practice in the most respected
law firms to government service and then back. In the summer
of 1940 he was in private practice. He drafted the letter, with
Cohen's assistance, and rounded up the signatures. He had no
trouble persuading *The New York Times* to publish the letter.
Charles Merz, an editor of the newspaper, had been a Yale class-
mate.

Robert Jackson, the attorney general, had to be reached and
persuaded that the sale could take place without Congressional
authorization, then the President had to be persuaded. Neither
man required much effort. But curiously, as Jackson later told
the story, Winston Churchill did. Rather than sell the ships for
money, they would be "sold" for British bases in the Atlantic.
The deal was actually a wise one for England. Not only did she
receive the ships without having to pay any cash, she was relieved of posting ships at a series of bases in the Atlantic. Also,
the placing of American ships at these bases extended America's
line of defense into the Atlantic, bringing that line closer to

Europe. Still, for a time Churchill feared that the British people would object to the trade, believing that the United States might have taken advantage of their predicament. He continued to press for the giving of the ships to England without any cost.

In a transatlantic telephone conversation with Churchill, Jackson tried to explain that the President had legal authority to sell the ships but did not have the authority to give them.

"Empires just don't bargain," Churchill replied.

"Well," answered the American attorney general, "republics do!"

The President later told Churchill that "The trouble is that I have an attorney general—and he says I have got to make a bargain."

"Maybe," grumbled the Prime Minister in answer, "you ought to trade those destroyers for a new attorney general!"

But the trade went through. America supplied the destroyers and Great Britain leased some of her empire. The President dictated a memorandum on the agreement to send to Congress. When he had finished, he said to his secretary, Grace Tully, as she remembered it: "Grace, Congress is going to raise hell about this but even another day's delay may mean the end of civilization. Cries of 'warmonger' and 'dictator' will fill the air but if Britain is to survive we must act."

Churchill believed the destroyer deal persuaded Spain to remain neutral rather than enter the war on the side of the Axis. He also believed that the deal contributed to Germany and Italy joining with Japan in September, 1940, to organize the Tripartite Pact, as a means of surrounding the United States. Certainly it also made the British understand they were not alone in standing against Adolf Hitler. America was their friend.

There was some resistance to assisting England with the rifles and the destroyers. The extreme isolationists and pacifist groups were bitterly opposed. Frederick J. Libby, executive secretary of the National Council for Prevention of War and one of the grand seigniors of the peace movement, charged that the European war would end in a few months unless "direct American participation" prolonged it. "On the continent," Libby said, "Hitler's army, best equipped in history, cannot be defeated."

But Libby and the tiny movement he led were exceptions. Many Americans were willing to aid England, assuming that England paid for such assistance. Part of this was the traditional tie with the Anglo-Saxon nation. Part of it was the abhorrence of the Nazi system. And in 1940 much of it was the shock of the Nazi brutality toward England. Rather than risk invasion, Hitler decided to bomb England into submission. Cities like London and other residential centers were attacked night after night, with civilian and military targets being bombed indiscriminately, in an effort to force England to surrender. But bombing did not produce surrender; rather, it increased the determination to resist.

Sympathy for the victims of this blitz quickly build up in the United States. That sympathy soon would be translated into political action. The politically astute William Allen White wrote to a Congressman friend:

I have been going to write you for two or three weeks [to tell you] to watch your step about this war from now on. It is approaching England, and anything you say and any vote you cast may possibly have to be defended when the horror of the terrible war is descending upon Great Britain. Public sympathy will be rising for Great Britain and we will forget our isolationist tradition. Watch your step. Your political path is strewn with dynamite and step easy and look where you go. The ordinary inhibitions of the last two or three years about your vote on questions of foreign relations are all out. When they begin to bomb Wales and the casualty list of women and children and old men goes into thousands, watch for any vote that would seem to withhold sympathy or aid in that awful time.

This growing sympathy for England made the sale of large supplies of American arms and ammunition that much easier politically. And such sales were substantial. In a report dated February 19, 1941, for example, as the United States faced a request from the British for 900 million rounds of ammunition, George Marshall conceded that "We have to reduce the amount of ammunition for training to about sixty percent" of America's needs. The rationale behind this was the need to keep England fighting. It continued America's first line of defense.

There was, however, another side to the large sales of American arms and ammunition to England and to France before it fell to the Germans in 1940. The orders placed by those nations with American firms gave the industries an economic incentive to gear up for military purposes long before Franklin Roosevelt could persuade them to. The Congress might have been reluctant to give FDR needed funds to order arms for American troops, but there was little objection to American industry making a dollar. By the time the American government was ready to move, a firm industrial base for an armaments industry had been created by the British and French orders.

In a little more than two years after entering the war, England spent three billion dollars in the United States for arms. That included two hundred million dollars in direct assistance for capital improvements—buildings, modern machinery—to American corporations. The money went to the makers of airplanes, ammunition, machine tools, motor vehicles, and ships. The American military aircraft industry actually began to develop because of the $1.5 billion in British orders for airplanes placed after September, 1939. What would become famous as the American "Liberty" ship, a quickly-built cargo ship, was begun from a British design and a British contract. The manufacture of American tanks began with United States firms taking contracts to build British tanks. British funds also supplied incentive for the development of a modern machine tool industry and also for the training of skilled workers capable of handling those tools. The American rearmament effort may have been mothered by America's own defensive needs, but it was fathered by the British.

But all this was based on England being able to pay for what she purchased. England eventually would run out of funds. But giving the British armaments without being paid in return would violate the nation's policy of official neutrality. The administration, in 1940, did not believe it could do this. The formal neutralism of the United States was not hurting Germany, which had prepared for war and did not need American aid. The policy, however, did hurt England and France, which had not prepared for war and did need American assistance.

James Wadsworth, a Republican member of the House of Representatives from upstate New York, wanted to do something about changing this policy. Being a member of the minority party in the House and not belonging to the foreign affairs committee, he did not believe he could effectively lead a drive to change the policy. Wadsworth went to the State Department for a chat with Sumner Welles, the Under Secretary of State.

"Crisis may hit us this coming year," Wadsworth later recalled saying to Welles, "and it will hit us all the harder if we hang onto this neutrality policy until we are actually driven into war." Welles agreed, Wadsworth recalled, saying the policy was wrong.

Then Wadsworth said, "I have no influence on the Hill. I'm

a member of a small minority and I'm not a member of the foreign affairs committee, but wouldn't it be wise for the administration to confer with Democratic leaders in the House and Senate and warn them of this possible danger if the Neutrality Act
is to remain upon the statute books, and organize them for repeal
of the neutrality laws?"

"I think it should be done," Welles answered, "but I think you
had better come into the adjoining room and have a talk with
Secretary Hull."

Sitting across from Cordell Hull, Wadsworth repeated what he
had said to Welles.

"Wadsworth, we can't do it," the Secretary replied. "We
can't do it, I'm afraid."

"Why not, Mr. Hull?" pressed the Congressman. "Can't the
administration with its power and its large majorities in both
houses of Congress get to work on this thing? Why not, Mr. Hull?"

"Politics, Wadsworth. Politics."

The Secretary continued as Wadsworth recalled it, by repeat-
ing the cry of much of the American public: " 'Keep us out of
war.' "

This was politics. It was the kind of politics that tells a national
leader in a democracy that he cannot do what his constituents
oppose. Before Franklin Roosevelt could act and before he could
demand that Congress act, he must first persuade the American
people of the necessity of acting. And in 1940 the American people had not been persuaded.

In the next year they must be.

"We don't require in 1941 large armies from overseas," said
Winston Churchill at the beginning of that year. "What we do
require is weapons, ships and airplanes." Then he added, "All
that we can pay for we will pay for, but we require far more
than we will be able to pay for."

The statement was Churchill's. The problem was Roosevelt's.

Churchill once told W. Averell Harriman that "Few men are so
gifted as to understand the politics of their own land. No man
can understand the politics of another land." But the British
Prime Minister was underrating himself. He understood American politics extremely well. Before presenting the situation of
British cash being insufficient to pay for British military needs,
Churchill waited until the 1940 American presidential election
was over. Not only was Churchill then assured of a friendly audi-

ence in the White House, but the delay had been most discreet. A report that England was seeking credit could have turned the American election against FDR.

In December, 1940, Churchill sent a formal letter to the President explaining the British economic position. "I come to the question of finance," wrote the Prime Minister. "The more rapid and abundant the flow of munitions and ships which you are able to send us, the sooner will our dollar credits be exhausted. They are already, as you know, very heavily drawn upon by the payments we have made to date. Indeed, as you know, the orders already placed or under negotiation, including the expenditure settled or pending for creating munitions factories in the United States, many times exceed the total exchange resources remaining at the disposal of Great Britain." Then Churchill cautioned: "The moment approaches when we shall no longer be able to pay cash for shipping and other supplies."

Roosevelt received the letter while he was taking a post-election Caribbean cruise. He quickly understood the letter's significance. For hours he sat alone in a deck chair on the *Tuscaloosa*, rereading the message. The tropic sun did not warm him. For Roosevelt the problem never was should the United States assist England by extending her credit; he realized that the United States must, to save itself. The problem, rather, was how to persuade a reluctant Congress and a disbelieving public.

The extent of the British plight was becoming fully understood throughout the American government. "Get the money," said a civilian War Department official when presented with the blunt fact of a shortage of British funds blocking an arms delivery. "I would spend every cent I could get," the official continued, "legally or otherwise, if it would speed defense." At a December meeting in Treasury Secretary Morgenthau's office, there was a discussion of the British needs versus the remaining British assets. It was apparent that the United States, if it were to continue aiding England, must finance the war's cost.

"I was rather shocked at the depth we are getting into," recorded Secretary of War Stimson, who had attended the meeting, "and I told Morgenthau frankly at the meeting that I thought Congress ought to be taken into the confidence of the Executive— that the Executive should not go ahead on such an enormous project alone."

A few days later the *Tuscaloosa* docked at Charleston and

Roosevelt returned to Washington. He felt refreshed. He looked good. And he had an idea.

The next day he held a news conference. "I don't think there is any particular news . . ." he began. The veteran correspondents perked up. Knowing FDR, they knew that the line signaled a major news development coming.

Then the President began to chat informally. He said that most Americans understood that their first line of defense was England and realized that "from a selfish point of view of American defense . . . we should do everything to help the British Empire to defend itself." He then conceded having read "a great deal of nonsense" during the past few days about what the United States might do to assist England; there had been considerable speculation about loans and outright grants.

The President got down to business. "In my memory," he said, "and your memory and in all history no major war has ever been won or lost through a lack of money." Then he told this story:

In 1914 I was up at Eastpoint, Maine, with the family at the end of July, and I got a telegram from the Navy Department that it looked like war would break out in Europe the next day; and actually it did break out in a few hours, when Germany invaded Belgium. So I went across from the island and took a train down to Ellsworth, where I got on a thing known as the Bar Harbor Express. I went into the smoking room, and the smoking room of the Express was filled with gentlemen from banking and brokerage offices in New York, most of whom were old friends of mine; and they began giving me their opinion about the impending world war in Europe. And even though I was young, I had the sense to take up some—I suppose they should be called forms of wagers. These eminent bankers and brokers assured me, and made it good with bets, that there wasn't enough money in all the world to carry on a European war for more then three months—even money; that the bankers would have stopped the war within six months—odds of two to one; that it was humanly impossible, physically impossible, for a European war to last for six months—odds of four to one; and so forth and so on. Well, actually, I suppose I must have won those— they were small, $5 bets—I must have made a hundred dollars. I wish I had bet a lot more.

The President next emphasized his point that back in 1914 the "best economic opinion in the world" believed that continuing the war "was absolutely dependent on money in the bank." He said to the newsmen, "Well, you know what happened."

He explained that the United States would have to continue helping England in its own selfish interests but dismissed as "banal" the suggestions he had heard so far about providing the necessary funds to England. He then proposed this alternative: the United States to take over all British orders. As much of those arms as "the military events of the future" would determine would be sent to England, he explained. "Either lease the materials or sell the materials, subject to mortgage to the people on the other side," he said.

"Now, what I am trying to do is to eliminate the dollar sign, and that is something brand new in the thoughts of practically everybody in this room, I think—get rid of the silly, foolish old dollar sign. All right!"

What FDR really was suggesting was that the United States give England all the arms she needed and worry about being paid for them at a later date. Would the American people and the Congress go along with what appeared to be a giveaway program? Roosevelt thought they would if it were presented to them correctly.

Suppose my neighbor's home catches fire, and I have got a length of garden hose four or five hundred feet away; but, by Heaven, if he can take my garden hose and connect it up with his hydrant, I may help him to put out his fire. Now, what do I do? I don't say to him before that operation, "Neighbor, my garden hose cost me $15; you have got to pay me $15 for it." What is the transaction that goes on? I don't want $15—I want my garden hose back after the fire is over. All right. If it goes through the fire all right, intact, without any damage to it, he gives it back to me and thanks me very much for the use of it. But suppose it gets smashed up—holes in it—during the fire; we don't have too much formality about it, but I say to him, "I was glad to lend you that hose; I see I can't use it any more, it's all smashed up." He says, "How many feet of it were there?" I tell him, "There were 150 feet of it." He says, "All right, I will replace it." Now, if I get a nice garden hose back, I am in pretty good shape.

The President then summed up:

In other words, if you lend certain munitions and get the munitions back at the end of the war, if they are intact—haven't been hurt—you are all right; if they have been damaged or deteriorated or lost completely, it seems to me you come out pretty well if you have them replaced by the fellow that you have lent them to.

Franklin Roosevelt was suggesting the lend-lease program. In effect, the United States would assume responsibility for producing almost all the arms the British needed. If after the war the material was still in good condition, it could be returned; otherwise it would be replaced, paid for; or, as Franklin Roosevelt suggested to a friend, "If everything turns out all right, we can forget all about it."

By using the simile of a neighbor helping the man next door, Roosevelt had placed the situation in a perspective readily understandable to Americans. They were the kind of people who helped their neighbors in such a situation, not only because it was the decent thing to do but also to prevent the fire from jumping across the yard and burning down their own home.

Announcing a program and having Congress enact it into law, however, are two different things. Roosevelt had been brilliant with the first. He, and the men helping him, must be equally brilliant with the second.

Perhaps the most politically astute assistant FDR had was a man not in his administration. This was Felix Frankfurter. As a law professor at Harvard, Frankfurter had assisted the Roosevelt administration in transforming many of its grandiose welfare schemes into legislation, his keen legal mind capable of turning rhapsodic theories into the acceptable minutiae of legislative proposals. Roosevelt had appointed him to the Supreme Court in 1939. Although Frankfurter did not believe that Supreme Court justices should involve themselves outside the Court, particularly on issues that might come before the Court, he was able to overcome that reluctance when it came to assisting his friend and benefactor, Franklin Roosevelt, and the great cause he supported with Roosevelt, stopping Hitler.

On the afternoon of Friday, January 3, 1941, Treasury Secretary Morgenthau and Ben Cohen called on Justice Frankfurter. The justice carefully examined the draft of the lend-lease bill they presented him. There were, he said, a couple of changes that could help. One was altering the wording of the section having to do with the powers of the President so that they would not appear quite so strong. There was no reason to scare more people than necessary. He also recommended that the bill include a preamble, in nice quotable language, explaining the bill's contribution to national defense. That, he said, would enhance the measure's constitutionality. Since Frankfurter was one of the

nine men on the Supreme Court who would have to judge any
constitutional challenge to the law, on that point he spoke with
great authority.

The next day Morgenthau and Cohen took the bill to Sam
Rayburn, the Speaker of the House. He gave them his parliamen-
tarian for the afternoon to help with drafting the final form of
the bill. Within a few days it was ready for introduction in Congress. Shepherding a bill through Congress is a touchy business.
Success is not always dependent upon the public's reaction to
the proposed legislation, nor even upon the will of the majority
of the Congress. In both the House and Senate, committees must
examine the proposal, perhaps redraft it, approve it, then send
it to their parent bodies for approval. The first obstacle then was
the committees on Foreign Affairs in both the House and Senate.

The chairman of the House committee was Sol Bloom, a New
Yorker. The House Democratic leader, John W. McCormack
of Massachusetts, doubted whether Bloom was capable of guiding
the measure through the opposition of Republican and Democratic isolationists. At a strategy session he recommended that
the bill be routed through the Ways and Means Committee. As
an alternative, another person present suggested, Speaker Rayburn could fill four vacancies on the Foreign Affairs Committee
with persons friendly to lend-lease.

When the strategy session moved to the White House, Rayburn reported that House Democrats were insistent that the bill
go to Bloom's Foreign Affairs Committee. House members are
particularly sensitive to any apparent violation of traditional
procedures. The House being so large—435 members is an un-
wieldy body—its members believe they can only survive by a
rigid adherence to the rules. It was this belief that blocked any
attempt to bypass the committee which should have received it.

But if the bill went to the House Foreign Affairs Committee,
it must also go to the Senate Foreign Relations Committee. Walter
George of Georgia, chairman of that committee, told the President that if he were lucky, the bill would emerge from his committee with only one or two votes to spare. That was too tight a
squeeze. McCormick then made a suggestion. Usually a presidential bill is introduced in the House and Senate by the chair-
men of the committees involved, Bloom and George in this
case. McCormack recommended that he, as majority leader in
the House, and Alben Barkley, as majority leader in the Senate,

sponsor the bill. This had never been done before, and more than twenty-five years later McCormack said he did not remember doing it since.

The purpose was to emphasize the importance attached to the bill as well as give it flexibility. The members of the Foreign Affairs committees wanted jurisdiction over the bill. They wanted the publicity that would come to them from the hearings. They also wanted the feeling of importance that would come to them from handling a major piece of legislation. Also, because of their deep involvement with foreign relations, they had a strong desire to continue shaping legislation in that field. But they had to promise not to be too rough on the bill; otherwise it would go to another committee.

Bills in Congress are numbered in order of introduction. Rarely has there been a case of a bill numbered out of order; there is, in fact, no formal record of a bill being numbered out of order. The lend-lease bill was numbered out of order, however, when it was introduced in the House the morning of January 10. A total of 1,764 bills had been introduced up to that morning. When a House clerk received the lend-lease bill for numbering, he should have affixed a number in the 1760s to it. Instead, he numbered it 1776, knowing that enough bills would be introduced during the day to go beyond that number. By his act the House clerk related lend-lease to visions of embattled Minutemen fighting for their liberty.

Although Roosevelt's Democratic Party appeared to have strong majorities in both houses of Congress, there was a large number of isolationist Democrats, like Senator Burton K. Wheeler, of Montana, who would oppose the lend-lease bill. When these were added to Republican opposition senators, the potential "no" votes were significant.

And the Republicans were against the President. One of the best analyses of the Republican position was made by Wendell Willkie a few days before FDR's third inaugural. Sitting with some friends in a New York apartment, Willkie went over the list of Republican leaders. He referred by name to Herbert Hoover; Robert A. Taft, a rising political star from Ohio; Alf M. Landon; Thomas E. Dewey, who was beginning to attract attention to himself in New York; and some of the Congressional leaders. He described the lot of them as isolationist. There were several reasons for this, Willkie explained. First, Willkie himself supported the President's internationalist position. This means, Willkie said, that anyone planning to challenge him for the Republican nomination in 1944 must automatically tend to take the opposite position. Second, he continued, the businessmen who make up the backbone of the Republican Party still resented FDR's interference with their untrammeled pursuit of profits and feared war measures would increase that interference. Also, Willkie told his friends, businessmen were coming around to the appeasement theory, that the war could be "fixed up." Now that Hitler has unified Europe, the businessmen were thinking, it might even be easier to do business with Europe. Finally, he said, businessmen were scared that a war economy would demand huge taxes and result in confiscation of their fortunes.

Willkie described Herbert Hoover as the "brains" of the isolationist movement. Then he listed Roy Howard of the Scripps-Howard newspapers as "general manager or field marshal" and Bruce Barton, the nation's leading advertising man, as "contact man." Willkie said that the isolationists had decided to make a major stand against the lend-lease bill. Roy Howard, Willkie recounted, had telephoned him and said the lend-lease bill was a chance for Willkie "to show up that blank-blank as a dictator."

Willkie had, instead, supported lend-lease. Howard, as Willkie told the story, then telephoned him again and asked him to dinner. Over dinner Howard said he wanted to warn Willkie that the Scripps-Howard newspapers were going to "tear your reputation to shreds." Willkie said that kind of talk, mixed with cajolery, continued for about three hours. Willkie said he managed to keep his temper, but added that "if Howard wasn't such a little pip-squeak I'd have felt like knocking him down."

The opposition to lend-lease then had the leadership of an ex-President, the public relations know-how of a newspaper publisher, and an advertising executive, plus a goodly number of influential businessmen. It was from this last group that the isolationist groups such as America First had developed to oppose FDR's policies.

But the lend-lease bill had on its side such Congressional professionals as John McCormack, Sam Rayburn, and Alben Barkley—as well as Franklin Roosevelt. Having learned a good deal about handling Congress in his eight years as President, FDR no longer sent bills to Capitol Hill and then waited for a subservient Congress to act. Now he was inviting wavering members of Congress to come to the White House for a chat. He could not coerce a member of Congress, but he could talk to him, flatter him, explain the bill's purpose. This approach was helpful with members who had doubts about the lend-lease proposal.

Senator James E. Byrnes, Democrat of South Carolina, one of the bill's shepherds in the Senate, sent regular progress reports to the President through a White House aide. In February, Senator Byrnes reported that a Democratic senator previously opposed to the bill now supported it. "I do not know how to account for this change," said Byrnes, "except that the Senator went to the White House and upon his return left instructions to be paired in favor of the bill. I suspect a man named Roosevelt."

On another occasion, a presidential friend suggested that the President call in Senator Albert B. "Happy" Chandler, a Democrat of Kentucky, to settle a feud Chandler was having with the Democratic senatorial leaders. The friend suggested that the President's "felicitous touch" could "bring Happy out openly and probably vigorously for the bill." The friend received a note from a White House assistant informing him that "everything is smooth and lovely."

The President had some assistance. Lend-lease was helped by the extremism of the opposition, principally Burt Wheeler. The Montana Senator appeared on radio discussing lend-lease and said, "The lend-lease program is the New Deal's Triple-A foreign policy; it will plow under every fourth American boy." Wheeler's thesis was that Franklin Roosevelt was leading the nation to war. FDR believed that by saving England he was saving the United States, perhaps from war and certainly from defeat.

Roosevelt was not above grappling with Wheeler. He described the Wheeler attack as "the most untruthful, the most dastardly, unpatriotic thing that has been said in public life in my generation." Wheeler later was to confess that his words "did sound somewhat harsh." He also reported Joe Kennedy's comment to him that "If the President hadn't criticized that speech of yours, there wouldn't be five thousand people who remembered it. Now five million people will remember it."

The Wheeler attack was not the only example of the opposition allowing the administration forces to turn an attack to its advantage. During the House debate, a Missouri Democrat named Dewey Short, an ardent isolationist, told his fellow representatives that "I never knew I would live to see the day when a good Irishman like John McCormack, from Massachusetts, would openly admit that Great Britain is our first line of defense." The comment was intended to embarrass McCormack with his Irish constituents because of his co-sponsoring lend-lease. But John McCormack was a match for that kind of thing, any day. He answered Short in the House the next afternoon. "And, by the way," said McCormack of Short, "he gave me a characterization yesterday that I consider a great compliment—the Irishman from Boston. There is one greater compliment that he could give me—by characterizing me as 'The American of Irish descent from Boston'!" The House of Representatives gave John McCormack a standing ovation, and he had no trouble with his constituents.

The President was willing also to compromise, to appear to give members of Congress something so they could claim a victory of sorts over the President. The clue that a compromise would be acceptable came toward the end of January at a press conference when FDR was asked to comment about reports that the lend-lease bill would be amended. Rather than respond strongly with a denunciation of any weakening moves, the President shrugged off the question. "I would have to know what the language was," he said, "and I haven't had anything of that kind." By declining to say no, the President had indicated he would accept amendments.

Rayburn worked out several amendments with his fellow House members. All appeared to restrict the President's power. They placed time limits on the lend-lease programs, called for regular reports to Congress, and detailed Congressional authority to end the program. That last amendment was forced on Rayburn by Republicans. Once these amendments were adopted, the bill easily passed the House. The vote was 260 to 165. The 260 "yes" votes included twenty-four Republicans who were defying their party leaders. That vote was a mark of their political courage as the 135 Republicans who voted against the bill indicated the party was largely unified against lend-lease—a fact that would be significant when the bill was voted on in the Senate.

The House amendments accepted by the President did not make the bill palatable to the Republicans. They believed FDR had originally asked for more power than he wished, only so he could appear to make a retreat on those minor issues. The Senate, the Republicans decided, would be the crucial field of battle.

Herbert Hoover had a session with Harold Burton, the freshman Republican senator from Ohio, that was typical of the ex-President's efforts to lobby behind the scenes against the bill. Hoover and William R. Castle, a State Department official in Hoover's Cabinet, invited Burton to join them for a private dinner. An ex-President and an ex-Under Secretary of State were big company for a freshman senator. According to Burton, after a lengthy discussion of the lend-lease bill, Hoover "gave me a list of seventy-nine suggested amendments" to the lend-lease bill. Burton did not record his reaction to the amendments. But he later declined to join the Senate Republicans caucusing against the measure.

There would be two major lines of attack against lend-lease. The first was that England had enough assets to pay for the military arms she needed, if she were only willing to convert those assets into cash. Many people in the United States, including some in the Roosevelt administration, could not appreciate that England was nearly broke. Even FDR had some problems with it. Early in January he had suggested that the British put up perhaps two billion dollars in payment for goods already ordered as a token of the British good faith. Secretary of State Cordell Hull argued that the British could do this, and Treasury Secretary Morgenthau sent Sir Frederick Phillips of the British government to see Hull and explain why England could not make any such payment. But Sir Frederick was not very persuasive, considering the destitute position his nation was in. Hull described Sir Frederick as "reticent" and said, "I still got nothing virtually from Sir Frederick in the way of either arguments or facts or figures."

But Henry Morgenthau was not so reticent. With his sharp features, his dark clothes, and his banker's demeanor, he presented a convincing picture of fiscal conservatism. He appeared before Congress and presented an elaborate explanation of why England simply no longer had the funds with which to pay for her military orders. The British Empire's expected deficit for 1941, he said, would probably be near $1.5 billion. If Britain were to eliminate all her holdings, he continued, that deficit would not be made up. Also, he continued, England already was placing sixty percent of her national income into the war effort. England, he said, simply was running out of money.

"The facts are," Secretary Morgenthau told the Senate committee, "that they will not place orders that they cannot pay for. Therefore, the ordering has practically ceased."

By the time the lend-lease bill was being considered, the British Purchasing Mission had ordered approximately $2.7 billion worth of supplies in the United States. Payments by the mission totaled $1.3 billion, which represented payment in entirety for all goods received. From January 1, 1941, until March 12, 1941, the British would pay an additional $382 million for goods delivered in that period. The payments were in dollars and usually 25 percent had been paid when the orders were placed. England had raised the money by selling its securities and investments in the United States.

Great Britain had holdings in the United States totaling $1.5 billion, which would be used to pay for goods already ordered. Another two billion dollars in Canada also was available to England, but this was being used up at a regular spending pace by the British purchasing military equipment in Canada. Britain also controlled what was believed to be a substantial amount of wealth in Latin America. A Treasury Department estimate placed that wealth at $3.5 billion. That was demonstrated to be a false figure. Most of the Latin American assets existed only on paper. Those that had some value could only be sold at a great loss.

The picture that emerged as the hearings and debate continued was not that of a rich England trying to retain her wealth by mulcting a gullible United States. Rather the picture was of England exhausting herself in her fight against Hitler. The argument that England could pay for the war herself turned out to be a defeat for the isolationists.

The second line of attack against the lend-lease bill was that it gave Franklin Roosevelt too much power when dealing with American military forces. Senator Charles W. Tobey of New Hampshire dramatized this line when he publicly asked the President for a "candid statement" about the possibility of the President turning American naval ships over to the British.

In the past Roosevelt would have treated such a grab for publicity on the part of Tobey with disdain. But again Roosevelt was much more willing to deal with members of Congress and also the stakes were high. Rather than publicly answer Tobey with sarcasm, FDR answered him privately with courtesy "because you are an old friend of mine." And then FDR was quite frank.

All I can tell you in confidence is that there is no intention [to give American ships to the British] at the present writing. If you were in my place and I were in yours, you would probably tell me, as a Senator, that you were the Commander-in-Chief of the Army and Navy and that you were not the seventh son of a seventh son!

Actually I am not a crystal gazer and naturally I decline to say what I would do under new circumstances in the future. Suppose between ourselves we agree to the simple fact that both of us are trying to do all we can to prevent this world from being dominated by the Axis powers, including Japan, and that both of us are doing our utmost to keep the United States out of war.

The major attack against the supposed extensive grant of power to the President came in mid-February, and then it was a more serious blow than could have been anticipated. Roosevelt had always believed that the lend-lease bill would pass Congress without serious change. "My best information," he wrote Churchill in January, "is that the bill at present has a safe majority in both Houses." He could not predict a date for passage, he explained, because a Senate filibuster could delay passage. But the President was confident of ultimate passage. He was, that is, until mid-February.

Senator Robert Taft, the Republican isolationist from Ohio, was against the bill, as expected. By itself his opposition was not significant; no one anticipated he would support the bill. But he was smarter than only to vote against it. He understood that a number of Democratic senators, particularly from the South, feared FDR's growing power. He capitalized on that fear.

As the bill stood, Taft argued, the President could give to the British materiel originally purchased for the American forces. If, for example, Congress appropriated two billion dollars for airplanes needed by the Army Air Corps, FDR could turn all those airplanes over to the British. This would force the Congress to appropriate another two billion dollars to keep the American air force at the needed strength. Taft enlisted Senator Harry F. Byrd, a Democrat of Virginia, in an effort to block that power. Byrd's joining with Taft was neither a surprise nor a serious blow. The Virginia Senator and the President, although nominally of the same party, had not been in agreement for years. His opposition to a Roosevelt plan was expected. But they got some further assistance, a serious defection from the presidential ranks, in Senator Byrnes of South Carolina. Byrnes had been the administration's workhorse on Capitol Hill; he was "Mr. Fix-it." His sudden defection would not only claim his own vote but that of a number of Democratic senators who were accustomed to following his lead.

The price Taft, Byrd, and Byrnes wanted before they would support the bill was an amendment saying that only funds voted specifically for aid to foreign governments could be used to pay for materiel that would go into the lend-lease pipeline. Also their proposed amendment would say that no military equipment originally manufactured for American forces could be disposed of under lend-lease without specific Congressional authorization. The administration understood that the amendment would gut the bill, denying the President power to send the equipment needed at the time it was needed. Roosevelt was bedded down with one of his frequent attacks of flu and could not lead the battle against the amendment.

A young Treasury Department aide, Edward Foley, who had worked on the original draft of the bill, managed to come up with an acceptable compromise. Rather than have the President seek specific authorization from Congress for an action under the lend-lease program, the President would be free to act unless the Congress specifically forbade him from doing so. The compromise was almost a classic of a kind created so that no one emerge a loser. The Southerners, Byrd and Byrnes, came from states in which there was much pro-English sentiment. They were glad to stop blocking a bill that extended assistance to England. At the same time they could say to their conservative constituents that they had made a dent in the presidential powers in the bill. If FDR used his powers under the bill arbitrarily, Congress had the power to act against him.

During the maneuvering in Congress isolationists across the nation were strong in their opposition, stressing the theme that the bill gave FDR too much power, that it turned him into a dictator. That became the catch phrase. The lend-lease bill was the "dictator bill." Robert Wood, the Sears, Roebuck executive who headed the America First Committee, began the attack with the charge that the President wants "a blank check book with the power to write away our manpower, our laws and our liberties."

Another isolationist group, American Peace Mobilization, said of lend-lease that "Never before . . . have the American people been called upon, as they now are, to suspend their right of self-government in time of peace, in order to allow one man to decide whether or not he shall plunge this nation into war."

The usual weapons against legislation were amassed. There were letter-writing campaigns, petitions, committees, and speakers made available to any group opposed to the bill, and the opposition received a favorable press in those papers with isolationist tendencies. On March 2, 1941, for example, the Chicago *Tribune* headlined a story "Church Groups Wage Fight on Dictator Bill." There was no question in the minds of the *Tribune* editors that the lend-lease bill was indeed a means of turning FDR into a dictator. The story began: "Nine out of every ten of the 244,000 Christian clergymen of all churches of the country were declared yesterday to be opposed to the administration's war dictator bill."

Organized labor, usually a supporter of FDR's legislative proposals, was badly divided. William Green, president of the American Federation of Labor, favored lend-lease and refused an invitation to testify against the bill. "It is my opinion," he explained, "that the general principles of this measure should be enacted into law." But Philip Murray, president of the Congress of Industrial Organizations, opposed the bill because it appeared to give the President power to ignore all the labor legislation passed since 1933—passed because of FDR. Some local CIO groups, such as the Detroit and Wayne County Industrial Union Council, representing three hundred thousand members, criticized the bill as "the most dangerous threat to the liberties and peace of our Nation."

The lend-lease bill was not a dictator bill. There was nothing in it beyond what it said. It authorized the President to extend military aid to England in America's own self-interest. Its major practical effect was to team the United States and England in a joint effort against the Axis powers. The United States would supply guns while Britain supplied manpower and blood. By American standards that was a good bargain, accepting the premise that the United States was on the German list for conquest. The validity of that premise could have been a much better subject for debate rather than the hackneyed charge, made ever since FDR first came to the White House, that Roosevelt wanted to be a dictator. But the opposition was so mesmerized by its distrust of "that man in the White House" that it permitted its passion to submerge its reason. It did not create a good debate; it barely questioned the basic premise behind the bill at all. And that sterility of the opposition contributed to the bill being passed by an overwhelming vote. On Saturday night, March 8, the Senate approved the lend-lease bill by a vote of sixty to thirty-one. The bill then returned to the House of Representatives for its approval of amendments added by the Senate.

Once the Senate had acted, FDR was ready to move. He sent Churchill a note. "Notwithstanding some delay," it said, "the ultimate passage by vote of sixty to thirty-one is highly satisfactory. Final concurrent action by the House followed by my signature should take place Tuesday evening. Confidentially I hope to send estimate for new orders and purchases under the bill to the House on Wednesday. Best of luck."

Passage of the lend-lease program made a substantial contribution to keeping England in the war. Not only did England manage to keep its status as a combatant but the promise of future aid encouraged her to become more aggressive in the war. Even Republicans in Washington heard reports that around the world those nations fighting the Axis, or already conquered, were stimulated to greater opposition against the Germans, Italians, and Japanese. Some neutral nations, such as Turkey, which had been considering the possibility of entering the war on the side of the Axis, now determined to hold onto their neutral status.

Harold Macmillan, an official in Churchill's government and later a prime minister himself, pointed out another aspect of lend-lease in his memoirs. It may have come too late. Through 1941, he correctly stated, even after the passage of lend-lease, England continued to pay cash for most of the supplies it received because they had been ordered under the old "cash and carry" system. "In the end," he wrote, "we got what we wanted, and some of the supplies, like the Sherman tanks, were worth their weight in gold. But, in the long run, we paid a high price for saving the world from Nazi tyranny. Our dollars came in fact to an end and we ceased, for the time being, to be an exporting country. We sacrificed our own future to protect the future of civilization."

Among Americans the concern was that the shipment of even greater supplies to England would strip the United States arsenal bare. Secretary of War Stimson, once discussing this situation, said,

"The difficult and critical nature of such a decision for men legally responsible for the defense of our own country can be readily perceived. It is not unlike the painful decision which must be made by a commander in the field when he has to determine how much of his limited reserves he can afford to send forward in response to the importunate calls for help from his fighting line and how much of these reserves must be retained for the final critical moments of the combat."

The isolationists feared what would come next. "I dreaded giving up the ghost on the battle against the lend-lease bill . . ." said Senator Gerald Nye, Republican of North Dakota. "It seemed to me to be a thing which meant everything to our future. Just what the next challenge will be remains to be seen, but we ought to be mindful of the fact that incidents can come awfully fast from now on." And Herbert Hoover correctly pointed out to a friend that the legislation would channel the public into accepting the status of contributing to the Axis defeat.

The passage of lend-lease had come at a time when the Axis powers, particularly Germany, were beginning for the first time to understand that the bite of war can be a nasty one. A few days before the Senate passed the bill, Adolf Hitler determined to encourage Japan's entry into the war against England, even, Hitler said, if this meant the entry of the United States into the hostilities. Only a Pacific war could divert enough of England's military power to assure a German victory in Europe.

Germany's big pitch for Japan's assistance came at the end of March when Japan's foreign minister, Yosuke Matsuoka, was passing through Berlin on his way to Russia. Joachim von Ribbentrop, the Nazi foreign minister, would see Matsuoka first, and then Hitler would come in for what was hoped to be the final "clinching" argument. With their devotion to Aryan superiority, the Nazi leaders could not have thought much of the Japanese. For them that was unfortunate. Matsuoka would outsmart them.

Matsuoka had been born in 1880, and spent his teen-age years in the United States. Living in Portland, Oregon, he went to school at the University of Oregon, from which he received a law degree, embraced Christianity, made close friends with several Americans, worked at a variety of odd jobs, and then returned home. Little about this period of Matsuoka's life is known. If he met any racial prejudice that turned him against the United States he did not report it in later years. Whatever happened to him after graduation from the American university, he returned to his homeland and was always an enemy of the United States.

He joined the diplomatic corps in Japan and worked in many world capitals, including a period in 1914 at the Japanese embassy in Washington. In the 1920s he became a director of the South Manchuria Railway Company, and then a vice president of that company. Still later, he would be president of the company. While in Manchuria, Matsuoka became associated with a number of the more militant leaders of Japan's army, including Hideki Tojo. These military men were dreaming of a "new order" in Asia with Japan as its leader. This concept of a powerful Japan to be achieved by military means appealed to Matsuoka. He returned to Japan in the early 1930s and re-entered the foreign service. In 1933 he was the chief Japanese delegate to the League of Nations. When the League criticized Japan for aggression in Manchuria, Matsuoka led his delegation in the Japanese walkout from that organization.

By the time he became foreign minister, he had a reputation for being a shrewd, hard-boiled negotiator. The unwary did not always realize his ability when they first encountered his urbane, roly-poly appearance and apparently friendly attitude.

He arrived in Berlin on March 27, 1941. Immediately Ribbentrop began his sales pitch, aimed at persuading Japan to enter the war against England. This would have forced England to divert her energies to the Far East and made her more vulnerable in Europe to Germany. But Ribbentrop did not say that. Instead he boasted to Matsuoka that Germany was in the final stages of the war against England. Hitler had amassed the strongest military power the world ever had known. The Luftwaffe was superior to the British air force. Soon new German battleships would be moving against the British. On the European continent itself, there was no military force of value to stand against the Germans. And although Ribbentrop was forced to concede that there might have been a few small troubles in Africa when the Italians met the British, he assured Matsuoka that these were minor. He concluded his presentation with the statement that the Germans had at last won the war, and that the capitulation of England was only a matter of time. Of course, Ribbentrop acknowledged, he could not say how much time, but he was certain that it would come.

Then Ribbentrop came to his main point. The Fuehrer, he explained, believed that it would be advantageous if Japan entered the war against England immediately. A quick attack on Singapore would bring the British to defeat. Ribbentrop insisted that FDR would not attack Japan.

After lunch, Matsuoka had his audience with Hitler. Hitler went over much of the same material that Ribbentrop had, but with less control in his voice and his actions. He demanded that Japan enter the war against England.

Matsuoka refused.

Japan understood the significance of the American fleet in the Pacific much better than did the Germans. For Japan to have entered the war then, while the American fleet still was active, would have meant the defeat of Japan ultimately—despite anything Germany said it believed to the contrary.

Germany and Japan had two different objectives at this time. Germany wanted, first, the defeat of England, and, second, the United States to be kept busy in the Pacific. This could be accomplished by the entry of Japan into the war. But Japan did not care about England as much as it did about the United States, realizing that the United States was the chief power in the Pacific that must be challenged. Anything Germany wanted to the contrary, Japan would not make that challenge until it believed it was capable of winning. For Japan winning meant the elimination of the United States as a power in the Western Pacific. This required the destruction of the American fleet, based at Pearl Harbor, and the destruction of the American military bases scattered along the Pacific islands. It did not require and it was never contemplated that Japan invade the continental United States or even destroy America's ability to wage war, only destroy her ability to wage war in the Western Pacific. Yamamoto, the Japanese navy chief, eventually would decide that ravaging the American west coast would be necessary to persuade the United States to negotiate. But he was thinking of hit-and-run raids, not marching to Washington as he had suggested to a friend at the beginning of 1941.

Matsuoka quickly demonstrated his disregard for German interests. On his way home from Germany he stopped in Moscow. While there he signed a treaty with Russia. The two countries,

Japan and Russia, pledged not to attack each other. For Japan this treaty assured that it could go to war in the Pacific without fear of an attack from the northwest. For Russia the treaty assured that it could face the dangers in Europe without being concerned about threats on its Asian borders. But for Hitler, who then was planning his attack on Russia, the treaty meant Russia would not have to face a two-front war. He was furious at the treaty and repeatedly insisted that Japan break it, but Japan refused, for reasons unknown to Hitler.

Matsuoka's concern in his meetings with Ribbentrop and Hitler was a matter of timing. He would not pledge Japan to attack the United States until Japan felt confident of victory. That confidence would come with the time that Admiral Nomura was buying in Washington.

Hoping to compromise the difference between the United States and Japan, FDR had suggested in his first meeting with Nomura that the Japanese ambassador and Secretary Hull talk privately. The two men then began a series of confidential and unpublicized meetings, usually in Hull's hotel living quarters.

These Hull-Nomura talks, as did further sessions between Nomura and FDR, had a quality of unreality about them. Neither side addressed the other. Nomura insisted that Japan had no military intentions, that it was not desirous of moving into Southeast Asia, nor of conquering China, and certainly had no wish to enter into a war with the United States. Hull answered that such disclaimers were difficult to believe when the Japanese fleet continued to move closer to Southeast Asia, with the Japanese hold on China becoming tighter, and while Japanese leaders such as Matsuoka continued to deal with the Germans and to make bellicose statements toward the United States.

In dealing with Matsuoka, the Roosevelt administration apparently had forgotten that, while at the University of Oregon, Matsuoka had been an accomplished poker player. He had not played the game as FDR did, for relaxation; he played it seriously, for the money he desperately needed to stay in school. And a good poker player bluffs and misleads. Matsuoka did both. When two American Catholic priests were leaving Japan after a visit there, they talked to numerous prominent government officials, including Matsuoka. All the priests heard, including from Matsuoka, was that Japan desired better relations with the United States. Returning to the United States, the priests brought this information to the attention of the administration. FDR was skeptical, but no possible approach toward a peaceful settlement in the Pacific could be ignored. So the Hull-Nomura talks were encouraged.

There were approximately fifty of these private talks, in the confines of the Secretary's study, without the press being aware of them. Each man came with only a few aides and spoke frankly and bluntly. The conversations never became noisy, however. The two men, Hull and Nomura, always showed courtesy and respect toward each other.

Joseph W. Ballantine, a State Department expert on Japan, was one of the aides attending these sessions. "These conversations were a very, very wearisome affair," he later said. "From eight o'clock to ten o'clock at night, I'd be talking with Mr. Hull and talking with the Japanese. Of course, I couldn't take any notes at all, unless there were some specific thing mentioned that they wanted me to record. Then I would go down to the State Department at ten o'clock at night and type out my recollection of the conversation, and the next morning I'd be down there at 8:30 in the morning, dictating a memorandum of conversation which made up the record. Some of these records of conversations were fifteen printed pages."

As these conversations were beginning, Japan sent an espionage agent, a naval ensign named Takeo Yoshikawa, to Hawaii. Grossly incompetent, Yoshikawa still managed to send back messages to Tokyo about movement of American military ships at the naval base at Pearl Harbor. At this time also, the United States had intelligence reports of the German pressures on Japan to move against the British possessions in the Pacific.

But also the lend-lease program was beginning. America was being the good neighbor lending its garden hose to its friend across the ocean. And America's first line of defense—England— was being strengthened. A few weeks after Congress had approved the program, FDR was examining the first list of nonmilitary equipment requested by the British under the lend-lease program. He ran his eye down the list. There were such items as tar, kettles, pumps, graders, and fire hoses. "Actually fire hose," said the President, "at a total cost of about $300,000. I thought it was a rather nice little coincidence."

APRIL: "... *the most hair-trigger times ...*"

$\mathbf{F}$RANKLIN ROOSEVELT was cautious, much more cautious than many of his advisers. This showed in April when Navy Secretary Knox submitted a speech for clearance. The speech suggested that the United States insure delivery of lend-lease goods to England. This would have meant convoying the goods to England and engaging German attack vessels in battle. FDR said "No" to the speech, explaining: "The last is a little premature because we cannot yet insure the delivery. As you and I know, we are going to help the safe delivery."

A few weeks later there was another example of Roosevelt's caution. Sumner Welles, the Under Secretary of State, persuaded FDR to send a statement to Congress extending the Monroe Doctrine to include much of North Africa. The purpose was to keep that continent out of German hands. FDR discussed it with Secretary of State Hull, who was against it. The message, Hull explained, would challenge Germany to move into those areas and precipitate a conflict. When that argument was presented to him, FDR accepted it as valid, and the statement was not sent to Congress.

There was no need for haste. War would be difficult to avoid. That same month the Japanese ambassador to Peru had a session with an official in that nation's ministry for foreign affairs. What would be Peru's reaction if Japan and the United States became involved in war? the ambassador asked. When the Peruvian official said he expected his nation and other South American nations would join the United States, the Japanese ambassador looked startled. This conversation was reported by the Peruvian to the

American ambassador in Lima who informed the Secretary of State.

That kind of report increased the pressures on FDR to end the Japanese threat by negotiation. Obviously Japan planned to fight if he did not do so. So Secretary Hull continued the long and wearisome private sessions with Nomura, hoping that the Japanese would show some willingness to negotiate.

Still, Japan continued the secondary problem. Keeping England as the barrier between Nazi Germany and the western hemisphere was the primary one. Previously this had posed the problem of how to finance aid to England, which had been solved by the lend-lease program. Now it posed the problem of making certain that aid reached England—"to help the safe delivery" in FDR's words.

For England, control of the seas was a fact of history, a tradition, and a vital necessity. As long as she controlled the seas around her island home, an invader could not enter. Supplies could be brought in. The wounded and children could be evacuated. The convoys, each of some sixty merchant ships, four miles across and almost two miles deep, were England's highways of salvation. The enemy of the convoy was the wolfpack. These were groups of German submarines moving silently beneath the ocean waters in search of prey: English ships to attack. And they found them. During the first eight months after the war's start, Germany destroyed almost two hundred British ships, about five percent of its entire merchant fleet. During the first six months of 1941 British merchant losses amounted to almost three million tons, about one-fifth of the tonnage of the British merchant fleet when the war began. England was losing control of the seas.

Early in the year, when the lend-lease bill was before Congress, newspapers carried reports that FDR had, as a price for passage, agreed to an amendment forbidding American ships to convoy merchant vessels across the Atlantic. Henry Stimson read the accounts and telephoned the President to ask if they were true. "He said *no* decidedly," Stimson reported, "and that no such proposition had been put to him."

The question of American ships convoying supplies to England arose again in March for FDR when a newsman asked him about reports that he was considering authorizing convoys. FDR shrugged off the question. "I haven't paid any attention to them yet," he said of the reports.

Early in April the President decided to initiate the "patrols" of the Western Atlantic. He called a session with Secretary of War Stimson, Harry Hopkins, and some of his military advisers for Thursday, April 10. FDR began the session by saying that more assistance must be given to the British convoys. He continued that he considered it too dangerous to ask Congress for authorization to use American Navy vessels to actually convoy the British transports. He explained that he did not believe Congress would extend any such authorization, and the implications of such a defeat would be enormous. British morale would suffer and German attacks on British ships would intensify. Stimson disagreed with FDR about Congressional reaction, but he did not say so.

What the President did at that session was initiate the policy of American patrols of the Atlantic. Pulling out an atlas, a line was drawn midway between the westernmost bulge of Africa and the easternmost bulge of Brazil. The line was extended northward, turned toward the east when it met Greenland on the map. To the west of the line, the United States Navy would patrol the Atlantic. American ships and airplanes would follow British convoys. If they spotted a German raiding vessel, a submarine, or any unidentified ship, the Americans would notify the British.

The President did not discuss these plans immediately with many people. He explained to an aide the next day, as the aide recorded it, that "Only four members of the Cabinet knew about them, and the President doubted that he would tell the others because they could not keep their mouths shut."

A few weeks later, however, when the plans were well along, the President did explain his patrolling plans to his Cabinet. Realizing perhaps that the majority of his Cabinet hoped he would take even more aggressive action, the President concluded with, "Well, it's a step forward."

"I hope," Secretary Stimson quickly said, "you will keep on walking, Mr. President. Keep on walking." Even the President joined in the laughter that filled the room.

Stimson considered FDR a fumbler. After he had worked for him for a period, he said of the President, "He has no system. He goes haphazard and he scatters responsibility among a lot of uncoordinated men and consequently things are never done." And another time Stimson said that "The only fault I have to find with the President is that he is irregular in his habits of consultation. He has a regular group of three—or five counting in Marshall and Stark—who are his official advisers, Hull, Knox and myself, and the two military men, and here he is going along with them and suddenly he stops and makes his decisive decision without calling us into conference again. It was probably a right decision for the time being but it is not the right way to do it."

The War Secretary was not the first to learn that there was a haphazard quality to Roosevelt. Nine years earlier, when FDR had hoped to win the Democratic presidential nomination for the first time, Felix Frankfurter commented, "I am wondering what will come out of Chicago. If FDR is nominated, it will certainly prove that there is no limit to the amount of fumbling one can do and still win a game."

Roosevelt continued his "fumbling" as President. The White House seemed in a constant state of chaos. Government agencies failed or succeeded and his attitude toward them was the same. Lines of authority overlapped. People with specific assignments found they were overruled by someone with a similar assignment, or one totally different. A policy paper entered the White House, was digested, and emerged as something entirely different.

That FDR was not as good an administrator as, say, Herbert Hoover, has never been disputed. Francis Biddle, who became Attorney General in 1941, did not believe that administrative ability was an attribute necessary or even desirable in a President of the United States. To him, Roosevelt practiced the far more difficult art of driving a score of subordinates, few of whom could be described as tame, keeping their actions in perspective with the needs and the will of the country, settling their disputes, soothing their egos, while at the same time balancing the need for competent appointments with the necessities of politics.

Roosevelt was an experimenter. He did not care about means, only that they were legal and proper. When his aides informed him that a desired action faced a roadblock, he would respond, "There's always a way to get through it." He was more concerned about achieving results. Parts of the New Deal program were dismal failures. Not only was legislation overruled by a conservative judiciary but many programs did not achieve as promised. But in total, the New Deal was a reasonable success. The gross national product in 1933 was fifty-six billion dollars. Eight years later it had doubled. In 1933 American consumers spent forty-six billion dollars. Eight years later this figure also had doubled. Investment by the public did even better, jumping from about one and one-half billion dollars to more than eighteen billion dollars. Wages had doubled. The rate of unemployment had been cut from twenty-five percent of the working population back to ten percent.

This success had been caused in great part by what Felix Frankfurter described as Roosevelt's "fumbling." Because Roosevelt was not wedded to any specific plan, was not attracted by any one technique, was not completely loyal to any one man, he was free to experiment until he found the approach best suited to his purposes and the curing of the nation's ills. He led the war against the economic depression by enlisting the best minds he could find, giving them free rein to develop ideas, fight with each other over approaches, and then finally stepping in personally to support the technique that had evolved from that throbbing mass of intellectualism.

Roosevelt articulated the nation's ambitions, then called on individuals to help him realize those ambitions. He provided those individuals with energy, political support, encouragement, and praise when they succeeded. If they failed, they were welcome to stay with him and try again on another problem—although many, because of personal ego problems, declined to do so. FDR's flaw in personnel matters was that he could fire no one. It was this "fumbling" that had enabled the White House to successfully battle the Depression. And it was this same "fumbling" that would be FDR's approach to preparing the nation for war.

He had not sought the position of a wartime leader. He had not planned to seek a third term and break the tradition begun with George Washington that a President should not serve more than eight years. After being reelected in 1936, he had spoken of leaving the White House on January 20, 1941, not beginning another four-year term then. After the Congress, in 1937, refused to approve his plan to enlarge the Supreme Court so as to give it a more liberal membership—the famous "Court-packing" episode—Roosevelt saw his party slipping away from him. More important, it could slip away from the liberalism, the social welfare concept, that had characterized his approach to government.

This fear of his party returning to the conservatism from which he had wrenched it grew stronger in 1938. In the elections that year FDR tried to purge several Democratic Congressmen who had not supported his programs. He failed.

As the 1940 election approached, the possibilities for the Democratic nomination were not such to offer FDR much enthusiasm. Joe Kennedy was interested, but Roosevelt believed his isolationist tendencies would be bad for the nation. Also Kennedy was a Catholic and the political estimate was that it was too soon after the unsuccessful and divisive 1928 campaign of Al Smith to try another Catholic. The same religious problem worked against James A. Farley, who had been FDR's campaign manager and his Postmaster General. Working against Farley also was his split with FDR before 1940. Roosevelt believed that he himself had been the only issue in the 1936 election, and his overwhelming victory then meant to him that other Democrats better fall in behind him, or face being politically ostracized. That happened to Farley. It also happened to John Garner, who hoped to be nominated in 1940 despite being more than seventy years of age.

Against what seemed to FDR a lackluster group of possibilities was his own driving egotism. It is presumptuous for a human being to believe that he has the capability to be President of the United States. Fortunately for the nation there are capable people who have enough self-confidence to believe they can handle the job. Roosevelt had more self-confidence than most persons, even than most persons who have been President. Well he should have. He had conquered the infantile paralysis that had crippled him. His success against that disease was so great that many Americans never were aware that he spent most of his time in a wheelchair or with ninety-pound braces on his legs.

He had been an effective governor of New York, then combined such diverse groups as the religious and racial minorities of the northern cities and the Southern aristocrats in the Democratic Party of the 1930s. He had won a hard-fought election contest in 1932, then went on to reap the greatest public accolade ever bestowed on a presidential candidate with his stunning victory in the 1936 election. His New Deal had pulled the nation out of the Depression. If he could not lead the United States in the troubled 1940s, who could?

So he permitted his name to be entered at the 1940 Chicago convention, even encouraged his nomination somewhat. He did not look forward to another campaign and was not really enthusiastic about another four years in the White House. The physical toll on him was great. But the situation at the time, the other candidates available, and his confidence in his own abilities persuaded him to accept nomination for a third term.

When the tradition against a third term was begun by George Washington, the young American nation had had much bitter experience with kings, rulers who could not be ousted from office. That experience influenced Washington to shape the Presidency as a man of the people who would serve in his exalted office, and then leave after no more than eight years. But the tradition against a third term also had a negative effect. It denied the American people a free choice. They could have anyone as their President—except the man who had just served eight years in office. And that man might very well have been the most suitable choice. Would a man serving more than two terms as President become too powerful? Perhaps. But so could a man serving only his first term. The presidential powers are there, waiting to be seized or developed. They are available to the man who holds the office, whether he has held that office one day or eight years and one day. There is a Congress, a federal judiciary, and, ultimately, the American voter to watch over him and to make certain his actions do not go beyond proper bounds.

An argument against a third presidential term more valid than Washington's in modern America was the sheer physical challenge of filling the job. One can be President, as some were, in a lackadaisical fashion—assigning responsibility to others, demanding that troublesome problems be solved before being brought to the president. But that was not FDR's way. He was intensely interested in most details of the work in his Cabinet departments. He wanted to hear from his friends, what they thought of the domestic situation or of affairs in Europe. And, to keep the communication lines open, he answered them, keeping up a voluminous correspondence. Personality disputes, philosophical arguments, bureaucratic hassles, all found their way to the man who sat behind the big desk in the oval office of the White House. He tossed them all from hand to hand, tilting his head to one side before he answered a question, pointing his cigarette holder jauntily toward the sky, his ebullience apparently unchallenged.

When he could, he escaped to the sea he loved. He said a few weeks after his 1941 inaugural:

I try to get away a couple of times a year on these short trips on salt water. In Washington, as you know, the working day of the Presidency in these days averages about fifteen hours. Even when I get to Hyde Park or to Warm Springs, the White House office, the callers, and the telephones all follow me. But at sea the radio messages and the occasional pouch of mail reduce official work to not more than two or three hours a day.

So there is a chance for a bit of sunshine or a wetted line, or a biography or a detective story or a nap after lunch. Above all there is the opportunity for thinking things through—for differentiating between principles and methods, between the really big things of life and those other things of the moment which may seem all-important today and are forgotten by the world in a month. That means that if today the fellow next to you catches a bigger fish than you do, or vice versa, as sometimes happens, you don't lie awake at night thinking about it.

He still was a late riser, not waking usually until nine o'clock in the morning. Then, sitting up in bed, eating his breakfast, he held court. The secretaries and assistants came in, both to report and receive instructions. He arrived at the White House office at about eleven A.M., and stayed there until five o'clock. Then, if there was time, there would be a massage or swim and a short nap. Before dinner he enjoyed a cocktail and boasted of his prowess as a bartender as he fixed his friends their favorite drinks. Like most men who boast of their bartending ability, he overrated himself. "The President," reported Harold Ickes, "makes a perfectly terrible dry martini." But if he was a bad bartender, Roosevelt was a gracious host and men enjoyed coming to social evenings at the White House, not only to bask in the aura of being near the Chief Executive but also because they enjoyed it.

Roosevelt's graciousness was a visible manifestation of his inbred good manners. Herbert C. Pell, an American diplomat and an old friend of FDR's, told this story about Franklin Roosevelt in 1941 that exemplifies those manners.

"I came in and was talking to the President by the fire when the President of Haiti was announced," said Pell. "I naturally withdrew as these two chiefs of state were in conversation. President Roosevelt asked me to join them." Pell pointed out that usually, "even if the two Americans speak French, they'll carry on their own conversation, their questions and answers to each other, in English regardless of the fact that the third party in the conversation hasn't the slightest idea of what they're talking about." But with FDR this was not so. FDR, Pell, and the Haitian President spoke in French. "It was one of the very few times," said

Pell, "that I have been in conversation in a group where, if there was a Frenchman who could not speak English, the two Americans present had the decent manners to carry on conversations between themselves also in French." Pell added, "It seems an odd thing to have found this—what I should consider elementary good manners—in the President and in hardly anybody else."

Francis Biddle told a story about George Norris which demonstrates Roosevelt's instinct for decency. Norris had been a liberal senator long before liberalism was fashionable and FDR's respect for him bordered on awe. In 1936 Roosevelt had supported Norris for re-election even though Norris was not a Democrat; with a liberal and a man like Norris, FDR considered party labels superfluous.

But in 1942, Norris, then age 81, was defeated for re-election. The President realized that the important thing was to give Norris a feeling of usefulness. FDR worked out a complicated scheme having the chairman of the Tennessee Valley Authority switched to a federal judgeship and Norris appointed in his place. FDR believed the job would be a wonderful way for the man who had fathered TVA in Congress to end his career.

The President assigned Biddle the job of approaching Norris about the new assignment. At the same time, Biddle was to ask Norris for advice about several matters before the Justice Department. The important thing, FDR told Biddle, was to build up Norris, to seek his advice, since he must be lonely and feeling out of things.

Biddle also offered another example of Roosevelt's courtesy. Harold Ickes could not be present at one Cabinet meeting and sent a young assistant to sit in for him. As Roosevelt looked around the Cabinet table he spotted the assistant but could not identify him immediately. FDR whispered to Henry Morgenthau, asking the name of the young man who seemed somewhat nervous by the company in which he unexpectedly found himself. Morgenthau, who did not know the young man's name, asked Biddle.

"Fortas," Biddle whispered back. Morgenthau passed it on to FDR.

The President grabbed at a scratch pad. "Not his last name," he wrote, "his first name."

Back came Biddle's answer. "Abe."

And when, going around the Cabinet table, Franklin Roosevelt came to the nervous young Under Secretary of the Interior, he asked, smiling and friendly, "Well, Abe, what's been going on in Interior?"

This consideration for the other person, this concern for the other man's feelings, pervaded many of Roosevelt's actions. Basically he was a decent man who wanted to help his fellow man. And those who needed help understood this and appreciated it. Biddle remembers a scene of Negro women holding up their children so that they could see Franklin Roosevelt. This is a friend, the mothers seemed to be saying, remember him.

This decent man also was the shrewdest political master on the American scene. Who else could have joined the Bourbon South and the northern minorities into an effective political organization? Who else could have brought the liberal labor organizations and the conservative Democrats into a party strong enough to elect a President? And then, when the need to prepare for war came, FDR had not hesitated to call on Republicans such as Henry Stimson and Frank Knox.

He did not stop there. To replace Joe Kennedy as ambassador to England, he chose a Republican, John G. Winant, who had been a governor of New Hampshire. The selection of Winant touched all the important bases for FDR, pointing up the President's political mastery. Winant was a Republican, which made the administration more bipartisan. He was a liberal, which placated the New Dealers. And he had been recommended for the post in England by several prominent Britishers. These included Harold Laski, British economics professor, and Aneurin Bevin, the Labour Party leader. Their recommendations assured Winant being well received in England. At a news conference, FDR tried to eliminate any political connotation to his selection of Winant. "I think it is a great mistake," the President told newsmen crowded around his presidential desk, "to make a lead in any story that he was a Republican; he was appointed because he was an American. I think there is a nice distinction there." Roosevelt joined in the laughter at his own slip of the tongue. But then he became serious. "I could say the same thing if he was a Democrat," the President insisted. "He was appointed because he was an American of very wide experience." The President continued after a moment, "I realize that this is Washington and people do have to talk about Republicans and Democrats; but in a crisis like this I don't think it is a very good line to take."

Those comments of Roosevelt's, of course, were window dressing. He did want good men, but he also wanted good Republicans as a means of wrapping the Republican Party into support of his policies. He did this because he realized that only a national government could prepare the nation to defend itself.

As shrewd a politician as he was, Franklin Roosevelt at times became a demagogue—a trap into which many politicians fall. For FDR it had happened in the 1940 election. He was having difficulty then with those voters, not identified with any particular ethnic group, who feared that his re-election would mean war and the sending of their sons, husbands, and loved ones to the battlefields of Europe. The Republican candidate was Wendell Willkie, the Wall Street lawyer who was listed in *Who's Who* as a Democrat. Willkie was a liberal and an internationalist. If he had been elected, his foreign policy probably would have been little different than that of FDR's. He also was an honorable man of good reputation. But he wished very much to be elected President. He waged a strong, bitter, and personal campaign against the President. His principal charge was that Roosevelt was a warmonger leading the United States into the European conflict.

The pre-election polls showed FDR's popularity down in every part of the nation. In some areas, it had dropped only a few percentage points, such as in New England and the South where it had gone down only three percent during his second term. In several areas the popularity drop was more severe and politically threatening. In the Middle Atlantic and the Pacific Coast states the drop was nine percent. In the Rocky Mountain states FDR's popularity was down ten percent, and in the west central states it had declined by eleven percent.

By the end of October, a few days before the election, it was apparent that the Willkie campaign was having an impact. Reports of voter desertions were ominous and even once loyal Democratic members of Congress were disassociating themselves from Roosevelt and his foreign policy.

Roosevelt had previously said he would not send the youth of America into foreign wars. "But how often do they expect me to say that?" he demanded of his advisers. "It's in the Democratic platform and I've repeated it a hundred times."

Robert E. Sherwood, the playwright who was writing speeches for FDR, answered, "Evidently you've got to say it again—and again—and again."

Franklin Roosevelt knew a good phrase when he heard it. He had just heard one.

That night he made a major address in Boston. Speaking to the "mothers and fathers of America," Franklin Roosevelt asserted, "I have said this before, but I shall say it again and again and again: Your boys are not going to be sent into any foreign wars."

This was Franklin Roosevelt the demagogue. He had used that promise of not sending American men to fight foreign wars in previous speeches, but then he always had added "except in case of attack." But this night in Boston he dropped that qualification, that weakening of his promise. An aide asked why. The aide remembered FDR's face as being drawn and gray. Roosevelt would not concede, even to a trusted aide, that he had been frightened by Willkie.

"It's not necessary," FDR snapped. "If we're attacked, it's no longer a foreign war."

Franklin Roosevelt, then, was a gracious and a decent man, a political man who regretted that he allowed himself at times to be a demagogue. To the Presidency he had brought a creativity rather than an administrative order. And in 1941, although he was known as a President involved primarily with domestic issues —the New Deal—he had had a long interest and involvement in foreign affairs.

When a teen-ager at Groton, he had written his parents once of going to Boston to have his teeth straightened and of having missed a "hare and hounds chase." And then he added, "Hurrah for the Boers! I entirely sympathize with them." The Dutch farmers in South Africa had been successful in their battle against the British empire builders, and even then Roosevelt was on the side of the underdog fighting to protect his home.

His interest in foreign affairs while at Groton led him to take the negative side of the question: "Resolved, that Hawaii be promptly annexed." The young FDR opposed annexation because he believed the United States should not acquire colonies as European nations had.

The argument had been made that Hawaii was needed as a coaling station for the American fleet in the Pacific. FDR had an answer for that. "Now it is not generally known," he said in 1898, "that Pearl Harbor, a port in one of the islands, belongs to the United States. All that is needed is a little inexpensive dredging and we shall have a coaling station without annexation." He did not think much of the argument made then that Japan was interested in the Hawaiian Islands. "She has disclaimed any intention of seizing the islands," young Roosevelt said, "and it would indeed be a foolish enterprise for her, for any armies in Hawaii would be as lonely as Robinson Crusoe."

That was a reasonable position in 1898. By 1941, however, it was no longer reasonable. Roosevelt had realized that and changed his position; most of the American military did not.

FDR's initial personal experience with war came during the First World War. He had come to Washington in 1913 as Assistant Secretary of the Navy. He believed that the United States should prepare for war so that, if it came, America would be ready. He figured out what supplies would be needed, which plants could produce them, and how to find the necessary raw materials. He dealt with the working men to prevent strikes and keep productivity at a high level. He realized that the submarine was the new weapon of war and demanded submarine chasers to counter it. His statements in those years reveal that, even then when few could visualize the shape of the new world to come, Roosevelt understood that the prudent nation prepared for the worst.

"Conflict, like anything else in modern civilization," he said in 1913, "is so complicated that preparation is essential. That is why we have our navy, our army and our militias, and that is why some of us think ahead. No one desires war today. We are all striving—army and navy alike—to prevent its occurrence. But no one can guarantee to the American people that there will be no more war." And two years later, in 1915, he returned to that theme. "It is better for us as a nation to feel that we are perfectly safe," he said, "than it is for us to live in fear by reason of the fact that all the downstairs windows are unlocked and that the burglar and enemy may at any time enter."

Roosevelt did not wear a military uniform during the First World War. He envied those who did, however. In September of 1918, his boss, Secretary of the Navy Josephus Daniels, sent him to Europe on an inspection trip. While at St. Nazaire in France, FDR talked with "good old Admiral Plunkett" about returning to Europe in uniform with an assignment in the Naval Railway Battery. The Admiral asked FDR if he could swear well enough in French to swear a French train onto a siding so a naval train carrying American guns could get through. "With certain inventive genius, I handed him a line of French swear words, real and imaginary," FDR later said, "which impressed him greatly."

Admiral Plunkett offered FDR the rank of lieutenant commander. FDR returned to the United States, was bedded down with a bout of flu for three weeks, then asked Navy Secretary Daniels to release him from his civilian job so he could put a uniform on. Daniels grudgingly gave his consent; he did not wish to lose his valued assistant. FDR then went to see President Woodrow Wilson. Wilson said that he had already received the first hints of an armistice and that FDR was too late to go into uniform. That ended his military ambitions.

What Roosevelt saw in Washington during those years impressed him deeply. When war did come in 1917, the United States was ill-prepared to fight it. Although the threat had loomed large, few had rallied to meet it. About a dozen years later, Bernard M. Baruch wrote a pamphlet saying that in the event of another war the traditional supply-and-demand economy of the United States must give way to a controlled economy. Baruch spoke with great authority. He was the Wall Street financial genius who had been called in to run the nation's economy during the First World War. Roosevelt, then governor of New York, wrote him a "Dear Bernie" note. "I am greatly interested in that fine pamphlet of yours," the note said. "I do hope that something will come of it for it is not either right or worthy of this country to be back and get into the same kind of a jam as we had in 1917 in the event of another war."

After he entered the White House in 1933, Roosevelt's interest in foreign affairs increased. In 1936 he wrote to the American ambassador in Germany:

Everything seems to have broken loose again in your part of the world. All the experts here, there and the other place say "There will be no war." They said the same thing all through July, 1914, when I was in the Navy Department. In those days I believed the experts. Today I have my tongue in my cheek. This does not mean that I am become cynical; but as President I have to be ready just like a Fire Department!

And then he added, as he would in the coming years, his offer to work for a peace of lasting quality.

If in the days to come, the absolutely unpredictable events should by chance get to the point where a gesture, an offer or a formal statement by me would, in your judgment, make for peace, be sure to send me immediate word. But the peace must be not only peace with justice but the kind of peace which will endure without threat for more than a week or two.

The dangers were evident. "These are without doubt," FDR said to another friend, "the most hair-trigger times the world has gone through in your lifetime or mine."

Hair-trigger times. One man could give an order and convulse the world in agony. Franklin Roosevelt understood this, although most of his countrymen did not. In England, Winston Churchill also understood this. But in the 1930s he was a prophet without honor in his own nation.

In 1937 the unawareness—perhaps the unwillingness—of the American nation to recognize the danger of war was dramatized. The Congress was passing a Neutrality Act, designed to keep the United States from taking sides in any military dispute between nations. The President told Hull to add a provision. FDR wanted this section to read that if American property destined for a neutral were seized on the high seas and transferred to a belligerent ship, then the President would have the power to impound in the United States a like amount of property belonging to that belligerent nation. It was a *quid pro quo* arrangement he wanted. If a nation steals from the United States, the United States will retaliate.

But the State Department asserted that all kinds of problems might be created. The officials there conjured up potential difficulties. Perhaps even, they suggested, a war. In a note to the Secretary of State, FDR replied that his provision "goes along with the common law and statutes which provide that if one individual's property is seized by some other person . . . the original owner can get an order to impound the assets of the individual who has taken his property."

Hull reports that FDR did not press the issue any further. He could not, of course. Once the measure went to Capitol Hill, where the isolationist sentiment was strong, the State Department's opposition would quickly be discovered and the provision would be dropped.

But if Roosevelt could not pull a reluctant Congress along with him in the 1930s, he could do much to educate the American public to the dangers across the oceans and also to alert that public to its responsibilities. By the fall of 1937 there had been considerable pressure on FDR to make a speech on the international situation—the warlike sounds of Germany, the aggressiveness of Italy and Japan. This pressure came from the more internationalist-minded members of his official family, such as Harold Ickes and Cordell Hull. Those two Cabinet members particularly were worried about the growth of isolationist sentiment in the country, especially in the Midwest. When the President planned a cross-country tour, Hull suggested that he make a stop in a large Midwestern city and give a strong speech stressing the theme of international cooperation. The President asked Hull and his staff at the State Department to work up a draft.

Chicago was chosen as the site for the speech somewhat by accident. Ickes was scheduled to dedicate the Outer Link Bridge, a public works project, on October 9. But he arranged to have the dedication changed to October 5, the day the President was passing through the city, so that the President could use the occasion for his speech on international cooperation. In talking over the world situation with FDR, Ickes, as he later recalled it, compared the danger of Germany, Japan, and Italy to the danger from a contagious disease in a community. Ickes added that people had a right to quarantine the carrier of a disease. Ickes recalled the President remarking, "That is a good line; I will write it down." It became one of the more famous lines of the Roosevelt years.

> The peace, the freedom, and the security of ninety percent of the population of the world is being jeopardized by the remaining ten percent, who are threatening a breakdown of international order and law. Surely the ninety percent who want to live in peace under law and in accordance with moral standards that have received almost universal acceptance through the centuries, can and must find a way to make their will prevail. . . .
>
> It seems to be unfortunately true that the epidemic of world lawlessness is spreading. When an epidemic of physical disease starts to spread, the community approves and joins in a quarantine of the patients in order to protect the health of the community against the spread of the disease.

The word "quarantine" caught the public's attention, as FDR undoubtedly realized it would. Newspapers bannered the word in their headlines. Commentators spoke of FDR's "quarantine" speech. But the reaction was mixed. Ickes, who claimed to have suggested the word, believed that the speech had encouraged other peoples around the world to be more resistant to the military aggressors. Hull, on the other side, believed the speech did more harm than good. The "quarantine" approach, he later asserted, was too strong for the time and scared Americans into becoming more isolationist than they had been.

A positive reaction came—curiously for 1937—from Frank Knox, then publisher of the Chicago *Daily News* and only one year from the presidential campaign in which he had run for vice president on the Republican ticket against the Democratic slate headed by FDR. The day after the speech, Knox wrote to a friend in the State Department that "I feel very thoroughly in accord with the declarations of the President. . . . I am gratified that he has decided to lead the moral sense of the world in a stinging reprobation of murder of innocent women and children and defenseless civilians in an undeclared war."

All those reactions were exaggerated. Words would not encourage anyone to be more resistant to aggressors as Ickes said; actions and assistance would. Nor would a word like "quarantine" frighten America into isolation, as Hull charged. That same negative reaction would have been produced by any word or phrase that FDR used in developing his theme of the civilized nations of the world cooperating together against the uncivilized. Nor did the speech, as Knox suggested, make FDR the leader of the world's moral sense. But the value of the speech was described in another line by Knox. "It is high time," he said, "that civilized humanity found a voice."

FDR had become that voice. It was modest. It led no one— then. But it was a start. The speech served notice that here was a rallying point. Here in the United States, it was saying, is a beginning. This was the first call to arms. And while many did not like it, while many thought it exaggerated, while many believed it dangerous, no one could say that he had not heard the first call.

But military power, unfortunately, is only influenced by a greater quantity of military power. And if the United States could sound a trumpet, it could not field an army in 1937. So those who should have paid the most attention to Franklin Roosevelt's warning ignored it. "The general direction," said FDR a few weeks after his quarantine speech, "seems to have got worse instead of better and there is no question that the German-Italian-Japanese combination is amazingly successful—bluff, power, accomplishment, or whatever it may be."

Early the next year Roosevelt decided on a daring diplomatic plan. His scheme was to call together the leading European nations for a peace conference, in hopes of preventing by dicussion the looming war. If it had come off, it would have been a dramatic grandstand play. It also would have been much more. Winston Churchill, in his account of the events leading up to the Second World War, has best explained the significance of Roosevelt's proposal and also the personal dangers to FDR.

Mr. Roosevelt, was indeed running great risks in his own domestic politics by deliberately involving the United States in the darkening European scene. All the forces of isolationism would have been aroused if any part of these interchanges had transpired. On the other hand, no event could have been more likely to stave off, or even prevent, war than the arrival of the United States in the circle of European hates and fears.

The plan failed when the Neville Chamberlain government in England refused to cooperate.

Chamberlain's foreign secretary then was a young man named Anthony Eden, who believed Chamberlain's refusal to be a mistake. Years later, when he had become Lord Avon, Eden recalled that moment in history with a newspaper reporter. "One cannot tell," he said, "what the conference's immediate effect would have been on Hitler and Mussolini. But I believe that had the United States then concerned itself with European affairs, in however moderate a form, this would have been a deterrent to the dictators and an encouragement for the free nations. Certainly, this was one of the turning points on the road to war."

Realizing perhaps the truth of his cousin's comment about the "big stick," FDR in 1938 began to think in terms of rearming the United States. Not even a President, however, no matter how powerful he is, can snap his fingers and have his wishes transformed into reality. Billions of dollars that did not appear to be available must be found. Manpower, brainpower, industrial power must be organized. In a democracy, this means the people must be aroused.

FDR's first task was his own government. Its members were chosen not only for their ability and their loyalty to the President but also for the political strength they brought to the national administration. The Secretary of War then was Harry H. Woodring, an isolationist who was not interested in expanding the army. Cordell Hull was reluctant to take action that might antagonize another world power. But such men could not be dismissed abruptly. Each represented a factor in the political strength of Roosevelt and of the Democratic Party. Dropping Woodring meant losing, or at least weakening, the party's hold on the Midwest. Hull, from Tennessee, was a party stalwart; dropping him would mean a revolt in the ranks. Charles Edison of New Jersey, who became Secretary of the Navy, represented the conservative businessmen who still clung to the Democratic Party in the hope that it would once again become the political party they remembered.

The art of politics is the art of leading; it is not the art of making pronouncements and then looking backward to see if the people are following. FDR understood that. "The President," he once said, "is the Commander-in-Chief and he, too, has his superior officer—the people of the United States." Again and again he returned to that essential theme: in a democracy, action must have popular support. Once when the Senate was balking one of his actions, FDR said to Frances Perkins: "You know, you can always do this kind of thing if you only give people time to think about it. Don't rush them. Don't press them to do it before they are ready. Give them time to think. The facts justify the action." And when the Senate finally acted favorably, FDR commented, "This is a lesson in patience. You have to give men an opportunity to understand for themselves in their own way. You can't rush them. Not in a democracy."

Roosevelt has been accused by his enemies of aspiring to become a dictator. But much more than did his critics, FDR understood the role of leadership in a democracy. He perhaps expressed this understanding best when he made a speech in 1932 before the Commonwealth Club in San Francisco. He said then:

Government includes the art of formulating a policy, and using the political technique to attain as much of that policy as will receive general support; persuading, leading, sacrificing, teaching always, because the greatest duty of a statesman is to educate.

In 1938 Hitler demanded the dismemberment of Czechoslovakia. Winston Churchill, who was not a member of the Neville

Chamberlain government in England, privately advised that government, "We should tell Germany that, if she sets foot in Czechoslovakia, we should at once be at war with her." His advice was ignored and England at Munich exchanged Czechoslovakia for the promise of "peace in our time."

"You were given the choice between war and dishonor," Churchill then told the English people. "You chose dishonor and you will have war." Churchill was correct. Adolf Hitler had been given a clearance for conquest. War now could not be stopped, except by complete surrender.

Again FDR acted, appealing to Hitler for a conference at a neutral site. Hitler scoffed at the President of the United States. The United States had nothing with which to back up its words. The big stick was made of paper.

Roosevelt understood this. After the Munich agreement and its threat of disastrous consequences, he told a Cabinet meeting that Hitler never would have acted as he had if the United States had planes to put in the air. The President spoke then of five thousand war planes on hand and the ability to produce ten thousand more a year. Of course there were no five thousand planes. The Army Air Corps* numbered its planes in the hundreds. The capacity to build new airplanes was almost nonexistent. This situation, the President told his Cabinet, could no longer be tolerated. America must rearm. From almost nothing, Franklin Roosevelt said, a defensive war machine must be developed.

The call to arms had gone beyond mere words.

The reports of an impending world war grew stronger. Bernard Baruch returned from Europe to report to the President that neither England nor France was capable of fighting Germany. Harold Ickes, on a trip to Europe, had a long talk with William Bullitt. Bullitt, the experienced diplomat, told Ickes that war was inevitable.

Still, Americans were reluctant to accept the inevitable; war, they were certain, would not come to Europe. In July, 1939, there was a meeting at the White House with the President,

---

* A word on terminology. In 1941 and before there was an Army Air Corps. Later there would be an Army Air Force, which produced a report referred to in this text. Still later, of course, there was an independent Air Force. At this time also there was no Defense Department, but a War Department, which handled the affairs of the Army, and a Navy Department.

Secretary of State Hull, and several leaders of Congress, including Senator William E. Borah, Republican of Idaho. In 1941 Franklin Roosevelt, with obvious enjoyment, told what happened at that meeting.

"You know," FDR began, "once upon a time there was a fellow . . . who had a great deal more information and was a much more reasoning person than any of the people . . . it's obvious whom I am talking about. His name is Senator Borah—in many ways a very great statesman, and certainly with experience and information that was far better than most of the speakers."

And then Roosevelt described "the famous conference upstairs" two years earlier when the Secretary of State said, as FDR quoted him, "From our information we really believe regretfully that a war will break out this year." Then, FDR continued, Senator Borah turned to the Secretary of State and said, "I am sorry, Mr. Secretary, my information is better than yours. There will be no war this year." Six weeks after Borah made that pronouncement Germany invaded Poland to begin the Second World War.

Roosevelt laughed at this point in the story. Then he said of William Borah, "And yet he had been on the Foreign Relations Committee and everything else, and had been there for years and years—nearly forty years. In the Senate he certainly had far more information than any of these people that are going around making speeches today; and of course his error has become a classic."

When the war began with the German invasion of Poland, England and France accepted their responsibilities and declared war on Germany. Once again the fields of Europe would be ravaged by the aggressions of the German nation and once again a generation of young men would die. And when it would all be over, when the last gun had stilled, no one would be able to offer a satisfactory answer to the question of "Why had it begun?"

The European war gathered momentum, then slowed to such a degree that it was described as a "phony war." Then it picked up in severity through 1940. Roosevelt was not surprised at the increased pace. He recalled the years he had spent as a youth in Germany attending German schools.

I, too, went to a school—a village school—in Germany and, indeed, spent almost every summer there until I was fourteen years old.

In those early nineties, I gained the distinct impression that educa-

tion and outlook under the old Kaiser and under Frederick was quickly
and almost suddenly changed when Wilhelm II came to the throne.
When I was eleven in 1893, I think it was, my class was started on
the study of *Heimatkunde*—geography lessons about the village, then
about how to get to neighboring towns and what one should see, and,
finally, on how to get all over the Province of Hesse-Darmstadt. The
following year we were taught all about roads and what we would see
on the way to the French border. I did not take it the third year but I
understand the class was "conducted" to France—all roads leading
into Paris.

The talk among us children became stronger each year toward an
objective—the inevitable war with France and the building up of the
Reich into the greatest world power. Even then we were taught to
have no respect for Englishmen and we were taught that Americans
were mere barbarians, most of whom were millionaires.

The Germans entered Paris three months after the President
made those comments. All roads had led to Paris.

In May, 1940, when the European war was almost nine months
old, Franklin Roosevelt could not help but speak out against
those who had criticized him for being an alarmist in the years
before actual hostilities had begun.

I was a sort of—who was the fellow? John the Baptist—a "voice
crying out in the wilderness" all last summer. I was perfectly sure that
there would be a war. . . . And there was a most awful howl of protest
all over the country, as you know, at that time. I was accused of being
an alarmist, accused of wanting to send troops to the other side and
things of that sort—I am quite accustomed to that sort of thing—and,
after all, today we are faced with the complete fulfillment of that because practically the whole of Europe is falling into the hands of a
combination headed by the Nazi school of thought and school of
government with a pretty close association and affiliation with the
Communist school of thought and school of government, and a third
school which is balancing very carefully on the edge of a knife at the
present time, the Fascist school of thought and school of government.

One of Roosevelt's close associates at the time, Robert Jackson,
later commented that FDR "didn't want this country in war if
it could possibly have been avoided, but he thought we should
have a free hand as far as international law was concerned
to follow our policy."

If Roosevelt wanted to push the United States into the war,

he had many opportunities. Through 1940 and 1941 his Cabinet secretaries and other aides were constantly suggesting to him that he take actions that would provoke an attack against the United States. In October, 1940, for example, Secretary of War Henry Stimson suggested that the American fleet

. . . fully equipped and with its train of supplies complete, move across the Pacific by a nonprovocative route which would avoid the Marshall and Caroline islands and accept the pending invitation of the British to establish itself at Singapore.

It would, thereby place itself between the Japanese fleet and any possible union with the Italian fleet and the other Axis forces in the Mediterranean and near East. . . .

And what would be the result of such a movement?

First, Stimson said, British morale would be greatly increased. He then pointed out that

If any naval hostilities against our coast or possessions in Hawaii or the Philippines should result, it would produce a situation in which the Japanese were the avowed aggressors and any resulting action by our naval forces would have behind them the full sentiment of sympathy from our population. . . .

If the Japanese should be foolish enough to attack Hawaii or the American coast they would give our Navy an Heaven sent opportunity for fleet action far away from the Japanese bases. Therefore, nothing more than raids need probably be expected, and raids would be comparatively impotent and easily disposed of. Even a Japanese attack upon the Philippines would give our Navy a far better opportunity for successful action than would be presented if we should wait until Japan took the offensive with our fleet remaining in American waters.

This was the suggestion for a "preventive" war also raised by Joseph Grew.

Roosevelt resolved to resist this kind of pressure as long as he could. Harold Ickes frequently badgered the President about the United States' policy of selling oil to Japan. The oil was being used as part of Japan's war machine. FDR opposed turning off the American faucets. He understood that Japan would have its oil, one way or the other. If it could not purchase oil from the United States, it would take military action in the Pacific to acquire oil supplies from other sources. On occasion the pressures for the

United States to take a provocative action would transform FDR's usually calm attitude into one of exasperation. When Edwin Pauley, an American oil man, suggested to Ickes that the United States take any action to prevent Japan from grabbing at the oil in the Netherlands East Indies, Ickes passed the note on to FDR. Roosevelt snapped in reply, "If I could spend a week with Pauley—eight hours a day—giving him the history and the present facts relating to the pros and cons of the Far East and their relationship to the pros and cons of the Atlantic—and now Russia—he then might be beginning to graduate from the ranks of the amateurs." The view from the White House was not one for amateurs.

Sometimes, instead of exasperation, there would be anger. The story of his "stab in the back" speech is an example. In June, 1940, when Germany appeared triumphant, or almost so, over France and England, Italy declared war on those two nations. The declaration was a tawdry act. Mussolini obviously believed he could come in at the end and pick up some of the spoils. FDR had scheduled a speech for the night of June 10 at Charlottesville, Virginia. The speech was written before the news came of the Italian declaration of war. Roosevelt was so incensed at Mussolini's act that he sat down and inserted a line in the speech text reading, "On this tenth day of June, 1940, the hand that held the dagger has struck it into the back of its neighbor."

Cordell Hull, the Secretary of State, was not in Washington at the time, so Sumner Welles, the Under Secretary, was asked for a departmental opinion on the sentence. Welles objected vigorously. The phrase was not diplomatic. There also was an unspoken objection, apparent to any person knowledgable about politics. Either Roosevelt or another Democrat would be running for President in a few months. Was it wise politics to anger a large segment of American voters of Italian origin?

The line was taken out of the speech.

Roosevelt traveled that day to Charlottesville with his wife Eleanor and his press secretary Stephen Early as his only companions. As the presidential train cut through the Virginia countryside, FDR brooded about Italy's act, his own reaction to that act, and the restrictions placed upon him by diplomacy and politics. He spoke of his feelings to his wife. Perhaps he did so because he knew what his wife's reaction would be. Eleanor

Roosevelt was as decent a person, as religious a person—in the sense of understanding her obligation to other people—as was Franklin Roosevelt himself. But she felt free of the diplomatic and political restraints that tied him.

"Well," she said to him, "if your conscience won't be satisfied unless you put it in, I would put it in."

And he did.

"On this tenth day of June, 1940," he said, his words crisp and clear, spat out as a gun spits out bullets, "the hand that held the dagger has struck it into the back of its neighbor."

The language was not diplomatic. Sumner Welles never became reconciled to it, but Roosevelt was overjoyed. "For once," he insisted to Harry Hopkins and some other friends, he had said "exactly what I think of an evil action." But Franklin Roosevelt spoke not only for himself. As President, he spoke for the United States. And this time, then, the United States had spoken out clearly to condemn an evil action and to call on men to have certain moral standards. At the time of the quarantine speech in 1937, Frank Knox had asserted that "It is high time that civilized humanity found a voice." That voice now was becoming louder and more distinct.

But there was one area in which this most decent man did not speak as loudly and clearly as perhaps he should have. This area was the plight of the Jews in Europe. To have helped the Jews would not have required an army, probably not even an airplane. As early as 1933, at a rally in New York City, an American Jewish leader said:

It is difficult for Americans—Jews and Gentiles alike—to understand the silence of President Roosevelt in the face of one of the great human disasters of our time. The tragic and needless sufferings of the Jews in Germany are such that it should have been impossible for the President of the United States not to have spoken a word of warning and condemnation to the German government.

Felix Frankfurter, an American Jew who had been born in Vienna and whose relatives in Austria experienced the horrors of Hitler's violent anti-Semitism, once directed the same question to FDR privately. FDR answered then that he doubted whether he could publicly express his abhorrence of anything that was done in a foreign country toward its own nationals. Did he really have the right, Roosevelt was saying, to criticize Germany for the way it treated Germans who happen to be Jews?

When Adolf Hitler came to power, Germany had a history of anti-Semitism. So did the United States. When the Olympic games were to be held in Germany, for example, the question arose of whether the United States should enter the Olympics if the Nazis denied Jews equal opportunities in the games. The question was most emphatically answered by the American Olympic Committee. Absolutely, the United States would enter.

Jewish ghettos existed in Europe. They existed in the United States also. The areas in the United States where Jews could buy homes were severely limited. Most sales contracts for homes carried clauses forbidding the resale of the house to Jews, Negroes, and occasionally to Italians. One of America's greatest industrialists, Henry Ford, had spent a considerable part of his fortune in the 1920s attacking Jews. In the 1930s one of the most popular of Americans, judging by his radio audience, was the Catholic priest Charles E. Coughlin. He was a vicious anti-Semite. The sickness of racial prejudice was not confined to one nation.

But there was a difference, and it was significant.

When the Nazis came to power in Germany, they inflamed the anti-Semitism in that nation, practiced it, and encouraged the German people to express that anti-Semitism in violent acts. The moral collapse of Nazi Germany was not caused by a few roughnecks parading through the streets shouting obscenities, challenging the law as well as elemental standards of decency. The cause, instead, was the encouragement of lawlessness by responsible officials. At the moment when a German policeman either stood passive or joined in the attacks against the minority members, knowing that he was doing as his superiors wished him to do, the downfall, the collapse of morality in Germany, began. The slaughter of six million innocent Jews came in the 1940s, but it was foreshadowed by the sometimes isolated, sometimes organized, acts of violence against German Jews by their fellow countrymen in the 1930s. When the slaughter came, the German people accepted it as a natural development of the lesser forms of bestiality they had practiced.

By contrast, in the United States the movement was away from anti-Semitism. Violent acts committed against Jews in the United States were not condoned by public officials. The United

States was striving desperately for a higher state of civilization, a state in which religious and racial prejudice would not exist. And it was a tribute to the American people that they had chosen a man who would assume leadership of this drive toward that higher state of civilization rather than do as the German people had done when they chose a leader who traveled in the other direction.

If Roosevelt believed he could not act publicly to help the German Jews, he never hesitated to make his own personal feelings known. In 1933 an American diplomat in Vienna, George H. Earle, told newsmen that Americans had little sympathy with the rising anti-Semitism in Germany. His remarks were quickly criticized, even in the United States, as being a diplomatic blunder. Technically they were. Diplomats do not criticize internal affairs of nations. Shortly after the incident, however, Earle received a letter from the President. "I am delighted, from all I hear, to know that you are doing such a fine job" began the President almost casually. "Strictly between ourselves," FDR continued, "I am glad that you committed what some have suggested was [a] diplomatic blunder. I can assure you it did not embarrass me at all!" To another American diplomat a few years later, FDR wrote, "What a plight the unfortunate Jews are in. It gives them little comfort to remind them that they have been 'on the run' for about four thousand years."

In 1935, when the European warlords were condemning Jews and persons with Jewish ancestors, Franklin Roosevelt seized a chance to say that among his ancestors "In the dim distant past [there] may have been Jews or Catholics or Protestants." And then he said, "What I am more interested in is whether they were good citizens and believers in God—I hope they were both." And in 1939, when Roosevelt appointed Felix Frankfurter to the Supreme Court, newspapers around the world reported not that a man named Frankfurter had been appointed to the Court but that a Jew had been appointed.

Anyone who wished to know could discover where Franklin Roosevelt's sympathies lay.

In 1938 there was an abrupt change in the situation regarding the Jews inside Germany. Up to that time Nazi persecution of German Jews had been primarily economic. Taxes had been imposed upon Jews and not upon Gentiles. Restrictions were placed upon Jews trying to operate businesses and the authorities had looked in another direction when Jews were physically attacked. In 1938, however, using the murder in Paris of a German diplomatic official by a young Jew as an excuse, the government organized, encouraged, and participated in an attack upon innocent Jews within the borders of Germany that went beyond the acts of previous years. There was murder, pillage, and destruction. The pogrom has become known as *Kristallnacht*, so named for the broken glass from synagogue windows that littered the street.

When *Kristallnacht* had ended, the Jewish-owned shops and homes and synagogues destroyed numbered in the hundreds. The dead and wounded Jews numbered in the dozens. The Jews imprisoned in concentration camps numbered in the thousands. The Nazi government was pleased at the result. The people of Germany, who had largely supported the pogrom, were pleased at the result. When *Kristallnacht* had ended, there was no doubt Adolf Hitler had succeeded in bringing out the worst in the German people.

Even the American State Department agreed that the United States should react to the pogrom, in contrast to its general position of ignoring such issues. The department prepared a three-sentence statement for the President to issue. It read, "The news of the past few days from Germany has shocked public opinion in the United States. Such news from any part of the world would inevitably produce a similar reaction among the American people. With a view to gaining a firsthand picture of the situation in Germany I asked the Secretary of State to order our Ambassador in Berlin to come home for report and consultation."

The statement was not good enough for Roosevelt, the Christian country gentleman who believed in the Golden Rule, the apostle of decency. When he issued the statement to the press, it had a significant change. This sentence was added in the President's name: "I myself could scarcely believe that such things could occur in a twentieth century civilization."

And there it was again. In Frank Knox's phrase, the voice of civilized humanity had spoken once more.

The American ambassador was never sent back to Germany. While the action was not a formal severing of relations between the two nations, it was a well-understood act of displeasure. The civilized nation, or the nation at least striving toward a civilized state, would not deal diplomatically with the nation moving away from that state.

Still, later historians agreed that Franklin Roosevelt did not do as much as he should have done and probably not as much as he could have done to ease the plight of the Jews in the 1930s. Arthur D. Morse, in his study *While Six Million Died*, has pointed out that thousands of unfilled places existed on American immigration quotas which German Jews could have filled, and he has also documented how the State Department placed every obstacle possible in the path of any Jews seeking to immigrate to the United States. That department was described at the time by Harold Ickes as "a conglomeration of ambitious men consisting mainly of careerists who, because they are career men, feel no obligation to follow Administration policy. I believe that, in substance, it is undemocratic in its outlook and is shot through with fascism." It was Roosevelt's State Department. If he is to receive credit for the positive actions of his administration, he must also be scored for the negative actions.

There were, however, several mitigating factors. FDR had to deal with a nation, the United States, which continued to have a strong anti-Semitic strain. It was not unusual in an American movie house in the late 1930s, when the screen showed Nazis murdering Jews, for at least part of the audience to cheer.

There were also political dangers. The American people, filled to their ears with the dangers of communism and fascism, were fearful of "foreigners." At one time in 1941 the Justice Department asked American citizens to report any evidence of sabotage. Thousands of reports flooded federal offices. They were nonsensical, based on prejudice, directed usually at people with foreign-sounding names.

Roosevelt also had problems with Congress. In the late 1930s and early 1940s FDR was trying to persuade Congress to appropriate the funds needed for rearmament. Congress believed the national mood isolationist. Suspicious of FDR, believing his every move to be a thrust for personal power, the Congress was reluctant to support any action that might involve the nation more deeply in the affairs of Europe.

And there still was another factor, the most important. The tragedy that befell the European Jews in the 1940s simply could not be anticipated in the 1930s. It is barely believed three decades later. Nora Levin, in her study called *The Holocaust*, documents how the Jews did not believe it was happening to them at the moment that it did. In 1938 Roosevelt had criticized what by comparison were a few acts of government-sanctioned vandalism and barbarism by saying that he himself could scarcely believe such acts could take place in a modern civilized nation. Roosevelt and most Americans simply could not grasp that ultimately six million noncombatants would be killed because of the way they chose to worship God in the privacy of their homes and their temples. Americans were too decent a people to grasp that vision.

And that was the man, Franklin Delano Roosevelt, who was taking the cautious steps forward he believed necessary to defend the United States.

MAY: *". . . an unlimited national emergency exists . . ."*

AS FDR moved cautiously he was being pulled in two directions. Wendell Willkie in May called on the United States to insure delivery of its cargoes to England. FDR had turned down that recommendation the previous month when made by Navy Secretary Knox in a speech text. "Whether it be by convoy, airplane accompaniment of merchant shipping or whatever method the Army and Navy experts deem best," Willkie said, "I do not believe the present use of the Navy for patrolling is enough to prevent our production from going to the bottom." While Willkie and the other interventionists were pulling FDR one way, the isolationists tugged in the other direction. Hamilton Fish, the Republican who represented Roosevelt's Hyde Park district in Congress, publicly dared FDR to send a bill to Congress requesting authorization to convoy merchant ships to England. Fish claimed the bill would be defeated in the House by seventy votes. FDR refused to accept the dare. If he had sent a bill and it had passed Congress, there would have been no restrictions on his insuring delivery of war materiel to Britain. But if the bill had lost, as Fish claimed it would, then FDR would be hardpressed even to claim authority for the patrols he had ordered. Chances were that Fish's claim that the bill would be defeated was an accurate assessment. The America First Committee was becoming stronger and stronger. Rallies at which senators like Burton Wheeler and Gerald Nye, the author Kathleen Norris, and the aviation hero Charles Lindbergh spoke were attended by thousands of cheering persons. Their speeches were broadcast over radio to millions of other Americans and were published in newspapers across the nation. The Committee's power was an unknown quantity but an awesome one. When Willkie called in May for greater intervention, two members of FDR's Cabinet made somewhat similar speeches. Stimson and Knox, the two Republicans in the Cabinet, publicly called for the repeal of the neutrality laws. Cordell Hull, the Secretary of State, criticized both men at the next Cabinet session, telling them they were stirring up a needless controversy. The controversy, Hull said, was needless because the American public was not yet ready to agree to any additional intervention in the European war. FDR told the Cabinet session he agreed with Hull.

At the same time, indications became even stronger that the choice of whether or not to intervene was being taken out of the hands of the United States. Clarence Dillon, one of the nation's most prominent financiers, called the White House. He told a presidential aide that the Japanese had approached his company to handle the sale of two insurance companies they owned in the United States. The Japanese, Dillon reported, were interested in "an immediate bid." Dillon continued, "I thought this might be of real interest to the President, as it looks like the Japanese are selling out their assets over here in a hurry. We had purposely cabled them a low offer for immediate acceptance, to see what would happen, and they accepted immediately."

It was against that kind of background that the Hull-Nomura talks dragged on through May. The position the United States took in the talks was, basically, that Japan not move against Indochina and other European possessions in the Pacific and that it withdraw from China. If Japan did so, the United States would begin to talk about improving commercial relations and political ties with Japan. This was too much to ask of Japan at this time. Its war with China by then was too much of a national cause and withdrawing from China would have been too much of a defeat. But the United States could not accept less. To do so meant conceding the military aggression of Japan to be irreversible. The possibility that Japan would, after succeeding with China, stop military aggression was remote.

Even the conciliatory tone used by Nomura in his meetings with Hull irked his superiors in Japan. "Before Nomura left Japan," Foreign Minister Matsuoka said in May to his fellow government members, "I gave him a written memo, and that memo suggested the exact opposite of what he is doing now." Some years later Matsuoka described Nomura as "impossible." Japan believed it could afford to be nonconciliatory. With the signing of the treaty the previous month with Russia, its way south had become clear. If Japan could not win control of Asia and the Western Pacific by negotiation, it would win by military means.

The lack of rapport between Nomura in the United States and his superiors in Tokyo was understood in Washington, and this understanding that war could come unexpectedly created the urgency behind the rearmament effort. But that urgency was felt by government, not by the leaders of American industry who must manufacture the equipment for war. Roosevelt tried to make them understand the seriousness of the situation. Often he met with small groups of American business leaders; he felt he was persuasive in such gatherings. A session he had this month with a small group is typical of such talks. If the war "goes the wrong way," he said, if "the Axis powers win," then "it is going to hit business far more than any one thing has ever hit them. It will hit them far worse than a mere ending of all of these emergency orders. . . . [We] will get 'put in a vise,' a 'strait jacket,' by the Axis powers; and I don't think that the seriousness of that situation can be underestimated."

The defense effort required cooperation by industry and government. Roosevelt was willing to go more than halfway. He was not an enemy of business. When not in politics, FDR had been a New York lawyer dealing with large corporations. Most of his close friends, outside of the political world, were from the Wall Street circle of big businessmen, their bankers, and their lawyers. Not everyone in his administration was quite so friendly. Many of the New Dealers had been fighting big business most of their lives; they did not welcome the prospect of shaking hands, even for the duration.

Less than a week after the European war began in September, 1939, Harold Ickes lunched with Ben Cohen and Tommy Corcoran, two of the most prominent of the New Deal workhorses, as well as Robert Jackson. The subject at the luncheon was whether Roosevelt would permit big businessmen to come into the government and assume control of it as the luncheon companions believed Wilson had allowed during the First World War. "The situation," Ickes thought then, "is something for the liberals in the administration to be very anxious about."

FDR understood the fears of the New Dealers and realized he

must tread carefully or else face the prospect of his administration collapsing. At one time in 1939 Henry Morgenthau suggested to him that he bring in Nelson Rockefeller and Donald M. Nelson of the Sears, Roebuck company to help with procurement. The President then did not believe he could move quite so openly. "You don't want to get too many of these kind of people in," he said, referring to Rockefeller and Nelson. He suggested to Morgenthau that they find people who had always supported the Democratic administration. The President then explained that he did not wish to create the impression that the J. P. Morgans of Wall Street were running Washington. "We have to be careful," he told Morgenthau, "that J. P. Morgan does not get control, not that I have anything against J. P. Morgan because I am talking to him all the time myself . . . but the public need not know that."

Going halfway himself, FDR wanted industry to come the other half. Despite the Depression, the United States by 1941 was the greatest industrial complex the world ever had known and in that year was achieving its greatest economic success. Because American businessmen had benefited most from the free enterprise system, FDR believed he had the right to anticipate that the American industrial machine willingly and quickly would contribute to the defense effort. He was disappointed.

When FDR decided to rearm the United States, he had been faced with the problem of industry and money. Roosevelt remembered the First World War when there had been much profiteering by some industrialists willing to contribute to the war effort only at an outrageous cost. He wanted to prevent that from happening a second time. There were, however, many legitimate questions. Millions of Americans had money invested, through small and large stockholdings, in American industry. They expected a return on their investment. This meant that even if industry turned to war work, it must earn a profit. Also, gearing up for the war effort meant expenditures for new plants and new equipment. Who should pay for this? And there would be a loss of markets; civilian consumers would get out of the habit of buying certain products. Such problems must be considered.

The "consideration" process had begun early. In 1939 the Navy lobbied for a sixty percent tax writeoff for companies expanding to fulfill Navy contracts. The President and Treasury Secretary Morgenthau were willing to go along with a tax writeoff, even a generous one, but they said flatly that sixty percent was too high. The acting Secretary of the Navy then was Charles Edison, a businessman who could not understand why there were objections to the sixty percent figure. Harold Ickes, who had been present at the Cabinet meeting when the issue was thrashed out, cracked, "It is astonishing how the American businessman is willing to jump in upon the slightest excuse and enrich himself at the expense of the country."

The consideration process continued in 1940. Congress then passed a law permitting the War and Navy departments to begin the contract awarding process with a letter of intent. This was a document from the military service to a particular company, promising to award a contract for a specific item to that company. It was helpful to the defense effort. The company could start hiring the men it would need. It could build the plant facility, design the machinery; all this would be done before or while the company and the military service were engaged in the lengthy contract negotiating process. It meant that once the negotiations were completed and the contract signed, the company could begin work immediately. This represented a tremendous saving of time. But there was a disadvantage for the government. Once the letter of intent had been signed, the government was, in effect, stuck with that contractor—and the price that contractor would charge. The "negotiation" process became a give and take process in the sense that the government gave and the company took. An Army Air Force study of procurement in that period sums up the situation succinctly: "The letter of intent put the government at a disadvantage in negotiating and, on that account, was very acceptable to the contractors."

The next consideration was an increase in the amortization rate. Any company can amortize (write off) its capital investment. A machine ultimately will wear out. If it cost one thousand dollars originally and is considered to have a life span of ten years, it is costing one hundred dollars a year. That one hundred dollars a year can be deducted from the company's yearly earnings. That is amortization. Speeding up the amortization process permits a company to write off a plant or a machine with a life span of, say twenty years, in only five or ten years. As the United States began rearming, industry wanted an amortization period of five years rather than the sixteen years then allowed. This meant that industry would be receiving huge tax deductions in the period in which it expected to earn its biggest profits. Also it meant that at the end of the five year period the private industry would have a complete facility, entirely paid for through tax credits, that it could turn to civilian production.

There was a reasonable case for some step-up in the amortization rate. The argument was made to the President that Germany had an amortization rate of seven years and, since American industry was expected to accomplish the same armaments job in less time, it should have a faster tax writeoff. The President also was told that nobody anticipated the war would last sixteen years. American industry, this argument continued, did not want anything for nothing, but it did wish some protection on its investment. The protection it was demanding, of course, was becoming a guarantee of profits.

The last part of the consideration given to industry in 1940 was the end of competitive bidding. Again, the case made was based to some extent on reasonableness. Prior to the rearming effort, the War and Navy departments would publicly advertise for bids. "The hallowed requirement that contract awards be preceded by advertising for bids may now be omitted at the discretion of the Secretary of War," explained Robert Patterson. "The system of competitive bidding is supposed to bring out the lowest bidder and to assure the government the lowest possible price, which is all very well when times are quiet. But in an emergency, economy in time takes precedence over economy in cost. Congress has given the Secretary authority to buy goods or services by negotiated contract, in the same way that a business house buys, and care is taken in the War Department to guard against favoritism." Patterson continued that the change "will save days, weeks, and in some cases months in contractual procedure; and time is the hub around which our whole armament program must rotate." Then Patterson summed up with this slogan: "Maximum production in minimum time."

Once the government began negotiating with specific companies, it was developing a system under which a company had a hammerlock on the product. Only one company was manufacturing a weapon under the negotiated contract system and if the government needed more of that weapon, it had to pay that company's price. In an effort to assure that industry would not gouge the government and also that it would have enough incentive to bid for a negotiated contract, the government began the cost-plus-fixed-fee system. The government pays for the cost of manufacturing the item plus a fixed fee, a certain percentage, which is the manufacturer's profit. Since that profit was a percentage of the cost, the manufacturer found it to his financial benefit to have the product cost as much as possible. It also was to his advantage to count as many costs as possible in the estimate of the product's overall cost. The government would pay all such costs and then hand the manufacturer a percentage of that total as part of his profit.

Patterson, under whom most of these contracts were issued, conceded that "the cost of the government is frequently greater than it would have been if the situation had allowed us to make a lump sum contract on competitive bid." But, said Patterson, they must be used "in cases of urgency, where there is no time to prepare detailed plans and specifications, or where there is no experience available as to what would constitute a fair price." By May, 1941, the War Department became concerned at a move in Congress to prohibit the cost-plus-fixed-fee contracts, and Robert Patterson began a strenuous lobbying campaign with the Democratic leaders in the House to end the move. Patterson won when the House, by only a four-vote margin, decided against prohibiting the cost-plus-fixed-fee contracts.

Harold Ickes said such considerations were "abandoning advanced New Deal ground with a vengeance."

Once the considerations had been exacted, the American businessman began slowly edging toward Washington. Some even were surprised at what they found. One corporate executive later wrote of his Washington experiences that "I lost ten pounds and a lot of personal prejudices." The executive conceded being shocked that he had once written of Harry Hopkins that "he has the clearest, coolest mind of anyone I have ever seen here." Considering that Hopkins, as the dispenser of the WPA funds, had been thought of as the nemesis of American industry, that was high praise.

Of the civilians overseeing defense production, many did not receive compensation from the government but continued to be paid their regular salaries from their employers from whom they were on leave. There was no subterfuge involved. John D. Biggers filed a memorandum with the government stating as a matter of public record "that I have not resigned my position as President of the Libby-Owens-Ford Glass Company but have been granted leave with pay in order that I may respond to this call to government service." He received a formal reply that it was understood by the government that persons like himself "would be permitted to continue their relations with their respective firms or corporations and to receive compensation therefrom during the period of their employment" by the government.

The government needed these "dollar-a-year" men to assist in organizing the defense effort. It could not afford to pay them attractive enough salaries. So it gratefully accepted these donations by private industry.

There were many Americans, however, who believed that the dollar-a-year-man system was basically wrong, that it permitted and even encouraged favoritism. One senator, Kenneth McKellar, Democrat of Tennessee, sponsored legislation to end the system. Another senator, Harry S. Truman, Democrat of Missouri, demanded a list of all dollar-a-year men, their regular employers, and details about their work for the government. Bill Knudsen, who was the shepherd for the flock of these dollar-a-year people, maintained stoutly that "There is no direct connection between government contract awards and the former business affiliation" of any of the people assisting him in the defense effort, with or without government salary.

During 1941 the number of dollar-a-year men in Washington fluctuated, but usually stayed near one hundred and fifty. Obviously the possibility of scandal was great; they were dealing with large contracts. But it is a credit to these people that no scandals developed. Not everyone believed that. Philip Murray, the labor leader who headed the Congress of Industrial Organizations, charged that federal defense agencies were "infested" with corporation executives who were sabotaging the defense effort by working inside government to get "fat, juicy, profitable contracts" for their own companies. But, while mistakes were made, the charge of malfeasance in office was not proved.

Most of these dollar-a-year men were Republicans. That was a matter of both humor and concern to FDR and the Democrats. With newsmen, FDR joked about the situation. At one press conference, after he had announced that Harry Hopkins would head the lend-lease program, a reporter asked if Hopkins would be paid.

The President laughed. "Yes, sure," he said. "He's a Democrat! What a foolish question."

When the laughter ended, Roosevelt continued, warming to his theme:

That was what I said to Bill Knudsen the other day. In about the fourth or fifth list of these dollar-a-year men, they were all listed as Republicans except a boy who had graduated from Yale last June and never voted, and I said, "Bill, couldn't you find a Democrat to go on this dollar-a-year list anywhere in the country?" He said, "I have searched the whole country over. There's no Democrat rich enough to take a job at a dollar a year."

Knudsen also told that same story in his official biography. The point was the same in his version, but the incident was not quite so friendly. According to Knudsen, the President asked him to clear all appointees with the White House. Then a few days later, as Knudsen told it, a man from the Democratic National Committee visited him and directed that good Democrats be given the key production jobs. Knudsen ignored the demand and had no trouble with his appointments. He figured that Franklin Roosevelt did not really care about political affiliation but had to make certain gestures to keep his party happy.

Bill Knudsen was almost correct.

FDR did himself try to find some Democrats "rich enough" to come to Washington. To a New York businessman who was also a friend as well as a Democrat, FDR confessed that "I am somewhat appalled by the fact that at least nine out of ten men being brought here by the production people are not only Republicans but are mostly violently antiadministration Republicans." He asked his friend to "dig out for me the names of twenty or thirty Democratic businessmen who have had successful experience."

If FDR was "appalled" at the number of Republicans working for him, he was furious to find that some Democrats who had opposed him also were working in the war effort. Being a politician, FDR understood and respected the opposition. He could not respect those Democrats who were willing to ride his coattails to victory in elections and then opposed him in Congress. Jesse H. Jones, who headed the Reconstruction Finance Corporation, discovered this early in 1941. An ex-Congressman named Robert Luce, a Democrat from Massachusetts, had been hired by the RFC. "I do know," FDR told Jones, "you have never had a worse enemy than was Luce in Congress. He had a perfect record of opposition. In the meanwhile, your New Deal supporters are unable to get jobs."

Jones balked at firing Luce, throwing back at Roosevelt that the defense production agencies were hiring many Republicans. FDR conceded that was true. "However," he continued, "most of these men are employed for special business purposes and are not policy-forming like people in similar positions in the regular permanent agencies of the government." Roosevelt continued that regular agencies should employ people "who believe in us—not just lip-service." He concluded to Jesse Jones with "What to do?"

But it was and remained Jones's decision, as Bill Knudsen's employees were his decision. Franklin Roosevelt jettisoned politics for the duration and gave industry the considerations it demanded. It was against this background that he went about building a war production machine.

The contribution of American industry to that machine is exemplified by what happened to the American military airplane. In the late 1930s and early 1940s the symbol of the new warfare was the airplane. Hitler had made it his first weapon; his Luftwaffe swept into Poland and obliterated its will to defend itself, and then blitzed England in an attempt to do the same to the English people. The Royal Air Force had been England's first military defense; the Spitfires with their tired pilots continued to go into the air to save their island home.

In early 1940 President Roosevelt had been bluntly told by George Marshall that the United States did not have an adequate air force. The Army could count 2,800 airplanes, of which one thousand were considered combat craft. Some of those could not even be flown and few were equal to the German planes. The Navy's air arm was in little better condition. With war possible at any time, the United States was in a desperate position. If German divisions were to land on the American coast, the President was told, there would not be sufficient aircraft to block their advance.

A few days later the President went before Congress to ask that the nation develop an aircraft industry capable of producing fifty thousand airplanes a year. The figure stunned the nation. Fifty thousand airplanes was more aircraft than the United States had produced since the Wright brothers first flew at Kitty Hawk.

It was far more than the productive capacity of the aircraft industry. In 1938 that industry had produced 1,800 planes. By 1940 the industry had more orders but little additional capacity to fill them. At the time the President called for fifty thousand planes a year, the industry was producing between four hundred and fifty and five hundred aircraft a month—or approximately one-tenth of his target. The fifty thousand figure also far exceeded the orders for three thousand aircraft then placed by the military services.

The figure had been pulled out of the air by the President. But it was not a casual act on his part. He realized that members of the Air Corps as well as the public had to be jarred out of their complacent attitudes. The United States had to realize that business-as-usual would no longer be sufficient. The President believed that the American people as well as the armed services must understand that they would have to strive for new targets. And they were targets that the timid and the uncertain found unbelievable. So FDR chose a figure to shock the timid and the uncertain into the full realization of the future.

In the years before the war the planners in the Army Air Corps had been living in an unreal world. War, if it ever came, would be a minor endeavor and the nation could be nonchalant. The planners acknowledged that, in the event of a conflict, aircraft production must be increased but they arbitrarily decided that the aircraft industry would split its production down the middle, one-half for military use and one-half for civilian use. "It is obvious," said an Army Air Force study made after the war, "that these rules were not based upon anticipation of total war."

The industry responded to this kind of planning in the 1930s as expected. It did not concern itself with large-scale production. It was not even interested in bidding on military contracts. The aircraft industry produced a relatively small number of military aircraft each year, most of the planes manufactured by hand operations rather than by the assembly-line process developed by the Henry Ford company almost forty years earlier.

By 1940 the civilian planners and even the military planners had realized that production capacity would have to be increased enormously to meet the demands of a modern defense. Even then, however, there was an unwillingness to think beyond the past. The expansion plan produced for the Army Air Corps was based only on increasing the floor space of aircraft plants and multiplying the number of shifts the men would work. It did not even consider the increased production possibilities of going to an assembly line system. Roosevelt grasped that a new, bold approach was necessary. Production planning must be taken out of the hands of the traditional military planners. The military bureaucracy, stultified by a caste system that gave promotions whether deserved or not, was incapable of doing the job that needed to be done.

It was then that Roosevelt had called in Bill Knudsen. Knudsen's job was to serve on the Advisory Committee to the National Defense Council. The Council was a World War I agency resurrected by FDR in the spring of 1940 to spark defense production. The makeup of the Advisory Committee showed the political genius of Roosevelt at its best. The agency was not a good administrative body because FDR realized that the political impact of the group was more significant than its administrative qualities. The committee's effectiveness would be dependent primarily upon the ability of its members to persuade various segments of the American economy to volunteer for the war effort. So FDR, in choosing committee members, selected persons influential in all areas of American life. With Knudsen, a pre-eminent business leader, on the Advisory Committee, FDR also needed a labor leader. A problem existed, however. There were two major labor organizations, the American Federation of Labor and the Congress of Industrial Organizations, and they were bitterly opposed to each other. Frances Perkins, FDR's Secretary of Labor, recommended to FDR that he pick two labor representatives, one from the AFL and the other from the CIO. FDR rejected that idea. He realized that two labor representatives would mean that the feuds between the AFL and the CIO would be carried on in the Advisory Committee. FDR believed he had some rapport with the union leaders and could handle any objections from them to his choice. So he then selected Sidney Hillman. Like Knudsen, Hillman had arrived in the United States as a poor immigrant boy. Knudsen climbed to the top in industry; Hillman moved in the same direction in the labor movement. He worked in Chicago, first as a tailor, eventually becoming president of the Amalgamated Clothing Workers, a CIO union.

The clothing workers union was small, compared to the industrial unions such as the auto workers, which would have the brunt of the war work. Miss Perkins pointed this out to FDR as an argument against Hillman's selection. To FDR it was an argument in favor of Hillman's selection. As a labor leader, Hillman would have the confidence of other labor leaders. Because his own union was not overly involved in defense work, other union leaders would understand Hillman was not operating from selfish motives.

The other members of the committee were chosen equally for political reasons. Edward R. Stettinius, Jr., came to the committee with a background that included firm connections with the Wall Street banking houses which would have to advance industry much of the cost of rearming. Leon Henderson was an economist with a wide background in government; he would know the federal bureaucracy. Chester C. Davis had come from the South Dakota farmlands to become head of the Agricultural Adjustment Administration, a New Deal agency. He knew the farmers well and they knew and trusted him. Ralph Budd was a railroad president and a director of the Association of American Railroads. He would know how to move defense products across the nation. Harriet Elliott had an academic background and also a reputation for fighting for the underdog. She would be an equalizer on the board, watching that all rights were protected.

At the Advisory Committee's first meeting in the President's White House office, back in May, 1940, Knudsen had asked who was going to be boss. The President answered, "I am." Then he took the committee members into the Cabinet room and introduced them to the Cabinet members. He also advised the Cabinet members to do as the Advisory Committee suggested. Knudsen was certain the Advisory Committee existed without legal authority. He was positive that its powers, if they existed at all, were vague. Its orders were even less clear. That was not the kind of assignment Knudsen was used to, but he figured he could handle it.

From the White House, when the meeting ended, Knudsen went to Fort Myer, in Virginia, to lunch with General Marshall. On the veranda of the chief of staff's quarters that spring day in 1940, the two men discussed war needs. From Marshall's point of view, the problem was simple. He needed everything. Listening to the general, Knudsen began to make up a list. He would concentrate immediately on those items needing a long period for manufacture. The airplanes and the tanks would come before the traditional items like clothing and trucks which could be produced quickly. A schedule of war priorities was being developed.

Knudsen had his staff operating in weeks, a speed which Washington found shockingly fast. Within months he had placed orders for the $10 billion in defense contracts authorized earlier by Congress. The whole operation was an incredible feat, completely astounding the city of Washington. Thousands of problems developed, but they were ignored or solved over the telephone by pleas or bluster. The very fact that the committee had no specific lines of authority, no hard-and-fast directives is what made it so successful. It had no limitations and made its own rules as it went along. Robert Patterson told a couple of stories about that period.

Buying military supplies while the civilian economy remains undisturbed is filled, as is production, with complications and confusion. The services competed with each other and with [British and French] purchasing agents from abroad. Contracts were signed and orders placed with no real assurance that they would be executed and delivered. Officers in the Army and Navy, as well as the patriotic civilians who hurried to Washington to help their country, worked impossible hours. Tempers were strained beyond reason. I sometimes think the imperturbable good humor of General Knudsen, not to mention his standing in the industry, was one of America's greatest war assets in the early days.

Patterson continued that at one point the Secretary of the Navy and the Secretary of War met with Knudsen to inform him that drastic action was necessary because of an aluminum shortage. "It can't be so bad as all that," replied Knudsen, picking up a sheet of paper. "See," he continued, "I have an order here from the Navy for 20,000 aluminum tables and 20,000 aluminum chairs."

At another conference, Knudsen was told that there was a critical shortage of copper. Knudsen picked up another piece of paper from his desk. It was a Navy requisition for three hundred cuspidors. "Can't the sailors spit out to sea?" he said.

Jesse Jones, head of the Reconstruction Finance Corporation, gives another glimpse into how the rearming effort was handled then. His agency received Congressional authority to contribute to national defense in whatever way it could. "With Bill Knudsen selecting contractors to build plants," Jones reports, "and with no red tape except a telephone request from him to me, later to be confirmed by letter, we had authorized more than $2.5 billion for the construction of [defense] plants" through the second half of 1940 and 1941.

What Felix Frankfurter had once called FDR's "fumbling" had proven successful again. Roosevelt had selected good men to do a tough job, permitted them to handle it as they saw fit, and the scheme was succeeding.

When 1941 began, FDR believed the public had come to accept the concept of production being watched over closely from Washington and moved to make the practice more formal. The Advisory Committee was replaced with an agency called the Office of Production Management, with Knudsen and Hillman as its heads and with representatives of the military services represented. FDR realized that the increased production for the war effort would bring new and greater friction between organized labor, which was trying to retain and strengthen the gains it had made in the 1930s, and management, which was interested in stopping such a movement and even chopping it back somewhat. The immediate problem for him was who was going to be head of the OPM: Knudsen, a management man, or Hillman, a labor man. Whichever he chose, management or labor, the public would interpret that choice as the side FDR personally favored. The problem was a tough one for a politician who needed labor's political support and management's support for the war effort.

FDR solved the problem by ignoring it. Asked at a press conference if the agency would have one or two heads, the President answered, "I have a single, responsible head. His name is Knudsen and Hillman."

Newsmen can count. That, they told the President, was two heads. But a President counts only when he wishes to. "No," he answered, "that's one head."

Management and labor were going to be equal, at least as far as the public was concerned. As for the private areas of disagreement, FDR would settle those when he must.

The basic problem Knudsen faced with industry was the same problem that FDR faced with the entire nation: making people realize that the war effort required a major commitment.

Dealing with a number of industries, Knudsen was obliged to work with each one until it realized the magnitude of the problem and committed itself to the solution. His dealings with the automobile and aircraft industries illustrate the tough job he had.

The aircraft industry had always looked upon the automobile manufacturers as potential competitors. Whenever it had been suggested that, in a time of national emergency, the auto makers switch to airplanes, the leaders of the aircraft industry balked. In 1938 they persuaded the Army Air Corps to adopt a policy of considering only aircraft manufacturers as prime contractors. If the auto makers were needed for the defense effort, they would be used only as subcontractors working for the aircraft people. By late 1940 Knudsen realized this would no longer work. The aircraft industry did not have the productive capacity nor the engineering ability to produce fifty thousand airplanes a year. Only the autombile industry had that kind of ability. But Knudsen had to move carefully with the auto manufacturers. If he suggested to them that they curtail production of civilian goods to produce, instead, military equipment, he was afraid the response would be negative. In September, 1940, Patterson had suggested to Knudsen that the auto industry stop bringing out new models, so as to have greater tool capacity for defense. Knudsen refused.

Knudsen used a different approach. In a meeting with the automobile manufacturers, Knudsen appealed to their patriotism, to their pride in their skill at mass production and to everything else he could think of. But the automobile industry came into the war effort, not because of such appeals, but because of other inducements. In January, 1941, the Office of Production Management decreed that there would be no restrictions placed on automobile production, at least in the first half of the year. But federal funds would be made available for new plants where the auto manufacturers could do their aircraft work. The guns would be imposed on top of the butter. After some months of this, Patterson commented:

The automobile industry has scarcely been used in the national defense program, despite the orders for airplane items and ordnance items placed with it. Those items are being manufactured at new plants built especially for such manufacture or at marginal plants. The proof that the industry as a whole has hardly been touched by the

rearmament effort lies in the fact that over five million civilian automobiles will be produced this year—breaking all or nearly all previous
records.

When a government official went to the Glenn L. Martin airplane factory in Omaha, he found that company discouraged by
its dealings with the automobile companies. "Martin placed the
real interest of these companies in the whole project at a
rather low level," read the report back to Washington, "indicating
he felt the primary need was to get them really desirous of doing
this job. So far they gave the impression their attitude was that
they had been dragged into the proposition and had no vital interest in the whole affair."

That was a reasonably accurate picture of the automobile industry in 1941. It did feel it had been dragged into the defense
effort. And it would only cooperate as long as its civilian production was not hindered. Its tool and die makers, for example, were
largely withheld from the defense effort until about October,
1941. This permitted the industry to tool up for its 1942 models.
As Robert Patterson had observed, it was the old story of business
as usual.

The automobile industry's reluctance to divert any of its civilian productive capacity to war needs showed when it suddenly
was confronted with what became known as the "Reuther
plan." Walter Reuther, a young official of the United Auto Workers union, produced a plan by which he claimed the auto companies could turn out five hundred airplanes a day without
interfering with their civilian production. The basic premise of
his plan was that the automobile industry was operating under
capacity and that production could be increased substantially if
the industry operated at its full potential. The automobile industry scoffed at the Reuther plan. The industry said that only ten
or fifteen percent of its tools could be used in nonautomobile
production and that the plants could not be used for the production of wings, tails and other airplane fixtures. Reuther had suggested a joint industry-labor management team and the industry
used words like socialism in referring to that suggestion.

Some years after this period, Robert Patterson commented on
the industry's rejection of the Reuther plan. Patterson had been
intimately involved in defense production, had solid credentials
as a Republican, and was not a particular friend of labor unions.

He charged that the auto companies were too quick to reject the Reuther plan and that Washington was too quick to listen to the companies.

"Looking back," he wrote, "I am now inclined to believe that we should have given more serious consideration to the Reuther plan." He also charged: "The automobile manufacturers, approaching their record production of 1929, did not taper off until late in 1941. They were using materials, labor and engineering skill, indeed, in tooling up for 1942. Urgently needed die and tool makers were withheld from defense work."

Although a former president of General Motors, Knudsen realized that any effort to bring the automobile industry into the defense effort must begin with Henry Ford. Ford had started the automobile industry, was still its patriarch and its leader. If his company were to become involved, the entire industry eventually would fall into line. Immediately after taking over his new job in Washington, Knudsen had spoken glowingly of the Ford company joining the defense effort and building a thousand airplanes a day. Edsel Ford, old Henry's son, was the nominal president of the Ford company and he hurried to Washington. The result was an announcement that the Ford company would produce Rolls-Royce engines, some of which would go to England and some of which would be used by the United States.

But they reckoned without old Henry Ford. Bitterly against the New Deal, strongly isolationist, violently antagonistic toward England, he said that his company never would produce airplane engines for England. He—and Henry Ford was the company—would do it for the United States but not for England. That was that. Knudsen was obliged to turn the contract over to the Packard company.

Knudsen had not given up on Ford, however. A few months later he did persuade the Ford company to accept a contract to build Pratt Whitney airplane engines. With the contract came $14 million in federal funds to build a plant for manufacturing the engines.

The value of having Ford in the defense effort was more than only having a pacesetter. The Ford company brought an industrial brilliance to the war effort. The name was Charles E. Sorensen. Like Knudsen, Sorensen was a Danish immigrant. He had joined the Ford company when it was housed in a two-story wooden factory in Detroit a few years after the turn of the century. One day there, he tied a rope to an automobile chassis and pulled it through the plant. Instead of the workmen bringing parts to the chassis, the chassis came to where the workmen were. From that was born the assembly line process of manufacturing which revolutionized American industry.

It was ironical that Knudsen would call on Sorensen. Knudsen had started in the automobile industry not with General Motors but with Ford. And then in a real life executive suite drama, he was ousted from Ford, with the connivance of Sorensen. Knudsen then went to General Motors and became its president. Any ill feelings that might have survived that coup were submerged for the war effort.

The problem presented to the Ford company was the B-24 bomber. The Army Air Corps needed them by the thousands, and they were being built on the west coast at the rate of one a day. Would Sorensen go out and take a look at the situation? The manufacturing process Sorensen found in California was alien to his mass production approach. The parts of the airplane would be made in various sections of the plant and then carried to a central point where they would be assembled into the bomber.

Sorensen went back to his hotel room that night and drew up a plan for producing the B-24 bomber by the assembly line process. He himself said that building the bomber after building a Ford was like building a skyscraper after building a garage. But the plan, he figured, would work. His production schedule was not a plane a day but one an hour. He took his plans to the government and asked for $200 million. He got it.

On March 28, 1941, hordes of workmen converged on an area west of Detroit called Willow Run, after a creek that ran through the area. The land was quiet, covered with trees. The workmen began leveling, uprooting the trees, building what would be called the Willow Run plant. More than four hundred bombers a month would come from its assembly line.

The Willow Run plant, however, would produce airplanes without disrupting civilian automobile production. Guns would not interfere with butter. In May, 1941, even Knudsen conceded the economy could not produce all the airplanes needed and all the automobiles wanted. He called for a twenty percent cutback in civilian production. This was not enough. And a few months later, Leon Henderson, who had become head of the Office of Price Administration, would call for a fifty percent cut.

The result of Henderson's action was a squabble between his agency and Knudsen's over who was boss in such matters. FDR solved the problem by creating a new agency with Donald Nelson in charge of priorities. Nelson rescinded the Henderson cut, which made Knudsen happy. At the same time, however, he began giving greater emphasis to defense priorities and allocations of materials for defense needs, which made Henderson happy.

Through the entire defense reorganization program, FDR continually came under criticism from his aides and his friends for apparently not doing enough. Early in 1941 Bernard Baruch lamented to Henry Stimson of how he wished "they would stop throwing away the experience of the past." Unless the war effort were "more intelligently organized," he insisted, "no man of authority is going to do the work quickly."

Baruch had been through the industrial mobilization process during the First World War and could speak with experience about that process' needs. In May, 1941, he sent a memorandum to the President specifically calling for more centralized authority in the Office of Production Management. He also lobbied among government officials, becoming waspish when the officials expressed a lack of understanding of what he was driving at. Perhaps only a man with the background of business success and government service as Baruch had could have said to Vice President of the United States Henry Wallace, "If you did some reading in the books I sent you, some of the things that lie in front of you will be less difficult."

If Baruch and the other critics knew what the defense effort needed, they did not understand what the American political system would allow. The United States in 1941 was not at war, as it had been when Baruch joined the defense effort in 1917. Many Americans did not believe war would come. In the summer, for example, there would be serious doubt whether Congress would extend the draft act. If Congress failed to do so, the United States simply would be without an army.

The nation was not ready to accept the kind of economic controls that would be necessary for a wartime economy. FDR's critics wanted him to snap his fingers and produce an economy geared entirely to the war effort: drastically reduced civilian production, price controls, strict limitations on the use of scarce materials.

But Roosevelt was a Democrat who understood that the American system did not permit anyone to seize such power. As well as anyone he understood the meaning of the war threat, but more than anyone else he understood the real meaning of the Presidency. The President could lead; he could not command. Concerned that the nation was not yet fully aware of the dangers it confronted and of the responsibilities it must assume, Franklin Roosevelt at the end of May declared an "unlimited national emergency." Just what the phrase meant was uncertain. When the eighth draft of the speech had come to him, a section read: "By virtue of the powers vested in me by the Constitution and the laws of the United States, I shall authorize and direct that each and every measure be taken in furtherance of defense and in the maintenance and perpetuation of the spirit of liberty throughout the world." FDR crossed out that section and wrote in its place:

We assert an abiding faith in the vitality of our constitutional republic as a perpetual home of freedom, of tolerance, and of devotion to the word of God. Therefore, with profound consciousness of my responsibilities to my countrymen and to my country's cause, I have to-night issued a proclamation that a total national emergency exists and requires the strengthening of our defenses to the extreme limit of our national power and authority.

On the next version he crossed out the words "a total" and substituted "an unlimited," and the proclamation became one for an unlimited national emergency. The legal assistants then began scurrying around to find laws which would give him additional powers. The President was pleased with the reaction the speech produced. He was not as interested in laws that might be found as he was in the response from the American people.

"It has been possible, as you know, for me to carry the country along slowly, but I think surely," he wrote to a friend, "and last week's speech met with far more approval—I should guess at least seventy-five or eighty percent—than if I had given it even two weeks before."

That same month of May, the month in which FDR was wrestling with American industry and declaring an unlimited national emergency, the Japanese Navy had completed its study of the feasibility of Admiral Yamamoto's plan to disable the American fleet by attacking it at Pearl Harbor. The plan was disapproved. There were too many objections. The plan would require Japan's committing almost all of its aircraft carrier strength, and if something went awry the loss to Japan would be enormous. There also was the problem of knowing exactly when the American fleet could be found at Pearl Harbor. The Japanese Navy staff preferred, instead, continuing to move south and to establish an island ring of defenses around Japan.

But Yamamoto was not done. He understood his plan was the only one that could lead to success for Japan. He would convince others of that.

JUNE: *"There will be serious political complications . . ."*

FRANKLIN ROOSEVELT'S determination to enlist Republicans in a national administration was tested in June when FDR received the resignation of Charles Evans Hughes as Chief Justice of the United States. As head of an independent branch of the American government, the Chief Justice can be one of the most powerful persons in Washington. There are few more important appointments a President can make than that of the man to preside over the Supreme Court. FDR's first inclination was to appoint Robert Jackson, one of his stalwart assistants and, at the time, Attorney General in the Cabinet. But FDR listened to the argument he knew he must hear. Felix Frankfurter, a close friend and admirer of Jackson's, outlined the situation to the President.

Rather than name Jackson, Frankfurter said, the President must elevate Harlan Fiske Stone from Associate Justice to Chief Justice. Said Frankfurter:

On personal grounds, I'd prefer Bob. While I've known Stone longer and our relations are excellent and happy, I feel a closer friendship with Bob. But from the national interest I am bound to say there is no reason for preferring Bob to Stone—quite the contrary. Stone is senior and qualified professionally to be Chief Justice. But for me the decisive consideration, considering the fact that Stone is qualified, is that Bob is of your political and personal family, as it were, while Stone is a Republican.

Now it doesn't require prophetic powers to be sure that we shall, sooner or later, be in war—I think sooner. It is most important that when war does come, the country should feel that you are a national,

145

the Nation's President, and not a partisan President. Few things would contribute as much to confidence in you as a national and not a partisan President than for you to name a Republican, who has the profession's confidence, as Chief Justice.

The sentiments of Frankfurter on the need for bipartisanship were identical to those of FDR. Stone received the appointment as Chief Justice, and Jackson was named an Associate Justice.

That month also the cause of national unity received a boost, as it would several more times, from Nazi Germany. On May 6, 1941, the American freighter *Robin Moor* sailed from a Brooklyn pier at noon. Bound for South Africa, she carried eight passengers, a crew of thirty-eight, and a general cargo ranging from steel rails to women's hosiery. On her sides were painted American flags and the big letters "U.S.A." Fifteen days later, on May 21, the *Robin Moor* was in the equatorial Atlantic, between South America and Africa, approximately halfway toward her first stop at Cape Town. A submarine surfaced. With its blinker, it ordered the American ship to stop, silence its radio, and identify itself. After a brief discussion between the officers of the two ships, the Americans were ordered to abandon their ship. When they did so, the submarine sank the *Robin Moor*. The crew and passengers were set adrift in lifeboats.

The United States first learned of the sinking almost three weeks later in June, when one of the lifeboats was picked up by a Brazilian merchant ship. The United States then learned that the American flag had been fired upon by Germans for the first time since 1918.

There is no adequate explanation for the sinking of the *Robin Moor*. The ship was well outside the announced area of the Atlantic which the Germans were blockading. Its nationality could not be mistaken. The act of firing on an American ship was contrary to Hitler's orders of the time. Some weeks later a few of the more vociferous isolationists in the United States claimed the ship was carrying goods declared contraband by Nazi Germany and which were ultimately destined for Germany's enemies. Such a description probably could have been made of most goods on the high seas, the demands of war being what they are. Even if true, however, this would not have been known to the German U-boat commander at the time he ordered the firing of the torpedo. Nor could it ever justify the leaving of the crew and passengers afloat for weeks under a hot sun. Humanity, as well as the traditions of international law, required that the U-boat make some effort to notify rescuers—but this it never did.

The German navy long had resented the restrictions placed upon it by Hitler against attacking American ships. The restrictions meant that the U-boats had less room in the ocean in which to operate and became better targets for British destroyers. The navy had argued with Hitler about these restrictions, even suggested that the entry of the United States into the war sooner rather than later would be advantageous to Germany. Whether the sinking of the *Robin Moor* was the result of a calculated plan by the commanders of the German navy to provoke the United States into the war, or whether it was an isolated act by an irresponsible U-boat commander has never been satisfactorily determined.

Roosevelt sent a message to Congress. He described the sinking of the *Robin Moor* as "a warning to the United States not to resist the Nazi movement of world conquest. It is a warning that the United States may use the high seas of the world only with Nazi consent." He concluded: "Were we to yield on this we would inevitably submit to world domination at the hands of the present leaders of the German Reich. We are not yielding and we do not propose to yield."

The words were strong, but the actions would not be. Harry Hopkins suggested to the President that the Navy be ordered to "establish the freedom of the seas, leaving it to the judgment of the Navy as to what measures of security are required to achieve that objective." The suggestion was for the Navy to be allowed to make war against Germany. The President rejected Hopkins' suggestion. He would not delegate his responsibility to the commander of a Navy ship.

Politically, Roosevelt often was considered an artful dodger in that he frequently seemed to sidestep problems. That was not a fair assessment. He would live up to his presidential responsibilities; that was why he turned down Hopkins' suggestion. But he was a shrewd enough politician to realize that one should not be boxed into a decision until it is necessary and until there appears a strong chance that the public will support that decision. He demonstrated that grasp of political finesse in June when he finally had to grapple with the labor union movement.

Roosevelt turned against the union members in June, 1941, because he was driven by one goal: the defense of the United States. That was a quality of FDR's; he could understand the major problem and direct his energies to its solution without being diverted by lesser problems. When infantile paralysis gripped him, he realized his objective must be to become mobile enough to escape the description of "cripple." When he became President in 1933, he realized the major problem was to restore confidence in the nation's economic health and the free enterprise system. This he did by a whirlwind of activity and legislation. And now, in 1941, the problem was to prepare to defend the United States. Roosevelt had not been scared off in 1933 by the possibility of angering the business community. He would not be scared off in 1941 by the possibility of angering the labor leaders.

The first major strike in a defense industry had come the previous November, affecting the Vultee Aircraft Company in California. A total of $84 million in defense work was delayed twelve days. The next serious strike involved the Allis-Chalmers company. Defense contracts totaling $45 million were delayed ten weeks with no settlement in sight by April. Violence had erupted at the plant sites in Wisconsin and the governor of that state was calling for federal intervention. Said Robert Patterson:

> We must face the facts. Each day that the Allis-Chalmers plant is shut, our vital powder program is being delayed. The important aircraft production of the Vultee plant was paralyzed for eleven days. Direct stoppages on our huge construction programs have been few in number, but the protracted strike in the lumber industry on the West Coast seriously delayed delivery of materials for some of our cantonments. The recent stoppage of work at the Lackawanna plant of Bethlehem Steel threatened our production of steel vital for ordnance and shipbuilding. . . . During the week of February 24 to March 1, it was estimated that on account of strikes 120,000 mandays of production were lost in plants working on supplies for the Army . . . they cause as much concern as do threatened shortages of basic metals. . . . We need every manhour of production, and there should be no strikes or stoppages.

But the strikes and stoppages continued.

Vice President Wallace exhorted labor organizations to greater efforts.

In time of great emergency, like the present, the people of the United States have the right to demand sincere and earnest effort from both labor and management to settle all differences among themselves or with the government with promptness and good will. There is as great patriotism in working overtime to settle a defense contract or strike as in working overtime to rivet the wing of a fighting plane.

The administration tried embarrassing the strikers. "The young men," Wallace said, "who have given up jobs which paid them three times, five times, or twenty times that which they are now getting in the army will not hold guiltless those who are impeding production." But neither patriotic appeals nor embarrassment would do the job.

There were several reasons for the strike wave. The AFL and CIO were struggling against each other for members, and many of the labor troubles in 1941 were caused by jurisdictional disputes between these two organizations. Other troubles were caused by naked grabs for power by labor union leaders. Robert Patterson records that a representative of a construction union visited him and suggested "that contracts carry a clause to the effect that contractor and sub-contractor will employ laborers who will work in harmony with the majority of the laborers on the job." Patterson added without further comment that the union leader expressed his conviction that "if these practices are put into operation, there will be no strikes of any of our work, either for increased wages or for jurisdictional troubles." The price asked at that meeting for labor peace was union control over hiring with all of the possibilities of corruption and payoffs that such a dictatorial system could impose.

More than these causes, there was something else. The labor union leaders realized that the defense effort would be a make or break time for them. All the gains that had come to them during the past ten years, at a cost of so much blood, jailings, and economic tribulations could be lost unless the unions stood fast. The attitude of American business leaders at the time was not such to suggest that any union gains surrendered during the war effort would be voluntarily returned when the war ended. Union men realized they were coming under heavy criticism. They also knew that profits accruing to business because of increased defense production were enormous. Industry could afford to accept the gains made by labor. As a matter of principle, however, it did not wish to.

It also was a matter of principle for the union members. They struck.

In the building of bombers, hundreds of subcontractors manufactured thousands of parts. A strike against one subcontractor stymied the entire production of a line of bombers. That is why, although there were not many strikes against aircraft manufacturers or their subcontractors, those that did take place were enormously effective. Strikes against other industries had even more serious repercussions.

In the spring of 1941, one of the most serious of strikes was against the Allis-Chalmers plant in Wisconsin, the company making turbine engines for destroyers and also powder for Army weapons. The causes of the strike are obscure and depend upon who is telling the story. A critic of labor reports that the causes were "a crooked plant election, stupid management, and communist [union] leadership." Henry Stimson, more sympathetic to labor, said the cause was the CIO, which was trying to unionize the company. "It is, purely, at bottom," he said, "an interdepartmental row but it involves a lot of smaller matters too, and misunderstandings between the different people who have tried to mediate and conciliate the strikers."

Whatever the cause, the government people concerned with building up the defense program believed it must be ended. Sidney Hillman tried his hand at negotiating, failed, and then called on Philip Murray, president of the CIO. He failed also. Frank Knox could wait no longer; he needed the turbines for his destroyers. After talking with FDR, Knox arranged to have 1,500 troops moved to a site near the Allis-Chalmers plant. When one last attempt at mediation failed, he and Knudsen went to see FDR. Their position was simple. All other efforts had failed. The government must seize the Allis-Chalmers plant. Roosevelt said no.

There was no question of the seriousness of the strike. "We have no case," Robert Patterson had said, "where immediate resumption of work is more essential than in the Allis-Chalmers case." Nor was there any surprise that government seizure was recommended to the President. The possibility had been discussed earlier at a Cabinet meeting. Knox had said at that session that he was prepared to take over the plant. Stimson said then that the Army had been ready for several days "to move at a moment's notice." Stimson also cautioned that troops should not be used unless the President was willing to go all the way—"any timid or half way use of the troops would simply bring discredit on the Army," he said.

But FDR must move cautiously. If troops were called in, labor leaders in the Wisconsin area were threatening to strike all defense plants. The violence and passions already exhibited there made clear to the President that the threat was not an idle one. Also there was a question then of the legality of such an act. Finally, FDR with his fine intuitive sense, realized that the public was not yet ready to accept the federal government seizing a privately-owned company, forcing its employees to work at bayonet point. Perhaps there was an unmentioned reason. FDR may not have yet been ready, personally, to turn against that section of the economy, the working man, to whom FDR had given so much and from whom FDR had received so much political support in return. He would come to this position, but like the nation, he could only come to it when there was no other choice. With the Allis-Chalmers strike, his restraint did pay off. The strike was settled a few weeks later without the necessity of sending in federal troops.

The Allis-Chalmers strike, it turned out, was only the opening gun in a year of labor strife, with FDR caught in the middle as he tried to balance the defense needs of the nation against the demands of union leaders. A major showdown came with the Ford plant. As Henry Ford had been the pacesetter for American industry in developing the techniques of mass production, he was also the pacesetter in labor relations. Early in his industrial career he had astonished the business world and established a new standard for labor to shoot at with the $5-a-day wage, an extremely good salary for the time. He also did such things, unique then for American industry, as hiring members of minorities and trying to develop jobs for handicapped persons. By the 1930s, however, his benevolent attitudes toward labor had ended. In their place were company spies, speed-ups, summary dismissal of senior employees without valid cause, and discrimination against employees who sought to join or organize a union. And then wages at Ford plants dropped below the industry standards. "So far," comments Ford's biographer Allan Nevins of the company, "had it lost the spirit and standards of the five-dollar-day."

The Ford company hostility toward unions showed itself on

May 26, 1937, in what became known as the "Battle of the Overpass." Some United Auto Workers union men were passing out union literature when they were attacked and seriously beaten by men in the employ of the Ford company. The union men considered their activities legitimate under federal law and brought action against the company before the National Labor Relations Board. In December of that year the Board upheld the union's position. The company immediately began a court challenge. Much of the American union members' reluctance to fight for their rights through the courts stemmed from that challenge. More than three years passed before the issue was finally settled. On February 10, 1941, the Supreme Court of the United States upheld the union's position. The company had been acting illegally when it blocked the distribution of union literature back in 1937.

Shortly after the court decision, the prospect of a strike appeared strong. Much of the difficulty in 1940 over whether a defense contractor must comply with federal labor law had originated in contracts with Ford. With each contract Ford received, while at the same time ignoring federal labor law, the unions realized that their protections were being rapidly diminished. Which did FDR want? The labor unions protected or bombers produced by Ford?

FDR tried to avoid answering the question.

"Take a question of a contract for the Ford Motor Company," he was asked, "and suppose Mr. Knudsen believes Ford should get the contract because of speed reasons, and Mr. Hillman thinks Ford should not get the contract because of labor reasons; in your view, what should be done?"

"The answer is," replied Roosevelt, "suppose that question did not arise, what would you say? You see, in other words, you would feel awfully cheap, wouldn't you."

But there came a time when FDR no longer could avoid answering the question, when he became convinced that a reliance on good will was not sufficient, when he must decide which he wanted, the labor unions protected or the bombers.

In January, 1941, the Ford company did lose a contract because of its labor situation. The contract was for a relatively small amount, $10,298,138 for Army trucks. The specific reason for losing the bid was that Ford struck from the agreement those sections requiring it to abide by federal labor law. "Labor provision does not belong in the specifications," said a Ford official. "The labor laws are the law of the land and we have to abide by them whether we like it or not. It would be as logical to insert a clause requiring us to obey the traffic laws." What Ford was saying was labor could fight its case through the NLRB and the courts. The last fight had taken four years, from 1937 until 1941, and who could tell when a fight beginning in 1941 would end.

The cancellation of this contract with Ford represented labor's high point. But it quickly began to fall. The contract had been turned over to a Chrysler subsidiary with charged $250,000 more than Ford. Immediately criticism came into the War Department, charging the department with wasting federal funds and delaying the defense effort only to appease labor. Several members of Congress called for an inquiry. It was from this point that the policy of ignoring federal labor law began its ascendancy.

That labor laws were no longer going to be a matter of concern was apparent the next month. Ford had sought and received a contract for a small military car. As the cars began to roll off the Ford assembly lines in February, union leaders demanded that the government cancel the contract on the basis that Ford was refusing to obey the federal laws guaranteeing labor unions certain rights. The government refused. It needed small cars. FDR would not intervene.

The Army recommended that the policy of considering whether a firm had violated labor laws be dropped. Although largely ignored, the policy irritated the procurement people. They never could be quite sure they would not be pounced on by politicians for violating the policy. FDR discussed the situation with Morgenthau, who sided with the labor unions. Any firm not complying with the labor laws, he said, should be barred from receiving defense contracts. FDR would not go along with Morgenthau. He realized that the United States could not have a defense effort without companies like Ford and some of the other large concerns that were involved in the labor disputes. FDR asked Morgenthau to meet with Donald Nelson, then in charge of purchases for the Office of Production Mobilization, and to come up with a joint recommendation. The plan recommended to the OPM by Morgenthau and Nelson followed Morgenthau's approach. Strict compliance with the labor laws would be demanded of defense contractors.

The OPM turned down the recommendation. Although FDR

had once told Bill Knudsen "I am" the boss, he made no effort to overrule that decision. Secretary of War Stimson then called for the complete end of the policy, and his point was carried. All Hillman could do was acquiesce and say that he had obtained assurances that contracts would not be awarded to "habitual violators" of the labor laws.

To union members there seemed little choice but to strike. That choice became more obvious when an Associated Press reporter caught up with Henry Ford in Georgia, where he was resting at his plantation home. "We do not intend to submit to any union," the reporter quoted Ford as saying, "and those who belong to one are being fooled." Ford described a union as "a big spider's web" and said, "Once inside the web the workman can't move. Freedom, freedom of speech and personal pursuits is the keystone of our American government." Plenty of his employees thought differently. "Freedom" to them meant the freedom to earn a decent wage, to feel secure and not to be at the mercy of a company policeman. Those were the freedoms sought by the union.

No one is quite certain exactly how the strike at Ford's River Rouge plant began. For several weeks union members and their leaders, particularly Walter Reuther, had been talking and planning for the possibility of a strike. Company officials were aware of this and tension between the two sides was developing rapidly.

On April 1 one union official was distributing union literature when he heard that 1,500 men had gathered at one office. He raced there to hear a report that some employees had been dismissed because of union activity. Walkouts exploded all over the eleven hundred acre plant. All the hostility toward the company police—hostility because of the machine guns on the plant roofs, low wages, the callousness of company officials, the fears of losing a home or of watching children go hungry, the desperation of men who realize suddenly this is a time no longer to discuss but to act—all this came to a climax on April 1.

The union's headquarters were in Detroit. Telephone calls came in with a rush. One building was deserted. Another was surrounded. Hundreds of workers were walking out of that plant; thousands from another. Reuther and the other union leaders realized that the spontaneous walkout had grown too big to be stopped, and there was little inclination to stop it. The showdown must come. This was it. Reuther and the others jumped to the front. "You are," the union leaders told their members, "officially on strike."

River Rouge was more than a factory. It was an industrial complex of proportions unequaled in the United States. It included open-hearth furnaces, a steel plant and rolling mill, a glass factory, a cement plant, as well as fourteen miles of roadways and ninety-two miles of railroad tracks. Henry Ford had developed it so that the raw materials could be brought to its docks, unloaded and started on the journey that would transform them into automobiles when they emerged from River Rouge. In its thirty-eight year history, River Rouge never had been struck until April Fool's Day, 1941. But this strike did not lack in effectiveness because it was without precedent.

The union planners set up roadblocks along the highways to River Rouge, effectively blocking scabs or workers not supporting the union either from entering or leaving the plant. It was not a gentleman's endeavor. The union lines were charged. They broke. They reformed. They held. Men fought with sticks, their fists, with stones and knives. But River Rouge was effectively shut down.

Old Henry Ford, then in his late seventies, wanted to use force to end the strike. But the days when an industrialist could call out his own private army to make war against union members had passed. Other company men appealed to the state and federal governments for assistance. Both refused. FDR would not be rushed into a decision not necessary to make. Once he went along with the premise that the federal government can break a strike with soldiers, he would be stuck with it. Every time a company was struck, its officers would hold out against the union demands figuring that the federal government would force a labor peace, less costly than what the union members wanted, at bayonet point. Roosevelt would be faced with that problem before the year was done, but he would not meet it before he must. The Ford strike was only a few days old, and so his answer to the plea for federal troops was that the defense effort was not yet seriously affected.

The nominal president of the Ford Motor Company was Henry's son Edsel. Unlike his father, he did not live in the past, but he had always lived in the shadow of his father, who continued to dictate the company's operations. Henry Ford's decision not to manufacture the Rolls-Royce engines had been over the objections of Edsel Ford. After the strike had progressed for a few days, Edsel Ford emerged as a stronger man than he had ever been before. He insisted on negotiations with the auto workers union. He stood firm before his father and ultimately the father —described by biographer Allan Nevins as "fast decaying"— gave in to the son.

The Ford strike lasted only ten days. When it was done, Michigan Governor Murray D. Van Wagoner hailed the agreement as "an historic step in establishing industrial peace in our country at a time when every good American citizen must place his country ahead of self." It did that and more. After Henry Ford had capitulated to the unions, no American industrialist could stay aloof from the union movement.

The agreement reached was for all sides to abide by an election. The Ford employees could choose whether they wanted to be represented by Reuther's auto workers union, another union, or by no union. Henry Ford hoped his employees would accept the third choice, that they would reject unionism and all the evils that he associated with it. But he was wrong. When the election was held in May, Reuther's union won overwhelmingly. The other union received a few votes; to the workers it was associated with company management. The concept of no union received only a comparative handful of votes. Sorensen, one of the men at the Ford plant who knew Henry Ford best, wrote that the outcome of that vote was perhaps the greatest disappointment Henry Ford had in his business life.

The only thing left was the formal signing of the contract. "We have decided to go the whole way," said Edsel Ford on Friday, June 20. The contract signed with the union, which he was announcing, included wage increases, a union shop, a dues checkoff system, and abolition of the company police who had been used to terrorize workers and union members. The fight between Ford and the unions was ended. Old Henry Ford did not take his defeat well. Sorensen records that Ford rapidly began to lose interest in the operations of the industrial empire he had created. "He stayed away from the plant," said Sorensen of Ford. "At luncheon, which I had with him every day at the roundtable, he would rush in and out. He was a different person."

Although the Ford strike and the subsequent settlement were the most significant as far as future relations between industry and labor, it was the cheapest for the President. The strike had not lasted long enough to seriously threaten the war effort and he had not had to consider the use of troops. Presidents, of course, always have at their disposal the use of federal troops for the quelling of domestic disturbances. But federal troops had not been used to stop a major strike since Grover Cleveland, also a Democrat, sent troops to Chicago to end the Pullman strike there in 1894. FDR did not wish to be the first President since Cleveland to use federal soldiers to stop a strike. But if he must be, he would. The issue could not be avoided in June.

In May, Secretary of War Henry Stimson had suggested that FDR make a public statement about the labor situation. ". . . I have this morning," he explained to FDR, "received a report . . . as to the condition on the West Coast. [It] says that our airplane manufacturers there are very much troubled over the government's alleged attitude on labor. . . ."

The city of Los Angeles, on the West Coast, had a mile-square municipal airport. On the southeast corner of the airport was the North American Aviation Corporation. This plant had eleven thousand employees and $200 million worth of government contracts. It was building bombers for the Army Air Corps, pursuit planes for the Army and for the Royal Air Force, as well as training airplanes. In February, 1941, the airplanes that rolled off North American's assembly lines accounted for one-fifth of all American aircraft production. The aircraft was too important to be stopped. On Thursday, June 5, it was stopped by a strike.

The contract between the company and the union—the United Automobile Workers—had expired at the end of April, but both sides had continued negotiating. The union promised its members would stay at work with the understanding that whatever settlement was reached would be retroactive to May 1. Federal conciliators from the newly established National Defense Mediation Board worked with both sides, hoping to achieve a settlement. Then, unexpectedly, the union charged that the federal board was stalling and ordered a strike.

The strike was called by the officers of the union local at the scene. They claimed that workers at the nearby Vultee plant had won higher wages by striking. The national officers of the auto workers union described the strike as a "wildcat" walkout, meaning that it was not blessed by the union's national officers. The national officers of the union also charged that the strike was a result of the "vicious underhand maneuvering of the Communist party." At least one of the local officers had registered a few years earlier as a Communist.

The pressures on FDR to use troops to end a strike had been growing. As Stimson's comments in May had made clear, much of American industry was concerned that FDR was willing to sacrifice the defense effort in order to keep his ties to organized labor strong. Also, some of the strikes had led to lengthy delays in deliveries, both of American defense items and of items needed by England.

If he were going to use troops, the North American strike was a good one for Roosevelt to begin with. The crucial defense needs were clear; the public could acknowledge that drastic action was necessary. A moral issue appeared to exist; the union had backed off from its agreement to continue working while negotiations were underway. Also the possibility of Communist domination of the union—a charge made not by someone like Henry Ford, who considered most labor leaders Communists, but by the national leaders of a militant union—would serve to strengthen public opinion behind the President.

On June 9, beginning at five o'clock in the morning, strikers circled the North American plant. They marched three abreast, almost in a military fashion, to block the plant's nine gates. Nonstrikers were expected to attempt to report to work that morning and the union members were set to bar them. Two hours later a small group of nonunion workers tried forcing their way through a gate but were turned back. By this time more than one thousand pickets were at the main gate while smaller crowds of defiant union members made effective obstacles to the other plant entrances.

At 7:45 A.M. the police threw tear gas bombs. They were not very effective against the strikers; the wind was bad and most of the gas was blown back on the police. The union leaders then moved among their men, passing out pieces of lead wrapped in cloth or swinging from the ends of women's stockings. There could be no more effective blackjacks. "Nobody goes through now," the union members shouted as they waved their weapons.

Los Angeles Mayor Fletcher Bowron and police chief Arthur C. Hohmann spoke together for a few minutes. Chief Hohmann was heard to say, "If I try to break that picket line I'll have a mob on my hands." The Mayor was heard to answer, "We've got to do it."

A few more words and then one hundred police officers forced their way through the tightly packed union lines. The policemen formed a narrow lane leading from the parking lot to the plant gate, a distance of about seventy-five feet.

"All right," a police sergeant yelled. "Anyone who wants to work, come on."

"Stop them!"

After the shouts from the union leaders, the strikers rushed toward the blue-uniformed lines. The policemen held them off for a moment; a few workers actually entered the plant; then all semblance of order gave way as the police and the strikers joined in a free-swinging battle.

"Let's go in," yelled one striker, "and take the plant apart."

Then there was another shout. The United States Army was coming.

The military did not make an immediately auspicious entrance. The first sign of America's armed might to arrive was an army truck, loaded with a few grinning soldiers and trailing a soup kitchen. The messhall had become separated from the main contingent and arrived at the scene of action first. But the other soldiers arrived a moment later, and they were not grinning. There were three truckloads of them, in battle dress complete with fixed bayonets at the end of their rifles. These were regular army troops who had seen action in China and their experience showed. They dismounted and formed a skirmish line with their bayoneted rifles held before them. They moved against the strikers slowly: twenty paces and then they would halt for a moment; another twenty paces and then another brief halt. The strikers moved back before those menacing bayonet tips. Occasionally some hesitated. Would they challenge the Army? They did not. In fifteen minutes the roads leading to the plant gates had been cleared.

At 10:25 A.M., a lieutenant colonel climbed atop a small building inside the plant walls. Using a microphone he read an announcement that the North American plant had been taken over in the name of the United States government. Franklin Roosevelt had become the first President in forty-seven years to use federal troops to end a strike.

No one was quite certain exactly what it meant, least of all FDR. "Of course," the President explained to newsmen, "it is our desire in the case of that particular plant, or any others that may eventuate in the future, that they will be returned to private management as soon as it is possible." The newsmen wanted to know if the President had taken legal possession of the plant or were the Army troops only there in a policing capacity. The President did not know. "I took action," he said, "as President and not as a lawyer." He explained that regular scale wages would be paid and that whatever settlement was reached would be retroactive to May 1, the contract expiration date. Whose money was being paid, the government's or North American's? "I don't know," answered the President. "Frankly, I couldn't tell you."

Later that day FDR met with Attorney General Robert Jackson, Sidney Hillman, and Henry Stimson to find answers to some of those questions. The four men agreed that when it became necessary to take possession of a plant, as they had just done, it would be wise to keep the practice fluid so they could adjust to each situation as it arose. The government, it was agreed, would have possession of the plant but would stay out of the operations of the plant as much as possible, relying on the company to act as the government's agent. Also the government would retain possession until it believed that the union difficulties were smoothed out. FDR's principal concern at that session was that a printed notice be distributed with each paycheck to the effect that the rate of pay was subject to revision and that any increase in wages ultimately agreed upon would be paid retroactively.

Although the administration had been unsure of itself in seizing the North American plant, there was no uncertainty about the impact of its action. Robert Patterson received a telephone report from the scene on Wednesday, two days after the seizure had taken place. "We won the first round," Patterson was told. "The plant is on a normal operating basis. Practically all the men are back at work. There will be 100 percent regular production on Thursday."

Navy Secretary Frank Knox wrote to a friend that "We met one of our most serious difficulties head on when we took over the plant of the North American Aviation Company. It has had a profound psychological effect and from now on, I think, our troubles from that source will grow less."

Republicans marveled—privately—at how FDR seemed to have jettisoned the labor unions which he had helped so much in the past and which had helped him. Where once he had spoken of shorter hours and a shorter work week for the laboring man, now he spoke of increased production and longer working periods. Where once he had offered assurances that the gains of labor unions would not be lost or weakened because of the war effort, now he was refusing to speak in those terms. He was speaking out against the presence of agitators in labor unions working for companies with defense contracts. He was willing to use army troops to end a strike.

His efforts appeared to have results. By July, 1941, a slowdown in the number of strikes would be noticeable to government statisticians. In the first six working days in July, for example, there were 72,700 man days lost because of strikes, compared to 230,200 days lost in the comparable period a month earlier. When the North American strike was in progress, during the first half of June, there were 377,700 man days lost on army contracts because of strikes. In the second half of the month, after the troops had been called out, that figure had dropped to 144,620.

The use of troops in the strike had freed FDR. He had done it once; he would do it again if he must. Every labor union leader who considered calling a strike against a defense plant would be aware of that. One union leader still willing to challenge Roosevelt was John L. Lewis of the coal miners. When his challenge to FDR came later in the year, it would be the last major clash between two old enemies. But Lewis was one of the very few who discounted the significance of FDR's action in ordering soldiers to take over the North American plant.

That order was one of the more important acts of 1941, demonstrating FDR's intention to rearm the United States no matter what friends he must turn against. Another of the more important acts of 1941 also took place that month. This was FDR's decision to assist Russia after Adolf Hitler sent the Nazi armies east.

Russia claimed to be a Communist nation, and within the United States there was a passionate fear of communism. Since the Russian Revolution of 1917 brought the Communists to power, the United States had been concerned with alleged attempts by Communists to grasp control in America. Subversion always is a legitimate threat. But in the 1920s and 1930s, the fear of Communist subversion seemed more a "hot" political issue, one that an enterprising politician could use to boost his own fortunes. The "red raids" of 1920, conducted by A. Mitchell Palmer, then the Attorney General, were, as Samuel Eliot Morison pointed out, a result of Palmer's decision that "the way to fame and power was to crack down on the 'Reds.' "

The worst epithet to direct at a person in this period was "Communist," whether it was an accurate description or not. Most owners of industry automatically considered labor union leaders to be "Commies," and that, went the argument, was reason enough not to deal with them. Members of Congress found they could do very well with their constituents by investigating "un-American" activities. The climate of fear, distrust, and hatred for communism created several problems. There was the stifling of dissent, something which had been so valuable to the United States. There was the ignoring of real problems by blaming them all on "Red agitators"; and, perhaps most importantly, there was a belief that Russia, with all its great land mass and people, would simply disappear if the United States tried to ignore it.

The Russian invasion of Finland in 1939, and the Russian-German pact in which the two nations agreed not to fight each other, added to the American horror of the Russian nation. The Russian-German pact had made it possible for Hitler to move into eastern Europe by assuring him that his forces would not have to fight the Russians.

In the early months of 1941 the possibility of Germany turning on Russia began to appear more like a reality. Hitler decided to do it because he believed the defeat of Russia would persuade England to capitulate. He also spoke of a war between Russia and Germany as a war between two great ideologies, communism and fascism—a war that must be fought and which Germany must and would win. The people of Germany had entrusted their fate to a madman, and Hitler's invasion of Russia demonstrated the extremes of his madness.

The premier of Russia was Josef Stalin, who was as crafty a politician and as brutal a ruler as the twentieth century had seen. While his brutality may have been a match for Adolf Hitler's, however, his craftiness was not. He did not believe Germany would break its agreement with Russia and attack. He was one of the few persons in responsible positions who did not believe that would happen.

England had learned that a German invasion of Russia was likely; it also learned that a date in June had been selected.

Churchill warned Stalin on several occasions, but Stalin discounted the warnings, believing that Hitler was only bluffing in an attempt to pull further treaty concessions from Russia.

On June 14, Churchill wrote FDR that an invasion of Russia by Germany was "imminent." Despite his own long-standing hostility toward communism, Churchill said, "Should this new war break out we shall of course give all encouragement and any help we can spare to the Russians, following the principle that Hitler is the foe we have to beat." He added: "I do not expect any class political reactions here and trust that a German-Russian conflict will not cause you any embarrassment." The fear of communism in the 1920s and 1930s never had been as great in England as in the United States.

The next day C. L. Sulzberger reported in *The New York Times* from Ankara that German-Russian relations "have approached a critical point . . . and sensational developments may be looked for in a very short time."

Henry Stimson was one of the few who believed the military pressures being built up on both sides probably would not result in war. "It seems to be nip and tuck," he wrote in his diary, "whether Russia will fight or surrender. Of course I think the chances are that she will surrender." But the United States would take no chances. On June 21 the State Department sent a telegram to the American Embassy in Moscow authorizing the moving of American citizens out of Russia "via Siberia—if possible." A few hours later it became much less possible.

The morning of June 22 the armed forces of Nazi Germany moved across the fifteen-hundred mile Russian border. Hitler planned to do what Napoleon had failed to do and what no other Western leader ever had done—conquer Russia.

Roosevelt immediately understood that the Russian bear was more than the Nazi leader could chew. "Now comes this Russian diversion," he told a friend. "If it is more than just that, it will mean the liberation of Europe from Nazi domination—and at the same time I do not think we need worry about any possibility of Russian domination."

Cordell Hull was at home ill when word reached Washington about the invasion. He quickly spoke to the President and then to Under Secretary of State Welles by telephone. There was no question that the United States would assist Russia in its war against Germany. As Churchill had said, "Hitler is the foe we have to beat." Stimson, who had not anticipated that the war between Germany and Russia actually would come, welcomed it when it did. "I cannot help feeling," he recorded in his diary, "that it offers to us and Great Britain a great chance, provided we use it promptly."

Just what that chance would be, however, was questionable. The American military believed that Russia could hold out against the Germans a minimum of one month and a possible maximum of three months. That was the official War Department prediction handed to FDR the day after the invasion began. The German armies were moving smoothly and swiftly into Russian territory. Because Stalin had simply refused to believe that a German attack might be forthcoming, the Russian armies had been almost totally surprised by the onslaught. Bridges had not been destroyed. Supplies had to be abandoned. Many Russian prisoners were taken. The Russians appeared to be in a rout.

"These Russians will be promptly mopped up," Herbert Hoover told a friend. "At the moment, we are listening to the claims of the greatest pair of liars who ever yelled defiances across battle fronts. . . ." And Hoover added in his letter that "It is, I believe, a historic fact that the Russians have never won a European war on the battlefield."

However, a few of the more astute observers noticed that, after the first few days, the Russian retreat became more organized. Its army was being saved. Also, its supply lines were shortening. The German supply lines were lengthening.

After the Russian-German war had progressed for about a month, William Leahy in France reported confidentially to FDR that from "a reasonably reliable source in the French War Ministry" had come an estimate that Germany has

to date suffered in Russia one million casualties, killed and wounded. . . . They should not be able to endure that rate of loss for a long time, and the few anti-Axis Frenchmen with whom I make contact hope and believe that winter will come in time to interfere with the German campaign and immobilize for months a great army in Russia. There is of course at least a chance of a winter collapse of the service of supply such as that which ruined the Russian campaign of Napoleon I.

In the United States, Joseph E. Davies, who had been American ambassador to Russia, also believed that the Germans ultimately would be stopped. Davies claimed that the extent of the

Red army's resistance would amaze the world. Hitler would conquer a large area of Russia, but then, said Davies, Germany's troubles would begin.

Against those observations were the military estimates that Russia could not stand before Germany. To those conflicting opinions FDR added his own opinion about a people's willingness to defend their homes and native land against an unwelcomed invader. The United States would bank on Russia stopping Hitler. Asked for comment about Russian resistance when the war was five weeks old, FDR replied, "I think only . . . that it is magnificent, and, frankly, better than any military expert in Germany thought it would be."

The problem, however, was more than deciding whether to assist Russia. Breckinridge Long, a State Department official and a personal friend of FDR's, summed up the other implications in his diary the day of the German attack. "There will be serious political complications here at home," he wrote, "because a goodly number of conservative groups will waver in their opposition to Hitler and a goodly number of the ultra-radical groups will want us to intensify our opposition."

The entry of Russia into the war, forced by Germany, had increased the conflicting political pressures on the Roosevelt administration. The conservatives who hated communism would, even more, try to pull the government away from what it construed to be its international obligations. The liberals, who were sympathetic to Russia, would urge even greater efforts by the United States in the international field.

In Congress, the reaction was mixed—but unpleasant. Many members believed, with Burton Wheeler, that the United States should stay aloof and hope Adolf Hitler and Josef Stalin destroyed themselves. Others would argue that America's enemy was not Germany but Russia. This was in conflict with the view that stopping the Nazi aggression meant aiding Russia.

The feelings of the bitter isolationists were summed up by one of their leaders, Amos Pinchot. An old supporter of FDR's, who had grown less and less enthusiastic about the New Deal as FDR's liberalism became more evident, Pinchot let fly with paper and oratorical attacks from his New York office. The isolationists should stress, he advised one of the movement's publicists, that there was an "unnatural marriage between Roosevelt and Stalin." This, he continued, "has led to a two-fold conspiracy" to push the United States into the war and "to liquidate democracy and private enterprise and set up a virtual dictatorship that will preside over our economic system."

On the other side, political pressures were built up for greater American intervention by those groups sympathetic with Russia or communism. The National Religious Committee of the American Peace Mobilization (APM) had charged in January that FDR's policy "will inevitably lead to war and the destruction of democracy." But on June 25, 1941, three days after the invasion of Russia, the committee called for "all possible assistance [being] extended to those nations which are fighting aggression."

The National Labor Committee Against War, another APM affiliate, published a newspaper called *Shop Talk*. In its first edition, dated April 26, 1941, it charged labor leaders with "promoting Get-America-Into-War Committees." On July 12 that same newspaper described the "total destruction of fascism" as "the great positive blow to be struck for peace."

The morning of Sunday, June 22, *The Worker*, the newspaper of the American Communist Party, ran an editorial saying "the American people want none of this war." That afternoon, news was received that Germany had invaded Russia. The next morning, *The Worker* denounced the invasion of Russia as "an attack upon the peoples of the United States and the entire world."

Robert Sherwood tells of going to a Fight for Freedom rally in Harlem one Sunday afternoon. Entering the ballroom, as he wrote the story, he had to walk through a Communist picket line denouncing the persons attending the rally as warmongers and as British and Wall Street tools. When Sherwood emerged from the rally, however, the picket lines had disappeared. That Sunday was June 22, 1941. While he had been inside the rally, news had come of the invasion of Russia.

An even more difficult problem for FDR than the reactions of the right and the left was the reaction of the Roman Catholic Church. Breckinridge Long, who had spent considerable time in Rome as American ambassador there, understood Vatican politics well. "The Vatican has had a clique," he wrote, "which was not bitterly opposed to Hitler—partly because he has under his military jurisdiction the largest Catholic population in the world. They seem to have influence enough now to win others in the Vatican to their side, for while the others opposed Hitler yet they were in violent opposition to Communism as the very negation of the law and philosophy of the church."

There were strong pressures on the Vatican to support what

was presented to it as Germany's "anti-Bolshevik crusade" against Russia. At the Vatican, Monsignor Domenica Tardini, secretary of the Congregation for Extraordinary Ecclesiastical Affairs, wrote: "These Americans ought to know that the Holy See is in a very delicate position. . . . As far as religious liberty in Russia goes, it is clear that until now it has been worse than trampled." The willingness to toy with Hitler's fascism because it might stop communism resulted in the failure of the institution of the Catholic Church to exercise the moral and political leadership of which it was capable. As a result, many Catholics throughout the world were unsure of their feelings toward Nazism.

In 1938 Pope Pius XI had issued an encyclical condemning any cooperation with communism. After the German invasion of Russia, many prominent Roman Catholics in the United States cited that encyclical when expressing opposition to the United States extending assistance to Russia.

The President believed the best way to deal with opposition from the Catholic Church was the most direct way. He wrote a letter to Pope Pius XII. The letter is FDR's basic defense for assisting one dictatorship, Russia, while opposing another, Germany. Immediately after the German attack, the need for such a statement was apparent. Herbert Bayard Swope, a former newspaperman turned wealthy crony of Democrats, volunteered the draft of such a statement to Harry Hopkins on June 23. Part of that draft was picked up, in essence if not in exact wording, by FDR in his letter to the Pope. The Swope draft said: "In the twenty-seven years since Russia became Communistic, our national interests and our way of life never have been seriously threatened by the Soviets. But in the two years of Hitler's mad drive for world enslavement, our very existence, as a free people, has been gravely endangered."

In his letter to the Pope, FDR first spoke of religious freedom in Russia. He said it was his understanding that "churches in Russia are open." While the President acknowledged that true religious liberty did not exist in Russia, he stated his belief that "Russia may as a result of the present conflict" recognize the value of religious liberty. Then, picking up the theme from the Swope draft, FDR acknowledged that both Russia and Germany were governed by dictators. But, he said:

I believe, however, that this Russian dictatorship is less dangerous to the safety of other nations than is the German form of dictatorship. The only weapon which the Russian dictatorship uses outside of its own borders is communist propaganda which I, of course, recognize has in the past been utilized for the purpose of breaking down the form of government in other countries, religious belief, et cetera. Germany, however, not only has utilized, but is utilizing, this kind of propaganda as well and has also undertaken the employment of every form of military aggression outside of its borders for the purpose of world conquest by force of arms and by force of propaganda. I believe that the survival of Russia is less dangerous to religion, to the church as such, and to humanity in general than would be the survival of the German form of dictatorship.

Roosevelt, apparently thinking of the 1938 encyclical, said in his letter that "It is my belief that the leaders of all churches in the United States should recognize these facts clearly and should not close their eyes to these basic questions and by their present attitude on this question directly assist Germany in her present objectives."

Pope Pius sent the President an answer. Its general wording, courteousness, and friendliness belie the animosity that was felt in some Vatican quarters. Monsignor Tardini, for example, derided FDR's talk about the future prospects for religious worship in the Soviet Union as "an attempted apology for Communism."

The Pope's letter to FDR made no specific reference to FDR's hint that he intercede with members of the Catholic hierarchy in the United States to change "their present attitude." In October, 1941, however, the Vatican did authorize the Most Reverend John T. McNicholas, Archbishop of Cincinnati, to make a public declaration explaining that the 1938 encyclical had not intended to condemn all forms of aid to "the people of Russia."

The charge that Russian communism was against religion was made by non-Catholics as well as by Catholics, and by many politicians who enjoyed the ring of the phrase "Godless Communism." In August, when FDR and Churchill would meet at Newfoundland to create the Atlantic Charter and promise a better world once the Axis were defeated, they would make no mention of "freedom of religion" as being one of their objectives. The various accounts of that meeting suggest the omission was unintentional. Harry Hopkins' biographer, Robert Sherwood, insists it was "an oversight." Probably it was, because FDR was too sharp a politician to make a mistake like that intentionally. However, the omission gave many of FDR's critics the opportunity to charge that he and Churchill had omitted any reference to religion for fear of offending Stalin and his "Godless" Communists. In later statements issued by FDR about postwar aims, freedom of religion always was prominently mentioned.

Against political and religious opposition, FDR determined to assist the Russian war effort. As always, he was making his priorities. And his priority was to do everything possible to defeat Germany; he would worry about Russian domination later.

At one Cabinet meeting FDR dressed down his Cabinet members, claiming they had not been cooperating in supplying the Russians with what they needed. "Runaround" is the word FDR used to describe the situation. Henry Stimson objected strongly. He pointed to a list of war equipment the Russians wanted and said that neither he nor the War Department staff had seen the list before. The argument droned on. The Russians had wanted pursuit airplanes. The United States had less than a hundred of the airplanes, but there were two hundred crated in England that the British weren't using. Stimson wanted to ship those to Russia. Then began a long harangue about the best way to ship the planes to Russia. Stimson thought FDR was "in a hoity-toity humor."

Stimson was correct. The next day FDR sent a memorandum to a staff member directing him to push the sending of the needed war materials to Russia. "Please get out the list and please," directed FDR, "with my full authority, use a heavy hand—act as a burr under the saddle and get things moving!" He added: "Step on it!"

The sense of urgency was great. Russia needed equipment immediately. If it received arms, ammunition, and planes in time to use them against the Germans prior to October 1, FDR believed that could be the decisive turning point. After that date, the President figured that the Russian winter would halt the German advance. So if Germany could be held until the beginning of October, Russia would be safe until the spring. His was a nonmilitary position. The War Department disagreed with his analysis. The expert opinion there was that Russia was finished. But once again FDR was placing his judgment against that of the experts. Once again he would win.

Aid to Russia was financed through the lend-lease program and through other devices. In one instance, for example, the Defense Supplies Corporation, a federal agency, ordered $100 million worth of raw materials from Russia for delivery over a four-year period. One-half that price—$50 million—was paid in advance so Russia would have dollars with which to pay for American goods.

The aid was extensive. In the fall of 1941 the American naval attaché in London recommended that the United States deliver seventy-two pursuit planes to the British, beyond the regular delivery schedule. FDR sent the recommendation to Stimson for action. The Secretary of War replied with a formal memorandum, stating that "All production of Army Air Corps P-40E's between now and July 1, 1942, has been committed to Russia." At the bottom of the typed sheet, Stimson scribbled: "In other words there ain't no Kitty Hawks for poor Army to give you. The British and the Russians already have them all."

FDR believed it advisable to develop a personal relationship with Stalin as he had done with Churchill. He went about it in the same way: he sent Harry Hopkins.

As Churchill had, Stalin understood Hopkins' importance and treated him accordingly. Prominent Soviet officials met Hopkins as he entered Russia and flew with him to Moscow. At the airport a large delegation of Russian officials met him. The newspapers covered his visit extensively, including printing photographs of Hopkins and descriptions of his visit on their front pages. Russia, of course, was using Hopkins' visit for its own purposes. The visit was a device to bolster the morale of the Russian people. The visit suggested that the United States was siding with the Russians; and, once it had, American aid would be forthcoming.

In the summer of 1941, Josef Stalin was sixty-one years old. His residence and his office were inside the Kremlin walls. He was then five feet, six inches tall and weighed 190 pounds. "Stalin" in Russian means "steel" and his chunky body looked that hard. He usually dressed in a tight-fitting soldier's jacket, baggy trousers, and highly shined boots. He worked hard and lived well. His day began at noon in his office and usually would end about four o'clock the next morning. He enjoyed the opera, ballet, the theater, and chess. Rather than the pipe he was usually photographed with, he smoked cigarettes almost constantly. He enjoyed drinking, preferring brandy to other forms of alcohol.

He seemed a modest and informal person, but there was no question in Harry Hopkins' mind, as he sat across from him, that Stalin was a leader in every sense of the word. Not only was there the history of Stalin, a history of a man who had forged a huge land mass into a nation and who had not hesitated to use whatever means were at his disposal in the doing, but also there was the attitude of command. Stalin expected to order and expected to be obeyed.

Hopkins decided the best way to approach this man was the direct method. Not bothering with any formal diplomatic talk, he immediately began asking specific questions about the progress of the war. Stalin gave forthright and detailed answers. He discussed the retreat of the Red army before the Germans, his own opinion of the ultimate outcome, and his armament needs from the United States. Stalin, still smarting from the suddenness of the unexpected German attack, spoke of "the necessity of there being a minimum moral standard" between nations. "Without such a minimum moral standard," he said, "nations could not coexist." Stalin continued that "the present leaders of Germany knew no such minimum moral standard and that, therefore, they represented an anti-social force in the present world." Stalin went on, saying, "The Germans were a people who without a second's thought would sign a treaty today, break it tomorrow and sign a second one the following day." He concluded his discourse with: "Nations must fulfill their treaty obligations or international society could not exist."

Harry Hopkins spent two nights and three days in Moscow. Stalin insisted that Hopkins not stay in the American Embassy, which had been bombed; instead, Hopkins had a room in the bomb shelter that had been developed in the subway. In addition to the usual pieces of furniture, Hopkins found his room came with "an unusual spread of food."

As the American aid began moving to Russia, FDR received reports like this one from William Leahy in Vichy France:

We sense a definite softening of the attitude of even the collaborationists toward America and a revival of hope among the people for an early release from bondage. If Russia should be forced to sue for peace and release the German Army for use elsewhere, the official attitude of Vichy toward America would, of course, change for the worse at once, and the eyes of officialdom here would turn again toward the Nazi bandwagon.

The invasion of Russia produced an entirely different reaction in Japan. On a map Russia seems to hang over Japan like a great reaching paw, ready to snatch up the series of small islands that comprise Japan. It was always a threat to any Japanese action. Once Germany attacked Russia, however, the possibility of Russia threatening Japan seemed remote; it was too busy defending herself against the Nazis. The military men in Japan realized this, and the navy wanted to begin the movement south, toward Indochina.

"We must build bases in French Indochina and Thailand in order to launch military operations," said the Japanese naval chief of staff when informed about the pending German attack against Russia. "We must resolutely attack anyone who tries to stop us," he continued, "we must resort to force if we have to."

Matsuoka, the foreign minister who had signed a treaty in April promising not to attack Russia, wanted to break that treaty immediately and join with Germany in the war against the Soviet Union. He was not a military man and did not understand how Japan had been freed to move south against Indochina. He was a diplomat, captivated by dreams of glory in being associated with Germany against Russia. "If we attack the Soviets quickly," Matsuoka said at a government conference on June 27, "the United States won't come in . . . first strike north, and then go south. If we go south, we will have to fight Britain and the United States."

But the military would not go along with him. "The Navy is confident about a war against the United States and Britain," was the answer given to Matsuoka, "but not confident about a war against the United States, Britain, and the Soviet Union. . . . In order to avoid a situation of this kind, don't tell us to strike at Soviet Russia and also tell us to go south. The Navy doesn't want the Soviet Union stirred up."

At this time Hitler pressured Japan to enter the war against Russia in violation of the Japanese-Russian pact. Japanese refusal was not based on any standards of "honor." Japan did not violate its Russian treaty because it was against her interests to do so. If it had been in her interests, the accounts of the government sessions make clear, it would have done so.

The machinations within the Japanese government were known in Washington. When Harold Ickes, for example, pressed FDR to cut off oil shipments and take other actions against Japan, FDR told him:

I think it will interest you to know that the Japs are having a real drag-down and knock-out fight among themselves and have been for the past week—trying to decide which way they are going to jump— attack Russia, attack the South Seas, thus throwing in their lot definitely with Germany, or whether they will sit on the fence and be more friendly with us. No one knows what the decision will be, but, as you know, it is terribly important for the control of the Atlantic for us to help to keep peace in the Pacific. I simply have not got enough Navy to go around—and every little episode in the Pacific means fewer ships in the Atlantic."

The day after FDR wrote that note to Ickes, the fight inside the Japanese government came to an end. Formal approval was given to the plan to move into Indochina.

JULY: *". . . the test of one's devotion to freedom . . ."*

ON JULY 21, Japanese troops occupied the southern part of French Indochina.

The French colonies were under the rule of the Vichy government and technically the Vichy government approved the Japanese occupation. But it was clear that the French had been coerced into giving this permission. William Leahy, American ambassador in Vichy, wrote in his diary on July 21:

> At five P.M. received a message from the Minister of Foreign Affairs to the effect that in view of the threats of immediate action by the ambassador from Japan, the French government has found it impossible to forestall or postpone Japanese occupation of bases in Indochina, and that the ambassador from Japan is today informed that France agrees to the use of bases in French Indochina by Japan.

The American government had learned the move was coming and had tried to prevent it. FDR had spoken with Nomura to see if he could persuade his government to stop the planned action. Roosevelt also said then that he would agree to a neutralization of Indochina so there would be no possibility of that area being used to attack the Japanese forces in China.

Japan had not responded to FDR's offer, however.

Still the United States did not go to war. Instead it imposed economic sanctions on Japan. This step had been urged on FDR for months by Ickes and others. Whether he had acted too late, a charge that history might make, disturbed FDR. In some extemporaneous remarks about this time, FDR explained his Far East policy.

Here on the east coast, you have been reading that the Secretary of the Interior, as Oil Administrator, is faced with the problem of not having enough gasoline to go around in the east coast, and how he is asking everybody to curtail their consumption of gasoline. All right. Now, I am—I might be called an American citizen, living in Hyde Park, N.Y. And I say, "That's a funny thing. Why am I asked to curtail my consumption of gasoline when I read in the papers that thousands of tons of gasoline are going out from Los Angeles—west coast—to Japan; and we are helping Japan in what looks like an act of aggression?"

All right. Now the answer is a very simple one. There is a world war going on, and has been for some time—nearly two years. One of our efforts, from the very beginning, was to prevent the spread of that world war in certain areas where it hadn't started. One of those areas is a place called the Pacific Ocean—one of the largest areas of the earth. There happened to be a place in the South Pacific where we had to get a lot of things—rubber, tin, and so forth and so on—down in the Dutch Indies, the Straits Settlements, and Indochina. And we had to help get the Australian surplus of meat and wheat, and corn, for England.

Roosevelt stressed then that "from our own selfish point of view" it was "essential" that a war be prevented from starting in the South Pacific.

So our foreign policy was trying to stop a war from breaking out down there. At the same time, from the point of view of even France at that time—of course France still had her head above water—we wanted to keep that line of supplies from Australia and New Zealand going to the Near East—all their troops, all their supplies that they have maintained in Syria, North Africa, and Palestine. So it was essential for Great Britain that we try to keep the peace down there in the South Pacific.

Next FDR referred to Japan.

Whether they had at that time aggressive purposes to enlarge their empire southward, they didn't have any oil of their own up in the north. Now, if we cut the oil off, they probably would have gone down to the Dutch East Indies a year ago, and you would have had war. Therefore, there was—you might call—a method in letting this oil go to Japan, with the hope—and it had worked for two years—of keeping war out of the South Pacific for our own good, for the good of the defense of Great Britain, and the freedom of the seas.

The imposition of economic sanctions against Japan meant that nation had three choices. Japan could meet some of the demands made by the United States, requiring it to surrender its imperialistic dreams; Japan could watch idly while it began losing its military power as the sanctions closed off important sources of oil; or, finally, Japan could seek to eliminate the United States as a power in the Western Pacific. This last choice meant war. The Japanese navy envisioned such a war as lasting perhaps two years before it must be ended by a negotiated peace. The leaders of the Japanese navy realized they had a brilliant strike force but that their nation did not have the industrial strength to sustain a long war. "If it is necessary to fight," Yamamoto said about this time, "in the first six months to a year of war against the United States and England I will run wild. I will show you an uninterrupted succession of victories. But I must also tell you that if war be prolonged for two or three years, I have no confidence in our ultimate victory." But although the leaders of the Navy recognized the dangers of such a war, they did not fear it and they would avoid it only on their own terms.

Robert J. C. Butow, one of the more respected students of Japan in this period, writes: "Bringing the talks in Washington to a successful conclusion was regarded as a matter of life or death for Japan." But, he continued, "the trouble lay in the nature of the settlement envisaged by the Japanese military and in their great haste to achieve what they had in mind."

The Asian situation could have been defused at any time by Roosevelt. All he had to do was give to the Japanese at the negotiating table what they threatened to take by force.

The United States would not reward aggression or acknowledge its fruits as permanent. Since the Declaration of Independence had been signed in 1776, said FDR to a radio audience on July 4, 1941, from his Hyde Park home, the "cause of human freedom swept across the world. . . . But now, in our generation—in the last few years—a new resistance, in the form of several new practices of tyranny, has been making such headway that the fundamentals of 1776 are being struck down abroad and definitely they are threatened here."

Of the argument that Germany would not attack the United States once it conquered Europe, FDR said that was "indeed, a fallacy, based on no logic at all." He then continued to describe that argument as "childlike fantasy itself" and "that misdirected faith" which had led other nations "to go about their peaceful tasks, relying on the thought, and even the promise, that they and their lives and their government would be allowed to live when the juggernaut of force came their way."

And then was his warning: "I tell the American people solemnly that the United States will never survive as a happy and fertile oasis of liberty surrounded by a cruel desert of dictatorship."

In July it was apparent that there simply was not enough productive capacity, real or potential, to continue producing civilian goods at an unabated pace and still meet the defense needs of the nation. There could not be enough skilled workmen, not enough raw materials, not enough sophisticated machine tools to staff both a Willow Run and a River Rouge, not enough to build all the airplanes the nation needed for its defense and all the automobiles the industry would like to sell.

Roosevelt said to Henry Stimson that month:

I am convinced that if we are going to get production where it must be . . . it is essential that we utilize for defense purposes a substantial part of the large durable goods factories in America that are now manufacturing items to meet consumer needs. I am convinced that we must have the services of the foremen, the skilled workers, existing engineering departments and, in fact, the going organization of these great plants if we are to get on as rapidly as our national interest requires.

FDR conceded there would be delays during the changeover and that there would be costs which, he said, "must be borne by the government."

He could not be quite so blunt in talking to the public which listened to constant warnings and his exhortations, responded briefly, and then largely lapsed into an enjoyment of the first "good times" it had known since before the 1929 depression. At a press conference almost two weeks later, he suggested that rather than use the word "curtailment" to explain the reduction of civilian products like automobiles and refrigerators, the word "substitution" be used. "In other words," he explained, "it's not a cutting off of the manufacturing, it is substitution of manufacturing something else with the same plants, and largely the same tools, and the same workmen. One article in place of another article." The words may have been gentler; the meaning was identical.

The shortages of military goods were real. The building of a weapon of war, the conversion of a peacetime industry into a wartime industry, is at least a two-year process. The impetus given to American industry by British orders, which had begun in late 1939 and early 1940, would not have an effect until late 1941. In the meantime, there were serious problems facing the United States. When the Army had begun its expansion in 1940, it immediately faced a shortage of uniforms and tents because there was not enough cotton and other fabrics. Aluminum for the expanding aircraft program and steel for heavy ammunition were in short supply. As orders for defense expanded, shortages increased, both in finished goods and in raw materials.

Many businessmen who were involved in the defense effort lacked the vision to see what would be demanded of them. Early in 1941, FDR had told a story illustrating this. The specific commodity was steel.

We got the very best advice we could on steel way back—when was it?—last autumn, from people who know steel, and we don't. They said that there were ample steel production facilities in the United States. We told them, "Hold on, now, you may have more steel to turn out— planes, ships, et cetera, than you think." They said, "We still think we have ample."

The President said that attitude continued until October or November, 1940. "It wasn't their fault, but the program developed faster than they thought," FDR said, kindly, "and in November I insisted that they review the whole situation, and then they came to believe that additional steel production was necessary, and since then they have picked up."

The shortages continued.

The Navy Department sent the President a confidential memorandum on July 7, 1941, regarding shortages. The information it supplied to FDR almost was frightening—this was at a time when Roosevelt was aware the Japanese would soon move into Indochina, most likely, bringing a conflict with the United States that much closer. Of steel, said the memorandum: "Shortage . . . is acute and is becoming more so every day." Aluminum and magnesium: "Delays caused by lack of these materials are becoming worse each day." Machine tools: "All bureaus report delays due to lack of machine tools . . . [varying from] a few months to one year." The report continued on with its alarming statistics. Forged armor for battleships was eight to fifteen months behind schedule. Another shortage was critical. Still another was desperate.

America had the resources, the skilled men and the factories to produce what was needed. It lacked the will. Roosevelt wanted the airlines to give up some airliners, those already delivered and some promised. Robert Patterson demanded that civilian use of aluminum be restricted to the barest minimum. Industry would not go along.

In a dictatorship the ending of civilian production would be simply a matter of issuing a decree. This could not be done in a democracy. FDR must persuade, demand, cajole, and then, ultimately, receive the power from Congress acting for the people. Even when the power was granted to him he must use it sparingly, and only after a substantial case had been built up to convince the public of the necessity for his acting. Whatever powers Congress grants to a president can be rescinded and undoubtedly would be if the pressure on Congress became strong enough.

There was pressure on the President for him to become, in fact, a dictator. Wendell Willkie, the titular leader of the Republican Party, was one of those in 1941 demanding that FDR appoint a man to oversee all facets of production in the United States, to determine priorities between civilian and military goods. FDR's old mentor from the First World War, Josephus Daniels, tried to console his former assistant against the wounds of such barbs.

FDR appreciated Daniels' efforts. "Of course," he said, "we have to put up, now and then, with people who have no idea what government as such means."

And while the shortages continued, the entry of politics into the defense effort further complicated FDR's problems. Roosevelt had hoped to eliminate politics as much as possible from the war effort. That had been one of his reasons for picking a Republican, Henry Stimson, to head the War Department. Stimson insisted on keeping politics out of the Department's operations and FDR backed him up. One of Stimson's assistants, Harvey Bundy, later recalled those years with Stimson as head of the War Department:

I can't remember the Secretary ever having any pressure from the White House one way or the other. I think I would remember had there been an issue that went up to the White House.

I never saw the President during the entire time I was down there. And I remember when I was appointed . . . The Secretary went over and told FDR that he was going to appoint me a special assistant, in spite of the fact that I had been a staunch Republican. And the only thing FDR said was, "I hope he won't have to see any senators!"

Bundy was asked if he believed having Republicans in the War Department encouraged Republican members of Congress to cooperate with the President.

"Well," said Bundy, "I think it established a nonpartisan attitude in the War Department and eliminated politics in the War Department. There was no patronage in the War Department."

If a Democrat had been in charge of the Department rather than a Republican?

Bundy answered: "I don't know. It's very much harder to avoid patronage if your own party is in power . . . the Republicans who might otherwise have been sniping at the Administration found it more difficult to snipe at the War Department. And the Democrats sniping at the War Department had to snipe at their chief who made the appointment. So I think it was helpful."

Not all sniping from the Capitol was eliminated. At one time George Marshall's plan to promote young but competent officers was threatened by Chairman Andrew May of the House Military Affairs Committee. Marshall had a keen intuitive sense about people and he had developed a roster of young military men who he believed could effectively assume command. But he needed enabling legislation from Congress to promote these men over more senior officers.

Over the years members of the military had developed close relations with members of Congress. The senior members of the military went to Chairman May and asked him to block the legislation Marshall needed. They did not want anybody promoted over them. May agreed. George Marshall turned for help to James Byrnes. The South Carolina senator managed to have the needed legislation reduced to one sentence which was added to an appropriations bill on the Senate floor. Few senators realized that the line had any significance. The appropriations bill, with Marshall's amendment attached, went to the House where it also was approved without Chairman May being aware that the legislation was attached to it.

On other occasions Marshall had trouble with the National Guard. The Guard units came from the states. An appointment to lead a Guard unit often had been a political reward, meaning that many of the National Guard units were headed by political hacks in uniform. When Marshall tried to oust these hacks, their political friends moved to block him. In vain Marshall argued with the politicians that their constituents would be better served when fighting men are led by competent officers.

"I don't understand your position," General Marshall said on one occasion to a Congressional delegation protesting the removal of a National Guard officer, "because I should think that your constituents should be your principal interest—and here it seems to me that you are only considering one constituent and ignoring all [your] other constituents who are members of the division. I am concerned with them."

But the discussion continued about the political implications of the officer's removal, and Marshall, finally in great anger, told the Congressmen, "I am not going to leave him in command of that division. So I will put it to you this way—if he stays, I go, and if I stay, he goes.

The political hack was removed from the National Guard unit.

On another occasion Senator Tom Connally of Texas stormed into Henry Stimson's office at the War Department. Two Texas generals of the National Guard were being relieved of duty and Connally would be damned if he would put up with that, as he made clear. Stimson started a telephone search for George Marshall, finding him at the airport about to board an airplane for Chicago. After talking with the chief of staff, Stimson explained to Connally that there had been no other course. One of the Texas generals was over age and the second had been given two chances at command and proven himself incompetent each time. That, said Stimson, with a firmness that matched Connally's anger, was that.

Marshall, backed by Stimson, had determined that politics would not be a consideration in the development of the new army. "There was not much Army politicking," recalled Harvey Bundy, "because George Marshall ran that show. It was perfectly apparent you had a very, very strong man as chief of staff." And when Marshall turned down the politicians, they went to Stimson. "People would try to get favors from him, but he wasn't a favor giving man," Bundy said of Stimson, "and that, Marshall always said to me, was the greatest thing that Stimson did for the War Department."

But being above politics did not mean one could be discourteous to politicians. They did appropriate the money for the defense program. So Marshall was taking time from his work to do such things as explain to Representative Ross A. Collins of Mississippi why an Army contract for work in that state had gone to a non-Mississippi company—"no single contractor, or group of contractors, in Mississippi, or adjacent states, was considered sufficiently equipped or experienced to do the job in the time available"; and explain to Representative Frances P. Bolton of Ohio why one National Guard contingent from that state was not attached to that state's guard division—"we must consider the efficiency of the whole."

Again and again political pressures were used against the War Department in hopes of milking some money out of the rearmament program. In February, 1941, for example, Representative Frank W. Boykin wrote a letter to Vice President Wallace advocating the building of bomb shelters. Perhaps the Alabama Democrat was motivated by the hope of saving millions of American lives in the event of attack. His letter indicates, however, that he was more interested in demonstrating that the shelter he proposed could be "Made of AMERICAN Cotton, by AMERICAN Labor, For AMERICAN Defense." Cotton at that time was in great surplus within his Congressional district.

The next month, according to Stimson's diary, the Secretary of War was interrupted by one of the more prominent members of the Senate with "one of the usual Senatorial interventions in the search for patronage." The Senator wanted to have one of the new airfields built "at his place" in his home state.

Another Senator went to see Bill Knudsen. He and some friends had raised a little money. Would Knudsen help them raise the remainder from the Reconstruction Finance Corporation, a federal agency, to build an airplane plant in the Senator's home state. Neither the Senator nor his friends had any experience building airplanes, but all the pending defense contracts were appealing. Knudsen talked them out of it.

Even FDR's opponents did not object to their areas cashing in on the defense program. One such was Roy Roberts of the Kansas City *Star*. Roberts knew his standing with the powers in

IT'S TRIPLETS! — By Talburt

WASHINGTON NEWS NOV 6 1940

COME TO PAPA

WHAT A MAN!

3RD TERM

2ND

OLD DEE VOTER

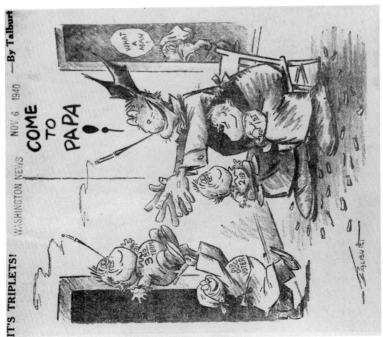

"TRADITION? WHAT'S TRADITION NOW?"

By Eubank.

Franklin Roosevelt, moved by his understanding of the foreign threats facing the United States and unhappy with the other possibilities for the Democratic presidential nomination, sought a third term—the first President to do so. The reaction to his victory is dramatized by these two cartoons. Some Americans were concerned by FDR's apparent arrogance in successfully overthrowing the two-term tradition. Others had a warmer response. (*Cartoons courtesy of the Franklin D. Roosevelt Library*)

The 1941 inaugural parade had none of the traditional color and razzle-dazzle that had
marked such festivities since the inauguration of Thomas Jefferson. Instead, it was all
military business, totally without pomp. The American military was showing itself to its
Commander in Chief. (*Courtesy of the United States Army*)

THE WHITE HOUSE
WASHINGTON

Jan. 20 1941

Dear Churchill

Wendell Willkie will give you this — He is Truly helping to keep politics out over here.

I think this verse applies to your people as it does to us:

"Sail on Oh Ship of State!
Sail on Oh Union strong and great.
Humanity with all its fears,
With all the hopes of future years
Is hanging breathless on Thy fate"

As ever yours

Franklin D. Roosevelt

Wendell L. Willkie, who had opposed Roosevelt for the Presidency a few months earlier, left for England early in 1941 on a fact-finding mission for the President. During a meeting with Willkie, the President scrawled out a note, reproduced here, and asked Willkie to deliver it to Churchill. "I think this verse," read the note, "applies to your people as it does to us: Sail on, O Ship of State!/ Sail on, O Union, strong and great!/ Humanity with all its fears,/ With all its hopes of future years,/ Is hanging breathless on thy fate!" Churchill called the verse "an inspiration." *(Courtesy of the Franklin D. Roosevelt Library)*

The primary members of the defense effort in 1941 are shown here. Sitting, from left to right, are Harry Hopkins, William S. Knudsen, Vice President Henry A. Wallace, and Donald M. Nelson. Standing, from left to right, are James Forrestal, representing Navy Secretary Knox; Robert Patterson, representing Secretary of War Stimson; Leon Henderson; and Sidney Hillman. *(Courtesy of the Franklin D. Roosevelt Library)*

Philip Murray (left), president of the CIO, and William Green (right), president of the AFL, were willing to go along with FDR's defense effort. But John L. Lewis (below), president of the United Mine Workers, could not. Despite the nation's defense needs, he was ready to call a strike. *(Courtesy of the AFL–CIO)*

Don't Worry Adolf, I Am With You . . .

When Germany invaded Russia, the almost unanimous military opinion was that Russia would soon fall before the Nazis. Franklin Roosevelt, however, was willing to bank on Russia eventually stopping Germany. He insisted that the United States help arm Russia as it was doing with England. *(Courtesy of the Franklin D. Roosevelt Library)*

FDR sought to establish a personal relationship with Stalin in the same way he had developed such a relationship with Churchill—he sent Harry Hopkins. Hopkins, the man in the center, is shown arriving at Moscow Airport. *(Courtesy of the Franklin D. Roosevelt Library)*

One problem of rearmament was that the professional officers anticipated fighting the coming war as they fought the previous one. One such was General George S. Patton, Jr. Although he ultimately would become the brilliant user of the tank, in 1941 his heart belonged to the horse cavalry. In 1929 he had charged that talk of mechanized units replacing horse cavalry was mere "piffle," and his mind had not changed. In this photograph, taken on maneuvers in September 1941, he wears cavalry boots although his vehicle was the tank. *(Courtesy of the United States Army)*

The United States needed an army and a navy. To build these forces FDR called on men like General George C. Marshall and Henry L. Stimson. These men understood that they were not expected to pay homage to domestic politics. (*Courtesy of the Franklin D. Roosevelt Library*)

President Roosevelt and Prime Minister Churchill meet aboard the U.S.S. *Augusta* in August 1941. As shown here, Churchill hands to Roosevelt a message from King George VI. *(Courtesy of William Leavitt)*

☆ ☆ PRESENT ☆ ☆

[signature: Winston Churchill]

[signature: Franklin D. Roosevelt]

FRANKLIN D. ROOSEVELT,
    PRESIDENT OF THE UNITED STATES.

HONORABLE
    SUMNER WELLES,
    UNDER SECRETARY OF STATE.

ADMIRAL
    HAROLD R. STARK, U.S.N.,
    CHIEF OF NAVAL OPERATIONS.

GENERAL
    GEORGE C. MARSHALL, U.S.A.,
    CHIEF OF STAFF.

ADMIRAL
    ERNEST J. KING, U.S.N.,
    COMMANDER-IN-CHIEF,
    ATLANTIC FLEET.

MAJOR GENERAL
    HENRY H. ARNOLD, U.S.A.,
    CHIEF OF AIR CORPS.

HONORABLE
    HARRY L. HOPKINS

HONORABLE
    AVERILL HARRIMAN

RIGHT HONORABLE WINSTON CHURCHILL,
    PRIME MINISTER OF GREAT BRITAIN.

HONORABLE
    SIR ALEXANDER G. M. CADOGAN,
    G.C.M.G.,
    PERMANENT UNDER SECRETARY OF
    STATE FOR FOREIGN AFFAIRS.

ADMIRAL OF THE FLEET
    SIR ALFRED D.P.R. POUND,
    G.C.B., G.C.V.O.,
    CHIEF OF THE NAVAL STAFF

GENERAL
    SIR JOHN G. DILL, K.C.B.,
    C.M.G., D.S.O.,
    CHIEF OF THE IMPERIAL
    GENERAL STAFF.

AIR CHIEF MARSHAL
    SIR WILFRID R. FREEMAN, K.C.B.,
    D.S.O., M.C.,
    VICE CHIEF OF THE AIR STAFF.

LORD CHERWELL

[signature: Cherwell.]

A formal dinner party was held on the American ship the first night of the Placentia Bay meeting. Each person present signed the menu. At this dinner Churchill argued that the Second World War, unlike the First, would not require large numbers of men. The Americans understood that Churchill was only presenting the argument in hopes of persuading the United States to offer greater assistance. *(Courtesy of the Franklin D. Roosevelt Library)*

The war effort was taking its to[ll]
Franklin Roosevelt's health. The [first]
photograph shows him at age thirt[y-six]
as Assistant Secretary of the Navy in [1918.]
His features had changed little by [1944,]
but his face was more heavily line[d, as]
these series of pictures show. Only [fifty-]
nine years old then, he seemed [much]
older. In this year he talked to [Felix]
Frankfurter about if "they are to pu[t up]
any memorial to me." FDR was a[ware]
that he continued in what most [doctors]
would be a killing regime. (First p[hoto]
courtesy of William Leavitt; others [cour-]
tesy of the Franklin D. Roosevelt Lib[rary.)]

Criticism of Franklin Roosevelt that he was not an aggressive enough leader ignored his problems. The public was not backing him. Despite his pleas for sacrifice he was constantly reminded that he had promised not to send American youths to fight in foreign wars. Massing against him was a powerful group of isolationists, formed into the America First organization. At an anti-war rally in Madison Square Garden were, from left to right, Senator Burton K. Wheeler, Charles A. Lindbergh, Kathleen Norris, and Norman Thomas. Lindbergh particularly attracted many young people to the movement. He became so significant that FDR finally moved against him. *(Cartoons courtesy of the Franklin D. Roosevelt Library; photo by Wide World)*

"....it being quite
uncertain in what part
of North or South or
Central America, or even
possibly other regions,
it ultimately may be
necessary to use
them (American Troops)
Secretary Stimson
April 15 1941

"I have said it before and
I say it again and again
and again. Your boys are
not going to be sent into
foreign wars."
F.D.R. Oct. 1940

SOMEONE MUST BE WRONG

(Copyright, 1941, News Syndicate Co., Inc.)

NEW YORK POST
OCT 3 1 1941

I DEMAND A
NEW LEADERSHIP.
ROOSEVELT
MUST GO!

HITLER
CAN'T
BE
STOPPED

WHITE
HOUSE

LINDBERGH

AMERICA
FIRST

ROLLIN KIRBY

"SLIM" DISPOSSESSES THE PRESIDENT

Isoroku Yamamoto realized that if Japan were to win a war against the United States it must first destroy the American fleet at Pearl Harbor. He believed it could be done. *(Courtesy of the United States Navy)*

When Husband E. Kimmel was appointed commander of the Pacific fleet at Pearl Harbor, the belief was that the Navy was bringing some of its best men into positions of important command. One of the best the Navy had to offer, Kimmel always had taken his naval career seriously. When he graduated from the Naval Academy the class yearbook said of him: "He had the air of being his own statue erected by national subscription." *(Courtesy of the National Archives)*

General Walter C. Short was in charge of the Army at Pearl Harbor. His orders were to protect the fleet and the harbor. After being warned in October about the possibilities of an attack, he said, "I was probably just a little more watchful." *(Courtesy of the United States Army)*

This is Pearl Harbor moments after the attack. In less than two hours eight battleships were either sunk or heavily damaged, ten other naval vessels were heavily damaged, 188 airplanes were destroyed, and the lives of 2,396 Americans lost. The military commanders, Admiral Kimmel and General Short, were permitted to retire from the service. (*Courtesy of the United States Army*)

Washington would not be very high because of his opposition over the years to FDR. He called on William Allen White to present the case for the Midwest. "I know you are awfully busy," he said to White, "but if you could find time to write the President urging him not to forget the problems of the West in the allocation of the new plants you would be doing a great service to this part of the country." Sometime later Stimson recorded that White "came to see me about an airport in Emporia. A nice old fellow. He had not changed at all and was as kindly and friendly as always."

And that was how the struggle to develop a new army often went. Removing an incompetent should have been a relatively easy task, but it required the utmost in threats and strength. Promoting a talented officer required political finesse. Issuing a contract involved fighting with members of Congress, some reasonable and some not so. It required taking time from regular duties to placate prominent citizens. Rearming involved politics as usual as much as it did business as usual.

But the struggle succeeded, slowly. Marshall and Stimson understood they had a free hand, that a member of Congress, if rebuffed by them, would not turn to the White House where a partisan President would overrule his military advisers. Harvey Bundy could not recall FDR ever approaching Stimson on a political matter. The President had picked his men and then permitted them to be as strong as they could be.

As for party politics, FDR never accepted that members of his political party opposed his policies. Nothing irked him more perhaps in politics than did rebellious Democrats. He considered the Democratic Party of the 1930s to be largely his own creation, and he was not very far from wrong. It was he who had taken a political organization, moribund after three defeats in presidential elections, and rejuvenated it, broadened its base, and led it to resounding successes. To some extent in 1932, entirely in 1936 and 1940, FDR was the major issue in the presidential elections. When he ran for re-election, his opponents had not challenged his New Deal; both Alf Landon and Wendell Willkie had promised to retain his social welfare programs. Nor were his campaign speeches filled with specifics about his plans for the coming four years. He had only one approach. Here I am, said FDR, take me and the Democratic Party I lead for the next four years.

Roosevelt detailed his attitude on rebellious Democrats in the summer of 1941 in a letter which he sent to the National Convention of Young Democratic Clubs. Critical of appeasers, FDR said in his letter that those who fitted his definition of appeaser and still wore the Democratic label should be drummed out of the Democratic Party. His fellow Democrats understood him to be saying, "Let's get rid of the isolationists!"

His irritation with rebellious Democrats in 1938 had led FDR to make one of his great political mistakes—the unsuccessful attempt to purge those Congressional Democrats he considered disloyal. His defeat then was a blow to his political prestige from which he never recovered. In July, 1941, this irritation led him to make a second serious mistake—too strong an attack against Burton Wheeler.

More than toward any other Democrat, Roosevelt aimed his barbs about disloyal Democrats at Burton Wheeler. Wheeler was the "Yankee from the West." He had been born in Massachusetts but as a young man traveled west. He settled in Montana and began developing a career for himself as a courageous defender of the individual. Whether he was battling the huge mining companies that dominated the state's copper industry or the prejudices of a people gone wild during the First World War, Wheeler had established himself as a gutsy fighter. Montana elected him to the United States Senate where Wheeler continued to demonstrate his liberalism.

In 1924 he was a candidate for Vice President on the Progressive Party ticket. In 1930 Wheeler was one of the first Democrats of nationwide standing to endorse the governor of New York for the Democratic Party's 1932 presidential nomination. The governor was Franklin Roosevelt. An early New Deal supporter, Wheeler was a strong booster and a close associate of the President's. But the break came in 1937 over the President's plan to enlarge the Supreme Court. That issue brought out all the personal and philosophical animosities that had been seething within Wheeler. Not only did he oppose FDR on that issue but he led the opposition. For the Republicans it was politically wise to have a Democrat, particularly one with liberal credentials like Wheeler, to lead the fight against the "Court packing" plan. It lifted the fight, or appeared to lift it, out of partisan politics. FDR could neither forget nor forgive Wheeler's heresy. As the issue of intervention entered the politics of Washington and Wheeler moved to the side opposite that of FDR's, the split between them became too great for healing.

Wheeler did not consider the word "isolationist" to be descriptive of his philosophy. He was not advocating, he later explained, that the United States withdraw or have only minimal relations with the remainder of the world. Instead, as he explained it, he was advocating that the United States do everything possible to stay out of a war unless it was physically attacked. He also believed, he explained, that the United States should have done everything possible to promote peace among the nations of the world. Wheeler was the Democrat responsible for his party's 1940 platform pledge against sending American forces outside of the western hemisphere unless attacked. This growth of isolationism in the Midwest, led by Wheeler, persuaded FDR to choose a running mate from the Midwest in 1940 to counter this isolationist feeling. Burton Wheeler claimed that FDR's aides first sounded him out about joining the FDR ticket in 1940 as second man before the President actually chose Henry Wallace.

Robert Wood considered Wheeler to be one of the most effective speakers used by America First against FDR's policies. Wheeler traveled extensively to speak at America First gatherings and was perhaps second only to Charles Lindbergh, with whom he often appeared, in popular following. He was the most prominent Democrat to be associated with the America First group.

Early in 1941 FDR had exploded in anger at Wheeler when the Senator had charged that the lend-lease program would "plow under every fourth American boy." The two tangled again in July. Wheeler had sent out a large mailing, using his Congressional frank so he would not have to pay postage, urging the recipients to write letters to the White House objecting to any plans to send American troops abroad. There were no such plans at the time, but the Congress was then considering the draft extension. Wheeler's mailing had been designed to build up public support against the extension. Some of the mailings were received by soldiers in their training camps. Several soldiers objected to Wheeler's action and wrote him letters of protest. Others brought the letters to the attention of their officers. Ultimately, George Marshall received two letters of protest from soldiers at different camps. He turned them over to Henry Stimson. The Secretary called the White House to ask if other letters had been received there. None had. Stimson then spoke with the President. Stimson told FDR of the letters and that he planned to criticize them at his regular news conference at the War Department that morning. Roosevelt responded that he agreed with Stimson's approach. Roosevelt further suggested Stimson say that Wheeler's action came very near the line of treason.

Stimson was reluctant to go that far, but the tone of the President's voice suggested that perhaps he better. He drafted a statement saying he believed Wheeler's action in apparently trying to propagandize American soldiers through the mails came very near to subversive action against the United States if it did not come near treason. He distributed the statement to the press. Then the fireworks began.

The story was played prominently on the front pages of the nation's newspapers. Wheeler responded at first by calling Stimson an old man who should be removed as Secretary of War. FDR then supported Stimson. Stimson had made his charge on Thursday, July 24. FDR had backed him the next morning. This is Stimson's private account of what happened Monday, July 28:

> Today . . . Senator Wheeler has made a very bitter reply to my talk about his appeals to the soldiers last Thursday and I fear he has in many respects shown that I was wrong. He claims that there were no appeals sent out especially to the soldiers—that they were all in general circularization and that the only ones that went to the soldiers were a few accidental ones which happened to be misaddressed or done by the accident of the people who made the addresses. This is a pretty hard answer for me to rebut because I cannot get the facts. I had to stand the other day on the two letters which we had received and that made me a very insufficient case, generally. Wheeler swept the Senate with it and everybody who spoke—of the thirteen senators —spoke against me and in favor of him. That, however, was to be largely expected in an issue between a Cabinet officer and a member of the Senate.

Later Stimson issued a public apology. As he acknowledged privately, he did not have a good case against Wheeler. As he was forced also to acknowledge, a Cabinet officer does not do well in a personal dispute with a member of the Senate. The Senate is a closed body. Its members consider fighting among themselves acceptable, but they band together when one of their members is attacked from the outside. This is particularly dangerous when the attacker is someone like Stimson who needs Senate support for appropriations. Stimson had no choice but to apologize.

Burton Wheeler's successful drive against FDR's bill to enlarge the Supreme Court had been a slap at FDR's political prestige as well as at Roosevelt personally. Wheeler had just scored another point of the same kind.

The industrial development, the brighter professionals in command, the placating of the politicians—all were based on the premise that there would be an army of young Americans to fight. And this was the most serious problem with which to deal. The businessman could be appealed to by his love of profits and tax concessions to bring him into the war effort. The old soldiers who had lost their "self-starters" could be retired to pasture. The politicians could be appealed to on the basis of patriotism or bought off with some item of patronage. A young man in the army could be bought off with very little, and he could lose his life.

Felix Frankfurter once tried to console some friends of his. Their son had crossed over to Canada and enlisted in the army there to join the fight against the Nazis.

I cannot believe I am wrong in thinking that whatever feelings you and your wife may have about your boy's enlisting in the Canadian Army with the hope of early active duty, the dominant feeling must be one of pride. No utterance could be more offensive than the self-righteous insistence of all who belong to the America First suasion that they are against war—who isn't? It would be offensive were it not so childish. But it is inescapably true that those who place any interest above that of freedom, place man's destiny below the level of moral dignity. And the test of one's devotion to freedom may ultimately leave one no choice, as evidently your boy thought there was no choice.

There it was summed up: The price of freedom is the risk of death, and the price must be paid. Frankfurter had said it beautifully. But against that was an incident that happened when the first number was called under the draft law of 1940. The selection was by lot and when the number was read out, from the audience could be heard a woman's anguished scream. There is no answer to the fear of a loved one dying.

It was the awareness of this fear and the anguish it caused that had led FDR to make a demagogic promise in 1940 that American youth never would be sent to fight in foreign wars. It was a promise he understood he should not have made. As much as anyone, FDR knew that no responsible official in the American government could have made such a promise in the fall of 1940. FDR personally knew the pride of which Frankfurter had

written and also the anguish of fearing for loved ones. His sons
wore the uniform of their country in 1941.

And Roosevelt also knew he needed an army.

The answer to whether he would have an army, the answer to
whether the nation would answer his call to arms in an area
where it would hurt the most—the lives of its sons—that answer
would come in the summer of 1941. The House of Representatives
would vote to extend the draft and the outcome would be tan-
talizingly and frightfully close.

The people of the United States have a picture of themselves
as people good with guns. William Jennings Bryan had talked
during the First World War of a million men springing to arms
to defend the United States. There was a war song about Johnny
getting his gun. In movies and fiction the people of the United
States had seen themselves portrayed as the handsome hero
against whom no villain could stand. The reality was sharply different.

In 1940, when selective service was first proposed, a Democrat
wrote FDR advising against the draft, arguing that it would be
politically disadvantageous. FDR agreed that "it may very
easily defeat the Democratic national ticket—Wallace and myself." FDR continued that he had recently spent two days at one
of the Army's maneuvers, involving 94,000 men. "And anybody,"
he wrote, "who knows anything about the German methods of
warfare would know that [the American] army would have been
licked by thoroughly trained and organized forces of a similar size
within a day or two." What was wrong with the American Army?
FDR supplied the answer:

> The men were not trained in the high sense of the term to use the
> arms they had and that was largely because the officers and junior
> officers had not had the chance to carry out mimic warfare on the
> scale of a large army . . . the men themselves were soft—fifteen miles
> a day was about all they could stand and many dropped out at that.
> They could not be hardened up in the couple of weeks the maneuvers
> lasted—it would take a good long time to accomplish for them what
> the German armies are, practically all of them, capable of doing.
> These German armies have marched thirty miles a day continuously
> for a good many days on end.

Roosevelt frequently referred to the desperate need to have a
modern army, something not all Americans understood. "The

trouble with ninety-nine percent of us Americans—we are not very different from other people in the world—" he told Norman Thomas in 1941, "is that we think of modern war in terms of the conduct of war in 1812, or in 1861, or in 1898. . . . Very few people really came to understand the lessons of the World War—even though twenty years went by."

During the late 1930s FDR had sought funds for the modernization of America's military machine. He was forced, by a suspicious Congress and a reluctant nation, to be cautious in his requests and he succeeded only partially in achieving limited aims. The result was that on July 1, 1939, according to George Marshall, "The active Army of the United States consisted of approximately 174,000 enlisted men." Marshall went on to cite a list of deficiencies and concluded: "As an army we were ineffective. Our equipment, modern at the conclusion of the [First] World War, was now in a large measure obsolescent. In fact, during the postwar period, continuous paring of appropriations had reduced the Army virtually to the status of that of a third-rate power."

In George Marshall the President had found a chief of staff who was determined and capable enough to lift the United States Army out of that "third-rate" category. Marshall, then in his late fifties, was of the military—his professional career had been that of an American soldier—but he was not of the military bureaucracy that looked backward. He looked forward. He understood that modern warfare required a modern army and he resolved to build it.

He was a tall, thin man who wore civilian clothes. He did not have the flare of George Patton, nor did he have the charm of a colonel named Dwight David Eisenhower in whom Marshall had recognized ability. But he did have efficiency and purpose. He was a general who would not inspire on the battlefield but who would lead in the councils of war.

Marshall's biographer, Forrest Pogue, reports that Marshall and FDR were not friends in the social sense. That most likely was true. Marshall did not enjoy the poker-playing camaraderie of FDR's White House. He would not be seen in his shirtsleeves. He would not permit his emotions to show in public. He had disciplined himself ruthlessly. He found it difficult to understand the casual, almost negligent, manner in which FDR seemed to be conducting his office—the "fumbling," to use Felix Frankfurter's word. The difference was, of course, that George Marshall was an administrator. He did not make policy; he carried it out. FDR, in contrast, was responsible for policy. The ferment about him, which so many, including Frankfurter, had mistaken for fumbling, was an intellectual process from which emerged the broad policy lines which FDR expected his administrators, such as Marshall, to carry out. If FDR and Marshall never were friends, FDR recognized his chief of staff as a brilliant and courageous administrator, and a faithful one.

One of Marshall's great contributions to the war effort was to open up the lines of communication in the army. No longer did a stiff and unbending military protocol govern all. He kept track of the younger officers who showed promise and did not hesitate to place them in positions of command. Dwight Eisenhower is the most conspicuous example of this. But Eisenhower was not the only one. Dozens of other young officers suddenly found that intelligence and initiative were paying off. The War Department under Marshall was receptive to new ideas. When one officer came up with a new technique in antitank warfare, he found he could get a hearing. He was sent to Washington to work with the new commander of the Tank Destroyer Tactical and Firing Center. "If you can convince Colonel Bruce and his bright young men that you have an idea on technique of firing which will give better results than present," Marshall wrote him, "I will see that you have the means for developing it." The letter represented a new attitude toward initiative in the military.

While FDR realized the most compelling need was for an improvement in the Army, his heart belonged to the Navy. He loved the sea, whether sailing as a young man near his summer home at Campobello Island or cruising as President on the *Potomac*. His federal service had begun with the Navy Department during the First World War. To George Marshall's chagrin, FDR often spoke of the Navy as "we" and of the Army as "they."

As his chief of naval operations he appointed Harold Stark. Stark had the nickname, incongruous for a tough sailor and graduate of Annapolis, of "Betty." Unlike Marshall, Stark was an old acquaintance of FDR's. They had first met in 1914 when FDR, as Assistant Secretary of the Navy, was cruising on the U.S.S. *Patterson*. Germany had just started her drive toward Paris. The young Navy man and the young government official, back in 1914, watched with dread the reports of the German ad-

vance and then, when the advance was slowed and ultimately
stopped, they experienced a feeling of relief. "In some ways it
seems like yesterday," Stark said to Roosevelt in 1938 in recalling
that incident, "in others, a very long way off. Here's hoping history does not repeat itself."

In 1939 when the Second World War began and history repeated itself with even more violence, FDR called on Stark to
be chief of naval operations. "It will be grand to have you
here . . ." said FDR to his old friend, "you and I talk the same
language."

They had talked the same language about the need for recognizing England as America's first line of defense. It had been
Stark who had first articulated what later resulted in the "Germany first" policy. And it was Stark who had first recommended
a meeting between the military leaders of the United States
and England that became the ABC conferences.

Leaders like Stark and Marshall could turn the War and Navy
departments into efficient training and planning units for modern warfare. But they needed men. There had to be a draft. The
few volunteer enlistments and the calling up of the National
Guard units in the states supplied only a few hundred thousand
men. If war came, the military men understood that Hitler
must be beaten on his home ground. This meant a large invasion
force. Although Churchill would deny this at the Atlantic Conference, most Americans there understood that Churchill was
under tremendous pressure to obtain American assistance and
was casting America's projected role in its most favorable light.

In July, 1940, the condition of the Army, to use Robert Patterson's word, was "critical." In numbers there were 250,000 men.
The National Guard, which was about to be called into duty,
would add another 250,000. A draft, the first peacetime draft in
the nation's history, was the logical—most responsible officials believed it the only—means of building up the armed forces.

The Congress then did pass a one-year selective service act.
It was sponsored in the House by a Republican, James Wadsworth of New York. He realized his party was not happy with
his sponsoring of the legislation; his act made it more difficult
for the Republicans to criticize FDR as a warmonger. But Wadsworth was allied with a growing number of Congressmen who
were beginning to place politics and personal gain aside for the
duration.

Even among FDR's foreign policy supporters, there was no unanimity about the draft. William Allen White, in the summer of 1940, was chairman of a group working to assist England—the National Committee to Defend America by Aiding the Allies. When FDR broached the subject of a draft to White, the Emporia newspaper editor did not give his assent. And his committee never endorsed the proposal.

Once the induction began, resentment toward the draft became stronger. There was no certainty of war against the United States and to many of the inductees America's military build-up was only to save Churchill. "I am sorry to say morale seems to be slipping a little in the Army," Secretary Stimson reported to FDR. "The absence of any concrete war objective, coupled with delays in getting their weapons, and lack of energy and imagination here and there among their instructors, are being reflected in the spirit of the men and I am seeing many letters on the subject."

Some of the morale problems were the result of the build-up coming too fast. "It is imperative," George Marshall wrote to the commander of the Fourth Army in the winter of 1941, "that everything possible be done immediately to make comfortable for the winter the personnel in Alaska now living in tent camps. This includes comfortable messing facilities, latrines, bath facilities, and adequate hospitalization to take care of any probable epidemic." Such things as barracks and sanitary facilities should have been adequate, of course, before troops were sent to Alaska. But the rush to rearm had been too great.

But George Marshall did not believe the soldier's morale was as bad as that of the soldier's parents. He was so concerned that he wrote the President, asking if something could not be done about the badgering and bothering of the War Department by the civilian population. Roosevelt was amused by the letter, and he responded to Marshall: "Got any ideas?"

Everyone, it seemed, had some words of advice about perking up the soldier's morale. Archibald MacLeish, the writer who was then Librarian of Congress, wrote to Eleanor Roosevelt suggesting that singing groups be started in the military camps. She asked FDR to discuss it with the appropriate military leaders. He did so. The night of Monday, February 17, 1941, Henry Stimson and some other top men from the War Department showed up at the White House for dinner. At the dinner Mrs. Roosevelt spoke about the value of bringing to the attention of the men in the military camps the folk songs of America, the cowboy songs and the Negro spirituals. She then called on representatives of the military services who dutifully testified to the value of singing for soldiers. When Mrs. Roosevelt finished, the President also made a few remarks, agreeing with his wife. Then the dinner guests were treated to a concert by various military groups. No one told Mrs. Roosevelt to her face, but the singing apparently was not very good that night.

The MacLeish idea never did catch on. Nor was there much else done in a serious and comprehensive way to improve the morale of draftees. Army camps by necessity were established in desolate areas where land was available and cheap. The few communities near these new camps were not used to having large influxes of young men, nor did they particularly welcome soldiers. Prostitutes gathered around the camps, and venereal disease rates were high. Low morale was a cause of much of the ill-feeling among draftees and of much of the parental concern for them.

Out of this dissatisfaction grew a movement known as OHIO— Over the Hill In October. October, 1941, was when the one-year program for the first inductees was scheduled to begin coming to an end, and the inductees were making clear that they wanted to be released from service on schedule or else they would desert. No outside barracks wall and no latrine in any army camp was complete without OHIO scrawled on it. The news media picked up the cry, and no newspaper or magazine was satisfied unless it had its own story on the disenchantment and the threatened desertions of the inductees. The stories and discouraged letters home from the soldiers were building up a momentum for ending the selective service program.

In the summer of 1941 the administration and the Congress faced the problem of extending the draft. Much of the nation believed the men should be allowed to return to their homes on schedule, after their one year's service was completed. A promise had been made and, this argument went, it should be kept.

The administration did not believe the promise had been quite that strong; it had been made conditionally, depending on the international situation. The situation had changed from the summer of 1940 to the summer of 1941 becoming even more serious. An army was desperately needed.

"I think it is a very simple choice to make," FDR said, "as to whether in times like these you want to disintegrate the Army of the United States or not. . . . Roughly two-thirds of it would go back to private life, and their places would be taken by a two-thirds fill-in of untrained officers and men, and that is why the matter is so serious."

George Marshall spoke of his concern to James Wadsworth, the House sponsor of the original bill a year earlier. The Army, he said, was already chartering ships to bring some units back from the Philippines and Alaska so their members could be separated from military service by the promised date. Marshall also told Wadsworth that he was discouraged at the prospect of losing a million draftees. They were beginning to get along pretty well, he explained, learning how to use their weapons and, at last, beginning to develop into competent soldiers.

To extend the service for the draftees beyond one year required Congressional legislation. Some members of Congress asked why the inductees simply could not be rotated. Draft one million men, train them, and then return them to civilian life after one year of service; then draft another million men and begin the process all over again. General Marshall explained why this could not be done.

In accordance with plans of long standing we have reached the point of availability of troops and materiel where we now can and urgently should organize and train certain task forces against the possibility of the necessity arising for their use. What is the status of these troops? The Regular Army divisions contain from 75 to 90 percent Reserve officers whose term of service is legally limited to twelve months. In other words, some 600 officers in a division under the law would soon be entitled to drop their present duties and return to their homes. The twelve months' service period of many, if not most, of the officers in the first priority divisions, is now nearly completed. Must we replace most of the trained officer personnel of a division—the leaders—at the moment of departure for strategic localities? In two of the Regular divisions we have restricted the enlisted personnel to three-year men, but in the others, of necessity, the number of selectees varies from twenty-five to fifty percent. . . .

The chief of staff concluded his plea to Congress this way: "I submit that the limitations referred to should be removed as quickly as possible if we are to have a fair opportunity to protect ourselves against the coldly calculated, secret, and sudden action that might be directed against us."

Almost as if in answer, on July 16, 1941, the House in a decisive vote of 199 to 96 defeated an innocuous measure to maintain the West Point military academy at authorized strength. The result was a shock to the War Department, and officials there quickly and properly read it as a sign that any move to extend the induction period for draftees would be opposed most strenuously. The members of Congress were going on record against militarism.

"It was supposed to be unpopular at home to keep these men in the service and to keep drafting more men," Representative Wadsworth later recalled in explaining the fierce opposition to the draft extension. " 'They'll all desert. There'll be riots. There'll be violence. We'll get licked at re-election,' " he quoted the opponents. "The isolationist feeling was still strong. [The isolationists said:] 'There's no necessity for our getting militarily strong in this country because we're not going to get into this war anyway.' "

In mid-July an Army major, a member of the general staff, did some scouting of the political winds on Capitol Hill. A member of the House Military Affairs Committee told him, "If the bill for the retention of selectees were to come up in the House within the next week, it is my opinion that it would be defeated five to one, despite any administrative pressure that may be brought."

A Congressman's secretary who had been on Capitol Hill for forty-one years told the Army major that never in his experience with Congress had he seen so much fear of legislation as was generally expressed by members of the House regarding the retention of selectees. The secretary said it would be "political suicide" for any member of Congress to support the draft extension.

As Congressional leaders surveyed the membership, they found it dominated by fear and politics. There was the fear of being defeated; for many members of the House, all of whom would be up for re-election in a little more than a year, their mail was running seventy-five to eighty percent against extension. The other factor appeared to be a desire to strike out against Franklin Roosevelt and the Democrats.

"I am really concerned," FDR told Henry Stimson.

Next to the President and Henry Stimson, George Marshall more than anyone understood the critical nature of the issue.

He asked Representative Wadsworth to arrange a meeting for him with some recalcitrant Republicans. The chief of staff and forty Republicans gathered at the Army-Navy Club. From seven o'clock until midnight, Marshall hammered away at them about the need for extending the draft. The result was that George Marshall learned some of the brutal facts of political life. For some Republicans, hatred of Franklin Roosevelt was too powerful.

"You put the case very well," said one Republican to Marshall, "but I will be damned if I am going along with Mr. Roosevelt."

Marshall was shocked and angry. "You are going," he answered, "to let plain hatred of the personality dictate to you to do something that you realize is very harmful to the interest of the country."

There never was any question of Roosevelt becoming personally involved in the legislative battle. The only significant question was when. "I have talked to the principal leaders," Marshall told FDR on July 16, "and have had many others queried on the subject, all, of course, confidentially. The consensus of opinion appears to be that a message from you as soon as possible would be highly desirable."

Fiorello H. LaGuardia, director of civil defense, reported to the President the next day that while the political atmosphere in the Senate appeared favorable, the situation in the House "is still doubtful." He also recommended a presidential message. Robert Patterson said a presidential message was "most urgent" and would help the bill's passage "particularly in the House where some of our friends are now lukewarm."

The next day, at a Cabinet meeting, FDR said the message would go to Capitol Hill. On Monday, July 21, President Roosevelt told the Congress that the Army faced disintegration while "the international situation is not less grave but is far more grave than it was a year ago." A strong army, he said, was needed to defend the western hemisphere. "To weaken our Army at this particular time would be, in my judgment, an act of bad faith toward our neighbors. . . . Time counts," said the President in closing. "Within two months disintegration, which would follow failure to take Congressional action, will commence in the armies of the United States. Time counts. The responsibility rests solely with the Congress."

FDR had made the draft extension a personal and a political

issue. He also had served notice that if a danger resulted from the failure of the draft to be extended, he would not hesitate to place the blame for that danger upon the members of Congress who had voted against extension.

The debate in the Senate was heated. Even the spectators were emotional. During one session the people in the galleries had to be warned to stop their demonstrations or face eviction. There would be applause from the galleries, usually when a senator called on the President to promise that American troops would not have to fight alongside Russians or in foreign lands. But the Senate prospect never was in doubt. A draft extension would be passed. There was some problem that the Senate, rather than approve the administration's extension, might go along with another approach. Senator Robert Taft of Ohio wanted only a six-month extension, rather than an extension at the discretion of the military leaders and the administration. His six-month amendment was defeated. Then Senator Harold Burton, Ohio's other Republican, offered an amendment that would have extended military service only one year. It also was defeated. Burton believed that if the isolationist group in the Senate had not been so implacable in its opposition to FDR and any draft extension, the one-year approach might have won.

"I have not checked all the names," Burton said later of the isolationists, "but if they had stayed with me, we probably would have won." Instead, the administration bill passed the Senate, forty-five to thirty. Alben Barkley had done his work well, and the isolationists had done theirs badly. Then the legislation went for action to the House of Representatives.

It was in trouble there.

AUGUST: ". . . *their hopes for a better future for the world*"

WHEN Harry Hopkins visited England in January, "I told him," said the President, "to express my hope to Churchill that we could meet some day to talk over the problem of the defeat of Germany." Before Hopkins could make the suggestion to Churchill, the Prime Minister himself began talking of meeting with the President. "Thus," said Roosevelt, "it may be truthfully said that the meeting was suggested by both Churchill and me."

They tentatively planned the meeting for March or April, but delays postponed it. In March the President could not leave Washington because of legislative problems; he was watching the precarious progress of the lend-lease bill at the beginning of the month. In April military conflict in Greece, and later in Crete, prevented Churchill from leaving England. Difficulties developed when May or June was mentioned. Finally in July a definite meeting date was set. It would be in August, either the eighth, ninth, or tenth. The areas mentioned had been either Bermuda or Newfoundland. Newfoundland was agreed on.

The actual site of Placentia Bay on the south coast of Newfoundland was an American choice. The British preferred Loon Bay on the north coast. But the United States pressed for Placentia because it was a new base, manned by the Navy, with a number of airplanes, minesweepers, and other ships, and fitted with radio communications. The British then agreed to Placentia.

The meeting, almost casual in its origin, produced a document known as the Atlantic Charter. Throughout the world's history there have been a handful of documents that have inspired men. One such was the English Magna Charta with its declaration of the rule of law. Another was the American Declaration of Independence with its flat assumption that "all men are created equal." Another was the Atlantic Charter. The Charter's value was that it set a standard to which nations could aspire. "No aggrandisement," it said, "territorial or other." It called for self-government, equality of trading opportunities between nations, better living standards for all people, "the final destruction of the Nazi tyranny," the "freedom from fear and want," and the abandonment by the nations of the world "of the use of force."

The words have a flat sound to them, but they were much more than words to a world in which the triumph of Nazism seemed inevitable. In France and Holland, the Scandinavian nations, Greece, eastern Europe, in China and in Southeast Asia, the words were bullets of hope fired by the voice of civilized humanity. They were the vow that victory ultimately would come and with it would be a better world. The words were weapons. They urged men to fight on in the hills and the alleys of their native lands. In all the nations which Hitler occupied he never was the conqueror. The people would not permit it. They knew that someday Hitler and his Thousand-Year Reich would fall. Franklin Roosevelt and Winston Churchill had promised it.

Both Churchill and Roosevelt brought military advisers as well as diplomatic assistants with them. In addition, Harry Hopkins, who had been on an assignment in Russia for the President, joined the Prime Minister in England and sailed with him on H.M.S. *Prince of Wales* to the rendezvous. Utmost secrecy was necessary because of the danger the Prime Minister could be in from attack if the Germans learned of the meeting. Roosevelt had a problem. While Winston Churchill was not constantly surrounded by newsmen, the American president always was—"the only exception," he explained, "being long distance cruises on heavy cruisers, when three newspaper men, representing the press associations, followed me on one of the escorting destroyers." Early in August, the President told a news conference that he intended to take a cruise on the U.S.S. *Potomac* but could not take the three wire service reporters with him because there was not sufficient room on the small escort ship.

FDR left Washington the morning of Sunday, August 3, taking a train to New London, Connecticut. There he boarded the *Potomac* and set sail. "Many persons saw me and we stood out of the harbor into the Sound in full view of thousands," FDR said, "my presidential flag flying from the main top." The next day, still seeking to establish that he was only on a pleasure cruise, launches were sent ashore and returned with the Crown Princess of Norway, her brother and her three children. "We went offshore two or three miles and fished in full view of the beach— the entrance to New Bedford harbor, and many passing yachts. At about 6:30 P.M. we returned . . . and I took the party ashore and was seen by several thousand people." FDR seemed to be enjoying the preliminary efforts at deception.

The next morning at dawn the President and his staff secretly transferred to a battleship, the U.S.S. *Augusta.* The *Potomac* would continue sailing in the waters of the northeastern United States with a man, in size and dress resembling Franklin Roosevelt, often seen fishing from it. But the President of the United States, at 6:40 that morning, was underway aboard the *Augusta* with its protective screen of destroyers.

At 11:25 the *Augusta* sailed past the Nantucket Shoals Lightship, then beyond the shallow waters where mines could be laid. Moving at a speed of approximately twenty knots, the *Augusta* carried Franklin Roosevelt to his rendezvous with the Prime Minister of England. The two men would join their voices in the cry of civilized humanity.

The efforts at secrecy, of course, did not work; they rarely do when Washington officials are involved. As soon as the President had told his news conference that he was going on a trip and not taking newsmen with him, astute persons in Washington understood something was happening. "There is a wild rumor going around town tonight to the effect that the President is going to meet Churchill somewhere up near Canada. . . ." wrote Henry Stimson in his diary that week. "Perhaps it's true," Stimson thought, "because for the first time Marshall failed to tell me where he went when he left last Sunday."

When George Marshall had left his home without explaining to his wife where he would be, she understood that something of importance was happening. Mrs. Marshall, wanting to avoid telephone calls from investigating newspapermen, joined her sister in Leesburg, Virginia. Mrs. Marshall thought her "hideout" was safe, but a New York *Herald-Tribune* reporter tracked her down and telephoned her. The sister answered the telephone and informed the newsman that the general was not there.

The *Herald-Tribune* man persisted. Did the sister know where the general was?

"That is funny," replied the sister. "I just bought a *Herald-Tribune* to try to find out."

"You win!" said the reporter and hung up.

With the President, Acting Secretary of State Sumner Welles, Marshall, and most of the top military leaders away from Washington the same week, it was obvious that the rumor about FDR meeting Churchill was true. The same day that Stimson confided the "wild rumor" to his diary, the German embassy in Washington cabled Berlin the same rumor. But the meeting's location continued a mystery; the best bets in Washington were somewhere in the mid-Atlantic.

The rumors became so strong that the British, one day after Churchill had left, considered making a public statement about the meeting. The statement, presented by Churchill's assistant Anthony Eden to John Winant, the American ambassador in London, said that "The meeting is taking place on board ship somewhere in the Atlantic."

FDR was cabled the message and asked his opinion. "Think highly inadvisable make any statement at this time," he quickly answered. "In my judgment all that need be said is that Prime Minister is on short vacation. References to accompanying officers especially bad. Any statement now is direct invitation to Germans to attack him and his party going and returning. When in doubt say nothing."

On Thursday morning the President's ship approached the coast of Newfoundland. That was a leisurely day for the President. He caught a "large and ugly" fish which could not be identified. He directed it be sent to the Smithsonian Institution for identification. There were also conferences with his military aides. There was one pleasant surprise. The President's son, Franklin D. Roosevelt, Jr., was a Navy ensign aboard the U.S.S. *Mayrant*. Without the President being aware of it, Ensign Roosevelt was detached from his ship and assigned to temporary duty aboard the *Augusta*. "I detailed him as my junior naval aide for the great occasion," said the President, "and he borrowed what I always call 'the gold spinach,' i.e., the aiguillettes, which a presidential aide wears on his right shoulder and all other aides wear on their left shoulder."

The Army would not be outdone. The next day, Captain Elliott Roosevelt of the United States Army Air Corps was flown down from Gander Lake to join the presidential party, and the President had two of his sons as his personal assistants.

The day Roosevelt had left Washington he had received a letter from King George VI of England. It carried the King's best wishes and expressed pleasure that FDR and Churchill were going to meet. "I am sure you will agree," the King said of Churchill, "that he is a very remarkable man." The day before the King had written his letter, a British army officer described Churchill as "rather like a boy who's been let out of school suddenly. He says it's the only holiday he's had since the war."

The trip with its secrecy, its air of intrigue, with its high stakes—as well as the chance for a few days at sea—all appealed to the adventurous Churchill. After boarding the *Prince of Wales*, he obviously enjoyed himself. He wore his yachting cap tilted rakishly, puffed vigorously on his cigar, and roamed the deck smiling at all he met. Churchill had the ability to relax. One who was with him on that trip reported: "You might have thought that he had not one care in the world. He possesses the ability to shut his mind at will either to worry or work and to live entirely in the present. He can come from a War Cabinet having made a great decision and enjoy an hour of Laurel and Hardy." One night aboard the *Prince of Wales*, Churchill joined the officers in watching the American film *High Sierra*, starring Humphrey Bogart as a wanted gangster who is fatally shot by a policeman at the end of the movie and goes tumbling down the Sierra mountains, bouncing from rock to rock in typical Hollywood style. After watching the bloody demise of Humphrey Bogart, Churchill shouted, "And a good time was had by all!"

Churchill also was sentimental. The British had produced a movie, starring Laurence Olivier and Vivien Leigh, about the British naval hero Lord Nelson. That also was shown to Churchill and his company. In the final scene, Olivier as Lord Nelson lies dying aboard his ship. The moment before his death, he is informed that victory is his and that England is saved from invasion. The movie was intended as propaganda, and it worked with Winston Churchill. He was seen at that moment to be unashamedly wiping tears from his eyes. This was the fifth time Churchill had seen the movie and it still moved him. When it was over he stood and said, "Gentlemen, I thought this film would interest you, showing great events similar to those in which you have been taking part."

The British ships arrived at Placentia Bay early the morning of Saturday, August 9. As the *Prince of Wales* cut through the water, Winston Churchill came on deck. He had obviously only awakened. He wore the one-piece coverall that would become famous as his "siren suit." The first cigar of the day jutted from his round face, and the fringe of hair around his bald head was still uncombed.

He stood on the open platform surrounding the enclosed Admiral's bridge, savoring the stimulus of the cold saltwater spray and the sound of the water rushing against the ship's hull. Only a few persons were up then. Churchill turned to one. "Can you see any sign of them yet?" he asked. There was an eagerness in his voice, a sense of excitement. "Of who?" asked the crew member. "The American destroyers," was the answer. Together they crossed from the port side to the starboard side of the bridge. They saw no American ship. Only a calm sea.

"In a few hours," thought the prime minister's early morning companion, "ceremony and anthems would begin, but in that quiet opening of the day, like a warrior awakened from his tent, he stood unarmed at dawn, surveying the scene, wondering what the day would bring forth."

The first meeting of the American and British ships took place at 7:30 that morning. A group of American destroyers approached the British ships. A formal meeting had been scheduled for nine o'clock, but the British were keeping local time and the Americans were keeping American time. The result was that the British ships were ninety minutes early and had to turn around and sail until it was time for their entrance.

When the British ships finally did turn into Placentia Bay, they saw a land with low hills shrouded in mist. It was much like the England they had left six days earlier. But here there was no war, no blackouts, no bombs, no deaths. The British ships were closer now and, rounding a point of land, they finally saw the American ships. In the center of the American ships was the *Augusta*, next to it the U.S.S. *Tuscaloosa*, then the battleship U.S.S. *Arkansas*. Covering the wide anchorage was a flotilla of destroyers, ready to escort the British ships. Overhead there suddenly appeared American seaplanes, covering the British ships with a formal and protective umbrella. The British had come to friends.

The *Prince of Wales* followed her American escort ship through a double line of American destroyers to a point abreast of the *Augusta*. The English could see the President now. He stood beneath an awning, taller than most men around him, dressed in a light brown summer suit, turning occasionally to speak with someone. Then, as the *Prince of Wales* steamed by, the President of the United States removed his hat and placed it over his heart in salute.

The Prime Minister, dressed in his British Navy uniform, stood on the quarterdeck aboard the *Prince of Wales* at rigid attention. He also saluted. On the American ship a band began "God Save the King." It was answered from the British ship with the "Star Spangled Banner." The *Prince of Wales* anchored at a buoy. At the moment of touching it, the ship's engines stopped. Then the giant anchor chains slipped from the ship into the Newfoundland waters. The hour was exactly nine o'clock—American time.

"We were a remarkable contrast," recorded an Englishman at the scene, "as we lay anchored side by side. The *Prince of Wales* was camouflaged; her guns protruded from their turrets like rigid pythons. The American ships were uncamouflaged and shone in peacetime grey. We had been in action, and our brass was either painted or tarnished, and our decks were not what they would have been in other days. The American ships were spotless. We admired the beautiful rubber steps of their pinnaces, the gleaming brass, the pine-white woodwork." Having lived since 1939 in a country at war, the Englishmen looked "as over a great gulf of experience—at such evidence of a country at peace."

At eleven o'clock the Prime Minister boarded the *Augusta*. As his foot touched the deck, the American band began "God Save the King." Winston Churchill, in his dark blue navy uniform, stood for a moment on the deck saluting. Silhouetted against the gray of the American battleship, he seemed at that moment the lone soldier moving proudly to his destiny. Then he disappeared to the men on board the *Prince of Wales* to re-emerge again under the awning with the American President. Through binoculars the scene seemed quite formal. The Prime Minister pulled from his pocket a letter from the King and handed it to the President with a slight bow. Suddenly someone moved. People began to shake hands. Everyone smiled. Winston Churchill pulled out a cigar and began puffing. Roosevelt fitted a cigarette into his holder and lit up. The two men, the British Prime Minister and the American President, seemed comfortable with each other. Everyone relaxed. The Prime Minister stayed for luncheon, then returned to his own ship early in the afternoon.

That afternoon a number of small boats left the *Augusta* and headed for the British ships. They carried 1,950 gift boxes. Each box contained two hundred cigarettes, an orange, two apples, and a half-pound of cheese. There was a carton for every British sailor. With each carton was a card reading, "The Commander-in-Chief, United States Navy, Sends Greetings and Best Wishes. Franklin D. Roosevelt, President of the United States."

When the American sailors unloaded the cartons on the quarterdeck of the British ship, they also had a treat. The Prime Minister moved among them. Would he pose for pictures with the Americans, the sailors wanted to know? Would he! Not only did Churchill pose but he helped arrange the sailors on either side of him. "How's that?" he shouted at the photographers. The photographers answered "fine," but Winston Churchill still was not satisfied. He waved his cigar at the sailors and commanded, "More tooth!" The American sailors thought as well of Winston Churchill and his conviviality as the British sailors thought of Franklin Roosevelt and his generosity.

Churchill returned to the *Augusta* for dinner that evening. The menu included vegetable soup, broiled chicken, spinach omelet, salad, and chocolate ice cream for dessert. When the meal was finished, Churchill commented informally on the difference between this war and the First World War. Great masses of men were used in battles during the earlier conflict. In contrast, war was now being fought, he said, by smaller groups of men using armored equipment, automatic weapons, aircraft, and improved communication techniques. He also spoke of Adolf Hitler's tactic of engaging nations one by one and spoke of the lost opportunities for cooperative action. The inference was, to some Americans at least, that the United States should join in the war against Germany.

At that dinner the first night the President had arranged that the place cards bear a particular verse. The card had the British and American flags crossed at the top and beneath the flags were these lines:

> Sail on, O Ship of State!
> Sail on, O Union, strong and great!
> Humanity with all its fears,
> With all the hopes of future years,
> Is hanging breathless on thy fate!

Those lines, first sent to Churchill by FDR early in the year, were a bond between the two men and a bond between the two nations.

Roosevelt and Churchill never became what could be described as close friends. They liked and respected each other. They were at times a fascinating match. FDR was the sly politician when he must be, avoiding making a promise that he did not wish to deliver. Churchill was the English bulldog pushing always for a firm commitment. But there were gulfs between them. Franklin Roosevelt was a head of state while Winston Churchill was only a minister. So, to FDR, Churchill would always be, after this meeting, "Winston." But to Churchill, Roosevelt always would be "Mr. President." And at this particular meeting, in Placentia Bay in August, 1941, there was another gulf. Winston Churchill's nation was at war. Its young men were being killed in battle. Its young women and children were being destroyed by bombs. Despite the money and the arms the United States was sending to England, it was not actually fighting. America was at peace. And the awfulness of war cannot be comprehended by those who have not lived it.

The next morning, Sunday, there was an event that all who experienced it believed to be the most dramatic of the Atlantic meeting. To some it was the most dramatic of their lives. Coming across the Atlantic, Winston Churchill had considered having a joint Sunday morning religious service aboard the *Prince of Wales* with American and British chaplains conducting the service together before a congregation made up of British and American sailors. When the President was broached about the idea, he readily consented.

The Prime Minister took personal charge of the service. He watched over the setting up of the chairs. He moved one an inch or two, adjusted the folds of the British flag that hung near the lectern. "We have a grand day for a church parade," he said, "and I have chosen some grand hymns." Shortly before eleven o'clock that morning boatloads of American sailors began arriving on the British ship. They joined the British sailors and strolled with them to the quarterdeck where the service was to be held. Churchill had given careful orders that there was to be no marching and complete informality. It was a wise decision on his part. The American and the British sailors mixed together in a friendly fashion, as if they all belonged to the same armed service.

But they did not. Almost exactly four months later the *Prince of Wales* would be sunk while fighting the enemy with the loss of one thousand men, many of those one thousand men this morning were standing beside American sailors. The British knew this could happen and probably would one day. But the Americans who stood next to them were not at war, had not experienced war, and so at this moment they knew it could not happen to them. The religious ceremony they were about to undergo jointly became one of those rare experiences that transcend the physical and become mystical. The British and the Americans became one. But that great barrier lay between them: Some knew they would die while others knew they would not.

The President boarded at eleven o'clock. He came on the destroyer *McDougal*, which could bring her deck level with the *Prince of Wales*'s deck. This enabled the crippled President, holding the arm of his son Elliott, to walk across a gangway. As his foot touched the British ship, the band played "The Star Spangled Banner" and an honor guard saluted. The President stood there motionless and bareheaded while the anthem was played. Tall, broad shouldered, handsome, even elegant in his dark blue suit, Franklin Roosevelt was almost the prototype that sunny morning of the traditional hero—or so it seemed to the desperate British who so much needed a hero.

When the anthem ended, Prime Minister Churchill stepped forward to shake the President's hand. Together they walked to the two chairs on the quarterdeck that had been set up at the head of the congregation. Once they were seated, their chiefs of staff and diplomatic assistants filled a ring of chairs behind them, then the sailors of the two nations were seated. The service began.

There were prayers, for the American President and for all those in power, a prayer for King George VI, and then the British chaplain said, "Let us pray for the invaded countries in the grief and havoc of oppression; for the upholding of their courage; and the hope of the speedy restoration of their freedom. . . ."

There were hymns. The American and British sailors stood side by side, bending over their hymn sheets, their hats off. One could not tell which sailor belonged to which nation's navy. Their voices carried over the ocean waves—"O God our help in ages past, our hope for years to come."

Captain John Leach of the *Prince of Wales* then read the Lessons. Churchill found the captain "a charming and lovable man and all that a British sailor should be." This morning the captain read from the First Chapter of the Book of Joshua: ". . . as I was with Moses, so I will be with thee: I will not fail thee, nor forsake thee . . . Be strong and of a good courage; be not afraid, neither be thou dismayed; for the Lord thy God is with thee whithersoever thou goest." Four months later, when his ship was sunk, Captain John Leach would die.

Next the sailors, the military leaders of the two nations, the President, and the Prime Minister joined in the singing of the second of the hymns Churchill had chosen. It was "Onward Christian Soldiers." Before the Second World War began, historians and other analysts explained why it would come. Once it had begun, they argued about why it had happened. When it would finish, they would explore the possibilities for blame. The arguments were and continue endless. But all the discussion can never obscure the very basic point about the war. Since man had organized a society with another man, he has been seeking ways to live in decency and peace. This was the meaning of his religion. It was and is man's most difficult struggle, to gain control of the animalistic instincts that he cannot cut from him. The Second World War was, up to its time, the fiercest outbreak of this struggle, and the men aboard the *Prince of Wales* and the other ships in Placentia Bay realized they must win this struggle. To lose meant to surrender all that man had gained in his climb upward.

> Onward Christian Soldiers
> Marching as to war
> With the cross of Jesus
> Going as before.

The wind lightly touched the American and British flags by the chaplains' lectern, gently entwining the Union Jack and the Stars and Stripes together. Churchill cried. Roosevelt looked intensely serious, completely enveloped by the church service.

> At the sign of triumph
> Satan's host doth flee
> On then Christian soldiers
> On to Victory.

There was a prayer calling on God to "strengthen our resolve, that we fight not in enmity against men but against the powers of darkness enslaving the souls of men, till all the enmity and oppression be done away and the peoples of the world be set free from fear to serve one another as children of our Father."

In the British navy it is ordered that a benediction be said every day. It closed this morning's service, for those young men who did not know war and those who had known it for two years, for those young men who did not need to anticipate death in battle and those who must always anticipate it.

O Eternal Lord God, Who alone spreadest out the heavens and rulest the raging of the sea; Who hast compassed the waters with bounds until day and night come to an end; Be pleased to receive into Thy Almighty and Most Gracious protection the persons of us Thy servants, and Fleet in which we serve. Preserve us from the dangers of the sea, and from the violence of the enemy; that we may be a security for such as pass upon the seas upon their lawful occasions; that the peoples of the Empire may in peace and quietness serve Thee, our God; and that we may return in safety to enjoy the blessings of the land, with the fruits of our labours, and with thankful remembrance of Thy mercies to praise and glorify Thy Holy Name; through Jesus Christ our Lord.

The service was over.

The meeting between the leaders of the two nations had several specific points for discussion. One was the military situation. For chief of staff George Marshall, the session was an opportunity to sit down with his British counterparts and discuss the course of the war, the lessons they had learned from it, and how they expected it to develop. Marshall later described these meetings as "quite general," and said that the participants "had not a great deal to say about materiel." The military discussions were more specific than that. The British spoke of the United States contributing manpower to the war. The Americans responded negatively to the suggestion. They believed they were doing as much as could be done by supplying the arms with which the English could fight. Also, the American armed forces were not then ready to fight. Finally, the Americans understood that in a democracy they could not force their nation into war. The Americans held this position during the talks even though the British tried an energetic sales talk. Large armies would not be needed, claimed the British officers echoing Churchill's argument. Small numbers of men with the most modern equipment, assisted by armed guerrilla bands from the occupied nations would be sufficient. The Americans were skeptical of this claim, believing that the German military force must be met by an equivalent amount of force.

The next problem taken up at the Atlantic meeting was Japan. England was fearful of war breaking out in the Pacific with Japan, meaning that England would be fighting on two fronts and that the supplies it received from its colonies and trading partners in the Far East would be lost to it. As the Atlantic Ocean was England's province, the Pacific was America's. Churchill wanted the United States to tell Japan, in effect, to pull back from its aggressive stance or face a war with the United States.

After the Sunday morning religious service, while FDR and Churchill were lunching aboard the *Prince of Wales*, the American Under Secretary of State Sumner Welles was meeting with Sir Alexander Cadogan of the Prime Minister's staff. Sir Alexander handed Welles the draft of a statement. It was proposed that the American President hand the statement to the Japanese ambassador when FDR returned to Washington. The statement read:

Any further encroachment by Japan in the Southwestern Pacific would produce a situation in which the United States government would be compelled to take counter measures even though these might lead to war between the United States and Japan.

The proposal was an ultimatum. The United States would be committing itself to war. FDR realized that this might someday be necessary, but he could not make such a commitment on this day. As long as there was a chance to avoid war, he must take that chance. In two days, FDR knew, the House of Representatives in Washington would vote on whether to extend the draft. Prospects were that the extension would fail to gain the votes of a majority of the House members and the United States then would be without an army. The list of shortages, which FDR had agonized over in July, continued to be a lengthy one. In addition to the moral question—the decision of whether or not to make war—FDR was faced with the blunt fact that he led a nation which, despite all his speeches and all his warnings, all his actions and all his declarations, still was not yet ready to accept that war must be prepared for.

The Japanese situation came to a head the next morning, Monday, in a meeting between FDR and Churchill. The President made clear he would not use the British draft. Instead, the President said, he would tell the Japanese ambassador that the United States did not approve of the recent aggressive moves by Japan but, also, would express the hope that the two nations could resolve differences peacefully. The actual note handed to the Japanese ambassador carried only the warning that if Japan continued its aggressive policies,

> The Government of the United States will be compelled to take immediately any and all steps which it may deem necessary toward safeguarding the legitimate rights and interests of the United States and American nationals and toward insuring the safety and security of the United States.

The statement was almost meaningless; a nation always has the right to protect itself and its peoples. Churchill, who had hoped for much more, accepted this position, however. He had no choice. As much as Roosevelt sympathized with England's position, and as much as he understood the imperative need for England to win the war, he would not permit England to force the United States into the conflict.

Some months later Winston Churchill, in a speech to the House of Commons, spoke of the Atlantic meeting and of having discussed with Roosevelt the matter "that the United States even if not herself attacked would come into the war in the Far East and thus make the final victory assured." That matter was discussed; it was the agreement Churchill hoped to gain. But such an agreement was not entered into by Franklin Roosevelt.

A final major point was that of trade. Both FDR and Churchill were committed to a liberal trade policy and wished to insert a paragraph stating that commitment in the final document, which would become the Atlantic Charter. But England, being the center of an Empire, had certain commitments to her dominions, including preferential tariff agreements. Churchill wanted to insert in the paragraph about free trade the qualifying phrase "with due respect for their existing obligations." This would be understood to mean that England was not renouncing her tariff agreements with the members of her Empire.

Sumner Welles argued that the insertion would destroy any

value that paragraph would have. He said that more than phrase-ology was involved. If the British and the United States govern-ments, he continued, could not do everything in their power to restore free and liberal trade policies, "they might as well throw in the sponge and realize that one of the greatest factors in creating the present tragic situation in the world was going to be permitted to continue unchecked in the postwar world." Church-ill agreed emphatically with that, or said he did. But, he ex-plained, he was up against an obstacle which he could not sur-mount. The member nations of the British Commonwealth would have to be consulted. They might or might not agree to the Charter statement about trade. But whichever they did, their responses could not be received before the Atlantic Con-ference ended. It was either accept the Churchill phraseology or delete the paragraph entirely.

This upset the free-trade members of the President's party, including Welles and, when he later learned of it, Secretary of State Hull. As Secretary, Hull had devoted most of his career to the fight against such agreements and was "keenly disappointed" that the final Charter draft included the phrase. FDR accepted the phrase Monday afternoon, explaining "time [was] of the essence." He won a point also. Not only would the paragraph refer to trade but also to "the raw materials of the world." The President believed access to raw materials would not be hin-dered by the "existing obligations" phrase, and "For me," he said, "that is consistent." He emphasized the word "me," appar-ently aware that Welles and Hull would not be satisfied with the paragraph.

Harold Macmillan, then an official in the Churchill govern-ment and later Prime Minister, offered a different explanation. "President Roosevelt's response was by no means as warm or as open as Churchill believed," wrote Macmillan, who believed that Franklin Roosevelt was prejudiced against the British Empire and "the liquidation of the British Empire was, whether con-sciously or unconsciously, one of his aims." Macmillan cited American pressure to end the British preferential tariff system with its dominions as proof of this prejudice.

Macmillan's charge against Roosevelt is harsh. If the United States wanted to end the British Empire, America could have demanded its liquidation in one subtle way or another as a price for its assistance. Actually, after the passage of the lend-lease act in early 1941, the United States exacted no price—subtle or otherwise—from England. The war did sap England's strength, and it never would recover that strength. But that loss of strength was not due to FDR's prejudice. He was not interested in ending the British Empire.

Also discussed at the Atlantic meeting was the possibility of an international organization to keep the peace once Hitler was defeated. The proposed draft by Churchill referred to an "effective international organization" assuring to all peoples "the means of dwelling in security." FDR would not go along with the reference to an international organization. He himself had supported the League of Nations at the end of the First World War and had campaigned in its behalf when he ran for Vice President in 1920. In 1933 he had privately confided his personal hopes for agreements between nations to eliminate weapons of war and "a world agreement providing for continuous international inspection." But he had also witnessed Wilson's defeat over the League, the defeat of the Democratic Party in the 1920 election; then during the 1930s he had witnessed the animosity in the United States toward international agreements that appeared to cost the United States some of its sovereignty. So, for the sake or what FDR described as "realism," he insisted that the reference to an international organization be dropped. Churchill agreed.

The subject of a statement to be issued by both governments had come up at the meeting Monday between FDR and Churchill. The Prime Minister originated the suggestion. Roosevelt responded favorably, suggesting that identical statements be issued in London and Washington, probably on Thursday. The President thought the statement should report that the two leaders had met and had general discussions about aid to nations under the lend-lease program. The President also suggested that the statement say that the meeting had produced no commitments between the two nations. Churchill objected to this last point. This again was a flare-up of the basic issue between the two men. As with the statement concerning Japan, Churchill was trying to push the United States as far toward war as he could. Naturally he would; the fate or England depended upon the United States. And FDR, fully understanding the Prime Minister's position, was refusing. The President explained that to suggest that agreements had been made would arouse the isolationist sentiment in the United States and harm the rearmament effort as well as the lend-lease program. Churchill answered that he understood the problem, but to state the negative side of the meeting so categorically, he continued, would have a serious impact upon morale in occupied nations as well as in beleaguered England. At FDR's suggestion they settled the question by glossing over it. The Charter began:

> The President of the United States of America and the Prime Minister, Mr. Churchill, representing His Majesty's Government in the United Kingdom, being met together, deem it right to make known certain common principles in the national policies of their respective countries on which they base their hopes for a better future for the world.

And then unfolded the Atlantic Charter with its promise of a better future, its promise of decency, sustenance, and peace. "All the nations of the world," it said, "for realistic as well as spiritual reasons, must come to the abandonment of the use of force."

The authors of the Charter did not look upon it as a "great statement." It was to them little more than a publicity handout, mimeographed and released. There was no handlettering on parchment, no signatures, no seals, none of the trappings of the formal state document. But the significance soon became apparent. "The profound and far-reaching importance of this Joint Declaration was apparent," wrote Churchill. He was referring to the fact of a neutral, the United States, joining with a belligerent, England, in calling so strongly for "the final destruction of the Nazi tyranny." And Henry Stimson correctly said the Charter "will serve as a rallying point for all good men in the democracies." He continued that "the mere fact of the meeting, regardless of what was accomplished by the mutual contacts, will have a powerful influence of encouragement for the forces of freedom throughout the world."

And that was the meaning of the Atlantic meeting and the Charter to the nations of the world. Here were the leaders of the two greatest nations of the world promising not to seize another nation's territory, guaranteeing the right of self-determination and of self-government, promising to take down the barriers to a free world trade, holding out the hope of a world in which fear and want no longer exist. This was a picture of a world toward which all men were willing to strive and which most nations sought. From this point on, Adolf Hitler found himself increasingly alone in the world. His vow of Germany astride the world could not balance the prospect offered by the Atlantic Charter.

Churchill himself best summed up the significance of the Atlantic meeting and the Charter. Speaking on radio after he had returned to England, he said to his countrymen:

> Would it be presumptuous for me to say that it symbolizes something even more majestic, namely the marshalling of the good forces of the world against the evil forces which are now so formidable and triumphant, and have cast their cruel spell over the whole of Europe and a large part of Asia? This was a meeting which marks for ever in the pages of history the taking up of the English-speaking nations amid all this peril, tumult and confusion, of the guidance of the fortunes of the broad toiling masses in all the continents, and our loyal effort, without any clog of selfish interest, to lead them forward out of the miseries into which they have been plunged back to the broad high-road of freedom and justice. This is the highest honour and the most glorious opportunity which could ever have come to any branch of the human race.

Roosevelt considered the meeting "eminently successful," saying,

> I think one of the subjects which perhaps all overlooked, both in the statements and comments, was the need for an exchange of what might be called views relating to what is happening to the world under the Nazi regime, as applied to other nations. The more that is discussed and looked into, the more terrible the thought becomes of having the world as a whole dominated by the kind of influences which have been at work in the occupied or affiliated nations. It's a thing that needs to be brought home to all of the democracies, more and more.

The President had accomplished what he had set out to do. He had adroitly bolstered the British position and provided a moral basis for the world to turn against the Nazi powers— without making a commitment for the United States to enter the war. A few weeks after the meeting, FDR was chatting with an aide and said he thought he was doing a better job of handling the British than Woodrow Wilson had done. He talked then about England, with the assistance of the United States, winning the war. Franklin Roosevelt was confident that it would happen.

The Atlantic meeting ended Tuesday afternoon. The English leaders lunched that day with the President, finished the Charter draft, and then the party moved to the quarterdeck of the *Augusta* at ten minutes of three. An American honor guard paraded and the band played "God Save the King." The Prime Minister and his party left the ship for the *Prince of Wales*. Two hours later they were sailing back to the war. As the battle-streaked ship moved slowly from the harbor, the British could hear the sounds of the American band playing "Auld Lang Syne," the traditional theme of good friends. They could see the President on the deck of the *Augusta* watching them leave.

Winston Churchill stood against the rail watching the American ship and the American President grow smaller in the distance. Churchill's mother had been an American and he had always felt a strong kinship with her land. He had come here to pull from that land the physical strength for his own people to carry on. They had the moral strength, but not the guns and planes and tanks by which modern wars are fought. Nor did they have the great numbers of young men who would be needed to sacrifice themselves on the fields and in the cities of Europe if Hitler was ever to be destroyed. All this, Churchill knew, ultimately must come from the United States. And, although no promises had been made and no understandings arrived at, Winston Churchill knew that eventually the United States would supply what it must. For the English and the American soldiers were the Christian soldiers of the hymn before whom Satan's host must flee. One could not deny such a responsibility. "Great things may come of it in the future," said the Prime Minister as he watched the American ship disappear. And of the President, he said to those with him, "You have seen a great man this day."

Whether great things would, in fact, come from America in the future was being decided that every afternoon in the chamber of the House of Representatives. The question before the House members was the extension of the draft. The Senate vote the previous month had indicated where FDR's troubles lay in the House. Of the forty-five affirmative Senate votes, thirty-eight were Democrats and seven Republicans. The Southerners supported FDR almost entirely. Joining them was a scattering of senators from Maine, Connecticut, New York, Illinois, Wyoming, Utah, and Washington. The Republican supporters came from Maine, Vermont, New Hampshire, and New Jersey. Those votes showed that Roosevelt had some support in New England and the Middle Atlantic states, solid support in the South, and meager support in the Middle and Far West. Those last two areas had a greater share of the vote in the House than they did in the Senate, meaning there was a firmer foundation for the opposition.

There was also dissension within the Republican Party on the House side of the Capitol. The House leader was Representative Joseph W. Martin of Massachusetts. An isolationist with strong anti-Roosevelt feelings, Martin was a shrewd political tactician who would not permit his prejudices to overcome his political sense. He wanted to prevent the Republicans in the House from taking a formal party position on the draft extension. Martin realized that if the Republicans split badly on the final vote, or if the extension were approved, the Republicans would suffer a serious blow to their prestige. But the isolationists in the party would not be stopped. They insisted on a party caucus. At the caucus the House Republicans approved a resolution condemning FDR's foreign policies.

At the same time the House Republicans met, the national leaders of the party—Herbert Hoover, Alf Landon, and some others—issued an appeal to the Congress to place restrictions on the President. Among the House Republicans, however, that appeal had a negative impact. Some of the Republicans, favoring the draft extension, were able to sow enough discord to blunt its message. The Hoover-Landon statement, they said, was only a power play to take the party leadership away from Wendell Willkie, who was supporting the President's foreign policy. By the time the issue came to a vote in the House that Tuesday afternoon, no one could be sure what the Republicans would do.

Politicking among Democrats on Capitol Hill had been the most strenuous members had seen in years. Sam Rayburn, the Speaker of the House led the fight. He picked up a telephone and when an uncertain Congressman answered, Rayburn began peppering him with questions. Would the Congressman vote for an unlimited extension of the draft? an eighteen-month extension? a year? Then, after the "no" had been sounded, Rayburn (still too new at his job to have earned the affectionate title of "Mr. Sam" that came in his later years) began to talk, to coax, to bluster. He succeeded, usually, in getting a promise to "think it over." Then John McCormack, the House Democratic leader, called the Congressman. "We can get the eighteen-month extension," he said, "if you'll vote for it." If the Congressman continued obdurate, the next calls came from the Democrats back home, the state and county leaders. They explained that one does not balk the administration which is dispensing so many federal favors. When all else failed, Representative Pat Boland of Pennsylvania, the party whip, sat down with the member. "What are you going to do?" he demanded. And with his question was the vision of all the favors that the party hierarchy can extend to a member of Congress.

The tactics were not having a visible effect. The members did not like coercion. They did not like the suggestion of dishonesty, of trading their vote for federal patronage. They did not like the pressure. Another approach was needed, and it would be found at the last minute. It was one that politicians ordinarily scoff at.

The day of the vote Henry Stimson was nervous. "All through the morning I was at work trying to find out what the situation was on the Hill," he recalled, "and helping as far as I could. I talked with Wadsworth in the morning. He said he didn't know what it was going to be. . . ."

Many years later John McCormack recalled that vote. "We couldn't know how it would turn out," he said. "It was too close. On a close vote you usually know you're five or ten votes either way. We knew we were one or two votes on this one. When it's that close, you can't make any predictions because someone is likely to change and not even know why he did it."

The afternoon of the vote the galleries in the House chamber filled quickly. There were soldiers, watching and waiting to know when their term of service would end. There were mothers, who had arrived in organized groups, carrying small American flags. As the House members assembled, there was no question that the galleries were against the draft extension. In this the galleries only represented what appeared to be the attitude of the "folks back home." The members' mail, the visits from constituents, all the indications were that the only safe vote, politically, was a "no" vote.

There is a tradition in the House that members should vote their constituencies. This means that the party leadership never expects the House members to take an action that might mean their defeat in the next election. On this day the Democratic Party leadership broke that tradition. Whatever may happen to you, Sam Rayburn insisted to the members who gathered around him in the corners of the House chamber or in the Speaker's room, vote to extend the draft. His bald head glistended in the light. His big eyes bulged. Vote "yes," he insisted, whether you come back here after the next election or not. You cannot permit, he argued, the army to be disbanded. Rather than appeal to political safety or promise patronage, rather than call for party loyalty or offer a reward from the pork barrel, Sam Rayburn was appealing to the member's patriotism. Four members switched their positions from "no" to "yes." Two others said they could not change their "no" votes but, if necessary, they would take live pairs with two absent members. This, in effect, meant the withdrawal of their "no" votes and the reducing of the negative tally by two. Would these switches be enough? No one could be sure. As McCormack said: "We couldn't know how it would turn out. It was too close."

The roll in the House is called alphabetically. Each member, if he is present, answers either "aye" or "no" to his name. The tally clerk who sits in front of the Speaker's chair keeps a running count of the vote. Since his is the only official count, he is the only one who knows how the count is going. The voting process is a slow one. Approximately a half hour is required to call the names of all 435 House members and record their votes. It can be a long half hour when the fate of the nation's existence appears to hang on an uncertain outcome. Sam Rayburn stood and walked behind the tally clerk to observe the vote count. His chunky body was motionless, his round face without expression as he watched the votes recorded. As soon as the last member's name had been called, the Speaker returned to his desk and faced the House of Representatives.

If the draft extension had not been approved, the United States would have been saying it was not serious about its defense. It would have been saying it was not serious about defending the western hemisphere and its own shores. It would have been saying that it was not prepared to block Japan's aggressive steps in the Pacific. It would have been saying that, if need be, it would not assist England to defeat Germany. If the extension had not been approved, the United States would have been saying that it would not respond to Franklin Roosevelt's call to arms.

"On this vote," Sam Rayburn announced, "203 members have voted 'Aye,' 202 members have voted 'No,' and the bill is passed."

Selective service had been extended and the United States Army had been saved from disintegration.

The House exploded in an an uproar of shouts, demands, applause, and boos from the galleries. One member demanded a recapitulation of the vote. Rayburn had to grant it; the vote was too close to refuse. The clerk then droned out the names of those who had voted for the extension and the names of those who had voted against extension. The outcome still was the same, 203 to 202. Then a Republican member jumped up. He had been present and voted, but he had not heard his name called when the clerk read the list of "no" voters. Had he been recorded? Slowly the clerk checked his tally sheet. For this moment, the House suddenly hushed. If the member had not been recorded, his "no" vote would bring the outcome to a tie, 203 to 203. But the member had indeed been recorded and counted in the "no" column. The vote was not changed.

"The vote stands," said Rayburn, "and the bill is passed." And then before anyone realized what he was saying, Rayburn added, "And without objection a motion to reconsider is laid on the table."

A motion to reconsider is a move to demand a new vote on an issue that has already been voted on. Laying it on the table means the motion to reconsider has been refused. Many members not having heard Rayburn, there was another Republican cry for a reconsideration of the vote. Usually such a second vote rarely changes the outcome and is ordinarily dispensed with. But with a vote count so close, the opposition believed it was worth making a try. The Republicans were shocked to learn that Rayburn had announced that a motion to reconsider had been killed "without objection."

"I beg to differ with the Speaker," said one Republican from the floor. "The Speaker did not announce that a motion to reconsider had been tabled."

"The chair has twice stated that he did make that statement," Rayburn shot back.

"I beg to differ with you," shouted the Republican.

Standing in the well of the House, armed only with the Speaker's gavel, Sam Rayburn glared out at the assembled members. He was their elected officer, the symbol of orderly procedure. If they challenged him, they would be challenging all their hope to operate a legislative body in a reasoned and efficient, as well as orderly, manner. That the members knew this was Rayburn's greatest strength. Actually it was Sam Rayburn's only strength.

"The Chair," he said in a tone of voice that immediately quieted the House, "does not intend to have his word questioned."

The debate over Selective Service officially had ended.

Of the 203 "aye" votes, twenty-one were Republicans—James Wadsworth and a few others he had managed to bring with him. The South was solidly behind the draft extension. Representative Frank Boykin of Alabama quickly shot off a letter to Steve Early at the White House: "When the Big Chief gets back, be sure and call his attention to the fact that the South and the Southwest saved the day on this Selective Service Bill." Who could tell? Someday the South might need a favor from FDR.

The vote itself was not quite as close as it appeared. If there had been three additional "no" votes, bringing the vote count to 205 to 203 against extending the draft, the extension still would have won in the end. First, the Democratic leadership had promises of two members to take live pairs with absent members. They would have withdrawn their two "no" votes from the official tally and the final count then would have been 203 to 203. In a tie the Speaker, who does not ordinarily vote, casts a ballot. Rayburn would have broken the tie in favor of extending the draft. Still, as John McCormack recalled years later, "That was too close for comfort."

Many of the isolationists considered the one-vote margin a slap to FDR personally and a rebuke to his policy. Certainly it was not an overwhelming show of approval. Still, FDR would not permit the slimness of that vote margin to weaken his policy. He would continue to build up America's strength and he would not reward aggression.

If he had chosen to reward aggression, he had the opportunity that month. Japanese Ambassador Admiral Nomura approached Roosevelt to suggest a meeting between the American President and Japanese Premier Fumimaro Konoye. The meeting had been suggested by Konoye. Opposed to war, Konoye more and more found himself under the control of the military leaders in Japan.

"The army is not necessarily in disagreement," Konoye was told. But, the military leaders concluded to him, "You shall not resign your post as a result of the meeting on the grounds that it was a failure; rather, you shall be prepared to assume leadership in the war against America." And the military believed that "failure of this meeting is the greater likelihood."

Konoye agreed to this. In his diary he described the proposed meeting as "an undertaking which must be carried out while being fully prepared for war against America." He continued that "Japan will insist, of course, on the firm establishment of the Greater East Asia Co-Prosperity Sphere."

That last phrase was Japan's description of her plans to dominate Asia and the Western Pacific. Konoye's original intention may have been to avoid war, but in the end the proposal was a trap for the United States. Either the United States must agree to Japan's plans or go to war. Once Konoye returned from the meeting to proclaim that the United States had not granted Asia and the Western Pacific as a fiefdom to Japan, there would be few in Japan daring enough to oppose war. The proposed meeting was actually a device to draw the neutral element in the Japanese government to the side of the militants. The Germans understood the Konoye offer in those terms. It was, their embassy reported to them from Tokyo, an effort to convince the Japanese people that every effort to avoid war had been made. It was a step toward war.

The United States understood that for FDR to meet Konoye under conditions then existing would pave the way for war. When Nomura suggested the meeting to FDR, Roosevelt replied that if the Japanese government halted its expansionist activities, a meeting perhaps could be arranged. The President then even went so far as to express his personal inclination to meet at Juneau, Alaska, rather than Hawaii as the Japanese suggested. An Alaskan trip would require the President being away from Washington only sixteen days while a Hawaiian trip would require more than twenty days.

But the United States was insisting on some sign from Japan that negotiations would take place and that the meeting would not be an excuse for the Japanese to make war. Joseph Grew, the American ambassador in Tokyo, believed the meeting should have taken place. Cordell Hull believed it should not, without some agreement beforehand.

Hull later explained to Grew that during the conversations with the Japanese ambassador in Washington, "the Japanese consistently showed that, while they were prepared to give lip service to vague generalities, they were not prepared to give up insistence upon a right to station large bodies of troops in large areas of China for an indeterminate period of time and to give up otherwise their purpose of carrying out the program of general aggression and domination by force on the whole Pacific area."

As the weeks wore on, the Japanese position hardened. From the American point of view any possible advantage to such a meeting seemed less and less likely. Eventually FDR sent Hull a note. "I wholly agree," it said, "with your pencilled note—to recite the more liberal original attitude of the Japanese when they first sought the meeting, point out their much narrowed position now, earnestly ask if they cannot go back to their original attitude, start discussions again on agreement in principle, and re-emphasize my hope for a meeting." The meeting was not held.

This was late in September. By that time any such meeting would have served little purpose. Unknown to FDR, the decision for war had already been made in Japan.

SEPTEMBER: ". . . we will immediately decide to commence hostilities against the United States . . ."

IN SEPTEMBER Japan chose war. She determined that she would not give up her imperialist ambitions in Asia as the United States was demanding, nor would she permit the economic sanctions ordered by FDR to dry up her oil supplies and other resources needed by a warrior nation. The only alternative available to her then was war.

This decision brought Japan's military leaders back to the plan of Admiral Yamamoto's, to attack Pearl Harbor and destroy the American fleet in one surprise move. During the first two weeks of September a war-plans conference was held continuously at the Naval War College in Tokyo. When the conference ended, the plans for the attack against Pearl Harbor were completed. Still, the military leaders were unsure. The element of risk was too great.

But Yamamoto would not be denied his revenge on the "barbarians." He argued, quite correctly, that if the American fleet were not destroyed, it was strong enough to break through any island ring of defenses. That defense ring was the only apparent alternative to the Pearl Harbor attack. When this did not completely convince his fellow officers, Yamamoto threatened to resign unless they accepted his plan. Against these arguments, the plan to attack Pearl Harbor was accepted.

The plan was based on several assumptions: first, that the main body of the American Pacific fleet could be found at Pearl Harbor the day of the attack; second, that a large strike force could move across the northern Pacific without being detected; third, that a reserve force could come to the rescue of the strike carriers if they were detected; and fourth, that the attack could destroy the land-based American airplanes as well as the fleet.

The Japanese then began listening to regular Hawaiian radio broadcasts which reported the movements of the American fleet. Crew members of Japanese ships that stopped at Honolulu were questioned. The Japanese embassy in Washington sent information. Gradually a picture of the American fleet at Pearl Harbor, its size and its scheduling, became available to the Japanese. The War College plans were military preparations only and were dependent upon the political decisions of the men who ruled Japan. But there was no difficulty from that quarter. In Japan there was perhaps only one man who could reverse the militaristic trend of his nation. He was a man of medium height, tending toward heaviness. Then forty years old, he was a devoted family man and fond of his scientific studies. A shy man with a fondness for writing poetry, his name was Hirohito and he was the one hundred and twenty-fourth Emperor of Japan. To the majority of his people he was a direct descendant of the Sun Goddess. To the military leaders of his nation, however, he was a figurehead. He did not rule Japan. They ruled it —in his name.

Whether it had to be like that is a question students of Japan have grappled with for years without producing satisfactory answers. In 1936 Hirohito had challenged his military leaders and done so satisfactorily. The issue then was punishment of a group of military officers convicted of treason. Hirohito insisted their death be by ignominious means; he would not tolerate any of the executed officers becoming martyrs. The military resented this, but made no challenge in the face of the Emperor's insistence. Hirohito would assert himself again in 1945, and again he would triumph over the military. But he did not do so in 1941.

Hirohito's biographer, Leonard Mosley, reports that the Emperor believed he should have blocked the Tripartite Pact with Germany in September, 1940, realizing that the alliance made inevitable Japan's entry into a war with the United States. But in the face of Matsuoka's and Konoye's insistence, the Emperor did accept the treaty. If that analysis is correct, then Hirohito was intensely aware of the repercussions of the diplomatic moves at that point and was also considering his own role in them. No events would take him by surprise.

On September 3, 1941, the Japanese naval chief of staff, Osami

Nagano, explained to his colleagues in the government that, because of American economic sanctions, the Japanese Empire was losing materials needed for its war machine. As time passed, Admiral Nagano explained, Japan would become progressively weaker. "Although I am confident that at the present time we have a chance to win a war," he said, "I fear that this opportunity will disappear with the passage of time." He then insisted that Japan establish a deadline for success at the negotiating table. "We cannot," he said, "let things be dragged out." The government then adopted the following resolution:

In the event that there is no prospect of our demands being met by the first ten days in October through the diplomatic negotiations mentioned above, we will immediately decide to commence hostilities against the United States, Britain, and the Netherlands.

That was the formal decision for war.

Two days later Prince Konoye, the premier, met with the Emperor to explain the policy adopted. Hirohito disagreed with the policy, saying it placed preparations for war over negotiations for peace. Konoye denied that emphasis was put on war. The Emperor then demanded that the military chiefs be brought before him. Of the army chief of staff, General Sugiyama, Hirohito asked how long a Japanese-American war would last. The army leader replied that hostilities in the South Pacific might last about three months.

Hirohito recalled that General Sugiyama had been Minister of War when the China Incident broke out in 1937. At that time, Hirohito continued, Sugiyama had said the China matter would be disposed of in about one month. Despite that assurance offered in 1937, Hirohito said, the incident still continued, after four years of fighting.

The general was startled by the turn of the questioning. He went into a long explanation of how military operations in China were hampered by the extensive land mass. If the Chinese hinterland was extensive, answered the Emperor, raising his voice, the Pacific was boundless. How, he demanded, could the general be so sure of military action ending in only three months? The general made no effort to answer. Admiral Nagano then joined the conversation explaining how bleak were the prospects for Japan. The Emperor asked if it were not true that both of them favored giving precedence to diplomacy. Both answered in the affirmative.

A formal Imperial Conference was held the next day, September 6, at ten o'clock in the morning. The military chiefs were asked if they were giving precedence to diplomatic moves or war preparations. One minister answered that diplomatic moves were being favored. But the Supreme Command—Nagano and Sugiyama, reversing their position of the previous day—remained silent. Suddenly the Emperor spoke up, something that rarely happened at such conferences. He expressed his regret that the members of the Supreme Command had not answered his questions. In the stunned silence that followed, he pulled from his pocket a piece of paper. On it was a poem written by the Emperor's grandfather, the Emperor Meiji. Hirohito read:

> Since all are brothers in this world
> Why is there such constant turmoil?

The Emperor said he hoped to introduce his grandfather's love of peace into the talks and then he lapsed into his traditional imperial silence.

Admiral Nagano was the first to speak. Again he stressed the military leaders' emphasis and hope for diplomatic means of ending the impasse with the United States. Despite what they said to the Emperor that morning, however, the October deadline remained. By that time either Japan would win what it wished at the negotiating table—which was free rein to conquer in the Pacific—or it would go to war. The Emperor made no other effort to stop the move.

In the Japanese government the military had a veto over the civilian. The Japanese constitution, as it had been implemented over the years, required that the cabinet have war and navy ministers, who were, respectively, a general and an admiral. The military groups, if they did not like the premier, simply refused to permit one of their officers to serve in the cabinet as a minister. This had happened in Japan's history, and the result was that the premier could not form a cabinet and a new premier, one more acceptable to the military, had to be appointed.

Joseph Ballantine, a State Department aide with much experience in the Orient, has described the Japanese army in this way:

The Japanese army in Manchuria is quite different from the Japanese army in Japan. You see, those generals were practically viceroys. Complete power. They weren't interfered with. Even the General Staff in Tokyo had no control over them. They had sources of income from various activities, such as narcotics traffic and prostitution and so forth, so they lived—personally they lived spartan lives, but they had that money for enterprises. Now, if a Japanese squad of cavalry felt like taking to the sidewalks instead of the middle of the street, they'd do it with impunity. Or they'd shut off a street if they wanted to. . . . Now, those people in Japan, those Americans who saw the Japanese at home and saw their nice ways, had no idea of the character of this absolute power, where there was no public opinion or social sanctions to curb their influence. There was nothing like that in Japan but in Manchuria the extent to which they could go to suppress any slightest opposition was boundless.

It was these Japanese army men who made up the center of the militaristic circle in Tokyo in the early 1940s. It was these men that Emperor Hirohito would have had to challenge if he had sought to insist on peace.

Hitler watched the course of Japanese-American relations with interest. His attitude toward a war in the Pacific had taken many turns. The German officer corps had a healthy respect for American military prowess, dating back to the First World War, when the Germans had seen the entry of the United States into the war transform a stalemated situation into a military victory for the Allies. They believed that the United States should be kept out of the hostilities until Germany was ready to take her on.

That also had been Adolf Hitler's position at the beginning of the Second World War. He insisted then that his navy not attack American ships in the Atlantic, even though such ships were carrying supplies to England, because he did not wish to provoke the United States into war. He had joined in the Tripartite Pact with Italy and Japan in September, 1940, agreeing to fight the United States if either Japan or Italy were involved in a war with the United States. But that Pact had been mostly bluff on Hitler's part; he had hoped to scare off the United States from assisting England.

In early spring of 1941, Hitler had more adventurous feelings toward the United States. He hoped then Japan would attack British possessions in the Pacific, meaning England would be less able to resist Germany in Europe and also, perhaps, that the

United States might enter the conflict. At the same time Hitler considered occupying the Azores Islands in the Atlantic, to use them as a striking point for long range bombers against the United States. Then came his attack against Russia in June. Wait until Russia is defeated, he said then, before taking on the United States. Besides, if Germany waits long enough, the United States will become so involved with Japan that Germany will have no worries on that score. "The Fuehrer declares in detail," recorded his Navy commandant, "that until Operation Barbarossa [against Russia] is well under way he wishes to avoid any incident with the U.S.A. After a few weeks the situation will become clearer, and can be expected to have a favorable effect on the U.S.A. and Japan. America will have less inclination to enter the war due to the threat from Japan which will then increase." By the fall of 1941, Hitler's position had turned again. He was willing for Japan to take whatever action it wished to, even at the risk of involving the United States in the war. Hitler realized then that a showdown between Germany and the United States, which was supplying the materiel that kept England capable of fighting, must come.

This was dramatized on September 4, 1941, when the American destroyer U.S.S. *Greer* and a German submarine fired at each other. The *Greer* was sailing toward Iceland. A few minutes before nine o'clock in the morning a British plane signaled the *Greer* that a Nazi submarine was submerged about ten miles ahead. The American ship began zigzagging and increased her speed. Forty minutes later her sound gear made contact with the submarine. The *Greer* maintained this sound contact for three hours. At ten o'clock the British airplane asked the *Greer* if she planned to attack. The answer was "no." At that point the British plane dropped its depth charges and flew back to its base for refueling.

More than two hours later the submarine began a series of maneuvers apparently designed to shake the American destroyer. The Americans actually saw signs of the submarine passing, at one point no more than about one hundred yards away. At twelve minutes of one, a sailor aboard the *Greer* spotted some bubbles that could only mean a torpedo had been fired. Flank speed, hard left rudder was ordered and the men of the *Greer* watched as the torpedo passed one hundred yards astern. The ship charged in to attack. She laid a pattern of eight depth charges, and less than two minutes later a second torpedo passed three hundred yards on the port side.

The American destroyer then lost sound contact with the submarine. But after two hours of searching the area, she again picked up the submarine's trail and dropped eleven depth charges. She apparently did not sink the submarine and then lost contact with it. The nineteen depth charges she had dropped were the first weapons deliberately fired by uniformed Americans against Germans. With the German attack on the *Robin Moor* and the contest between the *Greer* and the German submarine, the war at sea was on.

The shooting of the torpedoes at the *Greer*, FDR said, "occurred definitely on the American side of the ocean." The *Greer* was alone at the time and "clearly marked" as an American ship. Had the *Greer* acted within the limits of American policy by firing back when attacked? "What would you do," FDR replied, "if somebody fired a torpedo at you?"

The Germans claimed the *Greer* had fired first. Apparently the submarine had mistaken the depth charges dropped by the British airplane for an attack by the American destroyer; at least that is what the Germans claimed without explaining why the submarine had waited more than two hours before returning fire.

In a fireside chat to the nation the evening of September 11, FDR called the attack on the *Greer* "piracy—piracy legally and morally." In words recommended by Harry Hopkins, Roosevelt said, "When you see a rattlesnake poised to strike, you do not wait until he has struck before you crush him." Then in words inserted by himself, FDR said, "Do not let us be hair-splitters. Let us not ask ourselves whether the Americans should begin to defend themselves after the first attack, or the fifth attack, or the tenth attack, or the twentieth attack. . . . The time for active defense," FDR told the nation, "is now."

He then announced that the United States Navy would protect all merchant ships, whatever their nationality, "engaged in commerce in our defensive waters." The President insisted: "It is no act of war on our part when we decide to protect the seas that are vital to American defense. The aggression is not ours. Ours is solely defense."

The speech became famous as his "shoot on sight" order.

There was much criticism of Roosevelt for this order. Amos

Pinchot, the isolationist, charged in a letter to a friend that the speech "put the Germans in a position where they were amply justified" in shooting first at American ships. Other critics claimed FDR was waging an undeclared war against Germany. Perhaps those charges were true. The alternatives were the likely defeat of England and its potentially disastrous consequences for the United States, and American acquiescence in the invasion of ocean waters vital for American defense and commerce. But the question never answered by FDR's critics was at what point should the United States have stopped German ships? Halfway across the Atlantic? Three-quarters way across? Twenty miles off the coast of the United States? FDR's position was that the United States could tolerate no attack by German ships on American vessels.

The *Greer* incident dramatized two problems confronting the United States. The first was retaining some certainty that American supplies would reach England. During the summer FDR gradually had extended the line in the Atlantic Ocean behind which American naval ships continued "patrolling." British naval losses had been too great to allow England to convoy the merchant ships back and forth across the ocean. The more "patrolling" the United States assumed, the more lend-lease goods would arrive in England. And England still remained the United States' first line of defense; the supplies must get through. The second problem was one of freedom of the seas. The United States could not allow its ships to be fired on. Not only were questions of honor and economics involved, the United States could not permit Germany to coerce it into retreating back across the Atlantic Ocean. If the United States made one step backward, Germany would take two steps forward. That had been her pattern of action with every nation she dealt with since Hitler had come to power.

The *Greer* incident, for Hitler, meant that avoiding the inevitable showdown with the United States would be that much more difficult. If American ships were going to assist supplies to reach England, then Germany must engage those American ships in battle. This would lead to war. Adolf Hitler never had shrunk from the idea of war with the United States; he had hoped for it. The only question for him was one of timing. This was apparent from the Nazi activities in the 1930s.

In 1933, shortly after both FDR and Hitler came to power, an

American diplomat in Berlin reported that "The present German Government and its adherents desire peace ardently for the present because they need peace to carry through the changes in Germany which they want to bring about." The diplomat, George Messersmith, then warned: "What they want to do, however, definitely is to make Germany the most capable instrument of war that there has ever existed."

Through the 1930s the warnings continued. In 1935 the American ambassador to Germany, William E. Dodd, reported to FDR that Europe seemed balanced on the edge of a precipice and that nothing could restrain Hitler.

Not everyone in America accepted this view of Adolf Hitler and the Nazi movement he led, for a curious reason. The Depression that had swept Roosevelt and his New Deal into office in 1933 was a worldwide one. Germany felt it also. By the mid-1930s it appeared that Germany might have solved its problems more effectively with Nazism than had the United States with its potpourri of social-welfare programs. The German nation had no unemployment. The German people were not hungry. Their cities were clean, apparently without serious crime problems, and often most pleasant in appearance. The United States, in contrast, did not appear to have solved similar problems of unemployment, hunger, general poverty, and crime. "You could search far and wide through Berlin's sea of houses or Hamburg's huge harbor district, but you could never find a slum or anything approaching one . . ." wrote a young American reporter in Germany at that time. "Nobody was in rags, not a single citizen. They were well dressed, if not stylishly dressed. And they were well fed." The newsman, Howard K. Smith, dug deeper, however, and found the appearance of well-being a mirage. For Hitler, Smith realized, had solved the problem of unemployment "by exacting more of the people's income through exorbitant taxes and 'voluntary' contributions to phony schemes." And this money was used to buy armaments for Hitler's war machine. The Nazi economic system was not built to improve the welfare of the people or to strengthen the nation in any way except militarily. Its purpose was to wage war. And when it could not find enough nourishment within its own borders, it leaped across geographical and diplomatic barriers to feed from its neighbors.

The Nazi war machine was both an end and a means. It was

designed to conquer, and if it did not conquer then it could not survive. The mainspring of this war machine—the greatest war machine the world had yet known—had been described as "a peculiar fellow" by a First World War comrade. Then in his late twenties, and already with a record as one of life's spectacular failures, Adolf Hitler was a serious person with a long mustache. In the closing days of the First World War, as it became apparent that Germany was losing, other German soldiers began to think of returning home. But not Adolf Hitler. He, instead, sought an excuse for the German failure. For him there must be reasons other than that Germany had been wrong to have begun the war, or the possibility that Germany had waged it badly, or that its enemies had outproduced and outlasted it. There *must* be other reasons.

Throughout history men and nations which are too weak to acknowledge their own failures have turned to scapegoats. So did Hitler. His scapegoat was the Jews. Germany lost the war, he insisted, because the Jews had betrayed it. Over and over he shouted that, until there was no doubt left in his mind. And over and over he shouted that, until there was little doubt left in the minds of his countrymen. People have a tendency to believe what is easy for their egos, if not their intelligence.

Possessed of great oratorical abilities, as well as political craftiness, Hitler organized his own political party. As soon as he had a small following, he constructed an intricate political-military-industrial complex. He provided the political leadership and the organization needed to take command of the country. In exchange he received great personal power and was able to bring the German people toward the realization of the dreams of glory he held for them. The military provided the armed might. In exchange, the military leaders' prestige and power were enhanced as they became a vital ingredient in the fulfillment of Hitler's ambitions. The big businessmen contributed the funds, particularly in the beginning, to finance the whole operation. They realized that once the Nazi war machine began to move, they would reap huge rewards by selling armaments to that machine.

Even for the average citizen, there were tremendous attractions. In addition to the jobs the war-making machine provided, there were recreational events, concerts, and two-week vacations by the sea. And there was something more—a vision of the German astride the world, a vision of the German as master. The

German had been the defeated until Adolf Hitler promised him he could be the conqueror. The German had been the hungry and the cold and the unemployed until Adolf Hitler promised him the food and the riches of others. The German had been afraid until Adolf Hitler gave him a uniform and a gun behind which to hide his fears. And once the war machine did begin to move, the Germans became even more enthusiastic. Howard Smith reported that

In Berlin . . . the first effects of war were not the traditional ones of decay and scarcity, but a sudden leap upwards in visible prosperity. Berlin charwomen and housemaids, whose legs had never been caressed by silk, began wearing silk stockings from the Boulevard Haussmann as an everyday thing—"from my Hans at the front." Little street corner taverns began displaying rows of Armagnac, Martell and Courvoisier cognac from the cellars of Maxim's and others. Every little bureaucrat in the capital could produce at dinner a fine, fat bottle of the best French champagne. The first winter after the Norwegian campaign, the streets were filled with luxurious silver-fox fur coats wrapped around gleeful servant girls. A soldier coming home on leave was a fine sight to see. He carried in addition to his war kit, baskets, big cardboard boxes and cheap suitcases filled to overflowing with all kinds of goodies and luxuries from the front. . . . I am just pointing out what the horrors of war were like in Berlin. War was almost fun; like a football game except that you got more out of it. Shoes, hams, woolen sweaters, fine gowns, everything removable and some things that were not meant to be removed, were drained out of the serf lands with a careless abandon that might have shocked a Roman tyrant.

By the late 1930s Hitler's mustache had been cut back to the more familiar dirty wisp of hair beneath his nose. He was neither tall nor powerfully built, like Italy's Benito Mussolini before the good life available to dictators had sapped him. He was not personable. There was no charm; not even, in those days, much self-confidence. And this was the most frightening thing about him. He had none of the qualities usually associated with great leaders, and yet he was a great leader. His oratory, his craftiness, the demons driving him, combined to make him a leader that Germany neither could, nor wished, to deny.

Hitler would gain self-confidence. As he moved across Europe, diplomatically and militarily besting such nations as Poland, Czechoslovakia, and, especially, the more respected governments of France and England, he acted as if he had greater faith in the Hitler myth of invincibility that he had nurtured. This man planned that someday his Third Reich would extend across the Atlantic Ocean to the United States.

On March 8, 1939, Adolf Hitler met with several of his prominent military and economic officials. Germany, he explained to them, needed raw materials to enjoy a sense of economic health. Then, as one of the officials later confided to an American diplomat, Hitler continued: "In addition, in order to enjoy this well being, enemies of the German people must be exterminated radically: Jews, democracies, and the 'international powers.' As long as these enemies had the least vestige of power left anywhere in the world, they would be a menace to the peace of the German people."

Then Hitler explained his plan of conquest. First, there would be Czechoslovakia. "Poland," he said, "will follow." Next would come Hungary, Romania, then Yugoslavia. "This is the plan," he insisted, "which will be realized by 1940. By then Germany will be unbeatable."

And then?

"Germany," Hitler answered, "will settle accounts once and for all with her hereditary enemy: France. That country will be obliterated from the map of Europe. England is an old feeble country, weakened by democracy." There was a pause, and then Hitler, captivated by the vision before him, continued: "Thus, having for the first time unified the continent of Europe according to a new conception, Germany will undertake the greatest operation in all history: with British and French possessions in America as a base, we will settle accounts with the 'Jews of the dollar' in the United States. We will exterminate this Jewish democracy and Jewish blood will mix itself with the dollars." The harangue and the boasts grew stronger. "Even today, Americans can insult our people," Hitler vowed, "but the day will come when, too late, they will bitterly regret every word they said against us."

The report of that meeting came from William C. Bullitt. Had he been fed a line by some disgruntled official trying, for some unknown reason, to turn the United States against Hitler? Bullitt was one of the more respected members of America's diplomatic corps, as well as one of its most experienced. It was not likely that he could be conned by a self-seeking official. In addition, the story was confirmed—or at least reported again—a year later by Archduke Otto of Austria to Harold Ickes. Against the reports of this meeting, and the reports of many similar vows made over the years by Adolf Hitler, was his public disavowal of interest in the American continent. "America is for the Americans," he told an American newspaper correspondent. "Europe for the Europeans."

Which to believe? The reported remarks made privately or the public comments? Which to believe? That the lust for conquest would go on or that it would suddenly halt?

In 1941, a study made for the American State Department pointed out that Nazism had converted Germany "into an armed camp in which every person is subjected to military discipline and every major economic decision is motivated by military aims." After a lengthy examination of the German economy, the study continued:

Germany's trade with the countries of this hemisphere, although diminished in amount, was . . . used as a means of securing political influence. Moreover, the striving of private enterprise to purchase materials in the most profitable market on a basis of quality and price was overruled by political considerations aiming to secure special privileges for German trade . . . opportunities for that form of "peaceful penetration" which is a forerunner of penetration that is not peaceful. . . .

The entire German nation has been hammered into a machine for conquest. There is no way in which this machine now set in motion can be stopped except either by conquest of the entire world by it or its destruction before that objective is achieved.

If the rulers of Germany should win the present war and enslave not only the inhabitants of Continental Europe but also of the British Isles, they would have at their disposal a system of industrial establishments with a capacity at least equal to our own. It would then be necessary for us in self-defense to give up every hope of even maintaining our present standard of living so long as that menace might last. . . .

There is further reason for believing that a victory in the present war by the present rulers of Germany might be followed by attempted aggression against this country. The rulers of Germany realized before the present war started that Germany with its boundaries of that time could not be self-sufficient in all the requisites of war and cannot be made so. If the rulers of Germany should win the present war they would still be looking for *Lebensraum* in areas which have the material resources that Europe does not possess in sufficient amount.

Many of these resources are found in abundance in the Western Hemisphere—partly in South America, partly in our own country. The urge to conquest would still be present, and it is extremely likely that it would be directed across the Atlantic.

That last paragraph in the State Department report raised the possibility of a potential Nazi attack against the United States sometime in the future, using Latin American nations as a base. It was not a casual observation by an untrained diplomatic observer. There was too much evidence of Nazi penetration into the Latin nations. As Adolf Hitler rose to power in Germany, a deliberate effort was made to encourage Germans living in Latin American nations to reach positions of economic and political influence. To build up the relationship between those Germans living abroad and their native land, the German news service, called Transocean, was made available without charge to those communities large enough to support a German newspaper. German-language broadcasts in Latin America were financed and arranged by the Third Reich. The Latin American nations were looking for experienced military men to build up their armies; German officers were encouraged by their homeland to assist. Young Latin American students and military officers were brought to Germany to study, often at the Nazi government's expense. And while they were studying, the Nazis propagandized them to the glories of the future German world. Latin America needed an airline to link its cities; German money was available to finance it and German pilots were available to fly its planes—and make careful surveys of the terrain.

The German presence in Latin America during the late 1930s could not be ignored. In 1939 a prominent American Catholic priest, Maurice S. Sheehy, visited South America. "I recall the first night I spent in South America, at the Hotel Granada in Maracaibo," he later said, "in which a radio, tuned in only to German broadcasts, vilified the U.S.A. until the early hours of the morning. I saw the evidence of the tons of boiler-plate copy Hitler dumped on the cheaper press of the various countries in his effort to wean them away from a 'good neighbor' status. . . ."

The priest said in 1941 that "I have reason to believe . . . and I rely upon the best Catholic sources for this information, [that] Hitler has won over to the Axis one prominent South American nation."

Enrique S. deLozada, a former Bolivian government official turned American college professor, reported finding much the same thing. After being away from Latin America for two years he returned in 1941.

> What I found there was ominous for the United States. During the twenty-four month interval, the Nazi ideology has gained considerable ground at the expense of hemispheric solidarity. The "good neighbor" policy of Uncle Sam seems to have gone backwards. . . .
> Nazi propaganda flourishes everywhere, with "the Colossus of the North" in the villain's role. The old cry of "Yankee imperialism" has been streamlined by the Goebbels machine to "Yankee-Jewish plutocracy."

More than propaganda was involved. On June 17, 1940, Edwin C. Wilson, the American minister in Montevideo, Uruguay, telephoned Sumner Welles with an urgent message. The Nazis planned to overthrow the Uruguayan government. A dozen conspirators had been arrested; Montevideo was in turmoil. Nazi sympathizers, reinforced by other Nazis from Argentina, were gathering in the city. An uprising was threatened. Wilson's plea: Send a show of American military force. The plea was quickly reported to FDR. Without hesitation Roosevelt, who sometimes had been criticized for not acting fast enough, ordered the cruiser *Quincy*, then sailing off Cuba, to proceed to Montevideo. The uprising was aborted.

That was not an isolated incident. Roosevelt, never quite trusting his State Department, always kept his own lines of communication open. American diplomats were encouraged to write directly to him—friendly, chatty letters, which always produced an answer from him and which kept him informed promptly of what was happening in the world. This made him a one-man funnel for intelligence reports. When there were stories of German officers expected in the French West Indies, the military intelligence agencies learned of these from FDR. The Secretary of War and the Secretary of Navy received their orders direct from the President. "This should be thoroughly investigated by one of the intelligence services," FDR told them, "and should include not only Martinique and Guadeloupe but also the other smaller French Islands and French Guiana." The President added: "This is coming pretty close to home."

There were other very real threats. Early in 1941, the Nazis were ready to move against the Bolivian government. "The situation is ripe for revolt . . ." said one of the Nazi leaders. "I think, however," he added, "July is the most favorable for action." When, at the last moment, the attempt was discovered and aborted, there were five thousand men organized into tight Nazi bands. They controlled newspapers, radio stations, and had gained influence in the army.

There were not only revolts to contend with. In 1940 and 1941, the German movement across Europe appeared unstoppable. Adolf Hitler and his Nazis seemed to be the winners, and everyone wants to be with a winner. Brazil demonstrated that. General Marshall, the Army chief of staff, had visited that nation and found its government friendly toward the United States and responsive to American requests to station ships and soldiers within Brazil's borders. In the fall of 1941, however, the American naval attaché in Rio de Janeiro reported that the same Brazilian government General Marshall had found so friendly had turned decidedly unfriendly. It was, in fact, opposing any further development of the United States military in Brazil. In the months between General Marshall's visit and the attaché's adverse report, Hitler's march of conquest seemed that much stronger, that much more sure of victory, that much more difficult for a shaky political structure in Latin America to oppose.

The events in Latin America—the Nazi economic and propaganda penetration, the growing military influence, and the attempts at revolts—did not happen in a vacuum. They were the means becoming traditional for Nazis. Before military conquest there was economic penetration, propaganda, and political conquest. Only a fool would risk the chance that the United States was not on Hitler's list for conquest.

A Navy captain named Alan G. Kirk was not a fool. Stationed in London as the American naval attaché, he reported that "Safety of the United States would be definitely in jeopardy should British Empire fall, and would expect Italo-German combination to move swiftly in South America and Caribbean areas . . . safety of [the Panama] Canal seems paramount." That last point could not be ignored. Any Nazi incursion into Latin America threatened the Panama Canal, the vital American water link between the Pacific and Atlantic oceans.

Nor was Cordell Hull a fool. "We have irrefutable evidence," the Secretary of State insisted in 1941, "that this hemisphere and this country would be and are in serious and imminent danger." On what basis could the United States expect an attack against the western hemisphere? "It all depends," said the Secretary, "on whether Hitler conquers Great Britain. If he should, he would probably or possibly come into control of the high seas and would make his first attack in South America."

Roosevelt summed up the prospects this way:

If Great Britain goes down, the Axis powers will control the continents of Europe, Asia, Africa, Australasia, and the high seas—and they will be in a position to bring enormous military and naval resources against this hemisphere. It is no exaggeration to say that all of us in the Americas would be living at the point of a gun—a gun loaded with explosive bullets, economic as well as military.

Still, there were those who believed that business could be done with Hitler. Some thought, as did Joe Kennedy, that England was finished. Others conceived of the Nazi movement only as a bulwark against communism and the Soviet Union. They could have read with great profit some words written by Joe Kennedy's son, John F. Kennedy, a young man who had spent time in England when his father was ambassador there. John Kennedy had studied carefully the political problems in England during the late 1930s. Why, he wanted to know, did England sleep while Nazi Germany prepared for war?

The answer appeared first as a Harvard University thesis and then as a book entitled *Why England Slept*. "I am not an alarmist," wrote this young man, then barely more than twenty years of age. "I do not believe necessarily that if Hitler wins the present war he will continue on his course towards world domination. He may well be too exhausted, or he may be satisfied with what he has obtained. But . . ." and this was the significant warning "in the light of what has happened in the last five years, we cannot depend on it. A defeat of the Allies may simply be one more step towards the ultimate achievement—Germany over the world." And then Kennedy cautioned: "Therefore, if Hitler succeeds in winning the present war, the position of America will be remarkably similar to that of England during the last decade."

Saul Friedlander, one of the most careful students of American-Nazi relations in the early 1940s, has observed:

From the summer of 1940 on, one of the chief aims of German strategy and foreign policy was to prevent the United States from entering the war. . . . The whole of Hitler's policy points to his full awareness of the importance of the American factor in the event of a long war.

This does not challenge, however, what could be the only conclusion available to Franklin Roosevelt in 1941, and available also to reasonable men, based on the evidence and the facts before them, then and later. The question was not would Germany make war against the United States, rather it was *when* would Germany make war against the United States: before or after England fell? There may have been, if England fell to Germany, a change of intention on the part of the Nazi leaders, but as John Kennedy pointed out, "We cannot depend on it."

But many seemed willing to depend upon it. To FDR the rapidly developing dangers from abroad were real. "We, and all others who believe as deeply as we do," he said, "would rather die on our feet than live on our knees." And then on Labor Day he warned that "The task of defeating Hitler may be long and arduous. There are a few appeasers and Nazi sympathizers who say it cannot be done. They even ask me to negotiate with Hitler—to pray for crumbs from his victorious table. . . ." To others, however, the danger abroad did not seem very real. Charles Lindbergh appeared considerably more popular with the American public than did FDR. Walter Lippmann, even then perhaps America's most distinguished columnist, echoed the noninterventionist approach. The American army, he wrote in September, should be decreased in size and the United States should "concentrate our major effort upon the Navy, the air force and lend-lease." He was saying, in effect, that the United States should arm England and Russia and worry then only about an invasion of continental America. This was the concept known as "fortress America." Congress seemed disposed to heed the popularity of Lindbergh as well as the leadership of such intellectuals as Lippmann. Despite the unanimous military opinion about the necessity for extending the draft, for example, the House of Representatives had done so only by the narrowest of votes the previous month.

Domestic matters and routine jobs were shunted aside as the President turned almost all of his attention to the problem of grappling with the threat of war. His face became even more lined; the shadows under his eyes darkened. And then in September he was struck by two personal tragedies, and the always cheerful Franklin Roosevelt, for a brief moment, dropped his mask of ebullience.

On September 7, the President's mother, Sara Delano Roosevelt, died. The President and she had been very close, and he felt her death deeply. Almost three weeks later, on September 25, the President's brother-in-law, G. Hall Roosevelt, also died. He was Eleanor Roosevelt's only brother, and his funeral service was held in the East Room of the White House.

The day of the funeral, Friday, September 26, Felix Frankfurter received a telephone call from a White House assistant. Could the Supreme Court Justice come to see the President at 3:30 that afternoon, after the funeral? Of course Frankfurter could come. He arrived at the White House and was shown into the presidential office. FDR and he chatted casually for a few minutes while the President had his hair cut. "The President seemed under considerable strain and plainly enough he just wanted to talk," Frankfurter later wrote. After the barber left, FDR continued prattling for a few moments longer. The President had just received a letter pointing out that a local park had statues of four revolutionary war heroes and also one of Andrew Jackson. The President said he was directing that the Jackson statue be removed to preserve historical symmetry—but some other time, when money was more readily available. Then the President came to the main point of concern to him that afternoon.

"This leads me to say something that I want you to remember," he said to Frankfurter, "because you are much more likely to be here longer than I shall be."

Frankfurter laughed. "You mean," he answered, "that I shall remain on the Supreme Court longer than you will remain in the White House." Both men had been born in 1882.

The President smiled, but there also was a sharp tone in his voice as he answered. "No," he said, "that isn't what I mean at all. I mean in plain English that I am likely to shuffle off long before you kick the bucket. And if that should happen and if any memorial is to be erected to me, I know exactly what I should like it to be. Now please remember what I am telling you as my wish in case they are to put up any memorial to me. About half way between here and the Capitol is the Archives building. Now I have some relation to archives. And right in front of the

Archives building is a little green triangle. If, as I say, they are to put up any memorial to me, I should like it to be placed in the center of that green plot in front of the Archives building. I would like it to consist of a block about the size of this," and he placed his hands on his desk. "I don't care what it is made of, whether limestone or granite or whatnot, but I want it to be plain, without any ornamentation, with the simple carving 'In memory of. . . .' That is all, and please remember that, if the time should come."

"I shall indeed remember," Frankfurter answered, "and you deeply honor me in putting this wish in the keeping of my memory."

"Don't you think I am right in wanting that kind of a memorial and none other?" Roosevelt asked.

Frankfurter answered, "The founder of your party, Jefferson, left specific instructions for that beautifully simple memorial of his at Charlottesville, and I think your idea entirely comports with wisdom about such things."

When the Supreme Court Justice left the White House a few minutes later, he quickly penciled some notes of his meeting with the President. The next day he dictated an account of that session from those handwritten notes. The story, which Frankfurter was at such pains to report accurately, shows FDR for a moment turning away from world concerns to thoughts of himself. He was aware, at the age of fifty-nine, that he was engaged in what most likely would be a killing regime. With the two personal losses coming so close and weighing so heavily upon him, he acknowledged the consequences of that regime.

But such moments of personal concern could be permitted only occasionally. The President must cope with problems not of his making, and such problems left him little time for personal cares—particularly in the fall of 1941. Robert Sherwood reports that by this time the President was being pulled strongly in two directions, by the interventionists, such as Henry Stimson who wanted him to take bolder action, and by the noninterventionists, who wished him to relax his measures against the Axis powers. Roosevelt tried to resist both. The interventionists, he knew, would lead the United States into a war that the nation did not want and could not fight. The others would make the world safe for a Nazi-dominated holocaust which the United States probably could not survive.

FDR could handle the interventionists. They could cry for greater action, but only FDR could order greater action. He could not handle the noninterventionists so well, however. Roosevelt and most open-minded observers could see the war threat developing in both Germany and Japan, but America First by early September was doing an effective job in convincing the American public that the threat of war was not a serious one. America First, originally, tried to increase isolationist sentiment through the mails. Wayne Cole reports that while Gerald Nye's

greatest contribution to America First was as a speaker, he also co-operated in other ways. For example, like Wheeler and others, Nye let the committee representatives go through letters he received to prepare mailing lists of noninterventionists for use by America First. He made available at cost noninterventionist material reprinted from the *Congressional Record*. When ordered by America First chapters and others, these materials were sent in franked, sealed envelopes that could then be mailed without postage. Thousands of pieces of noninterventionist literature were distributed in this way.

The recipients of this literature were, in turn, urged to write to their representatives in Congress. "Letters or such cards as this," said one America First memorandum, "sent promptly to Congress may save your country." The sample read:

Britain today is the accomplice of Russia and this administration would have us become accomplices too.
Do you love Your United States?
Then save her from bondage.
The greatest threat to the United States is this administration; its gradual take over of industry and private wealth. This hushed, but Colossal Danger is now at work, already far advanced by strikes, which provide momentary excuse leading to the one sad end: Complete control of Labor, as of the Army; after which there will be no more strikes and no more walkouts—and no more United States.
Will this land of the free and home of the brave be so enslaved? Wake Up—You Stupid Americans, drugged by a dulcet voice, government controlled jobs, venial press and radio, and royal emissaries and visitors. . . .

But more than the mail campaigns and the newspaper advertisements, the rallies sponsored by the America First Committee were what gave the group its reputation for having touched a strong point in the American consciousness. Across the nation, in large cities and small, senators like Burton Wheeler and Gerald Nye, and public figures like author Kathleen Norris and Lindbergh, drew audiences in the thousands. "Keep us out of war!" chanted the speakers. And the crowds roared back approval. Radio stations broadcast the speeches. Newspapers reported them. The membership of the America First Committee may never have gone over a million at its best times, but the Committee's impact stretched to many millions.

There were a variety of reasons for this reaction, beyond the basic one of so many persons being opposed to war. Many followers of the Committee were not so much opposed to FDR's foreign policy as they were opposed to FDR. Criticizing his foreign policy was a means of branding him. He was leading the nation toward war while claiming to lead it toward peace, they charged. The European war, went this charge against FDR, was only an excuse for him to create a fascistic type dictatorship in the United States. Philip LaFollette, of the Wisconsin political family, gave a speech in the fall of 1941 that was typical. "Two years ago," he said, "the President and the War Party launched us on a course of action labelled 'steps short of war' to 'keep us out of war.' That was the most cunning of the many deceitful phrases employed in the propaganda campaign to get us into this war. . . . Every step taken in the past two years has been put over on us by the same fraudulent methods practiced by the European dictators." Particularly with Wendell Willkie, the titular leader of the Republican Party, supporting FDR's foreign policies and actually pushing for Roosevelt to assume even greater powers, the America First Committee became in 1941 the major organization attacking FDR.

In addition to using the Committee to attack FDR, others saw it as a means of attacking England. Great Britain had many friends in the United States, and it also had many enemies. The war in Europe, to England's enemies, was only a power struggle, and the United States would be better off outside of it entirely. That was the argument used against the lend-lease program early in 1941 by the America First Committee. The Committee did not take a formal position against the extension of the draft in 1941, but it made clear its informal position opposing the extension. Many of its officers spoke against the draft extension.

Also the America First Committee had considerable support

from pacifists, those who opposed the United States entering any war at any time. That was not the America First position; the Committee, for example, endorsed the concept of responding against attack and of defending the western hemisphere. Still it was opposing America's entry into the European war and that was enough to attract the pacifists to it—particularly because America First seemed to be attracting more prestigious names and more money and having a much greater impact than the older peace groups which had been around too long to have much glamor left.

Administration members did speak out against the isolationist movement. Frank Knox criticized the America First Committee before an American Legion convention. America First "was roundly booed," Knox reported, "and my appeal for support for the administration's national policies was unanimously adopted." Knox concluded in the fall of 1941 that "a good many of the isolationists are now running to cover." He made that report to an Englishman who probably needed the encouragement. In the United States there did not seem to be any great scurrying for shelter on the part of the isolationists.

Republicans like Knox, and perhaps Stimson, could be used against other Republicans, to blunt their criticisms of the FDR foreign policies, but only Roosevelt himself had the national prestige to take on the America First Committee, with its popularity extending through all parts of the nation, all economic groups, with its support from members of all political, ethnic, and religious faiths. America First was truly a national movement. Although small in terms of membership when compared against the United States' population, the diligence and brilliance of its leaders made it a most effective organization. But because FDR was the object of the America First attacks, he could not answer them effectively. Any answer from him, any counter-challenge he leveled seemed too self-serving in light of the charges against him of seeking greater political power. He could not defeat America First. America First must defeat itself.

This it did.

Back in January, John O'Connor had lamented that the isolationist movement lacked a leader, an articulate, fiery, and prestigious personality. The members of the movement had searched for such a man in late 1940 and early 1941. They found him in Charles Augustus Lindbergh, Jr.

As the "Lone Eagle," he had flown across the Atlantic Ocean in 1927 from obscurity to fame and wealth. The nickname "Lucky Lindy" was his. But he had not been lucky as much as he had been careful, intelligent, and prudent. That those qualities deserve more admiration than luck was overlooked as the American public sought a folk hero for the time and picked the lean, handsome, and charming Lindbergh for the role. The hero image continued as the "all-American" boy Lindbergh romanced and wed beautiful and wealthy Anne Morrow. Entering the airline business, Lindbergh became personally wealthy. Never had the American success story been so beautifully played out.

The people of the United States cannot leave their successes alone, and this was true with Lindbergh. The intrusions into Lindbergh's privacy stretched beyond the decent. When his family was engulfed by a great tragedy—the kidnapping and murder of his infant son—the public wallowed in his grief.

In the mid-1930s Charles Lindbergh and his family left the United States to live in Europe. Whatever bitterness he held could be understood. In addition to his charm, his courage, and his prudence—as well as his sadness—there were other qualities that appeared occasionally in Lindbergh that were less flattering. In the early 1930s the Congress was investigating the awarding of air mail contracts to certain airlines. Lindbergh was involved in the dispute with Congress. There was no suggestion of impropriety on Lindbergh's part, but many believed, as Felix Frankfurter did, that Lindbergh "is plainly the dupe of others."

During the mid-1930s Lindbergh became associated with Dr. Alexis Carrel, a brilliant scientist who had won many deserved international honors, including a Nobel Prize, for his medical explorations. Dr. Carrel had discovered a new way of sewing together the ends of an artery and had been associated in the perfecting of an antiseptic solution for wounds. In the 1930s he was working with the Rockefeller Institute in New York City on the cultivation of organs outside the body. He and Lindbergh worked together on the development of a perfusion pump, which was commonly and inaccurately described as an artificial heart. Perhaps because he was so brilliant Dr. Carrel had a disdain for those less than brilliant. Moving outside the medical area, he preached that all men are not equal—there are different levels of intelligence—and therefore they should neither be equal before the law nor have the same opportunities for education and suffrage. His message was not that the intelligent should rule but that they should dictate. He and Lindbergh were friends through the 1930s. As late as 1948, in a little-known book *Of Flight And Life*, Lindbergh still showed signs of Carrel's influence.

Lindbergh went to Germany in 1936 at the invitation of Colonel Truman Smith, the military attaché at the American Embassy in Berlin. Smith was concerned about the quality of information going to the United States about Germany's rearmament efforts, particularly the development of its air force. One morning while at breakfast, his wife read an item in a Paris newspaper about Lindbergh visiting a French airplane factory. If Lindbergh could visit French airplane factories, Smith thought, why not German ones? Smith wrote Lindbergh and asked him to come to Berlin. Lindbergh was a reserve colonel in the Army Air Corps and came as a military duty, according to Smith. The Germans were flattered to show off their growing air power to the world's most famous flyer, and Lindbergh was shown more than most Americans had seen of Germany's growing armaments industry. According to Smith, every morning of Lindbergh's visit, Lindbergh, Smith, and the embassy's air attaché met and reviewed the observations made by Lindbergh the previous day. These observations became the nucleus of reports sent to Washington.

Lindbergh made a second trip to Germany, in 1937. Again he toured German airplane factories and again he made valuable observations which became parts of reports to Washington. Smith reported to Washington that Germany must once again be considered a major air power. This was done on the basis of information supplied to him by Lindbergh. If the warnings Lindbergh's information implied had been heeded, the Second World War might have been a far different battle. In 1938, for example, he informed France that Germany had eight thousand warplanes and could build fifteen hundred a month. That same year he made much the same report to Joe Kennedy, then the United States ambassador in England. Through Kennedy's intervention, Lindbergh was formally able to present his impressions to the British government. Britain did not heed his warning as France did not.

The United States paid somewhat more attention. Charles Sorensen, the Ford Motor Company official who presided over Ford's entry into the warplane industry, used Lindbergh as a consultant and gives him much credit for the success of the air-craft produced at Willow Run. Sorensen also reports that General Henry H. "Hap" Arnold, head of the Army Air Corps, informed him that much of the Army's modernization of its air power after 1938 was the result of information supplied by Lindbergh.

In addition to the technical information he brought back, however, Lindbergh returned from Germany with a conviction that Germany was too powerful to fight. That is what he told Joe Kennedy. A European war must be avoided, said Lindbergh, otherwise European civilization would be destroyed and communism would overtake the continent. England and France simply did not have the air power to stand before Germany, Lindbergh told the ambassador in a formal report dated September 22, 1938. How much this report influenced Joe Kennedy's own opinion that England was finished—an opinion that destroyed his usefulness as ambassador—is not known.

Three years later, in 1941, when England at least had shown some ability to resist Nazism, Lindbergh was not willing to surrender the conviction of England's vulnerability voiced three years earlier.

My first realization of the dangers and problems that lay ahead came with a trip I made to Germany in 1936. . . . It was clear to me, at that time, that Germany had, or would soon have, by far the strongest army and air force in the world, and that she intended to use her military forces to increase her influence and expand her territory. Probably even more significant than the size of her army and air force was the fact that the people of Germany were ready for war, while the people of France and England were not. . . .

My estimate of the situation in Europe, and the best policy to follow, was different than that of most of my friends. After the Siegfried line was built, I knew that the French and British armies were no longer in a position to attack Germany successfully. I knew that the German air force was stronger than any combination that could be brought against it, and that England was in a disadvantageous position from the standpoint of air power. Hitler held weapons which Napoleon had lacked. He had aviation with which to strike at England and the British Navy, and he had modern communication and mechanical transport with which to overcome the great distances of Russia. It seemed obvious to me that these weapons changed the military balance and strategy not only of Europe but of the entire world.

By 1938, I had come to the conclusion that if a war occurred be-

tween Germany on one side, and England and France on the other,
it would result either in a German victory, or in a prostrate and
devastated Europe. I therefore advocated that England and France
build their military forces with the utmost rapidity, but that they permit Germany to expand eastward into Russia without declaring war.

Lindbergh's suggestion was that the Western powers permit
Germany to devour Russia while building up their own forces so
that, once Russia was defeated, Germany would not turn on
them. There is a cynicism to the suggestion. There also is a
naïveté—a naïveté that would show again and again as Lindbergh became more and more a spokesman for nonintervention.
If Hitler had succeeded in conquering Russia, the industrial resources and raw materials available to him would have meant
that no country could have stood before him.

While in Germany, in addition to gaining facts about German
military preparations and an impression of the strength of German air power, Lindbergh also was decorated by the German
government. This happened during his third visit, in October,
1938. It was one of the two most controversial events of his life.
The presentation took place at a dinner given by American ambassador Hugh Wilson for Hermann Goering, head of the Luftwaffe. There is a general acceptance of some of the facts in
this incident and a dispute over others. Lindbergh was surprised
at being presented with the decoration, which was the Service
Cross of the Order of the German Eagle with Star, Germany's
second highest decoration. That Lindbergh was unaware that
the decoration was to be presented to him is acknowledged. Truman Smith, writing of the incident about fifteen years later and
relying on his memory, reported that his office had been telephoned that afternoon and informed that the decoration would
be made. No officer was present at the time, he wrote, and the
secretary who took the message did not deliver it until the next
morning—when it was too late. There also seems to be agreement that Lindbergh, appearing at a diplomatic dinner, could
not refuse to accept the medal. The United States and Germany
did have diplomatic relations at the time. A war was not being
fought. The extent of the German barbarities against the Jews
was not yet understood. In 1941, when Lindbergh had come
under attack for having accepted the medal, Ambassador Wilson wrote him a letter saying to have rejected the decoration
would have been a breach of good taste.

There was more disagreement over why Lindbergh was present at the dinner. According to Smith, Wilson wanted to use
Lindbergh as bait to lure Goering to the dinner. Wilson hoped
to discuss with Goering ways of assisting German Jews and believed such a dinner would be the best way. Lindbergh himself
has said that assisting the ambassador was the motive for his presence. In 1941, when Harold Ickes was leading the Lindbergh
critics, Lindbergh wrote an open letter to the President. "Is it too
much to ask that you inform your Secretary of Interior that I was
decorated by the German Government while I was carrying out
the request of your Ambassador to that Government?" read
the letter. A week later, Ickes countered this by quoting a report made by Ambassador Wilson a few days after the dinner.
The report reads that "Colonel Lindbergh was in the city. He was
especially interested in meeting those persons responsible for
the development of the air forces. General Field Marshal Goering is chief of the air force. Hence he was present at my dinner,
as well as other leading members of this arm of the service."
That report does not deny but does contain the implication that
the Smith-Lindbergh account is inaccurate.

By 1941 there was even greater criticism of Lindbergh for
not returning the medal, which was in a St. Louis museum
along with decorations from many other nations. Lindbergh refused to return the medal and did not offer any explanation for
his refusal. He probably understood, correctly, that if he had
done so, his action would have been read as a surrender to the
demands of the Roosevelt administration and the others Lindbergh considered war advocates.

Also, Lindbergh was a proud man, as well as a brave one, who
was coming under increasing attack in the United States and
probably did not wish to concede he could be hurt. Some years
later he wrote Truman Smith that he did not believe the German medal caused him much difficulty. Lindbergh described
the medal, in that letter to Smith, as only a convenient object of
attack for his opponents. If there had been no decoration, Lindbergh claimed, his enemies would have found something else to
criticize him for. Perhaps. The night he received the medal, it has
been reported, his wife referred to it as "the albatross." Mrs.
Lindbergh's description of the medal's impact on her husband's
reputation is more accurate than Lindbergh's.

By 1939 Charles Lindbergh was a confirmed advocate of
nonintervention and was speaking prominently in the United

States against intervention. He was popular, appeared idealistic, and still had the aura of the "Lone Eagle" and "Lucky Lindy" hero about him. Felix Frankfurter was one of many interventionists who found Lindbergh's stature discouraging. "I think the time has come to treat with less romantic respect Colonel Lindbergh's views on issues for which mechanical skill and intrepidity are not adequate qualifications," Frankfurter said to a friend. "I am credibly informed that Lindbergh is in close communication with Senators Borah, Clark and Nye, and is likely to make continuing difficulty." The extent of that difficulty could not be grasped in 1939.

That Lindbergh developed as an advocate of nonintervention was not such a surprise to those who knew him. He had come out of the Midwest with its strongly isolationist tendencies. Also his father, Charles A. Lindbergh, Sr., had been identified with pacifism during the First World War. The senior Lindbergh had been a member of Congress then and strongly opposed American intervention. "No one can walk or march here to invade us," he said, "they must swim or fly if they come."

The senior Lindbergh believed that the mass of Americans had become "industrial slaves" and deserved a better economic deal than they were receiving. As for the war, it was only a means to make the rich richer. "Amid all the confusion, the lords of special privilege stand serene in their selfish glee, coining billions of profits from the rage of war, in shoving up the price of stocks and the cost of living," the senior Lindbergh said in Congress in 1916. "They coldly register every volley of artillery, every act of violent aggression, as a profit on their war stocks and war contracts, and discourage in every way possible any attempts to secure peace." When these views were collected in a book written by the senior Lindbergh and scheduled for publication while the United States was in the First World War, government agents entered the printing house and destroyed the page plates.

But if Charles Lindbergh was influenced by his father's pacifism, he did not appear struck by his concern for the masses. The 1941 edition of *Current Biography* reported that "Critics of Colonel Lindbergh, however, have looked in vain in his speeches for the same preoccupation with the 'little man'; the one thing he has yet to be called is Bolshevik." And William Allen White, whose experience and memory included the First World

War, commented to a friend that "It is sad beyond words that the son of a pacifist should become an imperialist."

Whatever Lindbergh's philosophy at the time, besides being an advocate of nonintervention, was difficult to determine. The Carrel theory of the superiority of the intellectual appeared to have had some impact. The visits to Germany may have had an influence also. Germany during the late 1930s had an orderly look to it. Some glimpse into his thinking of the time, or of the thinking that influenced him, may come from a thin book written by his wife Anne Morrow Lindbergh called *The Wave of the Future*. The book was published in 1940 and became a minor bible of the isolationist movement. In many ways it is a moving document by a sensitive writer. Reading it at one level, one comes away from it with a feeling that Mrs. Lindbergh is appealing for an improvement in the lives of Americans so the United States can avoid the cataclysmic changes that were then engulfing Europe. But there are other parts that seem less sensitive and more obtuse. She denied that the war in Europe was a conflict between good and evil. Mrs. Lindbergh asked if the barbarities and cruelties of the war were not merely the excesses of a new movement, perhaps a better way of life to come. While condemning the excesses, she said, perhaps the wave of the future should be at least acknowledged, studied, waited for. But she did not make a very convincing case. She cited the French Revolution as an example of violence giving birth to a welcome new order. But Mrs. Lindbergh did not suggest that the Nazi movement had raised any standard equivalent to the "liberty, equality, and brotherhood" motivation of the French Revolution. In her book she wondered if some new economic and social forces had not been discovered by Germany, but she made no effort to define what they might be.

She was not alone in this. Many people examined the orderly columns of German economic statistics and came to the same conclusion. Otto Nathan, an economist, wrote in 1944 that "Our horror and indignation at the insufferable brutality of Naziism, our complete rejection of all it stands for, should not obscure the *possible* importance of the economic experiments carried out under Fascist auspices, experiments which may take on new value and significance in a different political atmosphere."

But Nathan, like Mrs. Lindbergh, was seeing what he wanted to see. There were no new forces in Germany. The economic

philosophy in effect there was the old one of gearing an economy toward war. Make the nation into a war machine, then
conquer to feed that machine. Nor were the social forces new,
as Mrs. Lindbergh suggested. They were the old ones of racial
superiority, of inequality, of justice for some men and injustice
for others.

Mrs. Lindbergh concluded that the wave of the future could
not be stopped. To stand before it, she said, would be to risk
being ground into the sand.

There is almost an unreality to the Lindberghs and the other
isolationists. As long as the United States is not involved, they
argued, war is acceptable. Lindbergh wanted Hitler to fight
Russia and Burton Wheeler advocated that the United States
stand by while Stalin and Hitler destroy each other. And of
course, they all were sure, the United States need never be involved. The act of military aggression was a national code of
conduct that need produce only frowns from the United States
—until, of course, the aggression produced a crossing of the
American border. But it never would. They all were sure of
that. Oppression and murder of peoples may have been tragic,
but it was none of America's business—and, of course, the
virulence of genocide would stay neatly restricted within one
nation's boundaries.

The isolationists were betting that the tomorrow which was
engulfing Europe never would come to the United States. It
was a bet they might have won. But it also was a bet they might
have lost. As John Kennedy wrote at that time, Hitler might not
cross the Atlantic, but "in the light of what has happened in the
last five years, we cannot depend on it." In contrast to the isolationists, Franklin Roosevelt at this time was considering having
American airplane factories built west of the Allegheny Mountains and east of the Rocky Mountains to protect them from air
attack. He did not know then that Germany was ahead in the
development of an atomic bomb and that it would lead the world
in the development of rockets. Nor could he be certain that, if
England fell, Germany and Japan would cross the oceans to the
United States. But, as President, he could not bet that all of those
things would not happen. The isolationists could. The President
could not.

A bitterness toward Lindbergh had been developing within
Roosevelt for some time. At a Cabinet meeting in 1939, Acting

Secretary of the Navy Charles Edison had told the story of
Lindbergh and the German medal, but said that Lindbergh accepted the medal because he did not know what to do with
it. The President growled that *he* would have known what to do
with it! At that Cabinet meeting there was discussion of Lindbergh's losing his status as an officer in the Army Air Corps. It
was known that he planned to make a speech over radio, his first
one calling for a policy of nonintervention and attacking FDR's
policies. Secretary of War Woodring said Lindbergh had refused to submit his speech for clearance to the War Department
as required. The speech was given, but Lindbergh did not lose
his commission. During the next two years, even as his criticisms
of the Roosevelt policies became more frequent and stronger, his
commission was not revoked. He was too popular a figure to
punish in such a manner.

FDR had no affection for him. He realized that Lindbergh
was probably the one man who could lead the isolationist movement. He was not a politician, was not identified with any political party. He could not be faulted on that score. He came to
his position of leadership with some goodwill built in among the
American people. They admired his flight across the Atlantic in
1927, revered his success story, felt sorry for the tragedy of the
loss of his son. As a public speaker, the leader of a cause, he was
a relatively fresh face. Just turning forty, he was handsome and
retained much of the boyish charm that had first endeared him
to America. Also he could not be attacked for having any personal
motives. His advocacy of nonintervention would earn him applause from his fellow believers perhaps, but nothing else. Occasionally there were reports in the news media that Lindbergh
had political ambitions. Before the Republican nominating convention in 1940, Father Charles Coughlin's newspaper *Social
Justice* came out for a ticket of Wendell Willkie and Charles
Lindbergh. But no one took that ticket possibility or that en-
dorsement too seriously. The next year *The Nation* magazine
reported that Lindbergh was interested in entering politics. "Political circles there [Minnesota]," *The Nation* said, "feel certain
that Lindbergh will seek the Republican nomination for the
United States Senate in 1942." By the end of 1941, Dorothy
Thompson was writing, and *Look* magazine was printing, that
Lindbergh "has a notion to be our Fuehrer."

But these sporadic reports and charges did not tarnish the

image of Lindbergh as an idealistic young man without selfish motives. That made him a difficult man to beat, and this angered Franklin Roosevelt.

Hugo L. Black, who as a senator and then as an associate justice of the Supreme Court knew FDR well, has described him as "our greatest man" at the time. Even those who would agree with that description, however, acknowledge that FDR was also a man with faults. At times he would soar to peaks of egotism and at other times he would sink to unfortunate levels of pettiness. He would do this in dealing with Lindbergh. At a news conference in April, a reporter asked, "How is it that the Army, which needs now distinguished fliers, has not asked Colonel Lindbergh to rejoin?"

FDR perked up as a second newsman reported, "If I am not mistaken, I think [Lindbergh] is still on the reserve list."

"Still?" said FDR.

A third reporter said that he understood Lindbergh had resigned as a member of the service. FDR said he did not know. Actually, Lindbergh still held his rank in the reserve. FDR paused for a moment, and then all the dislike and all the anger at Lindbergh, all the pique and concern at the isolationist movement began to tumble from him. Being FDR, however, he neither swore nor shrieked. He told a story.

If you go back to the roster of the Army in the Civil War, we called on people there from liberty-loving people on both sides—both the Confederates and the North; and from outside this country we had people fighting for us because they believed in it. On the other hand, the Confederacy and the North let certain people go. In other words, in both armies there were—what shall I call them?—there were Vallandighams. Vallandigham.

The President was referring to Clement L. Vallandigham, the leader of those Northerners who sympathized with the South during the Civil War—the "copperheads." FDR continued:

Well, Vallandigham, as you know, was an appeaser. He wanted to make peace from 1863 on because the North "couldn't win." Once upon a time there was a place called Valley Forge and there were an awful lot of appeasers that pleaded with Washington to quit, because he "couldn't win." Just because he couldn't win. See what Tom Paine said at that time in favor of Washington keeping on fighting!

FDR had a chance to back off a few moments later when a newsman asked him, "Were you still talking about Mr. Lindbergh?"

The President would not back off. "Yes," he answered.

His friends among the newsmen in his office that morning joined in the laughter. But that was where the laughter over this incident ended. The reputations of the two men involved, Roosevelt and Lindbergh, were both tarnished by that remark. The publicity given to the FDR remark was sensational. It made the front pages of most newspapers, dominated the radio newscasts. Three days later Lindbergh sent the following letter, which he made public, to the President:

Your remarks at the White House press conference on April 25th, involving my reserve commission in the United States Army Air Corps, have of course disturbed me greatly. I had hoped that I might exercise my rights as an American citizen, to place my viewpoint before the people of my country in time of peace, without giving up the privilege of serving my country as an Air Corps officer in the event of war.

But since you, in your capacity as President of the United States and Commander-in-Chief of the Army, have clearly implied that I am no longer of use to this country as a reserve officer, and in view of other implications that you, my President and my superior officer, have made concerning my loyalty to my country, my character, and my motives, I can see no honorable alternative to tendering my resignation as Colonel in the United States Army Air Corps Reserve. I am, therefore, forwarding my resignation to the Secretary of War.

I take this action with the utmost regret, for my relationship with the Air Corps is one of the things that has meant most to me in life. I place it second only to my right as a citizen to speak freely to my fellow countrymen, and to discuss with them the issues of war and peace which confront our nation in this crisis.

I will continue to serve my country to the best of my ability as a private citizen.

The reaction to the spat between the two men was divided. The Newark, New Jersey, *Star-Ledger* editorialized against Lindbergh. "Lindbergh is no longer a Colonel in our armed forces," it said, "but he remains the wearer of Reichsfuehrer Adolf Hitler's *Verdienstkreuz*, the second highest decoration within the gift of Hitler. For his latest action, Lindbergh deserves a promotion—from Hitler." That kind of talk was fed

by the White House. "I understand from the press that Colonel
Lindbergh is returning his commission to the Secretary of War,"
said Steve Early to newsmen. "That leads me to wonder whether
he is returning his decoration to Hitler."

But most of the reaction then, and later, was critical of FDR.
The President's old friend, William Allen White, summed it up in
an editorial in his newspaper, the *Emporia Gazette*, when he
wrote:

> Each crowd—the isolationists and the interventionists—have the same
> idea, the retention of liberty in our land. Indeed, the whole criticism
> of the President rests on the fact that by applying the term "copper-
> head" to Lindbergh, the President revealed an unconscious intolerance
> which frightens people, makes them fear something pretty terrible
> ahead! It must have been a slip of the tongue. It must have been
> the petulance of a tired moment, the acrimony of a harried and bewil-
> dered man. But it hurt his cause by frightening lovers of freedom who
> feared for the President's tolerance at some future time of crisis
> and actual danger to freedom.

White's analysis was a valid one. It was even more effective
because White was known as an FDR crony, an internationalist,
and not as a friend of Lindbergh's.

That Lindbergh and the America First movement ultimately
came together was natural. The movement needed a leader.
Lindbergh needed a movement behind him. "As you know,"
Douglas Stuart wrote to Amos Pinchot in May, "Charles A. Lind-
bergh has recently joined the National Commitee [of America
First], and the response that has greeted him in Chicago, New
York, and St. Louis is one of the most phenomenal expressions
of public opinion in the history of the country." Lindbergh, as
Frankfurter had pointed out in 1934, had the failing of permit-
ting himself to become the "dupe" of others. During the next
few months he became responsive to the suggestions of Amos
Pinchot.

Then in his late sixties, Pinchot was a New York lawyer who
had a reputation as a liberal. He had fought in the Spanish-
American War, been a supporter of Theodore Roosevelt and his
Progressive Party, then had been a founder of the American
Civil Liberties Union as well as a supporter of Franklin Roosevelt's presidential candidacy in 1932. But like many wealthy
businessmen, Pinchot gradually realized that FDR was interested
not only in emergency economic action with which to fight the

Depression but also in permanent domestic reform. And like many of his contemporaries, Pinchot broke with FDR. An isolationist, as well as an FDR opponent, Pinchot was a member of the executive committee of the New York chapter of America First.

Pinchot expressed his admiration to Lindbergh for the way Lindbergh was speaking.

I want to take this opportunity to say that I am deeply grateful personally, and as an American citizen, for what you are saying, and, may I add, for the way you are saying it. You are unquestionably gaining power—fast. It is ironical, and will soon be so recognized generally, that the man, who, in June 1939, advised this country to mend its deficiency in air power—advice, which if taken, would not only have made us perfectly secure by this time, but enabled us to give some substantial help to other countries—should now be denounced by the very people who chose not to listen to him.

Shortly Pinchot was an adviser to Lindbergh. "I think you should go on the air," he told the flier in July, "and make an argument against undeclared war, and supplement and reinforce it by enlarging on your previous arguments as to the military disadvantages of abandoning the defensive position and spreading our forces, such as they are, thin all over the world."

Lindbergh was speaking regularly and, as Stuart said, he was finding "phenomenal expressions" of support. In San Francisco, Los Angeles, New York, crowds roared their approval at him. "Lindbergh was the most effective of all," Robert Wood recalled some years later. "He was the idol of the young people. Of course, he'd been over there. He knew the extent of the German preparations." But something was happening to Lindbergh as he spoke at these rallies. His denunciations of the Roosevelt administration's foreign policy became more strident. His warnings of the dangers the United States faced became more extreme. His search for villains become more irresponsible.

Perhaps understandably because of his own involvement with the news media in earlier years, Lindbergh did not trust the press. As early as 1939, he warned his fellow isolationists that

We will be deluged with propaganda, both foreign and domestic—some obvious, some insidious. Much of our news is already colored. Every incident and every accident will be seized upon to influence us. And in a modern war there are bound to be plenty of both. We must not only inquire about the writer and the speaker—about his personal interests and his nationality, but we must ask who owns and who influences the newspaper, the news picture, and the radio station. If our people know the truth, if they are fully and accurately informed, if they are not misled by propaganda, this country is not likely to enter the war now going on in Europe.

Again and again there appeared in his speeches this charge that the news media was being controlled by self-serving forces for propaganda purposes. In San Francisco:

Confusion is not an accidental fact in this war. It is the major weapon of the interventionists. They have flooded this country with propaganda for the purpose of drawing us into war. Our press, our radio, our book stalls, and our theatres are full of it. Our news is governed more by the formulas of propaganda than it is by the factual development of the war.

In Los Angeles:

Possibly the most ominous and deplorable development of the war, as far as the United States is concerned, has been the deliberate attempt to misinform and confuse our people. Some day, in the not distant future, the men who are responsible for this will be called to account by an aroused and enlightened nation. The attempt to involve our country in war by subterfuge and propaganda is not a crime to be passed over lightly. Public opinion will bring the charges, and history will be the judge.

With his charge of the manipulation of the news media, there was in the Lindbergh speeches and writings a touch of racism. In a 1939 radio speech he said:

Our bond with Europe is a bond of race and not of political ideology. We had to fight a European army to establish democracy in this country. It is the European race we must preserve; political progress will follow. Racial strength is vital—politics, a luxury. If the white race is ever seriously threatened, it may then be the time for us to take our part in its protection, to fight side by side with the English, French, and Germans, but not with one against the other for our mutual destruction.

He repeated much the same thoughts in his 1948 book *Of Flight and Life.*

These two strains—the touch of racism and the charge that the news media were being manipulated—came together in a speech Lindbergh gave in Des Moines, Iowa, on September 11. The speech was the second most controversial event in Lindbergh's life, and neither Charles Lindbergh nor the America First movement ever would be the same again.

Among the isolationists were many avowed anti-Semites. As some saw Hitler only as a menace toward communism, the anti-Semites welcomed Hitler as a means of destroying the Jews. These avowed anti-Semites in the United States were small in number but vocal. The America First Committee did not want them. There were several reasons. The Committee's position of advocating what it claimed was best for America would be seriously weakened if the charge could be made that America First was really interested in attacking a small group of Americans. America First was attempting to attract to its leadership the more responsible American businessmen; such persons did not publicly condone anti-Semitism even if they may have restricted Jews from joining their business, social, and residential worlds. And finally the people who were organizing America First would not themselves countenance anti-Semitism.

The America First organizers, however, realized that because of Hitler's treatment of Jews they might come under attack. They moved to stop such attacks before they could begin. Robert Wood prevailed upon Lessing J. Rosenwald, a Jew who was a director of the Sears, Roebuck Company, where Wood was chairman of the board, to join America First's national committee. But Rosenwald's membership did not last long. Perhaps because Douglas Stuart was so young he did not quite realize what he was doing when, simultaneously, he announced that Rosenwald had joined the national committee as well as Henry Ford. Ford's anti-Semitism had been so pronounced in the 1920s that asking a Jew to sit next to Ford, even in 1940, was too great a request. Ford had not only personally espoused anti-Semitism but had put a great deal of his money into disseminating anti-Semitic literature. Stuart would not have been personally aware of that. Rosenwald resigned from America First's national committee in December, 1940, because of Ford's presence. The committee then voted to drop Ford. Rosenwald was approached and asked to return, but he refused.

America First also tried to discourage anti-Semites from joining and refused membership to persons known to be anti-Semitic. It did not always succeed, of course; there were too many local chapters for that. But whenever the national chapter discovered that a local chapter had an anti-Semitic element, it demanded its ouster. On several occasions local chapters enlisted known anti-Semites as speakers, and the national chapter demanded that the anti-Semites not be permitted to appear before any group known as "America First." America First was so zealous that it occasionally was attacked as being a Jewish-dominated organization. In its zeal to be free of the charge of anti-Semitism, America First had trouble with Father Charles Coughlin and his followers.

Coughlin was a unique member of American society. A Catholic priest, he accepted the respect and courtesy Americans have always tendered to the clergy and used them as a shield behind which he built a basically anti-American movement. He was priest at the Shrine of the Little Flower Church in a Detroit suburb. More even perhaps than FDR, Coughlin had a voice perfectly suited to radio. He was the Huey Long of the airwaves, calling out the worst in people. He appealed to emotions, to prejudices, to lusts for power. Charles J. Tull in his authoritative *Father Coughlin and the New Deal* gives the best estimate of Coughlin's program.

Only an extremely loose interpretation would find clear similarity between his proposals and fascism. The priest was a frustrated, disgruntled demagogue lashing out at the world around him, but he was no fascist. In fact, to catalogue him left, right, or center is impossible; the man is simply too erratic to be so neatly classified a particular species of political animal.

Whatever his politics, Coughlin was an anti-Semite. His newspaper *Social Justice* was one of the more vicious publications in that genre. In November, 1938, speaking of Jews, it had charged: "Is it not true that a force, over which we Christians seem to have no control, has gained control of journalism, motion pictures, theatres and radio?" From then on, the attacks became worse. The policy of America First was to not welcome the Coughlin movement within its membership. But this was difficult to do. Many followers of Coughlin were strongly against intervention and wanted to join America First. Many of Coughlin's financial backers also wanted to contribute to the nonintervention movement. In New York City, America First leaders sought to block membership to Coughlin's followers. The committee's director for the eastern United States took a position not quite as strong, but still one solidly against the Coughlinites. He issued the following statement of policy:

> The Coughlinite situation has always been a difficult one for us. It has been our policy to not permit any Coughlin organization leaders to be in a position of leadership or direction in our local chapters. Of course, you cannot prevent their becoming members or working to get other members. The important thing is to handle the situation so that they do not in any way identify the chapter with the Coughlin movement per se. By all means do not permit copies of *Social Justice* to be sold at your meetings. While you perhaps cannot legally prevent this from being done on sidewalks outside the auditorium, you may be able to do it by direct request to the people who are intelligent enough to understand the situation. It is of particular importance that none of these [Coughlin] supporters be permitted to inject anti-semitism into the work of the chapter. We have the support of many Jewish people, and will not abide intolerance as a part of this movement.

One national director of America First stated flatly that America First had "no sympathy at all with Father Coughlin, his paper or anything it contains with relation to his movement." Coughlin, however, liked America First. His newspaper *Social Justice* endorsed the group, and Coughlin spoke positively about the group's purposes.

Because of all the difficulties with Coughlin, as well as problems of the other anti-Semites in the United States, America First knew it was dealing with a delicate issue. But by the second half of 1941 its members could begin to congratulate themselves for apparently having dealt with it satisfactorily.

Then Charles Lindbergh spoke at Des Moines on September 11.

Adolf Hitler always had seen the United States as being under the domination of Jews. Hitler believed that FDR was a puppet controlled by Jews. Also, Hitler liked to be told what he wanted to hear. From the German Embassy in Washington came a series of dispatches claiming that Lindbergh was leading the fight against the Jewish-dominated American government and that the Jews in the United States feared Lindbergh more than any other man. The reports were irresponsible and contributed greatly to Hitler's misunderstandings about the United States and its willingness and ability to fight.

Lindbergh personally had never been known to speak publicly in a manner that was construed as anti-Semitic. Actually, after his first solo across the Atlantic, he had become a friend of Harry F. Guggenheim, a wealthy Jew who was interested in aviation. When he began to speak against American intervention, many Jews who believed as he did supported him.

But then he spoke at Des Moines.

He began that night by saying that since the European war had begun in 1939, "there has been an ever increasing effort to force the United States into the conflict. That effort has been carried on by foreign interests and by a small minority of our own people, but it has been so successful that, today, our country stands on the verge of war." Although America did not wish to enter the war, he continued, "there were various groups of people here and abroad whose interests and beliefs necessitated the involvement of the United States in the war."

Who were these groups?

"The three most important groups who have been pressing this country toward war," said Charles Lindbergh, "are the British, the Jewish and the Roosevelt administration."

The British, Lindbergh said, wanted the United States in the war for natural reasons. Roosevelt wanted the United States in the war, Lindbergh charged, because Roosevelt needed a war hysteria to stay in power.

And what was the motive of the Jews?

It is not difficult to understand why Jewish people desire the overthrow of Nazi Germany. The persecution they suffered in Germany would be sufficient to make bitter enemies of any race. No person with a sense of dignity of mankind can condone the persecution the Jewish race suffered in Germany. But no person of honesty and vision can look on their pro-war policy here today without seeing the dangers involved in such a policy, both for us and for them.

Instead of agitating for war, the Jewish groups in this country should be opposing it in every possible way, for they will be among the first to feel its consequences. Tolerance is a virtue that depends upon peace and strength. History shows that it cannot survive war and devastation. A few farsighted Jewish people realize this and stand opposed to intervention. But the majority do not. Their greatest danger to this country lies in their large ownership and influence in our motion pictures, our press, our radio and our government. . . .

In selecting these three groups as the major agitators for war, I have included only those whose support is essential to the war party. If any one of those groups, the British, the Jewish, or the administration, stops agitating for war, I believe there will be little danger of our involvement. I do not believe any two of them are powerful enough to carry this country to war without the support of the third.

This speech destroyed America First and probably the entire isolationist movement as potent political forces. Lindbergh's remarks came too close to anti-Semitism to be ignored. His charge that the "greatest danger" posed by the Jews was their "influence" in "our government" came too close to the ravings of Hitler that the United States was governed by the "Jews of the dollar" for the followers of Lindbergh to feel comfortable. His assertion of Jews propagandizing through communication media they allegedly controlled was too much like the charges of Charles Coughlin "that a force, over which we Christians seem to have no control, has gained control of journalism." The company Charles Lindbergh had chosen for himself made other Americans feel decidedly uncomfortable.

Also, most Americans realized the charges were inaccurate. If any group in the United States was to be singled out as being among the most active agitators for war, it was not the Jews but the Southerners. England's greatest support in the United States came from below the Mason-Dixon line where the number of Jews was insignificant. This probably was due to the support the British had given the South during the Civil War. Whatever the reason, it was a fact. The charge that the Jews had "a large ownership and influence" in the communication media also did not hold. The publications at the time most interested in intervention were the magazines in the *Time-Life* empire, which were owned by gentiles. And, of course, Lindbergh's own speeches against intervention always had been prominently reported in the news media and usually were broadcast over radio. His side never had trouble reaching the American people through the news media. Anyone who listened to the radio or read a newspaper realized that.

There was another reason, much more significant, why the Lindbergh speech destroyed the movement he led. If Charles

Lindbergh was the best the isolationists had to offer, then his arguments against intervention and his charges against public figures had to be the best that the movement had to offer. And in the end, what the isolationist movement came down to, its major point, was only that the American people were being tricked into a war they did not wish by the British, by a power-hungry demon in the White House, and by a small group of Americans who could not even be admitted to the country club. The Roosevelt policies should have been debated and perhaps changed. The course in which the President was leading the nation should have been questioned and perhaps turned. The public should have been educated and perhaps persuaded. But once again the opposition was offering neither facts nor philosophies. Policy was not being countered by another policy. Leadership was not being met by leadership but by demagoguery. Americans, except for a small number, do not respond to this kind of approach. If this was the best the isolationists had to offer, it was not enough.

The career of Charles Lindbergh is filled with irony. He gained fame as the daredevil pilot who apparently jumped into his airplane and flew across the Atlantic Ocean by the seat of his pants. The truth was that he had carefully planned and prudently executed that flight. His feat in 1927 was one of intelligence and daring rather than stupidity and casualness. In 1941 he became a spokesman for the isolationists because, supposedly, he was knowledgeable about Europe and military power there. But rather than lead that movement with the intelligence and care he had shown in 1927, he simply jumped into his cockpit and flew by the seat of his pants.

A number of Jews belonging to America First were angered by Lindbergh's remarks—after all, they were not advocating intervention—and resigned. Others, however, wrote America First letters saying they intended to keep their membership in the organization and some wrote that criticism of Lindbergh for the Des Moines speech was unjustified. America First, for example, took pleasure in distributing an unsolicited letter from a Jewish doctor who had been president of a local chapter of B'nai B'rith, a Jewish service agency. "Let us read and reread the farsighted words—aye, prophetic words of that courageous and robust American, Col. Charles A. Lindbergh," read the letter. "Where, in the name of American good sense, can we find even the slightest suggestion of race prejudice in all his talks or writings?"

The problem created by the speech was not so much the anger of Jews but the fear of gentiles. Many rushed to proclaim that some of their best friends were Jews. The *Chicago Tribune*, long critical of FDR, in favor of isolationism, in support of Lindbergh, ran an editorial explaining that it was not anti-Semitic, that it hired Jews, and that it considered the Lindbergh remarks indiscreet. "Col. Lindbergh said that the Jews of America," concluded the editorial, "as a group, are working for war, altho he conceded that a few farsighted Jews see the folly of this course and oppose it. He might have added that other racial groups whose birthplaces have been overrun by Hitler are also working for war. But neither these other groups nor the Jews are unanimous in this."

In Iowa, where the speech had been given, according to a report to a Democratic senator, "the result of the meeting passing all differences of opinion has been that in Iowa, there is no definite antipathy to Jewish people, that for the most part they are successful businessmen and for the most part Republicans. Both they and many Republican leaders are thoroughly aroused at the injection of a racial issue into the campaign."

But it was America First that was most concerned. Since its organization a year earlier it had fought to keep any taint of anti-Semitism from its record. And now the only remark by a responsible isolationist official that could be construed as anti-Semitic had come from a leading America First speaker at a rally sponsored by America First. "As one who has the highest personal regard for Colonel Lindbergh," Douglas Stuart recalled many years later, "I remember being quite distressed that he had raised this issue. It seemed to me that we should keep the debate on the substantive question of intervention or nonintervention and try hard to avoid the emotional side issues."

America First, of course, had not had any opportunity to review the speech beforehand. Lindbergh was a free agent; he spoke as he pleased. But America First could not divorce itself from him; he was a member of its National Committee. The members of America First had two fears following the Lindbergh speech. One was that the speech would open the committee to attacks from interventionists. The second was that a large number of anti-Semites, held at bay in previous months, might now feel free to join America First and substantiate the charges anticipated from the interventionists. Two days after the speech, Amos Pinchot had a session with John Flynn, an America First official in New York City. Pinchot then reported to Robert Wood in Chicago that Flynn

is greatly worried about Colonel Lindbergh's Iowa speech. I talked with him the night before last, at length. I do not share his anxiety, and think that the situation in the Committee will simmer down if everybody sits tight. John is tremendously able and useful. But, as you know, he gets overexcited, at times, over comparatively inconsequential things, and suffers from some apprehension that his erstwhile radical friends will disapprove his course.

But Pinchot became more concerned than that report to Wood indicates. There was a luncheon at the restaurant of the Murray Hill Hotel in New York City on September 16. On the menu was scrawled out the first draft of a telegram from Lindbergh to Robert Wood. After being revised somewhat, the Lindbergh telegram, as sent, read:

Now that my Des Moines speech has come under attack, I feel that I owe it to you, to the America First Committee, and to myself, to say that, for the views expressed in that speech, I am personally and alone responsible. My manuscript was neither discussed with nor shown to any member of the America First Group.

Of course I did not attack England or the Jews, British or otherwise, on the basis of race or religion. The cruel and terrible persecutions of the Jews rightly stir feelings of profound resentment with which we all deeply sympathize. Nevertheless, this resentment should not be permitted to enter into the momentous decision between war and peace, which must be made by the American people solely on the basis of what is best for their country. Every Englishman must be stirred in his deepest loyalties by the existing crisis. But no matter what their feelings may be, or how influential the persons who express them, they should not be allowed to sway American policy.

Drawn from every race and tradition of Europe, millions of our citizens have friends or relatives who have suffered shamefully at the hands of European dictators. But these relationships cannot be allowed to sway the fateful choice between war and peace, which must be decided by the Americans, not on the basis of European issues, but on the question of what is best for their country.

A critical situation is upon us. The President without consent of

Congress or the public will, has declared what is, in effect, his own personal war against the Axis powers. This arouses the further issue, whether our democracy shall be destroyed from within by leaders who have seized upon an emergency to gather unto themselves dictatorial powers forbidden in our Constitution and hostile to the American character and way of life.

This telegram was designed to exonerate the America First Committee from responsibility for the Des Moines speech without Lindbergh having to retract anything he had said. The telegram, however, was never made public. "It is my recollection," said Douglas Stuart in 1969, "that we decided not to release the copy of Colonel Lindbergh's telegram to General Wood because we felt this would simply call more attention to a sensitive issue and prolong the debate of a question on which the majority of the America First Committee were not in agreement."

At a meeting of America First's national committee on September 18 in Chicago, the issue was thrashed out. Should Lindbergh be repudiated? Most members were against it. In the past few months, at least, Charles Lindbergh had become the creation of America First. That body could not disown him. But acting was not easy. Finally on September 24, almost two weeks after the speech had been given, America First issued this statement:

Ever since the nationwide effort to keep America out of war began, the interventionists have sought to hide the real issue by flinging false charges at the America First Committee and at every leader who has spoken out against our entry into the European conflict. The present attack on Colonel Lindbergh is merely another case in point.

Colonel Lindbergh and his fellow members of the America First Committee are not antisemitic. We deplore the injection of the race issue into the discussion of war or peace. It is the interventionists who have done this. America First, on the other hand, has invited men and women of every race, religion and national origin to join this committee, provided only that they are patriotic citizens who put the interests of their country ahead of those of any other nation. We repeat that invitation.

At least 80 percent of the American people oppose our entry into the war. The America First Committee has supplied to these millions of citizens a leadership which has thus far helped to avert disaster. Consequently, the aim of the war makers is to destroy the America First Committee.

Behind a smokescreen of groundless charges this nation is being led to war in violation of the Constitution of the United States.

There is but one real issue—the issue of war. From this issue we will not be diverted. We will carry on the fight until it is won.

Charles Lindbergh never spoke publicly of that Des Moines incident. In October, however, in a speech at Fort Wayne, he said that

In making these addresses, I have no motive in mind other than the welfare of my country and my civilization. This is not a life that I enjoy. Speaking is not my vocation, and political life is not my ambition. . . . I am moved by no personal interest or animosity. I do not speak out of hate for any individuals or any people. But neither have I tried to avoid facts in order to have my speeches politically popular.

Robert Wood, some years later, commented that Lindbergh's Des Moines speech "did us a good deal of harm, exposed the America First Committee to a good deal of criticism."

But the harm committed by Lindbergh was more than that. His speech demonstrated that the isolationist movement had no rationality. If war was coming, it was not because of the British, the Jews, or because of FDR; it was because, instead, totalitarian forces were willing to use military power to extend their domains. The impact of the Lindbergh speech quickly was evident in Congress. Always in politics there are a few persons who can be considered indicators of which way the public mood is flowing. They are so attuned to the spirit of their constituents, and so anxious for re-election, that they do not hesitate to switch their positions innumerable times if it insures their political longevity.

Everett Dirksen's Republicanism dated almost to his birth in Pekin, Illinois, on January 4, 1896. Eleven months later when William McKinley was elected President on the Republican ticket, Dirksen's father joyously gave his son the middle name "McKinley" in honor of the man who had rescued the nation from the evils of the Democrats.

Dirksen eventually went to Congress where he quickly established himself as a hard worker, a conservative Republican, and an isolationist. He became a "comer" on Capitol Hill, for good reason. During the lend-lease debate early in 1941, for example, it was Dirksen who realized that a number of Democrats had left the House floor for lunch. In a brilliant coup, he quickly brought up for a vote an amendment giving Congress power to rescind the lend-lease program. It passed before the Democrats realized they had been outflanked. He continued to oppose the President's foreign policy for the next several months. He was a particularly strong critic during the debate to extend the draft.

But in September there was a recess and the members of Congress went to rejuvenate their spirits among the people back home and to learn how their votes and speeches were being received. While they had been in Washington their constituents had read of both the *Greer* incident and of the Lindbergh speech. The members of Congress listened well to those voters. When the recess ended, Everett Dirksen symbolized the impact they had had. From being a forceful opponent, he returned from that recess as a supporter of FDR's foreign policy. "To disavow or oppose that policy now," he told the House, "could only weaken the President's position, impair our prestige and imperil the nation." Almost as if by prearrangement, the Republican members of the House stood up and applauded him. Before delivering the speech that marked his turnabout, Dirksen had discussed it with his Republican colleagues. There was a bitter exchange between Dirksen and Hamilton Fish in Fish's office. The New York Congressman refused to change his position as Dirksen had done. Dirksen left Fish's office, persuaded the Republicans to support him, and began a climb to the leadership of his party, while Fish's eminence in the party began a decline.

Mitsuo Fuchida had served in the Japanese navy for twenty-five years when, in September, 1941, he was transferred to the aircraft carrier *Akagi*. Fuchida had previously been on that carrier and was happy to return to his former comrades. He was given the job of commander of all air groups of the First Air Fleet. "This was an assignment beyond all my dreams," he later said. "I felt that something big must be afoot." He learned how big it would be very quickly.

"Now don't be alarmed, Fuchida," the operations officer soon told him, "but we want you to lead our air force in the event that we attack Pearl Harbor."

Fuchida's reaction was natural. "Don't be alarmed?" he later wrote. "It was all I could do to catch my breath."

OCTOBER: "... the Imperial Navy is itching for action"

ON OCTOBER 15, Roosevelt wrote to Churchill: "The Jap situation is definitely worse and I think they are headed north—however in spite of this you and I have two months respite in the Far East." The two-months' respite was based on the belief that Japan would not act until it was sure that Russia had been defeated. If Japan then moved against England, attacking her possessions and grabbing at her sources of raw materials in the Western Pacific, England probably would have been finished as a combatant against Germany in Europe—unless the United States came to her aid in Asia. That "unless" meant war for the United States.

The day after that letter was written, Prince Konoye resigned as premier and was replaced by General Hideki Tojo, perhaps the most militaristic of the army men who had served in Manchuria. Konoye wrote American Ambassador Joseph Grew that "I have had to resign owing to the internal political situation. . . . I feel certain, however, that the cabinet which is to succeed mine will exert its utmost in continuing to a successful conclusion the conversations which we have been carrying on up till today."

The new cabinet worked hard to give the impression that it still was interested in negotiations. Actually Tojo had become premier because he opposed negotiations, not because he favored them. He had been War Minister in Konoye's cabinet as the deadline for the end of negotiations neared—this was the first ten days of October which had been decided upon early the previous month. By October the formal deadline was pushed back to October 15. On October 12, Konoye had met with Tojo and begged him to agree to an extension. Tojo refused, arguing that any negotiations with the United States would require Japan to make some concessions in China.

The difference between the two men, Konoye and Tojo, was demonstrated by a conversation they once had regarding Japanese-American negotiations and the possibility of war. "Sometimes," Tojo said, "it is necessary for a man to risk his life in one leap."

"That might happen once or twice in the course of an individual's life," answered Konoye, "however, a person in a responsible position, when he considers a 2,600-year-old national polity and a hundred million subjects, cannot take such a risk." Tojo would take such a risk.

On the morning of October 14, the two men met again and Konoye renewed his plea for a delay in the deadline. When faced with the blunt prospect of war, Konoye wanted to back down. But Tojo told him, "I believe that the view of the Premier is rather overly pessimistic. This is because you are too well aware of the weak points of your own country. Is it not possible that the United States too has her weaknesses?" Konoye reported that his conversation with Tojo "threatened to lead us into violent disagreement over the problem of the withdrawal of troops." Finally Tojo said, "All that must be due to the difference in our characters."

On October 16, Konoye said that "careful reconsideration of the situation leads me to the conclusion that, given time, the possibility of reaching an agreement with the United States is not hopeless . . ." if Japan would agree to the ultimate withdrawal of her troops from China. In reply, Tojo "insisted that although he greatly appreciated my position and sincerity, it was impossible from the standpoint of preserving military morale for him to agree to the withdrawal of troops."

Faced with this reaction, Konoye had no choice but to resign. He could not govern unless the military supported him. To gain that support meant acting as a blind to mask war preparations. So Hideki Tojo became premier.

Known to his colleagues as "The Razor," Tojo was a man who understood nothing but military conquest. He is perhaps the classic example of the evils of the military man becoming the head of government. He would commit his nation to a course which could only lead it to disaster. But he understood none of this, or did not care to. He was totally dedicated to war.

Japan's decision for war would not be changed. Attacks by public officials in Tokyo on the United States were stepped up. Captain Hideo Hiraide, director of naval intelligence for the Japanese fleet, said in October: "The Imperial Navy is prepared for the worst, and has completed all necessary preparations. In fact, the Imperial Navy is itching for action."

The United States did not want the war to come. There were three reasons. First was the opposition to war generally. Henry Stimson and Harold Ickes were advocating war against Japan, but they were the extremists. Roosevelt knew that war might come and that it must be prepared for, and if at the end it were the only course, the President would not shrink from it. But he did not want it, as most Americans did not want war. Henry Stimson found FDR's attitude discouraging. The President, Stimson believed, is "entirely in the hands of people" who "are wedded to the idea that with our weapons [other nations] can win the war." Stimson was "perfectly certain" that the war could not be won without the active intervention of the United States.

Second, there was the question of timing. The United States in 1939 had begun preparing for war. From almost nothing, a gigantic military machine was nearing completion. If war must come, from the American viewpoint, it was more advantageous that it come in 1942 or 1943 when that military machine would have reached its peak.

Third, there was a tactical reason to oppose a war in the Pacific. George Marshall explained it some time later.

As a purely military proposition, it would be highly undesirable, if involved in war, that it should be on two fronts in widely separated parts of the world, and more specifically, that it should develop in the Pacific, where we knew the British had very little available means to resist aggressive action by the Japanese. . . . So a war on two fronts was to be avoided by us in our own view, if we could manage it, and every effort was to be made to gain us time in case war became inevitable.

For Roosevelt there was a political problem. He had always understood that a declaration of war was an action to be taken by the American people through the Congress and not by the

President. This was the meaning of his remark, as quoted by Churchill, "I may never declare war; I may make war. If I were to ask Congress to declare war, they might argue about it for three months."

FDR was concerned always that, after arguing for those three months, Congress might then refuse to declare war. During 1941 there had been many suggestions that he go before Congress and ask formal support in a decision to make war. But he always turned them aside.

William Bullitt had suggested to FDR in June that he go before Congress saying that—unless Congress voted otherwise within twenty-four hours—the United States would formally be at war with Germany. The President turned down the suggestion. He was rather polite about it. He explained that he might be able to carry the Senate but he doubted if he could carry the House. Harold Ickes grumbled that FDR "showed no disposition to venture." In addition to the Bullitt plan being unconstitutional, it was also a serious gamble. If the Congress had not gone along with FDR, and it most likely would have been affronted by his tactic and not gone along, then the Axis powers would act without fear of the United States. The Congress would have said it would not declare war to stop them. Even when FDR sought to have American merchant ships armed, his advisers counted votes in Congress and told him to move cautiously. To seek repeal of the entire batch of neutrality laws or to seek authorization for the convoying of ships would mean to court defeat in Congress. FDR followed that advice, and the close vote by which he won permission only to arm merchant ships showed the wisdom of that advice.

In the fall of 1941 the isolationist groups challenged FDR to seek a declaration of war. Through a series of advertisements and public letters they demanded that he go before Congress to ask for a declaration of war. The members of Congress, since the Lindbergh speech at Des Moines, were much more responsive to FDR, but not responsive enough to go along with a declaration of war. The isolationists were hoping that Roosevelt would commit such a *faux pas* as seeking a war declaration and turn the Congress against him. FDR did not rise to their bait. To lose on such a vote would mean that he could no longer present himself to the leaders of other nations as a spokesman for the American people. The other leaders—Hitler, the Japanese militarists, and even Churchill—would know that the people, through the Congress, had not backed him up.

But the choice for the Congress, for FDR, and for the American people was narrowing.

The day Konoye formally resigned, the U.S.S. *Kearny* was escorting a convoy in the North Atlantic. Three ships in the convoy were torpedoed, and the *Kearny* responded by beginning a depth bomb barrage that ran through the night. The next day a torpedo struck the *Kearny* on the starboard side but the crew managed to keep the ship from sinking. Eleven American sailors were killed and twenty-two were wounded. Those eleven sailors were the first men in American military uniform killed by Germans.

"We have wished to avoid shooting," said a grave President. "But the shooting has started. And history has recorded who fired the first shot. In the long run, however, all that will matter is who fired the last shot." Roosevelt made that statement on October 27. Four days later the Germans sunk an American destroyer, the U.S.S. *Reuben James,* about six hundred miles west of Ireland. The ship was the first American naval ship sunk by the Germans. More than one hundred men were lost.

The inevitable was coming much closer.

A clash between a Germany that sought to extend its borders by military means and a United States that was the only nation strong enough to act as an international policeman had threatened since the first German soldier crossed the line between his country and his neighbor's. Now the threat was on the verge of becoming a reality. Dozens of incidents had occurred, and, in later years, people would choose which incidents they wanted to accept as their justification or as the basis for their beliefs. But all the incidents went back to the original act of aggression. The United States did not approve of fascism. It did not approve of the acts of violence against the Jews within the borders of Germany. The people of the United States considered Hitler a comic or a maniac, or both. But none of these causes had pulled the United States to the point where American men were being killed and American ships were being sunk and where a war loomed. The single cause that had brought the United States to this point was the military aggression by Germany against her neighbors.

During the spring and summer of 1941, the United States had occupied Iceland and Greenland. There was no secret about

American motives. The United States was constructing a defensive line beyond which it did not wish to permit Nazi Germany to pass. Also, the United States not only was protecting itself but providing immediate assistance to England—America's first line of defense. As 1941 neared an end, it was apparent that more assistance would be required by England, increasing the dangers for the United States both in the Atlantic and Pacific oceans.

There was one bright spot in the international situation: the apparent competence of the commander of the Pacific fleet at Pearl Harbor—Husband Edward Kimmel.

He was considered the Navy's best. A tall, broad-shouldered, blue-eyed officer, he was known as "Hubby" to his friends; his military contemporaries believed him as good a product of the navy system as could be fashioned. He had done every job in the Navy, from desk work in Washington to warfare on the sea. His career had been long and illustrious, and when he was picked over forty-six more senior officers for the Pearl Harbor command the general view in Washington was that the Navy was getting rid of some of its fat and bringing its best men into positions of important command.

Kimmel had been born in Henderson, Kentucky, about one month after Franklin Roosevelt was born. His father was an Army major and Kimmel hoped for a West Point appointment. When this did not come through, he secured an appointment to the naval academy at Annapolis. He was a good student, an athlete, and serious about his naval career. When he graduated in 1904, the class yearbook said of him: "He had the air of being his own statue erected by national subscription."

When he was appointed to the Pearl Harbor post there were rumors that it was a political plum, an appointment made because Kimmel was a close friend of the President's. Kimmel later denied this, but said, "I thought if it was to be answered it should be answered by somebody else besides me." Actually Kimmel barely knew Roosevelt. They had first met in 1915 when Kimmel was fleet gunnery officer for the Pacific fleet. FDR, then Assistant Secretary of the Navy, came to the west coast for the opening of the San Francisco and San Diego expositions in celebration of the Panama Canal's opening. Kimmel, then a lieutenant, was assigned as FDR's aide and spent about ten days with him.

The next year, 1916, Kimmel was stationed in Washington and saw Roosevelt, as Kimmel later recalled it, "oh, three or four times." In September, 1918, Kimmel again met FDR at a luncheon in Europe and, said Kimmel, "I had no further conversations with him until June of 1941, six months after I had been appointed commander-in-chief [of the Pacific fleet]."

In the Pearl Harbor area were forty-three thousand Army troops under the command of Lieutenant General Walter C. Short. His orders, made clear to him many times, were to use his soldiers to protect the fleet and the harbor. On October 16, 1941, after the Konoye cabinet had fallen in Tokyo, Admiral Stark, the chief of naval operations, warned all Pacific commanders that the situation was "grave." He said then that "hostilities between Japan and Russia are a strong possibility. . . . Since the US and Britain are held responsible by Japan for her present desperate situation there is also a possibility that Japan may attack those two powers. In view of these possibilities you will take due precautions including such preparatory deployments as will not disclose strategic intention nor constitute provocative actions against Japan." The caution against alerting the potential enemy or provoking him was added to prevent Japan claiming it had an excuse for going to war against the United States.

General Short was shown that message when it was received at Pearl Harbor. He later said:

If you noticed, that message said there was a very strong possibility of war between Russia and Japan, and there was a possibility of war between the British and the United States, and Japan. In other words, their main emphasis there was war between Russia and Japan. That weakened, as far as I was concerned, the probability of immediate war between the United States and Japan, because apparently they had considered the strongest possibilty was between Russia and Japan.

As a result of that message did he take any new steps to further protect the fleet?

We had tightened up all our guards against sabotage, and measures against subversive measures, things of that kind, at the time of the freezing of the Japanese assets [in July], and we had never taken off a great part of those; and I figured when I got that message that we were all right, as far as this message was concerned—and I was probably just a little more watchful.

Watchfulness was required, and perhaps even more than that. Late in the month Secretary of the Navy Frank Knox was discussing the Pacific situation with a group of manufacturers holding war contracts. A collision between Japan and the United States, said Knox, could occur on very short notice.

NOVEMBER: *"This dispatch is to be considered a war warning"*

WINSTON CHURCHILL was as concerned about the Far East situation as was Roosevelt; he had read the fall of the Konoye cabinet the same way. War, the action seemed to declare, was closer. Early in November the English Prime Minister asked FDR to join in a stern warning to the Japanese against making any further advances into China. The American President refused. Roosevelt's explanation was that any additional remonstrances by the United States might provoke Japan into action. He did not want the Pacific powder keg to blow up. His course was one of prudence rather than bravado. Whatever the arguments for taking a "tough" line in international negotiations, FDR was faced with the prospect of having the United States' big stick turning out to be made of paper. Labor problems, for example, had appeared to be settled in June when FDR had called out troops to end the North American Aviation walkout. In November, however, John L. Lewis was threatening a coal strike that, if it took place, would stop the rearmament effort. Without coal, there would be no steel. Without steel, there simply would be no reasons for the defense factories to stay open. The President's advisers, at the same time, were informing him that his support on Capitol Hill, although growing, continued tenuous—too tenuous to risk a vote on whether the United States should convoy war materiel to England. According to the view from the White House then, the powder keg had to be kept unlit. So Roosevelt said no to Churchill's proposal for an ultimatum, believing he had no other choice.

But the choice had passed out of FDR's hands. The choice

was Japan's. At a Cabinet meeting on November 7, Hull reviewed the situation. Japan, he said, had adopted a much more bellicose tone. This was apparent in the intercepted messages, in the inflammatory statements made by Japanese officials in Tokyo, in the unyielding posture of the Japanese in the negotiations, and finally in the reports of Japanese military movements. This bellicose tone could be ignored by John L. Lewis and by those members of Congress who were reluctant to risk their political strength to vote for defensive action the United States must take.

That bellicose tone, however, could not be ignored by those men who sat around the Cabinet table that November 7. "In my opinion," said Hull, "relations are extremely critical. We should be on the lookout for a military attack by Japan anywhere at any time."

The October 15 deadline passed in Japan; the military had already begun preparations for war and would halt them only if the United States met all Japanese diplomatic demands by November 25. By that time war preparations would be complete. On November 16 Ambassador Nomura received coded instructions from his government.

I set the deadline for the solution of these negotiations . . . and there will be no change. Please try to understand that. You see how short the time is, therefore do not allow the United States to sidetrack us and delay the negotiations any further. Press them for a solution on the basis of our proposals, and do your best to bring about an immediate solution.

That message had been sent after a bespectacled and dapper man, complete with the diplomat's traditional Homburg hat, arrived in the United States from Japan. His name was Saburo Kurusu, and he had come to America, Japan announced, to help Admiral Nomura break the negotiations deadlock with the United States. He was the front man. He was the man who would talk publicly about working for solutions while privately his government set deadlines.

Cordell Hull had read that November 16 message the day before Kurusu came to his office to pay his first formal call. Unaware that the United States was decoding and reading Japanese messages, Kurusu did not know that his role in the United States was well understood. He must either persuade the United

States to give Japan what Japan was eager to take by war or he must lull the United States into complacency until Japan was ready to strike. After a brief discussion in the Secretary's office, they went across West Executive Avenue to the office of the President. FDR greeted them graciously and told Kurusu that he was anxious for a peaceful settlement in the Pacific. He then offered to mediate the problems between Japan and China. The talk dragged on. There were other discussions. As Hull recorded, "It was obvious to the President and me that [Kurusu] had come to Washington not for the purpose of stating any concessions to our point of view but to put backbone into Nomura's virtual demands that we accept Japan's terms."

Still, the American emphasis on peace continued. General Marshall had a background briefing with the press. He told the newsmen that the United States and Japan were on the brink of war. That was obvious to many of the reporters present; they had been saying that in their stories. Then Marshall explained that the United States was beefing up its forces in the Philippines. If allowed to complete the buildup, the United States could demonstrate to Japan how powerful it was in the Pacific and this might deter a war with Japan.

But the United States would not be allowed time. On November 20, Nomura and Kurusu came to Hull's apartment. They handed him a new proposal which they had just received from Tokyo. It was, they said, an attempt at a *modus vivendi*. It listed numerous demands the Japanese knew the United States would not accept: the United States would no longer assist China; the United States would restore economic relations with Japan; the United States would help Japan acquire the raw materials she needed from the Dutch East Indies. Japan, in turn, would move her troops from southern Indochina to northern Indochina, and then vacate Indochina at such time as a peace with China was achieved. The *modus vivendi* would give Japan all she wanted or needed.

On November 22, Nomura and Kurusu received a message from Tokyo. The deadline for ending reliance on diplomacy had been pushed back from November 25 to November 29. If the United States signed the *modus vivendi* by then, fine. If it did not, however, "things are automatically going to happen." The United States government had a copy of that message. Three alternatives were open. Reject the *modus vivendi*, ignore it, or try to talk some more. The first two probably would have given the militants in the Japanese government the chance to declare war. The last might buy some time. No one seriously considered accepting the Japanese offer. To do so would mean discarding China and perhaps also Russia. No Asian nation could have felt secure before an expanding Japan.

The stakes were high and Roosevelt felt uncertain. He remarked to Harold Ickes over lunch late in November that he wished he knew if Japan were playing poker or not. He just did not know whether Japan had a gun up its sleeve. "It seemed to me," Ickes thought later, "that the President had not yet reached the state of mind where he is willing to be aggressive as to Japan."

But FDR was being much more militant than Ickes realized. At a meeting Tuesday, November 25, FDR expressed concern about a Japanese attack being imminent. He guessed that one could come perhaps the next Monday, December 1, adding the observation that the Japanese were notorious for making sneak attacks. The possibility of the United States attacking Japan was not considered. The question before the War Council that day was how to insure that when the attack against the United States did come, it would have as little an impact on American defense forces as possible. Henry Stimson wrote in his diary of the council meeting this way: "The question was how we should maneuver them into the position of firing the first shot without allowing too much danger to ourselves." Japan already had decided to fire the first shot. The American problem was how to make that shot ineffective. The meeting broke up without the problem being resolved.

When Stimson returned to the War Department, he found a report from military intelligence that a number of Japanese ships were moving toward Indochina. He reported this to Hull and sent a copy to the President. The next day Stimson spoke to FDR over the telephone about the message. Stimson reported:

He fairly blew up, jumped into the air, so to speak, and said he hadn't seen the message and that that changed the whole situation because it was an evidence of bad faith on the part of the Japanese that while they were negotiating for an entire truce—and entire withdrawal —from China—they should be sending this expedition down there to Indochina.

The next day Hull met with Kurusu and Nomura to give them the American reply to their *modus vivendi* offer. This counter offer, although harsher than originally planned, contained some concessions by the United States. Japan would not have to withdraw from the Tripartite Pact, which had been a previous American condition. A trade agreement along liberal lines would be worked out, as would other economic measures to Japan's benefit. But the United States continued to insist on the principle at least of Japanese evacuation of the lands in China and Indochina it had conquered. The United States would not reward aggression.

Two days later, on Friday morning, while FDR was still holding early morning court in his bedroom, Stimson barged in. He insisted the President read the latest reports on the Japanese movements south. The President analyzed the situation. Sitting up in bed, he said the United States had three alternatives. Stimson interrupted him, saying he saw only two. First, the President continued, ignoring the interruption, the United States could do nothing. Second, he said, the United States could issue an ultimatum, and, with it, a promise to fight. The third alternative, the President said, was to fight at once. Stimson would not accept the first alternative, to do nothing. The President agreed.

At the War Council meeting a few hours later, it was agreed that an ultimatum would be drawn up. Japan had on the high seas, according to the intelligence reports, 25,000 troops heading for an unknown destination. They could be moving toward the Philippines, and so precipitate a war with the United States. They could be moving toward Indochina or toward Dutch or British possessions. The decision was to warn the Japanese to halt their troops or face American retaliation. FDR was not happy with that decision. He still wanted to avoid war. Once such an ultimatum was announced, however, the United States must go through with it. It was an irrevocable step toward war. He personally favored a message from him to Emperor Hirohito. He had written the Emperor on previous occasions. Stimson was strongly opposed to the idea. "One does not," he said, "warn an Emperor."

The story of the American-Japanese negotiations is filled with many might-have-beens. Some students go back as far as the late 1920s or early 1930s to find an incident where, if the United States or some other nation had acted differently, the negotia-

tions might have ended differently. Perhaps. Perhaps not. The
military had taken command of Japan's foreign policy. The military is trained to fight. It is geared to conquer. When the military
is kept under control by civilian authorities, those inclinations
toward war are valuable; they can be channeled into defensive
purposes. But when the civilians lose control of the military,
those inclinations are turned toward offensive purposes and
cannot be stopped. That had happened to Japan.

And, while the situation in the Far East grew more ominous,
the President could not ignore the problems in Europe. Adolf
Hitler, like his Japanese compatriots, was becoming more bellicose. A statement had come out of Germany, according to a
newsman at a White House press conference, that "America has
declared a shooting war on the Reich." The author of the statement seemed to be "Mr. Hitler himself," said the reporter. Any
comment from the President?

FDR could not afford to be bellicose, not with John L. Lewis
raising his bushy eyebrows menacingly and Congress still uncertain about how much of a commitment it wished to make toward saving England. "I don't know," answered FDR as noncom-
mittally as he could, "except what I read in the papers."

The immediate European problem for Roosevelt in November
was to determine whether the United States should convoy
lend-lease goods from port to port—from the American ports,
across the peaceful waters of the western Atlantic to the waters
of the eastern Atlantic where the German U-boats swarmed,
then finally to the British ports. Secretary of State Hull had asked
Admiral Harold Stark, the chief of naval operations, for a candid
military opinion about the impact of American convoying of the
British ships. Stark began by pointing out the obvious. More
shipping would arrive at the British ports. Strains on British manpower would be relieved. Morale of the British people would
improve while, at the same time, morale of Germans would be
harmed. Then Stark turned to the negative side. He always had
believed that the United States would insist that England be
saved, even if it meant fighting in the war. At the same time,
he believed the decision about war would be made in Germany
by Adolf Hitler. "I do not believe Germany will declare war on
us," he said, "until she is good and ready." Stark also believed
that "It will be a cold-blooded decision on Hitler's part if and

when he thinks it will pay, and not until then." He pointed out that Hitler "had no legitimate excuse in the world—except to serve his own ends—to invade the countries he has." It was against this background of personal belief that Stark estimated that American convoying across the Atlantic made it "probable" that Germany would declare war on the United States.

Franklin Roosevelt would not ask for Congressional authorization of convoys. He would not order convoys. He did, however, request Congress to change the neutrality laws to permit the arming of American merchant ships. If fired upon, they would be able to fire back. The America First Committee launched a massive lobbying campaign against the proposal. FDR's anger at the America First group finally became all-pervasive. He told Francis Biddle, his Attorney General, that he wanted a grand jury investigation of the Committee. Such a federal inquiry, FDR said, would show that much of America First's money came from German sources. Biddle would not go along with the suggestion. Such a revelation by a grand jury, Biddle believed, was wishful thinking on FDR's part. Also, the convening of such a grand jury would rile the isolationists in Congress to a greater frenzy of opposition to FDR's foreign policy, including his request to arm merchant ships. Better let it alone, he advised.

Biddle was correct; the loss of America First's strength, caused by the Lindbergh speech, was showing on Capitol Hill. The change in the neutrality laws to permit arming of American convoy ships was approved. In the Senate the vote was 50–37; in the House, 212–194. The opponents of the change claimed that the narrowness of the vote suggested FDR's position on Capitol Hill was not very strong. It was not strong enough for a war declaration, but it was stronger than it had been in August when the House had approved the draft extension by an even narrower vote. Congress reflects the American public and the American public was becoming more aware that the United States must risk sacrifice to avoid conquest. One American loath to risk sacrifice was John L. Lewis, the president of the United Mine Workers.

Perhaps it can be said more of Lewis than of any other man in this period that he could work with no one. He had led the walkout from the American Federation of Labor to form the Congress of Industrial Organizations, and then he would walk out of the CIO to be an independent. He had supported Franklin

Roosevelt, then opposed him. Lewis was a loner, driven by his passion to only one objective: the well-being of the coal miner. He himself began his career as a coal miner. His father had been a coal miner. He had seen the mines destroy the souls of the young children. He had seen the mines destroy the bodies of the workers because the operators wanted to save a few pennies by skimping on safety measures. He had seen it all: the company towns, the hired guns, all the brutality, all the arrogance, all the terror that marked the American free enterprise system at its worst. Whatever else would happen to him, whatever else would happen to the miners, and whatever else would happen to the United States, he never could forget what he had seen. It was an anguished scar cut deep within him.

In 1941 the big labor issue for the coal industry was compulsory union membership. The unions wanted such a system because it strengthened them, giving them a one hundred percent membership. Also, the unions argued, it was basically unfair to expect some company employees to strike, to pay union dues, to work toward the betterment of working conditions while other employees escaped all those responsibilities by not joining the union. Companies opposed compulsory union membership because they did not wish unions to be any stronger than necessary and, also, because many doubted whether it was morally correct to force a man to join a union.

In the spring of the year the independent coal mine operators had acceded to Lewis's demand. But the captive mines would not. These were mines owned and operated by the steel companies, principally United States Steel. The mine workers in these mines struck September 15. After a five-day wait, the union went back to work. But only, it said, for thirty days to continue negotiations. The truce period passed with no settlement. There was another walkout; this one for three days. Again the workers returned to the mines to permit another try at negotiation. That also failed. On Monday, November 17, the mine workers walked out again. This time the strike had a look of reality to it. There would be no on-again, off-again situation. This strike would be a long one.

The few days the mines had been closed since September had revealed the impact a strike in the coal industry would have on the defense effort. Coal was necessary for the manufacture of steel, and steel was the basic element in defense production.

Also, not only were the 53,000 miners in the captive mines involved, many of the 350,000 miners in the independent mines also had walked out in sympathy. The defense effort definitely was threatened. John L. Lewis, who had been president of the miners' union for twenty-two years, was, beneath his exclamatory eyebrows and bushy hair, one of the shrewdest labor tacticians in the nation's history. The few days his men had been on strike in September had demonstrated the impact on the defense effort of a prolonged coal strike. They had been arranged to scare FDR into forcing United States Steel to accept the union shop.

But FDR had a weapon also. His action in the North American Aviation strike had freed him. He had used troops once. He could do so again. No union member could ignore that fact or its significance. If the member struck too long, he would go back to work with a bayonet point jabbing at his back. FDR quickly determined that the nation would not have a prolonged coal strike. Troops would be used. Friday, November 7, FDR had met at the White House with Secretary of War Stimson, General Marshall, and some other aides, and had immediately made that position clear. The President said he believed Lewis was trying to turn the captive mine walkout into a general strike. That, the President said, would not be permitted. FDR said he wanted to call on the volunteer spirit of the American people and that he expected they would back him up, as the people of England had supported that nation's defense effort. Once troops had been sent in, FDR said, an Army officer should actually operate the mines. The Army men at the meeting had a map showing where the mines were located. At that meeting, there was discussion of which mines would be seized first. They were aiming in the beginning at the mines in Pennsylvania, then those in West Virginia; the mines in Alabama would be third.

A few days later the issue came up again in a meeting between Stimson and the President. The Secretary of War stressed that if the Army were called out it must be "allowed to win a complete decision. It must not have its prestige affected by a misfire or being called back when the job was half done. . . ." The President, Stimson recorded, agreed fully with that. Either Stimson misunderstood the President or FDR changed his mind. The next day, according to Stimson, FDR kicked "the whole thing in the nose." Instead of moving in a massive number of troops, as Stimson understood FDR's original plan to have been, the President now spoke of moving in only a few soldiers, in a piecemeal fashion. The President wanted to deal with each mine as trouble arose, but not with the mining industry as a whole. He stated that position at a Friday Cabinet meeting. And he and Stimson, in front of the Cabinet members, had a furious shouting session. Stimson called it the "hardest and hottest debate at Cabinet that we have ever had and I really talked out to the President more than I ever have." At the session FDR made his irritation at Stimson's outburst clear. Later, Stimson called FDR and apologized. The President assured Stimson there was nothing to worry about. Actually FDR was as concerned as Stimson that any ill feelings might linger on from their debate. When Stimson suggested bringing over an Army general the next morning to discuss the feasibility of seizing the mines, the President readily assented.

The next morning, at a forty-five minute meeting, the President agreed to the placing of troops near the mines, so they could be readily called out *en masse* if they were needed. The decision appeared to be a victory for the Stimson approach of a massive seizure of the mines—and it was, if soldiers must be used. The only concession FDR sought was that the presence of the troops must be hidden from the miners to avoid provoking them, until such time as the troops were needed. That meeting was the morning of Saturday, November 15, two days before the coal miners went out on strike, for what appeared to be the beginning of a lengthy walkout.

Roosevelt had one final ploy. He suggested to the steel companies and to Lewis that both sides submit the union-shop question to binding arbitration, winner take all. The companies agreed. Lewis refused. But the union leader explained that his refusal was only a personal one. The offer must be voted on by the union's two-hundred-member policy committee. That vote would be only a formality, or so everyone thought.

Every since FDR had called out troops to stop the North American strike, there had been no question that he would do so again, if necessary. The debate between him and Stimson over when and how to call out the troops was not carried on in a vacuum. It was carried on in official Washington. Everyone understood that the government was considering using troops in the coal strike, and that the only arguments were over details. The companies understood it. The news media understood it. The coal miners understood it. The two-hundred-member policy committee of the mine workers' union understood it. The question before them when they voted on Saturday, November 22, was not whether to accept binding arbitration. Rather, it was whether to accept binding arbitration or work at the point of an Army bayonet. The committee chose to accept arbitration. There would be no coal strike. FDR had won.

The mine workers knew they had been coerced, and they were not happy about it. That week there was a CIO convention in Detroit. When CIO president Philip Murray called for a standing vote to endorse FDR's defense program and foreign policy, every labor union delegate rose—except the mine workers' representatives. They sat immobile, silent and staring straight ahead. To them FDR never again would be a friend.

The day the two-hundred-man policy committee of the coal miners' union voted, November 22, a task force of the Japanese Imperial Navy assembled in Hitokappu Bay in the Kurile Islands. Mitsuo Fuchida was there. He had spent weeks wrestling with the problem of torpedoes. He had not believed they could be used against the American ships docked at Pearl Harbor because the water in the harbor was too shallow. But his superiors had insisted, correctly, that air-carried torpedoes would be the most effective attack weapon. Finally the problem was solved by the addition of more fins to the torpedoes to stabilize them. Then in mid-November the airplanes making up the First Air Fleet were taken aboard their carriers and the big ships began slicing through the Pacific waters until they reached the assembly point in Hitokappu Bay on November 22. The force consisted of six carriers, two battleships, two heavy cruisers, one light cruiser, nine destroyers, three submarines, and eight tankers. On November 25 they received this order:

The task force, keeping its movements strictly secret and maintaining close guard against submarines and aircraft, shall advance into Hawaiian waters and upon the very opening of hostilities, shall attack the main force of the United States fleet in Hawaii and deal it a mortal blow.

The next morning the task force began to move slowly out of the bay into the waters of the north Pacific. As the ships moved past the bay entrance, a patrol boat on guard blinked out the message, "Good luck on your mission." The *Akagi*, commanding the task force, replied, "Thanks." The task force moved at a midpoint between the Aleutians and Midway Island to avoid air patrols from either place. The three submarines were two hundred miles ahead, to warn if a ship were sighted. If the submarines did report a strange ship, the task force would change direction to avoid it.

In Tokyo, young men left the shops and offices where they worked to don their country's uniform. Throughout the Japanese nation there were mass meetings and inflammatory statements in the press. After American correspondents in Tokyo had been given an advance copy of a particularly hostile editorial—and were informed that the editorial reflected the Japanese foreign office position—Ambassador Grew remarked, "Nothing could better illustrate the childishness of the Japanese. They want and need an understanding with the United States and yet, even while efforts are going on to reach such an understanding, they continue to fill their press with hostile articles which tend to render an understanding impossible." Although there was no question that the Japanese would have been better off with an understanding between themselves and the United States, it was unlikely that they wished one at this point. Premier Tojo told his cabinet that Britain and the United States were trying to exploit East Asia. "We must," he cried, "purge this practice."

As November closed, *The New York Times* reported that "war in the Pacific between Japan and the United States probably was closer than at any previous time." Although the growing difficulty between Japan and the United States was common knowledge, officials in Washington were taking no chance on the American military being caught unaware. On November 24, Admiral Stark sent a formal message to Husband Kimmel at Pearl Harbor. "Chances of favorable outcome of negotiations with Japan very doubtful," it said. "This situation coupled with statements of Japanese Government and movements their naval and military forces indicate in our opinion that a surprise aggressive movement in any direction including attack on Philippines or Guam is a possibility."

That message was shown to Short. "I felt certain," the General later said, "that if the Navy Department believed an attack on Hawaii was probable, they would have mentioned it, the same as they did the Philippines. 'In any direction' might mean anywhere in the world."

Did he feel justified in deciding against ordering an all-out alert?

"I think very definitely that I was," Short answered.

Three days later, on November 27, the following dispatch came from Stark in Washington to the commanders in the Pacific:

This dispatch is to be considered a war warning. Negotiations with Japan looking toward stabilization of conditions in the Pacific have ceased and an aggressive move by Japan is expected within the next few days.

The number and equipment of Japanese troops and the organization of naval task forces indicates an amphibious expedition against either the Philippines, Tai or Kra Peninsula or possibly Borneo.

Execute an appropriate defensive deployment preparatory to carrying out the tasks assigned in WPL-46. Inform District and Army authorities. A similar warning is being sent by War Department. SPANAVO inform British. Continental districts Guam, Samoa directed to take appropriate measures against sabotage.

Stark later said the "war warning" phrase was placed in the first sentence to "accentuate the extreme gravity of the situation." The words "war warning" had never been used before and were only inserted after "considerable thought and discussion" in Washington. In Washington there might have been reliance on diplomacy and personal appeals between the heads of two nations, but officials there did not want their military men to be caught off guard. The war warning message, however, did not have the desired impact on Kimmel. Conceding that the "war warning" phrase never before had been used, he said that a number of warnings approximating a war warning had been used before. So of the November 27 war warning, he said, "I did not consider it an extraordinary term." He did not take any extra precautions. Kimmel insisted:

The so-called "war-warning" dispatch of November 27 did not warn the Pacific fleet of an attack in the Hawaiian area. It did not state expressly or by implication that an attack in the Hawaiian area was imminent or probable. It did not repeal or modify the advice previously given me by the Navy Department that no move against Pearl Harbor was imminent or planned by Japan. The phrase "war warning" cannot be made a catch-all for all the contingencies hindsight may suggest. It is a characterization of the specific information which the dispatch contained.

By late November Roosevelt determined to go before Congress and ask its backing in action FDR considered necessary: the issuing of an ultimatum to Japan. Bring back the troops moving south—or else. There appeared no other course. Hull advised, and the President agreed, that the message should not go to Congress unless everything else had failed. They could not permit the isolationists in Congress to charge that the United States had not sought to solve the problem by every diplomatic means possible. So FDR first sent a private request to the Japanese government asking for an explanation of the troop movements and of the continuing buildup in Indochina. He also had a draft worked up of a statement to go to Congress, if and when it was necessary.

FDR also decided to go ahead with his original plan to send a message to Emperor Hirohito. Although Stimson had not considered it a wise idea, the White House had received some information that a letter to Hirohito could have positive results. The information came from Joseph Davies, who had been American ambassador to Russia and who had known Saburu Kurusu in Europe. The day that Stimson advised FDR against sending a message to the Emperor, Kurusu came to lunch with Joseph Davies, who reported:

He was downcast. Things were not going well. It was a terrible situation, he said, and very difficult. Japan needed supplies. It was asking us for oil and other vital materials. Japan, however, was an ally of Hitler, and naturally there was a strong mistrust that any such supplies would be diverted to Hitler.

He could understand the difficulties. His wife was an American. He himself had lived long years in Chicago. He was eager and anxious to preserve the friendship between our countries. As he told me in Brussels, he said, he had no sympathies with the militarists in Japan. But he was loyal to his country, and a member of his country's Foreign Service. But, bad as it was, he still hoped that something could be done to avert war. He spoke of his meeting with the President. He had been impressed by his directness and force.

After lunch, we played golf. Leaving the eighteenth hole, Kurusu opened up. He recognized, he said, that our sympathies were with China and that we were convinced that the military in Japan were bent on conquests. But it was not as simple as that. Japan now wanted peace, and would do almost anything to end the war; but it could not "lose face." He was "terribly" worried, he said.

My reply was general and that, of course, war between our countries would be tragedy, and horrible to contemplate. It would be difficult to think that in a few months there should be war between our nations, and that personal friends, such as he and I, should become mortal enemies.

He stopped short and said abruptly: "Mr. Ambassador: There are only two men in the world who can possibly prevent this war—your President and my Emperor! They are the heads of state. Their actions cannot be controlled by anyone." He spoke with obvious feelings.

He went on: "Only those two men," he said again, "can stop it. If only your President would communicate directly with our Emperor! Why could not that be done? It must be done." They, neither he nor Nomura, the ambassador here, he said, could do it or suggest it.

I ducked it and changed the subject, and tried to give the impression that I did not get the significance of the indirect request. I decided on the instant to pass on the information to the President. In such delicate negotiations, however, I could not be placed in the position of taking a message to which a reply would be expected and when, if none came, would give information to Kurusu that might not be helpful to "our people who were on their job."

Joseph Davies quickly passed the information on to Steve Early at the White House and asked him to inform the President immediately. Davies added his belief that Kurusu was "on the level."

The incident suggests Kurusu was legitimately trying to prevent a war. There is another explanation. The two Japanese ambassadors had not hesitated to work behind the Roosevelt administration's back. Nomura had several meetings with a man in Washington known to be very close to Herbert Hoover. At these sessions Nomura would lament about how war could be avoided if only the United States better understood Japan's position. Résumés of these conversations were fed back to Hoover for use by him and other isolationist leaders. In late November, when Kurusu had that conversation with Davies, the job of the two Japanese emissaries was not to negotiate a settlement but to lull the United States into inaction. The United States was at this point waiting for a formal reply to its counter offer to the Japanese *modus vivendi* proposal. Waiting for a reply to a letter to the Emperor gave the United States that much more reason to be inactive.

The Japanese now were acting with a tremendous advantage. They knew when and where war would come. The United States knew that war probably would come but could not know when or where it would come. And the United States, being the nation it was, could not strike first.

That situation made it compelling on the President to do

everything he could to prevent war. At the end of November, Prime Minister Churchill again suggested that the United States and Britain jointly warn Japan "that any further act of aggression by Japan will lead immediately to the gravest consequences." But FDR turned down the suggestion. Such an ultimatum would only alienate the militarists in the Japanese government and give them an excuse, if they wished one, to go to war. Better to wait, the President believed, until after his message to the Emperor had been answered. There still was time, until at least the Japanese replied to the American counterproposal to the *modus vivendi*.

And in the north Pacific, Mitsuo Fuchida watched the ocean waters glide by the *Akagi* and wondered what the future would bring for him. He soon would know.

DECEMBER: *"X day will be 8 December"*

O N DECEMBER 1, an Imperial Conference was held in Tokyo. The next day the task force moving across the northern Pacific received this message: "X day will be 8 December."

December 8, Japanese time, was Sunday, December 7 at Pearl Harbor. The Japanese had learned that the American fleet usually returned to base on the weekend so that a Sunday attack was much more likely to catch a greater number of ships at the base. Also on the first day of the month the intelligence summary for the United States military forces included this item:

All service radio calls of [Japanese] forces afloat changed promptly at 0000, 1 December. Previously service calls changed after a period of six months or more. Calls were last changed on 1 November, 1941. The fact that service calls lasted only one month indicate an additional progressive step in preparing for active operations on a large scale.

And also that same day the America First Committee formally announced it would seek to become more of a political force. In the 1942 primary and general elections for members of Congress it would support noninterventionists. Its formal announcement said:

Efforts must be directed toward the renomination and re-election in 1942 of those Senators and Representatives in Congress who have kept faith with the people's mandate to avoid participation in the War. This program will be undertaken in a spirit free from partisanship and without regard to the political affiliations of the candidates.

On December 3, the Navy in Washington sent this message to Pacific commanders, including Husband Kimmel at Pearl Harbor:

Highly reliable information has been received that categoric and urgent instructions were sent yesterday to Japanese diplomatic and consular posts at Hongkong, Singapore, Batavia, Manila, Washington and London to destroy most of their codes and ciphers at once and to burn all other important confidential and secret documents. From foregoing infer that Orange plans early actions in Southeast Asia.

Despite the long series of warnings from Washington and the general knowledge about the deteriorating relations between Japan and the United States, no further defensive measures were taken at Pearl Harbor. Kimmel and Short had met several times following the November 27 message. From these discussions, however, little emerged. General Short assumed the Navy would conduct distant reconnaissance—patrolling sea lanes leading to Pearl Harbor by ship and airplane—as a direct result of the order to execute "an appropriate defensive deployment." The Navy was not so doing. Admiral Kimmel assumed the Army was engaged in an all-out alert; he did not know that the Army was alerted only against sabotage. Kimmel also assumed that radar was in full operation; actually it was only working from four to seven o'clock in the morning. In their conversations together neither Kimmel nor Short said anything to help the other understand what his own particular service was doing.

On December 5, two days before the planned attack, the Japanese war ships received their final refueling from the tankers, which then left the task force. Without the slow-moving tankers to hold them back, the warships increased their speed to twenty-four knots, aiming at the tiny speck in the central Pacific that was Hawaii. "The rise or fall of the Empire," said a message from Yamamoto to the members of the task force at this time, "depends upon this battle; everyone will do his duty with utmost efforts." Yamamoto at last would have his revenge against the "barbarians."

Fuchida, who would lead the assault, thought to himself: "Who could be luckier than I?"

And in the United States, the world of America and of Americans went on as if the danger threatening were not coming. The evening of Friday, December 5, William Leahy, the American ambassador to Vichy France, dined as the guest of the ambassador from Japan, Sotomatsu Kato, at a dinner at his apartment in the Hotel Majestic. Most of the other guests also were Japanese. "The Ambassador, Kato, appeared worried," Leahy thought, "but the general atmosphere was friendly and cheerful in spite of the fact that my country and Japan are on the verge of a declaration of war."

The next morning, in New Jersey, the Glendale-Ridgewood chapter of the America First Committee sent FDR a letter wanting to know "What is all this sabre rattling in connection with Japan?"

Even at the White House, the business of government went on as usual. The morning of Saturday, December 6, Roosevelt met with his budget director, Harold D. Smith, to discuss the upcoming fiscal-year budget. One item was for the recruitment of an additional forty thousand Marine Corps trainees. The President cut the figure back to twenty thousand. He explained that plans were under way for a special guard unit to relieve Marines of guard duty at various naval yards and stations. Then he and Smith discussed the National Youth Administration program. The President outlined a plan he was considering under which each youth, as he became twenty-one, would spend a year in military service or in some type of conservation work. The President then suggested that Smith see Representative Lyndon B. Johnson of Texas. Johnson, the President said, had a plan to combine the NYA with another conservation program. "Report back to me on Monday," the President said, "about what you and Lyndon Johnson agree to."

The President interrupted the discussion to take a telephone call from Navy Secretary Knox. After he had hung up, FDR told Smith that there were large Japanese convoys moving into the southern Pacific. The Japanese explanation of those convoys had just come in, FDR said, and was unsatisfactory, barely an acknowledgment of the President's query. The President said he was sending a message to Emperor Hirohito, but he was not optimistic. We might soon be at war with Japan, the President said, although no one knew.

No one in Washington could know. The decision was Japan's.

Henry Stimson had hoped to leave Saturday for a weekend on his Long Island estate. He had done so on most weekends. But this Saturday he decided against it. "The news got worse and worse," he wrote in his diary that night, "and the atmosphere indicated that something was going to happen."

That morning he and Marshall had discussed whether a group of thirteen B-17 bombers sitting on the west cost should be sent on to the Philippines. The situation was so tense that they feared the possibility of an attack on the airplanes over the Pacific. The decision was made to send the planes. They would stop at Hawaii en route. Their expected time of arrival there would be some time after dawn the next morning, Sunday, December 7.

George Marshall was exhausted by what had been a long series of crises. He was home that Saturday night to rest. He had left orders at the War Department to be called if anything of importance occurred. Nothing happened that was considered important by his subordinates and he would not be called.

A meeting of the War Council was scheduled for the next afternoon, Sunday, December 7, at three o'clock. The purpose was to discuss the message the President planned to send to Congress on Monday or Tuesday. The message would explain why Roosevelt believed it necessary to issue an ultimatum to the Japanese. In Washington the belief was that a few days still existed for such diplomatic efforts. The Japanese had not formally replied to the American counteroffer made late in November. In addition to the diplomatic effort, Franklin Roosevelt was trying a personal one. This was his letter to Emperor Hirohito.

"Dear Cordell: Shoot this to Grew—I think it can go in gray code—our least secret code—saves time—I don't mind if it gets picked up. FDR."

That was how the President passed on his letter to Hirohito. Addressed to "His Imperial Majesty the Emperor of Japan," the letter read:

Almost a century ago the President of the United States addressed to the Emperor of Japan a message extending an offer of friendship of the people of the United States to the people of Japan. That offer was accepted and in the long period of unbroken peace and friendship which has followed, our respective nations, through the virtues of their peoples and the wisdom of their rulers, have prospered and have substantially helped humanity.

Only in situations of extraordinary importance to our two countries need I address Your Majesty messages on matters of state. I feel I should now so address you because of the deep and far-reaching emergency which appears to be in formation.

Developments are occurring in the Pacific area which threaten to deprive each of our nations and all humanity of the beneficial influence of the long peace between our two countries. Those developments contain tragic possibilities.

The people of the United States, believing in peace and in the right of nations to live and let live, have eagerly watched the conversations between our two governments during these past months. We have hoped for a termination of the present conflict between Japan and China. We have hoped that a peace of the Pacific could be consummated in such a way that nationalities of many diverse peoples could exist side by side without fear of invasion; that unbearable burdens of armaments could be lifted for them all; and that all peoples would resume commerce without discrimination against or in favor of any nation.

I am certain that it will be clear to Your Majesty, as it is to me, that in seeking these great objectives both Japan and the United States should agree to eliminate any form of military threat. This seems essential to the attainment of the high objectives.

More than a year ago Your Majesty's Government concluded an agreement with the Vichy Government by which five or six thousand Japanese troops were permitted to enter northern French Indochina for the protection of Japanese troops which were operating against China further north. And this Spring and Summer the Vichy Government permitted further Japanese military forces to enter into southern French Indochina for the common defense of French Indochina. I think I am correct in saying that no attack has been made upon Indochina nor that any has been contemplated.

During the past weeks it has become clear to the world that the Japanese military, naval, and air forces have been sent to southern Indochina in such large numbers as to create a reasonable doubt on the part of other nations that this continuing concentration in Indochina is not defensive in its character.

Because these continuing concentrations in Indochina have reached such large proportions and because they extend now to the southeast and the southwest corners of that peninsula it is only reasonable that the people of the Philippines, of the hundreds of islands of the East Indies, of Malaya, and of Thailand itself are asking themselves whether these forces of Japan are preparing or intending to make attack in one or more of these many directions.

I am sure that Your Majesty will understand that the fear of all these peoples is a legitimate fear inasmuch as it involves their peace and their national existence. I am sure that Your Majesty will understand why the people of the United States in such large numbers look askance at the establishment of military, naval and air bases manned and equipped so greatly as to constitute armed forces capable of measures of offense.

It is clear that a continuance of such a situation is unthinkable.

None of the people whom I have spoken of above can sit either indefinitely or permanently on a keg of dynamite.

There is absolutely no thought on the part of the United States of invading Indochina if every Japanese soldier or sailor were to be withdrawn therefrom.

I think that we can obtain the same assurance from the Governments of the East Indies, the Government of Malaya, and the Government of Thailand. I would even undertake to ask for the same assurance on the part of the Government of China. Thus a withdrawal of the Japanese forces from Indochina would result in the assurance of peace through the whole of the south Pacific area.

I address myself to Your Majesty so that Your Majesty may, as I am doing, give thought in this definite emergency to ways of dispelling the dark clouds. I am confident that both of us, for the sake of the peoples not only of our own great countries but for the sake of humanity in neighboring territories, have a sacred duty to restore traditional amity and prevent further death and destruction to the world.

The letter was the final attempt by the squire of Hyde Park, the decent man who hoped to find decency within other men, to personally avert the holocaust that was coming. Where the diplomats had failed and where the military threats had failed, FDR hoped that he and the Emperor might succeed. The President hoped that he might be able to pull from Hirohito the strength to put an end to the madness that was engulfing the Japanese government. It was not a quixotic gesture. With the appeal was the promise of peace in Indochina, a promise to which FDR had pledged to secure the support of all nations that Japan might consider its enemies. That could have been enough, if the Japanese government was so inclined, to be claimed as a small point won, to be claimed as a reason to begin serious negotiations again.

Hull sent the message to Ambassador Grew in Tokyo at nine o'clock the night of Saturday, December 6, 1941.

In Washington attention had been given to the task force moving south in the general direction of Indochina. No one in Washington was aware of the second Japanese task force. This was the one moving across the north Pacific. For the men on board the ships in that task force, morning seemed a long time coming.

December 6, in the evening, was a regular weekend pass night for the military in Honolulu. Of the 75,000 military men in the area, at least 11,000 had passes—a usual number. The military police picked up thirty-eight soldiers for drunkenness and the Navy shore patrol arrested four sailors, also the usual numbers. Admiral Kimmel and General Short were at dinner parties away from their posts. Most of the other officers also were at Saturday night affairs. It was, by any standard, a typical Saturday night for the military. It was the kind of night the military spend when they are certain that tomorrow will bring no unexpected problems.

About thirty minutes after Cordell Hull had sent off Roosevelt's appeal to Emperor Hirohito, a Navy commander named Lester Robert Schulz presented himself at the second-floor study at the White House. He had a locked pouch, carrying a message for the President; the message was the first thirteen parts of a Japanese message to the United States. The American counteroffer was being answered. Now Commander Schulz unlocked the pouch at his side and handed that answer to the President. FDR was reading it as soon, if not sooner, than were the Japanese ambassadors who did not suspect that their secret code had been broken.

Roosevelt was seated at his desk. He had just come from a small dinner party he had hosted and was relaxing with Harry Hopkins. The President had been informed the decoded message was on its way. There were approximately fifteen sheets of typewritten paper, clipped together. The President took about ten minutes to read them through. The message was to Ambassadors Nomura and Kurusu and it instructed them to inform the United States government that Japan rejected all its offers. Negotiations were at an end. After reading the papers, FDR handed them to Harry Hopkins, who had been pacing nervously back and forth in the study. Hopkins read them and handed them back to FDR without speaking. The President commented then, stating the obvious. "This," Schulz remembered him saying, "means war."

Schulz stood silently while Hopkins and FDR briefly discussed the imminence of war, saying that the Japanese planned to strike when they were ready and at a time most opportune for them. The Indochina area was mentioned as the possible site for the outbreak of hostilities. It was the only area Schulz remembered being mentioned. "The time at which war might begin was not discussed," said Schulz, "but from the manner of the discussion there was no indication that tomorrow was necessarily the day."

Roosevelt spoke of his message to Hirohito, only describing it briefly. Harry Hopkins then said that since war undoubtedly was going to come at the convenience of the Japanese, it was too bad that the United States could not strike the first blow and prevent a surprise attack. Roosevelt nodded his head at that, but said: "No, we can't do that. We are a democracy and a peaceful people." Commander Schulz remembered that Franklin Roosevelt then raised his voice and said, "But we have a good record."

"The impression that I got," Schulz later said, "was that we would have to stand on that record. We could not make the first overt move. We would have to wait until it came.

The time in Washington was approximately 10:30 P.M.

In Tokyo, at about that moment, Ambassador Grew learned that President Roosevelt was sending a special message to Emperor Hirohito. The ambassador heard of the message first from a radio news broadcast. Then Grew received a priority message from Secretary of State Hull saying that the message would be coming shortly and should be handled with all speed. The telegraphed message from FDR to Hirohito had arrived in Tokyo at approximately noon December 7, Japanese time. That was ten o'clock Saturday evening, Washington time, about the moment Commander Schulz heard FDR say, "This means war." The presidential message, however, was not delivered to the American embassy from the Japanese telegraph office until more than ten hours after it was received. The delay was part of a continuing harassment by the Japanese of Americans in Tokyo. As soon as he did receive the telegram, Grew demanded to see Shigenori Togo, then Japan's foreign minister. No, Grew insisted, he did not wish to wait until tomorrow to see the minister. When he finally met with Togo, Grew requested an audience with the Emperor at which he could present the President's message. He and Togo discussed the message for a few moments, and

then Togo said he would present the request for an audience to
the Emperor. When Ambassador Grew left Togo's residence, the
time was 12:30 A.M., December 8, Japanese time. In Washington
the time was 10:30 A.M. December 7. At Pearl Harbor the time
was five o'clock the morning of December 7.

About an hour earlier at Pearl Harbor an American destroyer
on routine patrol duty outside the harbor entrance had been signaled by an American minesweeper. The minesweeper had discovered a submerged submarine. The destroyer, however, could
not make sound contact with the suspected submarine. It ordered the minesweeper to continue the search. The incident was
not reported to higher command. Three hours later, however,
the destroyer saw the submarine's conning tower. The American
ship opened fire. The incident was quickly reported back to the
Harbor Control Post. One officer was on duty there, a Navy lieutenant. He grasped the significance of what was happening. An
enemy submarine had been fired on at Pearl Harbor. That meant
war. He began telephoning his superiors. It was not quite seven
o'clock in the morning of December 7. More than an hour would
be needed for his message to reach the proper personnel. No
alarms were sounded.

In Washington, at approximately the same time—it was almost
noon Sunday there—a group of grim-faced Army officials were
meeting in George Marshall's office. They had just read the
thirteen parts of the Japanese message that FDR had seen the
previous night. Marshall had not been informed of the message
until this morning. Now also there was the fourteenth and final
part which had been intercepted at about five A.M. Washington
time and translated within two hours after that. This last part
directed Nomura and Kurusu to deliver the entire message to
Secretary of State Hull at one o'clock that afternoon. There could
be only one reason for the Japanese making such a point of the
time: That would be the moment for war to begin.

For weeks General Marshall and Admiral Stark had been sending out warnings to their Pacific commanders ordering them to be
ready for the outbreak of hostilities at any moment. Another
warning now would be sent out. In his authorized biography of
George Marshall, Forrest Pogue faults Marshall, and by implication others in Washington, for not making certain that commanders in the field actually did respond properly to the numer-

ous warnings of possible hostilities between Japan and the United States. It is difficult, however, to see what more could have been done. The American bases in the Pacific, particularly Pearl Harbor, were not commanded by novices but by experienced military men. They had been told over and over again that war with Japan could break out at any moment. They had been given as much pertinent information as Washington officials had. They had been told what were the most likely points of attack, but they also had been told that the attack could come at any place. They were experienced men—the American military commanders in the field. There had to be some reliance on professional competence.

About two hours earlier, 5:30 A.M. Pearl Harbor time, Mitsuo Fuchida, dressed in his aviator's uniform, entered the operations room of the *Akagi*. He reported to his commander in chief that "I am ready for the mission." The pilots began moving out onto the deck then, to their waiting airplanes. It still was dark and the sea had a heavy pitch and roll to it. Fuchida was asked whether he believed it would be possible to take off. "The pitch is greater than the roll," Fuchida replied. "Were this a training flight, the take-off would be delayed until dawn. But if we coordinate the take-offs with the pitching we can launch successfully."

He walked to his airplane. One of the maintenance men approached him and handed him a white cloth headband. "This is a present from the maintenance crew," said the man. "May I ask that you take it along to Pearl Harbor?" Fuchida nodded and fastened the scarf to his flying cap.

The *Akagi* turned to port, heading into the northerly wind. It was time for takeoff. Mitsuo Fuchida looked over his shoulder. He saw that the *Akagi* was flying its battle flag.

There were many problems with America's military machine, its Army, and its industrial strength in December, 1941. There were only seven Army divisions capable of being sent overseas. Much in the way of supplies was lacking. There were not enough guns and ammunition. There was not enough clothing, airplanes, radar sets—not enough of anything that goes into the making of war. Industry's contribution to the war effort still lagged. Only one-fifth of the automobile industry workers were engaged in defense work.

Many of the officers who had lost what Harvey Bundy called

their "self-starters" still were in positions of command. Army maneuvers in the Carolinas in November showed that the Army leaders did not know how to handle the tanks they had, could not communicate between the ground and the air forces, that they continued to spend too much time worrying about horse cavalry.

Still, in 1939 the Army had consisted of less than 200,000 men. By December, 1941, the army numbered 1,640,000 men. They were organized in modern divisions, were learning how to use new weapons, had begun to move as units. The George Pattons were saying goodby to the horses and becoming the masters of the armored cavalry. Brilliant leaders like Dwight Eisenhower were being pulled from obscure military posts and placed in command positions. If war came in December, 1941, the enemy would find the United States with an army. Two years earlier the United States had no army of which to speak. Now it had, potentially, the best army in the world.

Franklin Roosevelt was responsible for that change. He had selected good men, such as Henry Stimson and George Marshall, without regard to their political allegiance, and told them to build the United States an army. They had done so and he had backed them. In 1940 he had put his political future on the line by seeking a selective service bill. The next year he had risked his party's future by demanding that Democrats in Congress support that program's extension. He had won all of his political gambles and the United States had an army.

Industry was not yet giving its all in December, 1941, but it was ready to do so. In November, Harry Hopkins had written to a friend, "We are really getting on with our production program here now. Airplanes, tanks, ammunition and guns are moving rapidly and I think they are going to play an important part in the next few months."

Those Rolls-Royce engines that Henry Ford had refused to build were about ready to come off the assembly line at the Packard company. The Willow Run plant, which Ford had constructed with government funds, was ready to start producing bombers. By November, 1941, the Army Quartermaster General had completed camps and training grounds for 1,300,000 men. Construction had begun on forty-two new plants, to be owned and operated by the Army, at which would be manufactured military explosives. In the last six months of 1941 the Congress had appropriated $22 billion for military purposes, in addition to and compared to the $13.5 billion appropriated in the previous twelve-month period. This $35.5 billion in an eighteen-month span was more than the combined expenditures of the War and Navy departments during all of World War I.

As this money was being spent, American businessmen were coming to Washington to learn something about their government and their own responsibilities as citizens. They were developing plans to produce the greatest war machine the world ever had seen. In 1939 military airplanes had been produced by the tens each month. In late 1941 they were produced by the hundreds. And already, in December, 1941, the industrial strength to produce airplanes by the thousands existed.

Franklin Roosevelt was responsible for that change. He had brought in the best men—Bill Knudsen, Robert Patterson—without regard to their political allegiance. He told them to develop an industrial-military machine and then he had supported them. He only told them what to do, never how to do it. That last was their job, and they were all very good at it. There was another aspect of FDR's overseeing of the rearming effort. In building up its defense machine, the United States relied on the profit motive. There would be controls, priorities, taxes, but basically the Roosevelt administration relied on profits as the incentive for industry —the incentive which had been traditional throughout American industry. Other nations did not do so. England did not. Nor did Russia and Germany. There were many times, certainly after 1941, when FDR could have assumed the role of an economic dictator—on occasions there were demands that he do so. Bernard Baruch, the patriarch of Wall Street, and Wendell Willkie, the leader of the Republican Party, had made such demands. But Franklin Roosevelt refused to respond to them. He exercised a tremendous amount of power, exerted unprecedented authority and even dictated on a few occasions. But he refused to alter the basic free enterprise system of the United States.

And to the surprise of the business leaders, Roosevelt handled the unions for them—but in such a manner that the union members retained the rights they had gained in the 1930s. As the defense strikes had mounted early in 1941, the conservatives in Congress believed they at last had an opportunity to reverse the pro-labor trend of the New Deal. The conservatives believed that a good time to seek legislation stripping unions of some of their powers was when the public appeared riled at the unions for striking against the defense effort. Representative Howard W. Smith of Virginia, one of the leaders of the southern Democratic conservatives, had the most stringent bill. Mixed in with a number of reasonable measures, such as a thirty-day cooling-off period and a secret membership vote before a strike could be called, were a number of punitive measures. Jurisdictional strikes and boycotts would be illegal in defense industries. Any union that had a Communist or a fascist as an officer would be denied the benefit of the labor laws. The public had turned so against labor unions that the Smith bill did pass the House of Representatives. It never passed the Senate, however, and did not become law.

By his strong action, FDR had convinced the nation that he could and would handle the unions, that legislation would not be necessary; he would use troops if he must. The executive actions he took in time of national emergency would not become cemented in law. As he had done with the business community, FDR had brought the labor unions into the war effort without seriously diminishing the position they had achieved in American society. The working man would not have to face in the postwar world the despair he had known in the pre-New Deal world.

And if war came in December, 1941, the American people would be prepared for it also. The isolationists had run their course. They had had their chance to state their case. The American people were swayed by that case, but in the end they did not accept it. They had seen the bargaining go back and forth and the lines etch deeper into the worried faces of the leaders of the Roosevelt administration. In the end the American people would judge the record that had been made, and the decency they understood to be within Franklin Roosevelt, against the calumnies hurled at him, and they would know that if war came it had not been sought.

And Franklin Roosevelt was responsible for that. He had moved at all times cautiously and prudently, within the democratic framework of the American system. He had not acted to save England, as perhaps Winston Churchill would have wished, but to save the United States. He had resisted the pleas that he provoke war. By doing so he had avoided giving America's enemies the opportunity to claim a legitimate provocation. He had resisted also the pleas that he ignore the warfare engulfing Europe and Asia. By doing so he had educated the American people to their responsibilities as citizens of the world. He had led the American people, always a little ahead of them but never so far ahead that they could not catch up with him. "Government," FDR had said in 1932, "includes the art of formulating a policy, and using the political technique to attain so much of that policy as will receive general support; persuading, leading, sacrificing, teaching always, because the greatest duty of a statesman is to educate." He had successfully lived up to that definition.

Actually, if war came to the United States in December, 1941, the United States would be better prepared for it—militarily, emotionally, politically, in every way—than it ever had been prepared for any of its conflicts. The Revolution, the Civil War, and the First World War had not come to America as surprises, they were seen months in advance. Still, when they came, America was not ready to fight. This was particularly true of the First World War. After the war declaration in 1917, the United States had to develop an army, manufacture the weapons for that army to fight with, and learn the new techniques of combat. That would not be so if war came in December, 1941. Preparations were not complete. But they were well on their way.

And Franklin Roosevelt was responsible for that. It was perhaps his greatest contribution to America and the world. From a peaceful nation unaware of its responsibilities, he had forged a military power. He had politicked and persuaded, cajoled and threatened, bargained and bought. He had been subjected to more personal abuse than any other man in the nation. He had resisted those who could not wait to enter the war and fought those who wished to avoid war at all costs. He not only made it possible for the world to save the political system of democracy but, in Frank Knox's phrase, he raised the cry of civilized humanity and kept it strong until it became the cry of the world.

On the flight deck of the *Akagi* a small green light cut a circle in the darkness. The engine of the first plane began to roar, then moved slowly toward the end of the pitching flight deck and then with greater power, finally lifting into the air while the Japanese on board the carrier cheered. The Japanese planes circled over the task force, then turned due south for Oahu Island. The time was 6:15 in the morning. There were 360 planes.

Four years earlier the Black fleet under the command of the American admiral Ernest J. King had executed exactly the same plan of attack. But that had been only a mock attack, only to demonstrate that it could be done.

Fuchida used a radio-direction finder to guide him toward Hawaii; the device picked up some light music from a Honolulu radio station. The radio station obligingly announced the weather. The clouds were breaking over Pearl Harbor. The Japanese could not have asked for a better day.

On Oahu the radar station usually stopped at seven o'clock in the morning. This particular morning it was on a few minutes longer because an officer was training an enlisted man in how to operate the radar equipment. Shortly after seven the enlisted man noticed that the radar screen was picking something up. The officer told him not to bother about it. A group of B-17 bombers from the States was expected shortly. The American airplanes would have come from the other direction.

If there had been long-range patrolling by the Navy, as General Short of the Army thought there was, the Japanese might have been detected. If the Army was on a full alert, as Admiral Kimmel of the Navy thought it was, the radar blips might have been understood to be at least a matter of concern. If at Pearl Harbor there had been any response by the military to the "war warning" message and to the other alert messages that had streamed from Washington, it would not have required more than an hour to alert the command to the fact that an American ship had fired at a submarine at the base entrance shortly before seven o'clock that morning.

But none of these "ifs" had happened and so the Japanese air strike force flew toward its destination. At 7:40 A.M., Fuchida, flying the lead plane, pushed back the canopy of his cockpit. The wind caught at the white scarf that had been given to him by the maintenance crew, billowing it out behind the cockpit. Fuchida raised his hand and fired a single black flare.

"With this order," he said of the black column of smoke from the flare, "dive bombers rose to four thousand meters, torpedo bombers went down almost to sea level, and level bombers came down just under the clouds. . . ."

Pearl Harbor lay before them.

AFTERWORD

BURTON WHEELER'S isolationism came to an end with the Japanese attack on Pearl Harbor. "Let's lick hell out of them," he said. He was defeated the next time he ran for re-election.

Charles Lindbergh tried to regain his Army Air Corps commission, but Franklin Roosevelt never would acquiesce to the man he considered the Vallandigham of the Second World War. Lindbergh then went to the South Pacific as an observer for a manufacturer of military airplanes. Although a civilian, he flew combat missions. Since the war he has lived in selective obscurity. He wrote a dramatic account of his 1927 flight to Paris and co-operated with a glamorous film treatment of that flight. He declines, however, to write about or discuss his activities prior to America's entry into the Second World War. He declined to co-operate in the preparation of this book.

Father Charles E. Coughlin presented more of a problem for the Roosevelt administration. Francis Biddle, Attorney General after the war began, tells of calling in a prominent member of the Roman Catholic laity for assistance in quieting the Father. "The point was to win the war," Biddle said he told the layman, "not to indict a priest for sedition." The point of the conversation apparently was well made and Father Coughlin finally was quieted by the hierarchy of the Church he had so abused.

Many of the people active in the period before the war—such as Henry Stimson and Cordell Hull—served for part or all of the war, and then died shortly after.

George Marshall continued in the service of his country. After a brilliant record as an Army leader during the second World War, he became an equally brilliant civilian Secretary of Defense and then Secretary of State. For a brief period in the early 1950s he became the butt of Senator Joseph McCarthy's attacks. Marshall's position in history rightly survived having had such attacks made against him, while McCarthy's position in history was destroyed—he is relegated to the status of demagogue—because of his having made such attacks.

General Short and Admiral Kimmel, the Pearl Harbor commanders, were permitted to retire from the service. Kimmel claimed the surprise at Pearl Harbor was not due to any lack of responsible action on his part. Rather, he charged, the Roosevelt administration withheld information from him. The charge has been investigated dozens of times by friends of Kimmel and remains without any proof. The Navy, not officially but certainly informally, still will not accept that one of its best men could have done less than expected of him. To so acknowledge means acknowledging that the system by which the Navy produces officers is at fault. Kimmel's story is widely believed among career men in the Navy.

Douglas Stuart, the founder of America First, and many of its young members joined the United States military services and served their country in heroic fashion. Japan had taught them the lesson they did not believe from FDR: The United States could not escape its responsibilities.

Hirohito in 1945 forced the military leaders of his nation to surrender to the United States rather than commit Japan to a policy of national suicide. The authority he refused to exercise in the fall of 1941 when the war was beginning was used to good purpose when the war was ending. After the war Hirohito conceded he was not divine and was allowed to live, to putter in his scientific studies and in the councils of the leaders of his nation. The militarists in his country who survived the war were tried for war crimes and executed or imprisoned.

Mussolini was killed by his own people and strung up with a rope by his feet. Adolf Hitler committed suicide in a Berlin bunker. For the German people the Third Reich was dead and the apologies were just beginning.

At the end of the war Winston Churchill was ousted from the office of Prime Minister. He was called back again a few years later for a brief period. He died in 1965. At the time of his death perhaps no citizen was so beloved by the peoples of the world than this man who, in 1940 and 1941 when he had little else, had stopped the German bullets with his words.

The Second World War cost the United States billions of dollars and the lives of almost three hundred thousand Americans. When it ended, it could not be said that "the sacred fire of liberty," to use George Washington's phrase as FDR did in that 1941 inaugural address, engulfed the world. But it could be said that it still burned, and perhaps with a brighter flame.

Franklin Roosevelt died in April, 1945, a few months before the hostilities ended. Felix Frankfurter kept his promise to his friend. In the capital city of the United States there is a triangular patch of green grass in front of the National Archives building, on the Pennsylvania Avenue side, between Eighth and Ninth streets. In that patch of green is a slab of stone. The inscription says, "In Memory of Franklin Delano Roosevelt   1882   1945." Nothing else.

ACKNOWLEDGMENTS,
SOURCES, AND NOTES

ACKNOWLEDGMENTS

My appreciation to John W. McCormack, the Speaker of the House of Representatives, and to R. Douglas Stuart, Jr., for their assistance. My appreciation to Joseph W. Ballantine and to the late Robert E. Wood for permission to quote from their Oral History Research Projects at Columbia University. My appreciation to Mrs. Harvey H. Bundy for permission to quote from her husband's Oral History Research Project; Mrs. Bundy asked me to make clear that the project was an unedited tape recording. My appreciation to Mrs. Alan G. Kirk for permission to quote from her husband's Oral History Research Project; to Senator Claiborne Pell of Rhode Island to quote from the Oral History Research Project of his father, Herbert C. Pell; and to James J. Wadsworth for permission to quote from the Oral History Research Project of his father, James W. Wadsworth. My appreciation also to the Department of State for permission to quote from the Cordell Hull Papers; to the Franklin D. Roosevelt Library for permission to quote from the Roosevelt Papers; and to the Sterling Memorial Library at Yale University for permission to quote from the Henry L. Stimson Papers and Diary.

Research for this book was done at the following libraries and I am indebted to the staffs of all of them for their many courtesies and their efficiency which made my work so much easier: the Franklin D. Roosevelt Library, Hyde Park, New York; the Manuscript Division, Library of Congress, Washington, D.C.; the National Archives, Washington, D.C.; the Office of the Chief of Military History, Washington, D.C.; the Oral History Research Office, Columbia University; the Sterling Memorial Library, Yale University; and the Swarthmore Peace Collection, Swarthmore College, Pennsylvania.

Several of my sources must remain anonymous.

PRIMARY SOURCES

America First Committee Papers, a collection in the Swarthmore Peace Collection, Swarthmore College.

American Peace Mobilization Papers, a collection in the Swarthmore Collection, Swarthmore College.

Ballantine, Joseph W., "Memoir," a project in the Oral History Research Office, Columbia University.

Bundy, Harvey H., "Memoir," a project in the Oral History Research Office, Columbia University.

Burton, Harold H., "Papers," a collection in the Manuscript Division, Library of Congress.

Cater Files, a collection of military papers in the Office of the Chief of Military History.

Chief of Staff Files, a collection in the National Archives.

Citizens' Keep America Out of War Committee Papers, a collection in the Swarthmore Peace Collection, Swarthmore College.

Clapper, Raymond, "Papers," a collection in the Manuscript Division, Library of Congress.

Connally, Tom, "Papers," a collection in the Manuscript Division, Library of Congress.

Davies, Joseph E., "Papers," a collection in the Manuscript Division, Library of Congress.

Frankfurter, Felix, "Papers," a collection in the Manuscript Division, Library of Congress.

Green, Theodore F., "Papers," a collection in the Manuscript Division, Library of Congress.

Hopkins, Harry L., "Papers," a collection in the Franklin D. Roosevelt Library.

Hull, Cordell, "Papers," a collection in the Manuscript Division, Library of Congress.

Jones, Jesse H., "Papers," a collection in the Manuscript Division, Library of Congress.

Kirk, Adm. Alan G., "Memoir," a project in the Oral History Research Office, Columbia University.

Knox, Frank, "Papers," a collection in the Manuscript Division, Library of Congress.

Leahy, William D., "Papers," a collection in the Manuscript Division, Library of Congress.

Ministers' No War Committee Papers, a collection in the Swarthmore Peace Collection, Swarthmore College.

National Council for Prevention of War Papers, a collection in the Swarthmore Peace Collection, Swarthmore College.

Norris, George, "Papers," a collection in the Manuscript Division, Library of Congress.

Patterson, Robert P., "Papers," a collection in the Manuscript Division, Library of Congress.

Patton, George S., Jr., "Papers," a collection in the Manuscript Division, Library of Congress.

Pell, Herbert C., "Memoir," a project in the Oral History Research Office, Columbia University.

Pinchot, Amos R. E., "Papers," a collection in the Manuscript Division, Library of Congress.

Pringle, Henry F., "Papers," a collection in the Manuscript Division, Library of Congress.

Roosevelt, Franklin D., "Papers," a collection in the Franklin D. Roosevelt Library, including Press Conferences (PC), Speech File, President's Personal File (PPF), President's Secretary File (PSF), and Map Room Papers—Roosevelt-Churchill Correspondence.

Smith, Harold D., "Papers," a collection in the Franklin D. Roosevelt Library.

Smith, Col. Truman, U.S.A. (Ret.), "Air Intelligence Activities, August 1935–April 1939," Sterling Memorial Library, Yale University.

Stimson, Henry L., "Diary," Sterling Memorial Library, Yale University.

Stimson, Henry L., "Papers," Sterling Memorial Library, Yale University.

Wadsworth, James W., "Memoir," a project in the Oral History Research Office, Columbia University.

Wallace, Henry A., "Papers," a collection in the Manuscript Division, Library of Congress.

War Plans Division Files, a collection in the National Archives.

White, William Allen, "Papers," a collection in the Manuscript Division, Library of Congress.

Wood, Robert E., "Memoir," a project in the Oral History Research Office, Columbia University.

GOVERNMENT SOURCES

Anderson, Troyer S., "History of the Office of the Under Secretary of War," Office of the Chief of Military History.

Annual Report of the Secretary of War to the President, 1941.

Army Air Forces Historical Study Number 40, Office of the Chief of Military History.

Biennial Report of the Chief of Staff of the United States Army to the Secretary of War, July 1, 1941, to June 30, 1943.

Congressional Record, various bound volumes as cited in the Notes.

Craven, Wesley Frank, and Cate, James Lea, editors, *Men and Planes,* Chicago, 1955; a volume in The Army Air Forces in World War II series.

Craven, Wesley Frank, and Cate, James Lea, *Plans and Early Operations, January 1939 to August 1942,* Chicago, 1948; a volume in The Army Air Forces in World War II series.

Dictionary of American Naval Fighting Ships, v. 3, a publication of the Office of the Chief of Naval Operations, Naval History Division, Navy Department, Washington, 1968.

Fairchild, Byron, and Grossman, Jonathan, *The Army and Industrial Manpower,* Washington, 1959; a volume in The United States Army in World War II series.

First, Edythe W., "Industry and Labor Advisory Committees in the National Defense Advisory Commission and the Office of Production Management, May 1940 to January 1942," December 9, 1946; a pamphlet in the Historical Reports on War Administration: War Production Board, Special Study 24; National Archives.

Foreign Relations of the United States 1941, v. 4 and 5, Washington, 1956.

Greenfield, Kent Roberts, ed., *Command Decisions,* Washington, 1960.

Grundstein, Nathan D., "Programming of Defense Production of the National Defense Advisory Commission and Office of Production Management, May 1940 to December 1941," May 1, 1947; a pamphlet in the Historical Reports on War Administration: War Production Board, Special Study 31; National Archives.

Holley, Jr., Irving Brinton, *Buying Aircraft: Materiel Procurement for the Army Air Forces,* Washington, 1964; a volume in The United States Army in World War II series.

Inaugural Addresses of the Presidents of the United States, Washington, 1961.

Industrial Mobilization for War—History of the War Production Board and Predecessor Agencies, v. 1, Washington, 1947; National Archives.

Matloff, Maurice, and Snell, Edwin M., *Strategic Planning for Coalition Warfare, 1941–1942,* Washington, 1953; a volume in The United States Army in World War II series.

McAleer, James A., "Dollar A Year and Without Compensation Personnel Policies of the War Production Board and Predecessor Agencies, August 1939 to November 1945," April 20, 1947; a pamphlet in the Historical Reports on War Administration: War Production Board, Special Study 27; National Archives.

Sitterson, J. Carlyle, "Aircraft Production Policies Under the National Defense Advisory Commission and Office of Production Management, May 1940 to December 1941," May 30, 1946; a pamphlet in the Historical Reports on War Administration: War Production Board, Special Study 21; National Archives.

Smith, R. Elberton, *The Army and Economic Mobilization,* Washington, 1959; a volume in The United States Army in World War II series.

United States Congress, "Hearings Before the Committee on Foreign Affairs, House of Representatives on H.R. 1776 (the lend-lease bill)," 77th Congress, 1st Session.

United States Congress, "Hearings Before the Joint Committee on the Investigtaion of the Pearl Harbor Attack," 79th Congress, 1st Session.

Watson, Mark S., *Chief of Staff: Prewar Plans and Preparations,* Washington, 1950; a volume in The United States Army in World War II series.

SECONDARY SOURCES

Acheson, Dean, *Morning and Noon,* Boston, 1965.

Allen, C. B., "The Facts About Lindbergh," *The Saturday Evening Post,* Dec. 28, 1940.

Alsop, Joseph, and Kintner, Robert, "New Boss—New Army," *This Week,* Aug. 11, 1940.

Baker, Leonard, *Back To Back—The Duel Between FDR and the Supreme Court,* New York, 1967.

Baker, Liva, *Felix Frankfurter,* New York, 1969.

Barkley, Alben W., *That Reminds Me,* New York, 1954.

Beard, Charles A., *President Roosevelt and the Coming of War 1941,* New Haven, 1948.

Beasley, Norman, *Knudsen,* New York, 1947.

Biddle, Francis, *In Brief Authority,* New York, 1962.

Block, Maxine, ed., *Current Biography,* New York, 1940, 1941, 1942 editions.

Blum, John Morton, *From the Morgenthau Diaries: Years of Urgency 1938–1941,* Boston, 1965.

Burns, James MacGregor, *Roosevelt: The Lion and The Fox,* New York, 1956.

Butow, Robert J. C., *Tojo and the Coming of War,* Princeton, 1961.

Cantril, Hadley, *Public Opinion 1935–1946,* Princeton, 1951.

Casey, Rt. Hon. Lord, *Personal Experiences: 1939–46,* Australia, 1962.

Chicago Tribune, The, various editions as cited in the Notes.

Chomsky, Noam, *American Power and the New Mandarins,* New York, 1969.

Churchill, Winston S., *The Gathering Storm,* Boston, 1958.

———, *The Grand Alliance,* Boston, 1950.

———, *Their Finest Hour,* Boston, 1949.

Ciano, Galeazzo, *The Ciano Diaries, 1939–1943,* New York, 1946.

CIO News, various editions as cited in the Notes.

Cohn, David L., "Mr. Speaker," *The Atlantic Monthly,* Oct. 1942.

Cole, Wayne S., *America First,* Madison, Wis., 1953.

———, *Senator Gerald P. Nye and American Foreign Relations,* Minneapolis, 1962.

Coles, Harry L., *Total War and Cold War,* Columbus, Ohio, 1962.

Compton, James V., *The Swastika and the Eagle,* Boston, 1967.

Correspondence Between the Chairman of the Councils of Ministers of the U.S.S.R. and the Presidents of the U.S.A., v. 2, Moscow, 1957.

Davis, Forrest, and Lindley, Ernest K., *How War Came,* New York, 1942.

Davis, Kenneth S., *The Hero—Charles A. Lindbergh and the American Dream,* New York, 1959.

Dorough, C. Dwight, *Mr. Sam,* New York, 1962.

Emporia Gazette, The, various editions as cited in the Notes.

Fehrenbach, T. R., *F.D.R.'s Undeclared War—1939 to 1941,* New York, 1967.

Feis, Herbert, *The Road to Pearl Harbor,* Princeton, 1950.

Frankfurter, Felix, *Felix Frankfurter Reminisces,* New York, 1962.

Freedman, Max, *Roosevelt and Frankfurter,* Boston, 1967.

Friedlander, Saul, *Prelude to Downfall: Hitler and the United States 1939–1941,* New York, 1967.

Fuchida, Mitsuo, "I Led the Air Attack on Pearl Harbor," *United States Naval Institute Proceedings,* Annapolis, Md., Sept. 1952.

Gerhart, Eugene C., *America's Advocate: Robert H. Jackson,* Indianapolis, 1958.

Grew, Joseph C., *Ten Years In Japan,* New York, 1944.

Hellman, Geoffrey, "Roosevelt," *Life* magazine, Jan. 20, 1941.

Hitler, Adolf, *Mein Kampf,* Boston, 1943.

Hull, Cordell, *Memoirs of Cordell Hull,* v. 1 and 2, New York, 1948.

Ickes, Harold L., *The Secret Diary of Harold L. Ickes,* v. 1, 2, and 3, New York, 1953 and 1954.

Ike, Nobutaka, *Japan's Decision For War,* Stanford, Calif., 1967.

Israel, Fred L., ed., *The War Diary of Breckinridge Long,* Lincoln, Neb., 1966.

Johnson, Walter, *The Battle Against Isolation,* Chicago, 1944.

Jonas, Manfred, *Isolationism in America 1935–1941,* Ithaca, N.Y., 1966.

Josephson, Matthew, *Sidney Hillman,* New York, 1952.

Kahn, David, *The Codebreakers,* New York, 1967.

Kennedy, John F., *Why England Slept,* New York, 1962.

Klein, Burton, *Germany's Economic Preparations for War,* Cambridge, Mass., 1959.

Kramer, Dale, "Lindbergh Eyes Minnesota," *The Nation,* July 26, 1941.

Kuzuoka, T., *The Life of Fleet-Admiral Yamamoto-Isoroku,* Tokyo, 1943.

Langer, William S., and Gleason, S. Everett, *The Undeclared War 1940–1941*, New York, 1953.

Leopold, Richard W., "The Mississippi Valley and American Foreign Policy, 1899–1941: An Assessment and An Appeal," *Mississippi Valley Historical Review*, v. 37, Abilene, Kan., 1950–51.

Life magazine, various issues as cited in the Notes.

Lindbergh, Anne Morrow, *The Wave of the Future*, New York, 1940.

Lindbergh, Charles A., Jr., *Of Flight and Life*, New York, 1948.

Lindbergh, Charles A., Sr., *Your Country At War*, Philadelphia, 1934.

Look, various issues as cited in the Notes.

Macmillan, Harold, *The Blast of War 1939–1945*, New York, 1967.

Manvell, Roger, and Fraenkel, Heinrich, *Goering*, New York, 1962.

Marshall, Katherine Tupper, *Together—Annals of an Army Wife*, Atlanta, Ga., 1946.

Martin, Kingsley, *Harold Laski*, New York, 1953.

Mason, Alpheus Thomas, *Harlan Fiske Stone*, New York, 1956.

Morison, Elting E., *Turmoil and Tradition*, Boston, 1960.

Morison, Samuel Eliot, *The Battle of the Atlantic*, Boston, 1962.

———, *The Oxford History of the American People*, New York, 1965.

———, *The Rising Sun In The Pacific 1939—April 1942*, Boston, 1963.

Morse, Arthur D., *While Six Million Died*, New York, 1967.

Morton, H. V., *Atlantic Meeting*, New York, 1943.

Mosley, Leonard, *Hirohito—Emperor of Japan*, Englewood Cliffs, N.J., 1966.

Nathan, Otto, *The Nazi Economic System*, Durham, N.C., 1944.

Nation, The, various editions as cited in the Notes.

Nelson, Donald M., *Arsenal of Democracy*, New York, 1946.

Nevins, Allan, and Hill, Frank Ernest, *Ford—Decline and Rebirth, 1933–1962*, New York, 1963.

New York Herald Tribune, The, various editions as cited in the Notes.

New York Times, The, various editions as cited in the Notes.

Nichols, Jeannette P., "The Middle West and the Coming of World War II," *Ohio State Archaeological and Historical Quarterly*, Columbus, Ohio, Apr. 1953.

Nicolson, Harold, *The War Years 1939–1945*, New York, 1967.

Nixon, Edgar B., ed., *Franklin D. Roosevelt and Foreign Affairs*, 3 v., Cambridge, Mass., 1969.

Perkins, Frances, *The Roosevelt I Knew*, New York, 1964.

PM, various editions as cited in the Notes.

Pogue, Forrest C., *George C. Marshall: Ordeal and Hope*, New York, 1966.

Potter, John Deane, *Yamamato, The Man Who Menaced America*, New York, 1965.

Rauch, Basil, *Roosevelt From Munich to Pearl Harbor*, New York, 1950.

Reischauer, Edwin O., *The United States and Japan*, Cambridge, Mass., 1965.

Roosevelt, Elliott, ed., *F.D.R. His Personal Letters—Early Years*, New York, 1947.

——, *F.D.R. His Personal Letters 1905–1928*, New York, 1948.

——, *F.D.R. His Personal Letters 1928–1945*, v. 1 and 2, New York, 1950.

Roosevelt, Franklin D., *Public Papers and Addresses of Franklin D. Roosevelt, 1941*, New York, 1950.

Sherwood, Robert E., *Roosevelt and Hopkins*, New York, 1948.

Shirer, William L., *The Rise and Fall of The Third Reich*, New York, 1960.

Smith, Howard K., *Last Train from Berlin*, New York, 1943.

Sorensen, Charles E., *My Forty Years With Ford*, New York, 1956.

Terasaki, Gwen, *Bridge to the Sun*, Chapel Hill, N.C., 1957.

Time magazine, various editions as cited in the Notes.

Togo, Shigenori, *The Cause of Japan*, New York, 1956.

Tourtellot, Arthur Bernon, *The Presidents on the Presidency*, New York, 1964.

Trefousse, Hans L., "Failure of German Intelligence in the United States," *Mississippi Valley Historical Review*, Lincoln, Neb., June 1955.

Trivanovitch, Vaso, *Economic Development of Germany Under National Socialism*, New York, 1937.

Tull, Charles J., *Father Coughlin and the New Deal*, Syracuse, N.Y., 1965.

Tully, Grace, *F.D.R. My Boss*, New York, 1949.

Ward, Robert E., "The Inside Story of the Pearl Harbor Plan," *United States Naval Institute Proceedings*, Annapolis, Md., Dec. 1951.

Washington Post, The, various editions as cited in the Notes.

Washington Star, The, various editions as cited in the Notes.

Welles, Sumner, *The Time For Decision*, New York, 1944.

Wheeler, Burton K., with Healy, Paul F., *Yankee From the West*, New York, 1962.

Wohlstetter, Roberta, *Pearl Harbor—Warning and Decision*, Stanford, Calif., 1962.

NOTES

Preface

Page

vii   "once again was," Burns, p. 458.

vii   "as to maneuver," Beard, p. 566.

vii   "Japan's appeal to," Chomsky, p. 160.

January: ". . . the sacred fire of liberty"

Page

1   "With Thy favor," *Washington Star,* Jan. 20, 1941, p. 1.

1   "People sensed that," FDR to Endicott Peabody, Feb. 7, 1941, Roosevelt, *Letters 1928–1945,* v. 2, p. 1117.

2   Hitler quote, *N.Y. Times,* Jan. 1, 1941, p. 1.

2   Matsuoka quote, *N.Y. Times,* Jan. 21, 1941, p. 1.

2   Matthews quote, *N.Y. Times,* Oct. 4, 1940, p. 1.

2   Shirer quote, p. 871.

5   "When you feel," FDR to J. P. Kennedy, March 22, 1938, Roosevelt Papers, PSF: Kennedy.

5   Knudsen quote, Beasley, p. vii.

6   Knox quote, Knox to FDR, Dec. 15, 1937, Knox Papers, Correspondence, Box 1.

6   "The temptation to," Knox to FDR, Dec. 15, 1939, Roosevelt Papers, PSF, Navy: Frank Knox.

6–7   "any deep sense," FDR to F. Knox, Dec. 29, 1939, Roosevelt Papers, PSF, Navy: Frank Knox.

7   Frankfurter quote, Frankfurter Papers, Roosevelt 1940–1942, Box 34.

8   "We have two," Roosevelt, *Letters 1928–1945,* v. 2, p. 1100.

9   "Eleanor and I," FDR to Endicott Peabody, Feb. 7, 1941, Roosevelt, *Letters 1928–1945,* v. 2, p. 1117.

9   Twentieth Psalm, FDR comments to Rayburn and Barkley, *Washington Star,* Jan. 20, 1941.

10   "regular as a metronome," Block, 1941 ed., pp. 40–1.

11   "Though I speak," *N.Y. Times,* Jan. 19, 1941, p. 36.

11–3   Inaugural speech quotes and FDR reaction to word "isolation," Roosevelt Papers, Speech File, 1353.

13   Ickes quote, Ickes, v. 3, p. 416.

13   Burton quote, Burton Papers, Box 1.

14   "Above the rumble," Marshall, *Together,* p. 83.

14   Bundy quote, Bundy, "Memoir," pp. 163–4.

15   "The problem was," Bundy, "Memoir," pp. 169–70.

15   "Piffle to the," Patton Papers, Military Writings, Tanks, 1909–1944, Box 58.

15   "The advent of," Patton Papers, Military Writings, Armored Tactics, 1929–1941, Box 56.

16   "Let us assume," Patton Papers, Military Writings—1941, Box 54.

16   Nicolson quote, Nicolson, p. 163.

17   "On January 10th," Patterson Papers, Letter Book, v. 1, Box 24.

17   "Well, naturally, the," Roosevelt Papers, Text of President's remarks, meeting with Business Advisory Council, May 23, 1940, pp. 8–9, PSF, Harry L. Hopkins folder.

Page

18   "It was the," Patterson Papers, handwritten manuscript, p. 111, Box 94.

18   "Concerns engaged in," Army Air Force Study, p. 32.

18   "What do we," Patterson Papers, untitled manuscript, unpaged, Box 24.

18   "Prime contractors were," and "Well, these subcontractors," Army Air Force Study, p. 96.

19   "Large companies balked" paragraph, Army Air Force Study, p. 99.

20   Lewis-Hillman discussion, Fairchild, *Manpower,* p. 36.

20   "all work carried," Fairchild, *Manpower,* p. 36.

20   Ford-Jackson, Fairchild, *Manpower,* p. 37.

21   Patterson quote, Patterson Papers, Letter Book, v. 1, Box 24.

21   "It was difficult," Smith, *Mobilization,* p. 74.

21   Marshall quote, Testimony, Apr. 28, 1941, before House Appropriations Committee on Military Establishment Appropriation Bill for 1941; quoted in Watson, *Chief of Staff,* p. 37.

22   "My relief of," quoted in Pogue, *Ordeal,* p. 59.

22   "People have forgotten," quoted in Pogue, *Ordeal,* p. 34.

22–3 Comparison of 1941 and 1917 from Annual Report of the Secretary of War 1941, pp. 2–3.

23   "Democratic governments devote," Biennial Report of the Chief of Staff.

23   "free men will," Patterson address before the American Bar Association, Philadelphia, Sept. 8, 1940, printed in ABA Journal, Nov. 1940, p. 856, copy in Patterson Papers, Box 102.

24   "Most of these," Roosevelt, *Letters 1905–1928,* p. 296.

24   Woodrow Wilson quote, printed in Jonas, p. 2.

24   "can and should," FDR to Col. E. M. House, Sept. 17, 1935, Roosevelt, *Letters 1928–1945,* v. 1, pp. 506–7.

25   Cole quote, Cole, *Nye,* p. 76.

26   W. A. White quotes, White to Charles P. Taft, July 5, 1940, White Papers, Box 238.

27   "A young idealistic," Wood, "Memoir," pp. 86–7.

28   Wallace on R. E. Wood, Wallace to FDR, Apr. 21, 1939, Roosevelt Papers, PSF: Agriculture Department.

29   "It seems to," Wood to FDR, Oct. 6, 1939, Roosevelt Papers, PPF 1365.

29   "So, my dear," FDR to R. E. Wood, Oct. 12, 1939, Roosevelt Papers, PPF 1365.

29   "I have been," R. E. Wood to FDR, Feb. 7, 1941, Roosevelt Papers, PPF 1365.

30   O'Connor quote, J. J. O'Connor to Amos Pinchot, Jan. 24, 1941, Pinchot Papers, untitled folder, Box 71.

30–1 "I believe the," U.S. Congress, lend-lease hearings, p. 8.

31   "Frankly and definitely," Roosevelt Papers, Speech File 1351.

February: ". . . the United States fleet in Hawaiian waters can be destroyed"

Page

31   "It involved, in," Annual Report of the Secretary of War, p. 47 (the section in the report by G. C. Marshall from which this quotation is taken is dated July 1, 1941).

32   "Out in Hawaii," U.S. Congress, Pearl Harbor hearings, part 15, p. 1627.

32   "You are there," H. R. Stark to Adm. James O. Richardson, May 27, 1940, U.S. Congress, Pearl Harbor hearings, part 1, p. 261.

33   "inability to make," S. E. Morison, *Rising Sun*, p. 5.

34   "We must be," Watson, *Chief of Staff*, p. 124.

34   "It seems to," J. C. Grew to FDR, Dec. 14, 1941, Grew, p. 360.

34   "I believe that," FDR to J. C. Grew, Jan. 21, 1941, *Foreign Relations*, v. 4, pp. 7–8.

35   "It may become," Grew, p. 358.

35   "The Russo-Japanese," Togo, p. 105.

36–7 Yamamoto biographical details, Block, 1942 ed., pp. 898–9; Kuzuoka, pp. 2, 3, 7; Potter, pp. 6, 127–8.

38   "My Peruvian colleague," J. C. Grew to Cordell Hull, Jan. 27, 1941, U.S. Congress, Pearl Harbor hearings, part 1, p. 13.

38   "The Division of," U.S. Congress, Pearl Harbor hearings, p. 14.

39   "By golly, he," Kirk, "Memoir," p. 120.

39   "thinking out loud," Chief of Staff Files, Notes on Conference of 17 June 1940, Misc. Conf., Binder 3.

40   "I told him," Stimson Papers, Memorandum of talk with the President, Oct. 8, 1940.

40   "If war eventuates," U.S. Congress, Pearl Harbor hearings, part 14, p. 1001.

40   "My impression of," G. C. Marshall to W. C. Short, Feb. 7, 1941, U.S. Congress, Pearl Harbor hearings, part 7, p. 2968.

40   "I do not," Conference, office of Chief of Staff, Feb. 25, 1941, U.S. Congress, Pearl Harbor hearings, part 15, p. 1628.

41   Stimson-Marshall conversation, Stimson Diary, Apr. 23, 1941, v. 33.

41   "These instructions seem," FDR to Sumner Welles, Feb. 20, 1941, Roosevelt, *Letters 1928–1945*, v. 2, p. 1126.

41   "somewhat brief" and "He then handed," Hull Papers, Folder 230, Box 60.

41   "Admiral Nomura was," Ballantine, "Memoir," pp. 48–9.

42   "He is an," Roosevelt Papers, PC, Feb. 11, 1941, p. 3.

42   "marked spirit of," Cordell Hull memorandum, *Foreign Relations—Japan*, v. 2, pp. 387–9.

Page

44 "Just back from," FDR to Eleanor Roosevelt, July 26, 1917, Roosevelt, *Letters 1905–1928,* p. 354.

44 "The more I," FDR to Eleanor Roosevelt, Aug. 17, 1917, Roosevelt, *Letters 1905–1928,* p. 357.

44 "My Dear Churchill" letter, Roosevelt Papers, Map Room Papers—Roosevelt-Churchill correspondence.

45 "In May, 1940," paragraph, Ickes, v. 3, p. 176.

46 "But if American," W. S. Churchill to FDR, May 18, 1940, Churchill, *Hour,* p. 56.

46 "Excuse me, Mr.," W. S. Churchill to FDR, May 20, 1940, Churchill, *Hour,* p. 57.

46–7 "Wendell Willkie will," Sherwood, p. 234, and Churchill, *Alliance,* p. 26, and a copy of the note is among the Roosevelt Papers.

47 "These splendid lines," Churchill, *Alliance,* p. 28.

47 Monnet quote, *N.Y. Times,* Nov. 9, 1968, p. 31.

47 "Not everyone had," paragraph, Ickes, v. 3, p. 471.

47–8 Willkie-FDR conversation, Sherwood, pp. 2–3.

48 "The only way," Roosevelt Papers, Text of President's remarks, Meeting with Business Advisory Council, May 23, 1940, PSF, Harry L. Hopkins folder, p. 23.

48 "Now listen carefully," H. L. Hopkins to Jesse Jones, Sept. 23, 1940, Jones Papers, Hopkins folder, Box 14.

48 *Fortune* description, Block, 1941 ed., 405–6.

48 *Time* report, *Time,* Jan. 22, 1945, p. 17.

49 Early, Hopkins, and Roosevelt quotes, Forrest Davis, pp. 173–4.

49 "I am sending," FDR to H. L. Ickes, Jan. 4, 1941, Roosevelt, *Letters 1928–1945,* v. 2, p. 1100.

49 "any mission to," Roosevelt Papers, PC, Jan. 3, 1941, p. 6.

49–50 Frankfurter-Casey exchange, Casey, pp. 51–2.

50 "The President is," Churchill, *Alliance,* p. 23.

50 Laski memorandum to Hopkins, Hopkins Papers, Box 301, Hopkins in London File, Folder A.

50–1 "I suspect that," Ickes, v. 3, p. 429.

51 "The people here," Sherwood, p. 243.

51 "War might have," Patterson Papers, untitled manuscript, Box 24.

51 "In order to," War Plans Division Files, 4402.

52 ABC meeting, Matloff, *Strategic,* pp. 32–40, and S. E. Morison, *Atlantic,* pp. 45–6, and Watson, *Chief of Staff,* pp. 374–5.

53 "There can be no," Watson, *Chief of Staff,* p. 99.

53 "Are we not," Watson, *Chief of Staff,* p. 108.

53 "Three months later" paragraph, Forrest Davis, p. 157.

53–4 Plan Dog, Roosevelt Papers, PSF, Navy Department, and Greenfield, *Command,* pp. 35–8.

Page

54 "There was no" paragraph, Watson, *Chief of Staff*, p. 123, and Pogue, *Ordeal,* p. 127.

54 "Roosevelt accepted this," Memorandum by G. C. Marshall, Jan. 17, 1941, on White House Conference, Jan. 16, 1941, War Plans Division Files 4175–18.

54-5 "The ABC meetings" paragraph, U.S. Congress, Pearl Harbor hearings, part 15, pp. 1487–92, and Watson, *Chief of Staff*, p. 373.

55 "The secret was," Patterson Papers, untitled manuscript, Box 24.

55-6 "The one supreme," Hull Memorandum, March 15, 1941, Roosevelt Papers, PSF, Great Britain 1941–1942.

57 "Hoover's campaign for," Ickes, v. 3, p. 385.

58 British government statement, Press Release from British Embassy in Washington, Dec. 10, 1940.

59 Hull–Gaston Henry-Haye meeting, Hull Papers, Box 58, Folder 208.

59-60 Hull-Halifax meeting, Hull Papers, Box 58, Folder 214-a.

60 Leahy meeting with Red Cross representative, Leahy Papers, Box 10.

60 Leahy-Darlan meeting, Leahy Papers, Box 10.

61-2 "The efforts of," FDR to Wm. D. Leahy, March 19, 1941, Leahy Papers, Box 10.

62 "I feel as," FDR to Wm. D. Leahy, June 26, 1941, Leahy Papers, Box 10.

62 "In regard to all," Wm. D. Leahy to FDR, May 26, 1941, Leahy Papers, Box 10.

62 Leahy-Taylor meeting, Hopkins Papers, Memorandum by Myron C. Taylor, September 1941, Box 306, Book 5: Relations with French Folder.

62-3 Denny report, *N.Y. Times,* Oct. 19, 1941, p. 19.

63 "Germany used food" and following paragraphs, Wallace Papers, Louis Bean Folder, Box 1.

March: "Suppose my neighbor's home catches fire . . ."

65 Churchill-Hopkins exchange, Hopkins Papers, Box 303, Background of Lend-lease File.

65 Leahy quote, Leahy Papers, Box 10.

65 "There is no," J. P. Kennedy to FDR, Sept. 10, 1939, Roosevelt Papers, PSF: Kennedy.

66 "Immediately after Dunkirk," Biennial Report, p. 3.

66-7 "The United States" and following paragraphs, Anderson, pp. v—10–1, and Pogue, *Ordeal,* p. 51, p. 66, and Churchill, *Hour,* pp. 142–3.

67 "Give it an," Blum, *Morgenthau Diaries,* p. 155.

Page

67   Churchill comment, Churchill, *Hour,* pp. 142–3.

67   "After the rifles" paragraph, Churchill, *Hour,* pp. 23–5.

67   "Mr. President, with," Churchill, *Hour,* p. 401.

67–8   Cohen memorandum and FDR comment, July 22, 1940, Roosevelt Papers, PSF, Navy: Frank Knox.

68   "But England could" paragraph, Blum, *Morgenthau Diaries,* p. 179.

68   "A solution was" paragraph, Acheson, pp. 222–4, and Fehrenbach, p. 161, and Gerhart, p. 221.

68–9   Jackson-Churchill exchange, Gerhart, p. 217.

69   "Grace, Congress is," Tully, p. 244.

69   "Churchill believed the" paragraph, Churchill, *Hour,* pp. 521–3.

69   Libby quote, *Denver Post,* Apr. 16, 1941, clip in National Council for Prevention of War, Drawer 83.

70   "I have been," W. A. White to E. H. Rees, July 23, 1940, White Papers, Box 239.

70   "We have had," Watson, *Chief of Staff,* p. 315.

71   "In a little" paragraph, Memorandum by John Creedy of the British Supply Council in North America to Henry F. Pringle, Feb. 20, 1942, Pringle Papers, Box 1, Folder C.

71–2   Wadsworth-Welles-Hull session, Wadsworth, "Memoir," pp. 431–3.

72   "We don't require," *N.Y. Times,* Jan. 18, 1941, p. 1.

72   "Few men are," A. Harriman to National Press Club, Feb. 5, 1969.

73   "I come to," Churchill, *Hour,* p. 566.

73   "Get the money," Chief of Staff Files, Notes on Conference, Binder 8.

73   "I was rather," Stimson Diary, Dec. 3, 1940, v. 32.

74–5   News conference quotes, Roosevelt Papers, PC, Dec. 17, 1940, pp. 1–6.

76   "If everything turns," Forrest Davis, p. 119.

76–7   "Perhaps the most" and following paragraphs, Blum, pp. 213–5.

77–8   "The chairman of the" and following paragraphs, author's interview with Speaker McCormack, Sept. 14, 1968.

78   "Bills in Congress" paragraph, author's interview with Speaker McCormack, Sept. 14, 1968.

78–9   Willkie analysis of Republican opposition, Frankfurter Papers, Memorandum, Box 42, Willkie Folder.

80   "I do not," Roosevelt Papers, OF 4193, Box 1.

80   Chandler incident, Roosevelt Papers, OF 4193, Box 1.

80   Wheeler-FDR exchange, Wheeler, pp. 26–7.

81   Short-McCormack exchange, *Congressional Record,* Feb. 5, 1941, p. 600, and Feb. 6, 1941, p. 739.

81   "I would have," Roosevelt Papers, PC, Jan. 24, 1941, p. 4.

81   "Rayburn worked out" paragraph, Blum, pp. 224–6, and confidential source.

Page
82   Hoover-Burton-Castle session, Burton Papers, Diary entry for Jan. 28, 1941, Box 1.
82   "There would be" paragraph, *Foreign Relations 1941*, v. 3, pp. 4–5, and Hull, *Memoirs*, v. 2, pp. 923–4, and Roosevelt, *Letters 1928–1945*, v. 2, pp. 1103–5, and Blum, pp. 217–222, and Ickes, v. 3, p. 410.
82   Morgenthau on British financial difficulties, H. S. Morgenthau to FDR, March 15, 1941, Roosevelt Papers, OF 4193, Box 1.
82–3 "The facts are," quoted in Rauch, p. 306.
83–4 FDR to Tobey, Roosevelt, *Letters 1928–1945*, v. 2, p. 1122.
84   "My best information," FDR to W. S. Churchill, Jan. 16, 1941, Roosevelt, *Letters 1928–1945*, v. 2, p. 1107.
85   Taft amendments, Blum, pp. 226–8.
85   "a blank check," Cole, *America First*, p. 43.
85–6 "Never before . . . have" American Peace Mobilization Papers, Box 1.
86   *Tribune* headline, *Tribune*, March 2, 1941, p. 1.
86   Green comment, news clips, Jan. 30, 1941, in National Council for Prevention of War Papers, Drawer 83.
86   Murray opposition, *CIO News*, Feb. 10, 1941, p. 6.
86   Wayne County statement, National Council for Prevention of War Papers, Drawer 83.
87   "Notwithstanding some delay," Roosevelt Papers, FDR to W. S. Churchill, March 8, 1941, Map Room Papers—Roosevelt-Churchill correspondence.
87   Harold Macmillan comments, Macmillan, pp. 76–7.
88   "The difficult and," Annual Report, p. 7.
88   Nye comment, Pinchot Papers, Box 69, untitled folder.
88   Hoover reaction, confidential source.
88–9 Matsuoka biography, Block, 1941, ed., pp. 563–5; Roosevelt Papers, unsigned memorandum, PSF, Japan File; Butow, p. 75; Togo, p. 18; Mosley, p. 195.
89–90 Matsuoka-Ribbentrop-Hitler sessions, U.S. Congress, Pearl Harbor hearings, part 19, pp. 3645–6; Forrest Davis, pp. 215–8; Churchill, *Alliance*, pp. 182–8; Shirer, pp. 871–2, 883–4.
90   Yamamoto's plans, Potter, p. 185.
91–2 "These talks, as" and following paragraphs, Feis, pp. 171–5; Hull, *Memoirs*, v. 2, pp. 988–9, and 990; Forrest Davis, p. 212.
92   Ballantine comment, Ballantine, "Memoir," pp. 42–3.
92   "As these conversations" paragraph, Kahn, p. 13.
92   "Actually fire hose," Roosevelt Papers, PC, Apr. 15, 1941, pp. 1–2.

April: ". . . the most hair-trigger times . . ."

93   Knox speech incident, Roosevelt, *Letters 1928–1945*, v. 2, p. 1145.

Page

93 Welles incident, Hull, *Memoirs,* v. 2, pp. 959–60.

93–4 Peru incident, *Foreign Relations,* v. 4, pp. 118–9.

94 British ship losses, Churchill, *Alliance,* p. 148.

94 "He said *no,*" Stimson Diary, Jan. 26, 1941, v. 32.

94 "I haven't paid," Roosevelt Papers, PC, March 18, 1941, pp. 2–3.

95 "Early in April" paragraph, Stimson Diary, Apr. 10, 1941, v. 33.

95 "Only four members," Smith Papers, Conferences With the President, Apr. 11, 1941, p. 5.

95 "Well, it's a" and "I hope you" quotes, Stimson Diary, Apr. 25, 1941, v. 33.

95 "He has no," Stimson Diary, Aug. 4, 1941, v. 35.

95–6 "The only fault," Stimson Diary, Dec. 1, 1941, v. 36.

96 Frankfurter comment, F. Frankfurter to C. C. Burlingham, June 29, 1932, Frankfurter Papers, Box 8.

96 Biddle analysis, Biddle, pp. 186–7.

96 "There's always a," Perkins, p. 21.

99–100 "I try to," Roosevelt, *Public Papers,* p. 83.

100 "He still was" paragraph, Ickes, v. 3, p. 375; *N.Y. Times Magazine,* Jan. 19, 1941, p. 3; Hellman, pp. 66–73.

100 "The President makes," Ickes, v. 3, p. 342.

100–1 Pell anecdote, Pell, "Memoir," pp. 457–8.

101 George Norris anecdote, Biddle, pp. 196–7.

101–2 Fortas anecdote, Biddle, p. 176.

102 "This consideration for" paragraph, Biddle, p. 135.

102 Winant appointment, Confidential source; Roosevelt Papers, PC, Feb. 7, 1941, pp. 2–3.

103 "The pre-election polls" paragraph, Cantril, p. 602; Wallace Papers, Box 1, Louis Bean folder.

104 Roosevelt as demagogue, Burns, p. 449.

104 FDR/Boers, Roosevelt, *Letters—Early Years,* p. 358.

104–5 FDR/Hawaii debate, Roosevelt, *Letters—Early Years,* pp. 160–2.

105 "Conflict, like anything," Roosevelt, *Letters—Early Years,* pp. 251–2.

105 "It is better," Roosevelt, *Letters 1905–1928,* p. 272.

105–6 "Roosevelt did not" paragraph, Roosevelt, *Letters 1928–1945,* v. 2, pp. 1120–1.

106 FDR to B. M. Baruch, March 18, 1931, Roosevelt, *Letters 1928–1945,* v. 1, p. 184.

106 "Everything seems to," FDR to Wm. E. Dodd, March 16, 1936, Roosevelt Papers, PSF, Germany: Dodd.

107 "These are without," FDR to Breckinridge Long, March 9, 1935, Roosevelt Papers, PSF, Breckinridge Long.

107 "In 1937 the" and following paragraphs, Hull, *Memoirs,* v. 1, pp. 507–8.

Page

108–9   Quarantine speech background, Ickes, v. 2, pp. 221–2; Hull, *Memoirs,* v. 1, pp. 544–6.

109   Knox reaction, F. Knox to George Messersmith, Oct. 6, 1937, Knox Papers, Correspondence, Box 1.

109–10   "The general direction," FDR to Anthony J. Drexel Biddle, Nov. 10, 1937, Roosevelt Papers, PSF, Poland.

110   Churchill comment, Churchill, *Storm,* pp. 254–5.

110   Eden comment, *N.Y. Times,* Aug. 31, 1969, p. 14.

111   "The President is," quoted in Tourtellot, p. 341.

111   "You know, you," Perkins, p. 341.

111   "This is a," Perkins, p. 343.

111   "Government includes the," Roosevelt, *Public Papers,* p. xvii.

112   "We should tell," quoted in *N.Y. Times,* Jan. 6, 1969, p. 33.

112   "You were given," Block, 1942 ed., pp. 152–7.

112   "Roosevelt understood this" paragraph, Blum, pp. 48–9.

112   "The reports of" paragraph, Ickes, v. 2, p. 475 and p. 409.

113   "You know, once," Roosevelt Papers, PC, Aug. 22, 1941, p. 6.

113–4   "I, too, went," FDR to Arthur Murray, March 4, 1940, Roosevelt Papers, PSF: Great Britain, Arthur Murray.

114   "I was a," Roosevelt Papers, Text of President's remarks, meeting with Business Advisory Council, May 23, 1940, PSF, Harry L. Hopkins folder.

114   Jackson comment, Gerhart, p. 214.

115   Stimson recommendation, H. L. Stimson to FDR, Oct. 12, 1940, Stimson Papers.

116   "If I could," FDR memorandum to H. L. Ickes, printed in U.S. Congress, Pearl Harbor hearings, part 20, p. 4341.

116   "stab in the back" sources, Stimson Diary, Dec. 29, 1940, v. 32; Forrest Davis, p. 62; Churchill, *Hour,* pp. 132–3.

117   "It is difficult," Morse, p. 121.

117   FDR/Frankfurter, Frankfurter Papers, Box 34.

118   Olympic games situation, Morse, pp. 173–4.

119   "I am delighted," FDR to G. H. Earle, Dec. 22, 1933, Roosevelt, *Letters 1928–1945,* v. 1, p. 380.

119   "What a plight," Roosevelt, *Letters 1928–1945,* v. 2, p. 811.

119   "In the dim," FDR to Philip Slomovitz, March 7, 1935, Roosevelt Papers, PPF 2313.

120   "Even the American" and following paragraph, Hull, *Memoirs,* v. 1, p. 599.

121   Morse on immigration, Morse, p. 131.

121   Ickes on State Department, Ickes, v. 3, p. 216–7.

121   fearful of "foreigners," Biddle, p. 109.

May: ". . . an unlimited national emergency exists . . ."

123   Willkie quote, *N.Y. Times,* May 4, 1941, p. 1.

123   Fish challenge, *N.Y. Times,* May 21, 1941, p. 1.

Page

124   Dillon report, Memorandum from E. M. Watson to FDR, May 14, 1941, Roosevelt Papers.

124   "Before Nomura left," Ike, p. 45.

125   "impossible," Togo, p. 78.

125   "goes the wrong way," Roosevelt Papers, PC, May 23, 1941, p. 2 (the conference was with editors of business publications).

125   Ickes, Cohen, Corcoran luncheon, Ickes, v. 2, p. 716.

126   "You don't want," Blum, p. 98.

127   Ickes comment, Ickes, v. 3, p. 76.

127   "The letter of," Army Air Force Study, p. 27.

127–8   "The next consideration" paragraph, pp. 248–9.

128   "The hallowed requirement," address before the American Bar Association, Philadelphia, Sept. 8, 1940, reprinted in ABA *Journal,* Nov. 1940, p. 856, copy in Patterson Papers, Box 102.

129   "the cost of," R. P. Patterson to Rep. Walter G. Andrews, June 9, 1941, Patterson Papers, Letter Book, v. 1, Box 24.

129   Ickes quote, Ickes, v. 3, p. 295.

129   "I lost ten," J. S. Knowlson in *Atlantic Monthly,* quoted in Sherwood, pp. 288–9.

129–30   Biggers memorandum and reply, McAleer, pp. 23–5.

130   "There is no," McAleer, p. 26.

130   Murray comment, McAleer, p. 36.

130   "Yes, sure. He's," Roosevelt Papers, PC, Apr. 15, 1941, p. 8.

131   Knudsen version, Beasley, p. 257.

131   "I am somewhat," Roosevelt, *Letters 1928–1945,* v. 2, p. 113.

131–2   FDR-Jones exchange, Jones Papers, Roosevelt 1940–1941 folder, Box 29.

132–3   "In early 1940" and following paragraphs, Beasley, p. 229; Sitterson, pp. 1–3; Craven, *Planes,* p. 264.

133   "It is obvious," Army Air Force Study, p. 7.

133–4   "The industry responded" and following paragraphs, Army Air Force Study, pp. 5–6 and pp. 74–5; Anderson, pp. iv–20; Sitterson, pp. 26–7; Holly, p. 228.

134–5   "It was then" and following paragraphs, *Industrial Mobilization,* pp. 19–20; Perkins, pp. 355–7.

135   "I am," Beasley, pp. 237–8; Josephson, p. 505.

135–6   "From the White House" paragraph, Beasley, p. 247.

136   "Knudsen had his," Beasley, p. 304; Fehrenbach, pp. 118–9; Patterson Papers, untitled manuscript, p. 34, Box 24.

136   Patterson on Knudsen, Patterson Papers, untitled manuscript, pp. 34–5, Box 24.

137   Jesse Jones comment, Jones to B. M. Baruch, Aug. 29, 1946, Jones Papers, Baruch folder, Box 3.

137   "When 1941 began" paragraph, Beasley, p. 301; Army Air Force Study, p. 48, p. 62; Perkins, pp. 363–5.

Page

137 "I have a," Roosevelt Papers, PC, Jan. 7, 1941, afternoon meeting, pp. 6–7.

137–8 "The basic problem" and following paragraph, Army Air Force Study, pp. 10–11, p. 17; Craven, *Planes,* p. 321–2; Patterson Papers, Letter Book, v. 1, Box 24.

138 "Knudsen used a" paragraph, Patterson Papers, untitled manuscript, Box 24.

138–9 "The automobile industry," Patterson Papers, Letter Book, v. 1, Box 24.

139 Glenn Martin comment, Sitterson, pp. 69–70.

139 "That was a" paragraph, Army Air Force Study, pp. 83–4.

139 Reuther plan, Craven, *Planes,* p. 323; Sitterson, pp. 67–8; Army Air Force Study, pp. 85–6.

139–40 Patterson comment, Patterson Papers, untitled manuscript, Box 24.

140 Ford situation, Sitterson, pp. 28–9; Beasley, pp. 264–5; Nevins, pp. 174–6.

140–1 Sorensen biographical details, Washington *Post,* Aug. 14, 1968, p. 86; *N.Y. Times,* Aug. 14, 1968, p. 38.

141 B-24 incident, Nevins, pp. 182–8.

141–2 Henderson-Knudsen dispute, Army Air Force Study, p. 104; Roosevelt, *Letters 1928–1945,* v. 2, p. 1198; Ickes, v. 3, p. 591.

142 Baruch to Stimson, Jan. 14, 1941, Patterson Papers, Letter Book, v. 1, Box 24.

142 Baruch memorandum, May 7, 1941, Hopkins Papers, Box 299, "Book II: Ideas for Defense Effort" file; also see Smith Papers, "Conferences with the President 1941–1942," June 10, 1941, unpaged.

142 Baruch to Wallace, Sept. 8, 1941, Wallace Papers, Box 1.

143 "unlimited national emergency," Roosevelt Papers, Speech file, 1368, and Map Room Papers—Roosevelt-Churchill correspondence, and PSF, Ickes; H. L. Stimson to FDR, May 24, 1941, Stimson Papers; Sherwood, pp. 296–9; Blum, pp. 252–4; Frankfurter Papers, Roosevelt folder 1940–42, Box 34; *N.Y. Times,* May 28, 1941, p. 1.

143 "It has been," FDR to Arthur Murray, Roosevelt, *Letters 1928–1945,* v. 2, p. 1165.

143–4 "That same month" paragraph, U.S. Congress, Pearl Harbor hearings, Report, pp. 53–4; Ward, pp. 1272–80.

June: "There will be serious political complications . . ."

145–6 Stone appointment, Mason, pp. 563–8; Confidential source; Gerhart, p. 230.

Page
146–7   *Robin Moor* incident, Shirer, p. 882; *N.Y. Times,* June 15, 1941, Sec. 4, p. 1, and June 21, 1941, p. 6; Roosevelt, *Public Papers,* pp. 227–30; Sherwood, p. 299.
148   "We must face," Patterson Papers, Letter Book, v. 1, Box 24.
149   Wallace quotes, Wallace Papers, Boxes 75 and 76.
149   "that contracts carry," Patterson Papers, Letter Book, v. 1, Box 24.
150   "In the building" and following paragraph, Fairchild, pp. 62–3; Beasley, p. 306; *N.Y. Times,* Apr. 6, 1941, Sec. 4, p. 1.
150   Stimson quote, Stimson Diary, March 19, 1941, v. 33.
150   "We have no," Patterson Papers, Letter Book, v. 1, Box 24.
150–1   Knox-Stimson on troops, Notes on Cabinet meeting, Apr. 4, 1941, by H. L. Stimson, in Patterson Papers, Cabinet meetings folder, Box 6.
151   Nevins quote, Nevins, p. 155.
151–2   "The Ford company" paragraph, *N.Y. Times,* Apr. 6, 1941, Sec. 4, p. 7.
152   "Take a question," Roosevelt Papers, Jan. 7, 1941, afternoon meeting, pp. 6–7.
152–3   "In January, 1941," paragraph, *N.Y. Times,* Feb. 9, 1941, Sec. 4, p. 7; Nevins, p. 159.
153   "That labor laws" paragraph, Fairchild, pp. 38–40; Nevins, pp. 180–1.
153   "The Army recommended" paragraph, Fairchild, pp. 41–2.
154   H. Ford quotes, *N.Y. Times,* March 9, 1941, p. 34.
154–6   Ford strike description, Nevins, pp. 161–5; *N.Y. Times,* Apr. 6, 1941, Sec. 4, p. 1.
156   Strike settled, *N.Y. Times,* Apr. 12, 1941, p. 1, and June 22, 1941, Sec. 4, p. 2.
156   Sorensen on H. Ford, Sorensen, pp. 269–70.
157   "I have this," H. L. Stimson to FDR, May 26, 1941, Stimson Papers.
157–9   North American strike description, *N.Y. Times,* June 9, 1941, p. 1.
159   "Of course, it," Roosevelt Papers, PC, June 10, 1941, p. 2.
160   "Later that day" and following paragraph, Memorandum, June 10, 1941, Stimson Papers.
160   "We won the," Patterson Papers, Letter Book, v. 1, Box 24.
160   Knox comment, F. Knox to M. L. Deyo, June 13, 1941, Knox Papers, Correspondence, Box 1.
161   "His efforts appeared" paragraph, Fairchild, p. 66.
162   Morison on Palmer, S. E. Morison, *Oxford History,* p. 883.
163   W. S. Churchill to FDR, June 14, 1941, Hull Papers. Box 49, folder 145.
163   Sulzberger report, *N.Y. Times,* June 15, 1941, p. 1.
163   "It seems to be," Stimson Diary, June 17, 1941, v. 34.

Page
163   State Department message, June 21, 1941, Israel, p. 206.

163   "Now comes this," FDR to Wm. D. Leahy, June 26, 1941, Roosevelt Papers, PSF, France.

164   "I cannot help," Stimson Diary, June 22, 1941, v. 34.

164   American military reaction, H. L. Stimson to FDR, June 23, 1941, Stimson Papers; Forrest Davis, p. 251; Confidential source.

164   Hoover reaction, confidential source.

164   Leahy report, Leahy to FDR, July 28, 1941, Leahy Papers, Box 10.

164–5 Davies reaction, June 23, 1941, Davies Papers, June 18–Sept. 10, 1941 folder, Box 11.

165   "I think only," Roosevelt Papers, PC, Aug. 1, 1941, p. 1.

165   "There will be," Israel, p. 207.

165   Pinchot reaction, letter to John T. Flynn, Aug. 8, 1941, Pinchot Papers, untitled folder, Box 69.

166   "On the other" paragraph, American Peace Mobilization Papers, Box 1.

166   "The National Labor" paragraph, American Peace Mobilization Papers, Box 1.

166   *Worker* quotes, Forrest Davis, p. 246.

166   Sherwood anecdote, Sherwood, p. 303.

166   "The Vatican has," Israel, p. 208.

167   Tardini quote, quoted in *N.Y. Times,* March 26, 1969, p. 12.

167   Swope draft, Hopkins Papers, Box 303, "Russia Attacked" file.

167   FDR letter to Pope, Sept. 3, 1941, Roosevelt, *Letters 1928–1945,* v. 2, pp. 1204–5.

168   Tardini quote, quoted in *N.Y. Times,* March 26, 1969, p. 12.

168–9 "The charge that" paragraph, Sherwood, p. 361.

169   "At one Cabinet" paragraph, Stimson Diary, Aug. 1, 1941, v. 35.

169   "Please get out," Roosevelt Papers, PSF, Russia.

169–70 "Aid to Russia" paragraph, Sept. 11, 1941, Jones Papers, Box 30.

170   Stimson memorandum, H. L. Stimson to FDR, Nov. 12, 1941, Stimson Papers.

170   Hopkins in Moscow, Laurence Steinhardt telegram, Aug. 1, 1941, and H. L. Hopkins memorandum to FDR, Hopkins Papers, Box 298, "Book II: France Falls; England Stands Alone" file; H. L. Hopkins memorandum of conversations with Stalin, July 30, 1941, Hopkins Papers, Box 150, Hopkins in Moscow file; Sept. 8 and 10, 1941, Davies Papers, June 18–Sept. 10, 1941 folder, Box 11.

171   "We sense a" Wm. D. Leahy to FDR, Aug. 26, 1941, Leahy Papers, Box 10.

171   "We must build," Ike, p. 50.

Page

172 "Matsuoka, the foreign" paragraph, Ike, pp. 65–7.

172 "The Navy is," Ike, p. 59.

173 "I think it," FDR to H. L. Ickes, July 1, 1941, Roosevelt Papers, PSF, Ickes.

173 "The day after" paragraph, Ike, pp. 77–9.

July: ". . . the test of one's devotion to freedom . . ."

174 "At five P.M.," Leahy Papers, Box 10.

174 FDR-Nomura talk, FDR memorandum, July 26, 1941, U.S. Congress, Pearl Harbor hearings, part 20, p. 4373.

175 "Here on the," Roosevelt, *Public Papers,* pp. 279–80.

176 Yamamoto quote, Potter, p. 43.

176 Butow comment, Butow, p. 242.

177 "I am convinced," July 9, 1941, copy in Patterson Papers, Letter Book, v. 1, Box 24.

177 "In other words," Roosevelt Papers, PC, July 22, 1941, p. 4.

178 shortages, Smith, *Mobilization,* pp. 505–6; First, p. 77; *Industrial Mobilization,* pp. 91–2.

178 "We got the," Roosevelt Papers, PC, Jan. 3, 1941, pp. 7–8.

178–9 "The Navy Department" paragraph, printed in U.S. Congress, Pearl Harbor hearings, part 20, p. 4354.

179 Patterson/airliners, FDR to J. H. Jones, June 19, 1941, Jones Papers, Box 30.

179 "Of course, we," Roosevelt, *Letters 1928–1945,* v. 2, p. 1180.

180 "I can't remember, Bundy, "Memoir," p. 158.

180 "Well, I think," Bundy, "Memoir," p. 160.

180 "Not all sniping" and following paragraph, Pogue, p. 97.

181 Marshall/National Guard, Pogue, pp. 98–100.

181 Connally incident, Stimson Diary, Sept. 15, 1941, v. 35.

181 "There was not," Bundy, "Memoir," p. 153.

182 "People would try," Bundy, "Memoir," p. 145.

182 Marshall/Collins, Cater Files, 1940 folder.

182 Marshall/Bolton, Cater Files, 1941 folder.

182 Boykin/cotton, confidential source.

182 "one of the," Stimson Diary, March 19, 1941, v. 33.

182 Knudsen incident, Beasley, p. 251.

182–3 Roberts-White-Stimson incident, R. Roberts to W. A. White, July 25, 1940, White Papers, Box 239; Stimson Diary, Oct. 3, 1941, v. 35.

183–4 "As for party" and following paragraph, confidential source.

185 Wheeler definition of isolationism, Wheeler, *Yankee,* p. 378.

185 Wheeler impact on platform, Nichols, p. 143.

185 Wheeler as FDR running mate, Wheeler, *Yankee,* p. 22.

185–6 Wheeler-mailing, Ickes, v. 3, pp. 588–9; Stimson Diary, July 24 and July 28, 1941, v. 34.

187 Frankfurter letter, Frankfurter Papers, Lehman folder, Box 22.

Page
188   "it may very," FDR to L. B. Sheley, Aug. 26, 1940, Roose-velt, *Letters 1928–1945*, v. 2, pp. 1058–9.
188–9   "The trouble with," May 14, 1941, Roosevelt, *Letters 1928–1945*, v. 2, pp. 1156–7.
189   "The active Army," Annual Report, pp. 47–8.
189   Marshall description, relation with FDR, Pogue, pp. 15, 22–23, 457.
190   "If you can," Cater files, 1941 folder.
190–1   FDR/Stark early relationship, H. L. Stark to FDR, Sept. 28, 1938, and FDR to H. L. Stark, March 22, 1939, Roosevelt Papers, PPF 166.
191   "In July, 1940," Patterson Papers, unpublished manuscript, Box 94.
192   White against draft, Johnson, p. 92.
192   "I am sorry," H. L. Stimson to FDR, Aug. 15, 1941, Stimson Papers.
192   "It is imperative," G. C. Marshall to J. L. DeWitt, Oct. 28, 1941, Cater files, 1941 folder.
192   "Got any ideas?" FDR to G. C. Marshall, Sept. 23, 1941, Roosevelt, *Letters 1928–1945*, v. 2, p. 1211.
192–3   "Everyone, it seemed" paragraph, Eleanor Roosevelt to FDR, Jan. 9, 1941, OF 1413; Stimson Diary, Feb. 17, 1941, v. 33.
194   "I think it," Roosevelt Papers, PC, July 15, p. 3.
194   "In accordance with," Annual Report, pp. 56–8.
195   House vote, *Congressional Record,* July 16, 1941, p. 6113.
195   "It was supposed," Wadsworth, "Memoir," p. 443.
195   "In mid-July" paragraph, Memorandum of July 17, 1941, Chief of Staff files, Notes on Conference, Binder 19.
195   "I am really," FDR to H. L. Stimson, July 18, 1941, Stimson Papers.
196   Marshall-Republicans meeting, Pogue, pp. 152–3.
196   "I have talked," Roosevelt Papers, OF 1413.
196   LaGuardia/draft, F. H. LaGuardia to FDR, July 17, 1941, Roosevelt Papers, OF 1413.
196   Patterson/draft, R. P. Patterson to FDR, July 17, 1941, Roosevelt Papers, OF 1413.
196   FDR message, Roosevelt, *Public Papers,* p. 273.
196   "I have not," Burton Papers, Diary, Aug. 4–6, 1941, Box 1.

August: ". . . their hopes for a better future for the world"

198   "I told him," Roosevelt Papers, FDR's memorandum of trip, Aug. 23, 1941, PSF, Safe File: Atlantic Charter Meeting.
199   "the only exception," Roosevelt Papers, FDR's memorandum of trip, Aug. 23, 1941, PSF, Safe File: Atlantic Charter Meeting.

Page

200 "There is a wild," Stimson Diary, Aug. 6, 1941, v. 35.

200–1 "When George Marshall" and following paragraphs, Marshall, *Together,* pp. 94–5.

201 "German embassy," Friedlander, p. 265.

201 "The rumors became" and following paragraph, J. G. Winant to FDR, Aug. 5, 1941, and FDR to State Department, Aug. 5, 1941, Hull Papers, Box 49, folder 146.

201 "On Thursday morning" paragraph, Roosevelt Papers, narrative log of President's cruise, PSF, Safe File: Atlantic Charter Meeting.

201 "I detailed him," Roosevelt Papers, FDR memorandum of trip, Aug. 23, 1941, PSF, Safe File: Atlantic Charter Meeting.

202 King George VI to FDR, Roosevelt Papers, PSF, Safe File: Atlantic Charter Meeting.

202 Churchill description, Morton, p. 17.

202 "You might have," Morton, p. 43, pp. 80–1, p. 86.

202 "Gentlemen, I thought," Churchill, *Alliance,* p. 429.

202–3 British arrival, Morton, pp. 90–6.

204 Churchill boards *Augusta,* Morton, p. 98.

204–5 "That afternoon a" and following paragraph, Morton, pp. 101–2.

205 "Churchill returned to" paragraph, Sherwood, p. 353; C. W. Bundy's notes in War Plans Division 4402–62.

205–6 "At that dinner" paragraph, Marshall, *Together,* p. 96.

206 "The next morning" paragraph, Morton, p. 101.

206 "We have a grand," Morton, p. 110.

207–9 Church service description, Morton, pp. 110–7; Roosevelt Papers, narrative log of President's cruise, PSF, Safe File: Atlantic Charter meeting; Roosevelt Papers, E. M. Watson to C. E. Reidt, Aug. 29, 1941, OF 463-C, Box 15.

209 "The meeting between" and following paragraph, U.S. Congress, Pearl Harbor hearings, Part 3, p. 1236; Matloff, pp. 55–6; Pogue, pp. 142–5, Sherwood, pp. 358–9.

210–1 Japanese problem, Sherwood, pp. 353–5; U.S. Congress, Pearl Harbor hearings, memo by S. Welles, Aug. 11, 1941, part 4, pp. 1785–7, and memo by S. Welles, Aug. 10, 1941, part 14, pp. 1269–74, and S. Welles testimony, part 2, pp. 459–61; Churchill, *Alliance,* pp. 439–40.

211 "that the United States," quoted in H. L. Hopkins to FDR, Feb. 21, 1942, Roosevelt Papers, PSF, Winston Churchill.

211–2 "A final major" and following paragraph, Hull, *Memoir,* v. 2, pp. 974–6; Welles, p. 176.

212 "time [was] of," FDR to S. Welles, Aug. 11, 1941, Hull Correspondence, Box 49, folder 146.

212 Macmillan comment, Macmillan, pp. 120–1.

213 "Also discussed at" paragraph, Sherwood, pp. 359–60.

Page
214   "The profound and," Churchill, *Alliance,* p. 444.
214   Stimson comment, H. L. Stimson to FDR, Aug. 15, 1941, Stimson Papers.
215   "Would it be," Morton, p. 186.
215   "eminently successful," Roosevelt Papers, PC, Aug. 16, 1941, p. 5.
215   FDR/aide, Smith Papers, Conference with the President 1941–1942, unpaged.
216   "Winston Churchill stood" paragraph, Morton, pp. 120–1.
217   "There was also" and following paragraph, confidential source.
217–8 "Politicking among Democrats" paragraph, Memorandum dated Aug. 11, 1941, National Council for Prevention of War Papers, Drawer 84.
218   "All through the," Stimson Diary, Aug. 12, 1941, v. 35.
218   McCormack comment, author's interview with Speaker McCormack, Sept. 14, 1968.
218–21 Description of House vote, *N.Y. Times,* Aug. 13, 1941, p. 10; author's interview with Speaker McCormack, Sept. 14, 1968; Dorough, pp. 313–5; Cohn, pp. 77–8.
221   Boykin letter, Roosevelt Papers, OF 1413.
222   "The Army is," Konoye Diary, printed in U.S. Congress, Pearl Harbor hearings, Part 20, p. 4000.
222   "Konoye agreed to" paragraph, U.S. Congress, Pearl Harbor hearings, part 20, p. 3999; Ike, p. 124.
222   German understanding, Feis, p. 276.
222–3 "The United States" and following paragraphs, Hull, *Memoirs,* v. 2, pp. 1028–32; U.S. Congress, Pearl Harbor hearings, Hull testimony, part 2, pp. 425–6, and Konoye diary, part 20, p. 4001.
223   Hull to Grew, C. Hull to J. Grew, March 26, 1943, Hull Papers, Box 66, folder 292.
223   "I wholly agree," *Foreign Relations,* v. 4, p. 483.

September: ". . . we will immediately decide to commence hostilities against the United States . . ."

225   Hirohito analysis, Mosley, p. 133, p. 146, pp. 197–9; Ike, pp. xviii–xix.
225–6 Sept. 3 meeting, Ike, pp. 130–3.
227   Sept. 6 meeting, U.S. Congress, Pearl Harbor hearings, Part 20, Konoye diary, pp. 4003–5; Ike, pp. 133–6; Butow, pp. 257–9; Mosley, pp. 216–7, pp. 219–20; 234–5.
227   "In the Japanese" paragraph, U.S. Congress, Pearl Harbor hearings, Part 2, p. 568; Hull, *Memoirs,* v. 2, p. 2032; Churchill, *Alliance,* pp. 582–3.
228   Ballantine quote, Ballantine, "Memoir," pp. 12–3.

Page

228 German officer corps attitude toward U.S., Truman Smith, pp. 10–1.

228–9 "In early spring" paragraph, Shirer, pp. 878–81.

229–31 *Greer* incident, *Dictionary of American Naval Fighting Ships*, pp. 152–3; S. E. Morison, *Atlantic*, pp. 78–80; Roosevelt, *Public Papers*, pp. 374–6 and p. 391; *N.Y. Times*, Sept. 7, 1941, p. 1, and Sept. 12, 1941, p. 1; Sherwood, pp. 370–2; A. Pinchot to Stephen Wise, Oct. 28, 1941, Pinchot Papers, Box 71, untitled folder.

232 Messersmith quote, Hull, *Memoirs*, v. 1, pp. 235–6.

232 Dodd warning, Ickes, v. 1, p. 494.

232 "You could search," H. K. Smith, *Train*, pp. 9–10.

232 "by exacting more," H. K. Smith, *Train*, pp. 20–1.

233 "a peculiar fellow," Block, 1942 ed., pp. 377–84.

234 "In Berlin . . . the," H. K. Smith, *Train*, p. 117.

235 "On March 8, 1939," and following paragraphs, Roosevelt Papers, PSF, Safe File: William C. Bullitt (the report is dated March 12, 1939).

236 Archduke to Ickes, Ickes, v. 3, pp. 149–50.

236 Hitler quote, Forrest Davis, p. 131.

236–7 State Department study, Hull Papers, Box 48, folder 142.

237 "As Adolf Hitler" and following paragraph, Hull Papers, Box 76, folder 331.

237 Sheehy quotes, *PM*, May 1, 1941, p. 15.

238 deLozada quotes, *N.Y. Times*, March 28, 1941, clip in Wallace Papers, Box 75.

238 Uruguay situation, Forrest Davis, p. 121, Wohlstetter, pp. 87–8.

238 "This should be," Roosevelt, *Letters 1928–1945*, v. 2, p. 1147.

238–9 Bolivia situation, Forrest Davis, pp. 263–4.

239 "There were not only" paragraph, U.S. Congress, Pearl Harbor hearings, part 15, p. 1642.

239 Kirk quote, Wohlstetter, p. 88.

239–40 Hull quote, Hull, *Memoirs*, v. 2, p. 1001.

240 "If Great Britain," from FDR's Dec. 29, 1940 radio address, quoted in Forrest Davis, p. 173.

240 J. F. Kennedy quote, Kennedy, pp. 18–9.

240–1 Friedlander quote, Friedlander, p. 312.

241 "We, and all other," Roosevelt, *Public Papers*, pp. 226–7.

241 Labor Day speech, Roosevelt Papers, Speech File 1380.

241 Lippmann quote, *N.Y. Herald Tribune*, Sept. 20, 1941, p. 13.

241–2 "Domestic matters and" paragraph, Sherwood, p. 379, *N.Y. Times*, Oct. 19, 1941, Sec. 4, p. 1.

242–4 Frankfurter memorandum, Frankfurter Papers, Roosevelt 1940–1942 folder, Box 34.

244 W. Cole on G. Nye, Cole, *Nye*, p. 183.

244 "Britain today is," America First Committee Papers.

Page

245 LaFollette quote, Cole, *America First*, p. 55.

246 F. Knox on America First, Knox to Lord Beaverbrook, Sept. 19, 1941, Knox Papers, Correspondence, Box 1.

247 "Is plainly the," Frankfurter Papers, Roosevelt 1934 folder, Box 34.

247-8 Lindbergh's two trips to Germany, Truman Smith, pp. 18-9, 47-8.

248 Lindbergh's warnings. Kenneth Davis, p. 378; *N.Y. Times,* Jan. 6, 1969, p. 33.

248-9 Sorensen on Lindbergh, Sorensen, p. 292.

249-50 "My first realization," Lindbergh speech at America First rally in New York City, Oct. 30, 1941, text in Pinchot Papers, "Chapter Charter" folder, file 87.

250-1 Lindbergh and German medal, *N.Y. Times.* Oct. 20, 1938; Nevins, pp. 170-1; Truman Smith, pp. 91-93 and pp. 99-104; *N.Y. Times,* July 18, 1941, p. 6; Washington *Star,* July 25, 1941, p. A-2; Allen, p. 53.

252 "I think the time," F. Frankfurter to H. L. Stimson, Oct. 16, 1939, Stimson Papers.

252 Lindbergh, senior, quotes, Lindbergh, Sr., *Your Country,* p. 22, p. 50, p. 203, p. 209.

252 "Critics of Colonel," Block, 1941 ed., p. 513.

253 "It is sad beyond," W. A. White to B. M. Toon, July 9, 1940, White Papers, Box 238.

253 Nathan quotation, Nathan, p. 366.

254 "In contrast, Franklin" paragraph, Roosevelt Papers, text of President's remarks, meeting with Business Advisory Council, May 23, 1940, PSF, Harry L. Hopkins folder.

254-5 1939 Cabinet meeting, Ickes, v. 3, pp. 11-2, p. 20.

255 Lindbergh's possible political ambitions, Tull, p. 224; *Nation,* July 26, 1941, p. 72; *Look,* Nov. 12, p. 13.

256 Black on FDR, from text of "Justice Black and the Bill of Rights," broadcast on the CBS Television Network, Dec. 3, 1968, p. 10.

256-7 April news conference, Roosevelt Papers, PC, Apr. 25, 1941, pp. 10-1.

257 Lindbergh letter, Roosevelt Papers, OF 92, Box 1.

257 Newark *Star-Ledger* editorial, copy in Roosevelt Papers, OF 92, Box 1.

258 Early comment, *N.Y. Times,* May 4, 1941, Sec. 4, p. 2.

258 W. A. White comment, *Emporia Gazette,* May 5, 1941, p. 4.

258 "As you know," May 9, 1941, Pinchot Papers, Box 71, untitled folder.

259 "I want to take," A. Pinchot to C. A. Lindbergh, Apr. 22, 1941, Pinchot Papers, Box 69, untitled folder.

259 "I think you should," A. Pinchot to C. A. Lindbergh, July 14, 1941, Pinchot Papers, Box 69, untitled folder.

Page

259   "Lindbergh was the most," Wood, "Memoir," p. 90.

259–60 "We will be deluged," C. A. Lindbergh radio address, Sept. 15, 1939, printed in *Congressional Record,* May 20, 1940, p. 9820, daily edition.

260   "Confusion is not an," C. A. Lindbergh speech before America First rally, San Francisco, July 1, 1941, text in Pinchot Papers, Box 70, untitled folder.

260   "Possibly the most ominous," C. A. Lindbergh speech before America First rally, Los Angeles, Pinchot Papers, "Chapter Charter" folder, file 87.

260   "Our bond with," C. A. Lindbergh radio address, Oct. 14, 1939, printed in *Congressional Record,* May 20, 1940, p. 9821, daily edition.

260   "He repeated much" sentence, see Lindbergh, *Flight,* pp. 35–6.

262   Tull on Coughlin, Tull, p. 246.

262   *Social Justice* quote, printed in Tull, p. 196.

263   "The Coughlinite situation," Cole, *America First,* pp. 134–5.

264–5   C. A. Lindbergh's Des Moines speech, text in America First Committee Papers.

266   "Let us read," America First Committee Papers.

267   *Tribune* editorial, Pinchot Papers, America First Committee— Literature folder, file 88.

267   "the result of the meeting," copy in Wallace Papers, box 22, SA file.

267   Stuart comment, R. D. Stuart letter to author, March 24, 1969.

268   "is greatly worried," A. Pinchot to R. E. Wood, Sept. 15, 1941, Pinchot Papers, Box 69, untitled folder.

268–9   Lindbergh telegram, Pinchot Papers, Pinchot Articles folder, file 87.

269   "It is my recollection," R. D. Stuart letter to author, March 24, 1969.

269–70 "Ever since the," text in America First Committee Papers.

270   "In making these," text in Pinchot Papers, Chapter Charter folder, file 87.

270   R. E. Wood on C. A. Lindbergh, Wood, "Memoir," pp. 90–1.

271   "To disavow or oppose," quoted in Block, 1941 ed., pp. 227–8.

271   Republican support of Dirksen, confidential source.

271   Fuchida reaction, Fuchida, p. 939.

October: ". . . the Imperial Navy is itching for action"

272   "The Jap situation," Roosevelt, *Letters 1928–1945,* v. 2, p. 1223.

272   Konoye resignation, Churchill, *Alliance,* p. 591; Hull, *Memoirs,* v. 2, p. 1054; Grew, pp. 459–463 and pp. 481–2; Mosley, p. 226; Butow, pp. 285–91 and 300–1; Greenfield, pp. 111–2.

Page
272 "I have had to resign," quoted in Grew, pp. 456–7.
273 "The difference between" and following paragraphs, U.S. Congress, Pearl Harbor hearings, Konoye diary, Part 20, p. 4013.
273 Oct. 16 quotations, U.S. Congress, Pearl Harbor hearings, Konoye diary, Part 20, pp. 424–6.
274 Haraide quote, printed in Wohlstetter, p. 163.
274 G. C. Marshall quotation, U.S. Congress, Pearl Harbor hearings, Part 3, p. 1167.
275 "I may never declare," Churchill, *Alliance*, p. 593.
275 Bullitt suggestion, Ickes, v. 3, pp. 538–9.
275–6 "In the fall of 1941" paragraph, *N.Y. Times*, Nov. 7, 1941, p. 11; Sherwood, p. 382; Cole, *America First*, pp. 62–4; Pinchot Papers, Chapter Charter folder, file 87; confidential source.
276 *Kearny* and *Reuben James* incidents, *Dictionary of American Naval Fighting Ships*, p. 605, p. 609; S. E. Morison, *Atlantic*, pp. 92–4; Roosevelt, *Public Papers*, pp. 438–44; Shirer, pp. 882–3.
277 "I thought it," U.S. Congress, Pearl Harbor hearings, Part 6, p. 2715.
278 "The next year" paragraph, U.S. Congress, Pearl Harbor hearings, part 6, p. 2714.
278 Stark warning, U.S. Congress, Pearl Harbor hearings, part 14, p. 1402.
278 Short comment, U.S. Congress, Pearl Harbor hearings, part 32, p. 191.
279 "Watchfulness was required," *N.Y. Times*, Oct. 25, 1941, p. 1.

November: "This dispatch is to be considered a war warning"

280 W. S. Churchill to FDR, Churchill, *Alliance*, pp. 592–3.
281 Nov. 7 Cabinet meeting, Stimson Diary, Nov. 7, 1941, v. 36; Hull, *Memoirs*, v. 2, pp. 1057–8.
281 "I set the deadline," Hull, *Memoirs*, v. 2, 1063.
282 FDR-Kurusu meeting, Hull Papers, Box 60, folder 232.
282 Marshall meeting with press, Pogue, p. 202.
282–3 "On November 22" paragraph, Hull, *Memoirs*, p. 1074.
283 Ickes reaction, Ickes, v. 3, pp. 649–50.
283 Nov. 25 meeting, Hull, *Memoirs*, pp. 1079–80; Stimson Diary, Nov. 25, 1941, v. 36.
283 "When Stimson returned" paragraph, Stimson Diary, Nov. 26, 1941, v. 36.
284 "Two days later" paragraph, Stimson Diary, Nov. 28, 1941, v. 36.
285 "I don't know," Roosevelt Papers, Nov. 3, 1941, p. 7.
285–6 Stark memorandum, dated Oct. 8, 1941, Hull Correspondence, Box 49, folder 147.

Page
286 FDR re America First, Roosevelt, *Letters 1928–1945,* v. 2, p. 1241; Biddle, p. 189.
288 Nov. 7 meeting, Stimson Diary, Nov. 7, 1941, v. 36.
288 "allowed to win," Stimson Diary, Nov. 14, 1941, v. 36.
288–9 "Either Stimson misunderstood" and following paragraphs, Stimson Diary, Nov. 14 and 15, 1941, v. 36.
290 "The day the two-hundred-man" and following paragraphs, Fuchida, p. 940.
291 "war in the Pacific," *N.Y. Times,* Nov. 29, 1941, p. 1.
291 Stark warning of Nov. 24, U.S. Congress, Pearl Harbor hearings, part 5, pp. 2123–4.
291 Short comment, U.S. Congress, Pearl Harbor hearings, part 5, p. 2977.
292 "war warning" message, U.S. Congress, Pearl Harbor hearings, part 5, p. 2125.
292 Kimmel reaction, U.S. Congress, Pearl Harbor hearings, part 6, p. 2630 and p. 2518.
293–4 Davies-Kurusu meeting, Davies Papers, journal entry for Nov. 28, 1941.

December: "X day will be 8 December"

296 "X day will be," Fuchida, p. 942.
296 "All service radio calls," U.S. Congress, Pearl Harbor hearings, part 17, p. 2636.
296 America First statement, Text in Pinchot Papers, "Chapter Charter" folder, file 87.
297 "Highly reliable information," U.S. Congress, Pearl Harbor hearings, part 15, p. 1866.
297 "The rise of," Fuchida, pp. 944–5.
298 Leahy-Kato dinner, Leahy Papers, Diary entry for Dec. 5, 1941, Box 10.
298 America First letter, Roosevelt Papers, OF 4330.
298 FDR-Smith meeting, H. D. Smith Papers, "Conferences with the President 1941–1943, unpaged.
298–9 Stimson activities, Stimson Diary, Dec. 6, 1941, v. 36.
299–301 FDR letter to Hirohito, Grew, pp. 486–9; Mosley, pp. 264–5; Hull, *Memoirs,* v. 2, pp. 1094–5; U.S. Congress, Pearl Harbor hearings, part 2, p. 553.
302 "December 6, in the evening" paragraph, U.S. Congress, Pearl Harbor hearings, part 7, pp. 3294–5.
302–3 FDR-Schulz, U.S. Congress, Pearl Harbor hearings, part 10, pp. 4660–3.
304 Submarine incident, Ward, p. 1983; U.S. Congress, Pearl Harbor hearings, part 13, pp. 413–4; Wohlstetter, pp. 15–6.

Page

304 "In Washington, at approximately" paragraph, U.S. Congress, Pearl Harbor hearings, part 4, p. 1596; Pogue, p. 223; Marshall, *Together,* p. 99; Kahn, pp. 1–3, 12–3.

305 "About two hours earlier" and following paragraphs, Fuchida, p. 945.

306 Hopkins letter, to J. N. Hall, Nov. 12, 1941, Hopkins Papers, Box 303, Thoughts—Dec. 6, 1941 file.

307–8 "And to the surprise" and following paragraph, Fairchild, *Manpower,* p. 76; *N.Y. Times,* Nov. 14, 1941, p. 1, and Nov. 30, 1941, Sec. 4, p. 2; Perkins, pp. 365–7.

309–10 "On the flight deck" and following paragraphs, Fuchida, pp. 945–7.

Afterword

311 Wheeler comment, Wheeler, p. 36.
311 Coughlin situation, Biddle, p. 247.

INDEX

D